A Politics of
Presence

Studies in Anthropology and History

Studies in Anthropology and History is a series which develops new theoretical perspectives, and combines comparative and ethnographic studies with historical research.

Edited by James Carrier, University of Durham, UK.

Associate editors: Nicholas Thomas, The Australian National University, Canberra and Emiko Ohnuki-Tierney, University of Wisconsin, USA.

Titles in production

This book is part of a series. The publisher will accept continuation orders which may be cancelled at any time and which provide for automatic billing and shipping of each title in the series upon publication. Please write for details.

Peter Pels

A Politics of Presence

Contacts between
Missionaries and Waluguru in
Late Colonial Tanganyika

hoap **harwood academic publishers**
Australia ♦ Canada ♦ China ♦ France ♦ Germany ♦ India
Japan ♦ Luxembourg ♦ Malaysia ♦ The Netherlands
Russia ♦ Singapore ♦ Switzerland

Amsteldijk 166
1st Floor
1079 LH Amsterdam
The Netherlands

British Library Cataloguing in Publication Data

Pels, Peter
    A politics of presence : contacts between missionaries and
    Waluguru in late colonial Tanganyika. – (Studies in
    anthropology and history ; v. 22)
    1. Catholic Church – Tanganyika – Influence   2. Missions –
    Tanganyika – History – 20th century   3. Luguru (African
    people) – Missions – History – 20th century
    I. Title
    266'.009678

    ISBN 90-5702-304-0
    ISSN 1055-2464

To my parents, real and adopted

Tjits Gerritsma and Emile Pels
in Bussum, The Netherlands
and
Mama Mkoba and the late Mzee Petri Mloka
in Kiswira, Tanzania

Contents

ix

List of Maps and Figures

List of Plates

Acknowledgments

Reckoned from the start of my research at my admission to the Postdoctoral Institute for Sociology (now the Amsterdam School for Social Research), when I had never met a Holy Ghost Father nor yet set foot in Africa, this book has taken ten years to produce. It is a much improved version of my dissertation, defended in January 1993, and both during my dissertation research and after it I have accumulated a large amount of debts.

The research was funded by the Amsterdam School for Social Research (ASSR) and the Netherlands' Foundation for the Advancement of Tropical Research (WOTRO). I cannot list all the members of the Dutch province of the Congregation of the Holy Ghost who helped me with the Dutch part of my research, and will restrict myself to saying that the support of Father Joop Hogema and the collegiality of Albert de Jong exemplified their generosity. Leny Lagerwerff of the International Institute for Missiology and Oecumene in Leyden, and Jan Roes and Jan van Wel of the Katholiek Documentatie Centrum of the University of Nijmegen were also of great help. Life and work in Dar es Salaam would have been difficult without the hospitality of John Mlundwa, and the help I received from the late Joyce Ligunda, Mrs Lyaruu, and the staff of the Tanzania National Archives in setting up my research.

I thank Marjorie Mbilinyi and Anne Sefu for introducing me to *kaka* Adriani Nyawale. Adriani became my brother and provided me with a home, parents, more brothers and sisters, and a host of other relatives in Matombo. If I had a place in Tanzania I could call "home", it was the house he and his family had built in Kiswira village. His parents, Mama Mkoba and *marehemu* Mzee Petri Mloka, became my own. They settled me comfortably, pampered me with Luguru delicacies, and guided me into practical Swahili and Luguru life – this book is partly dedicated to them.

Thomas Martiniani and Camillus Kunambi were my research guides in Uluguru. Many Luguru elders helped me in my study of their culture and history. I especially thank Mzee Joseph Mloka, for welcoming me as chairman of Kiswira village, Mzee Kibuwi and

Mzee and Bibi Tendegu for their knowledge and friendliness, Mzee Pius Wendelini for his own history of Uluguru (Wendelini 1990), and Mzee Mikaeli Mlosa and Romani Karoli for making research at Zava possible and enjoyable. The late Bishop Adriani Mkoba put the energies of his priests at my disposal. Father Gumbo and Father Kubahari greatly facilitated work in Matombo and Tegetero. The community of Dutch missionaries remaining in Morogoro served as a kind of sally-port for research. Above all, I thank Father Theodor Winkelmolen. His tremendous support for this project – in putting the mission archives, the tales of his vast experience, and a table to note them down on, at my disposal – more than matched his scepticism about it. I cherish his friendship, and his criticism, very much.

Mr Henk Streefkerk drew the map of Uluguru. Noor van Mierlo did a great job on my photographic material. At the dissertation stage, Matthew Schoffeleers criticized an early version of Chapter Three, Willy Jansen, Annelies Moors and Luise White read and commented on Chapter Four, and Bonno Thoden van Velzen reacted to the whole manuscript with welcome encouragement and enthusiasm. My most meticulous and influential reader was Johannes Fabian, and my debt to him is evident from the following pages. As critic, native informant and meticulous corrector of my English, he was the single most important contributor to the dissertation.

In turning the dissertation into a book, I first of all have to thank Nicholas Thomas for his support in getting the book published in his series, and the staff of Harwood Academic Publishers. To both, my apologies for the delays in the delivery of the manuscript. Koen Alefs helped me check and cross-check the manuscript and prepare the index. Revised portions of the book were discussed at seminars of the Research Centre Religion and Society of the University of Amsterdam, the 11th Satterthwaite Symposium on African Religion and Ritual, and the Department of Anthropology of the University of Manchester. The Introduction and Chapter six were much improved by discussions with Prabhu Mohapatra, Dick Werbner, and with Jean and John Comaroff in the course of a wonderful day in the Peak District. I am especially grateful to my colleagues of the Research Centre Religion and Society of the

University of Amsterdam: Chapter three was much improved by one of Gerd Baumann's searching reanalyses of other people's material; Birgit Meyer has been an intellectual companion all along the way; Peter van Rooden paid me the complement of finding merit in what should be, to a true historian like himself, a piece of distasteful jargon; Patricia Spyer's understanding of what I was trying to do produced necessary critique and welcome reassurance; and Peter van der Veer first posed searching questions when I defended the dissertation, and pushed until this book was at long last ready for the press.

Material used in chapter two was first published as a photographic essay in *Critique of Anthropology* IX (1989): 33–47. The conclusion draws heavily on an essay published in *History and Anthropology* 8 (1994): 321–51. I gratefully acknowledge permission from Harwood Academic Publishers to republish Chapter three as a separate article in the *Journal of Religion in Africa* XXVI (1996): 163–201.

I thank Anke Kamerman for the months we shared in Matombo, for her patience with my physical and mental absences during research and writing, and for all the intellectual, moral and physical support. I thank my parents, Tjits Gerritsma and the late Emile Pels, for guiding my path to this book, which I therefore also dedicate to them.

CHAPTER ONE

Introduction: The Microphysics of Colonial Contact

On the 27th of October, 1949, Dr. Adolf Melchior climbed along the Mbezi river up to Tegetero mission, high up on the Northern slopes of the Uluguru mountains, in what was then called Tanganyika. He had been invited to attend the mission's anniversary by Bernard Hilhorst, the Bishop of the Vicariate of Bagamoyo. The Bishop, a worn man after fifteen years of incessant travel and administration of his diocese, was glad to be carried up to the mission in a hammock, but Dr. Melchior enjoyed the walk and continued on foot. He was joined by the Father of Tegetero, Piet Bukkems, who walked beside him, panting and chatting, "in full splendour".

That "in full splendour" no doubt requires further explanation, otherwise you might picture him in a black cassock or even in church vestments, and nothing is farther from the truth. Father Bukkems has been in Tegetero for years. He knows everybody and everything about them. He is not just their priest, but also their counsellor in worldly matters. He is the judge, doctor, vet, technician and above all: farmer. He helps the people as much as he can; he talks to them as often as he can, and that is often, because he is the only priest in Tegetero and, for years, was the only white man, with the negroes as his only contacts. He has come to know them as few others do; he came to understand and appreciate them. And the other way round, with the result that they chose him to become *mlunga*, headman, *mzee*, an elder of a clan, which is why he now belongs to the country's leaders, the nobility, so to speak. That was noticeable in this solemn reception! Father Bukkems, whose genteel name is Mzee Mwogera, appeared in full splendour: a blue turban, a big, stiff red-chequered sash on his right shoulder, a bangle on his left wrist and a smartly carved negro-axe on his left shoulder. All negroes we met greeted him with the obligatory reverential words which are the mlunga's due (Melchior 1950: 181–2).[1]

Melchior noted that it was difficult to be impressed by this "masquerade", but Father Bukkems was dead serious. Bukkems' colleagues disapproved of his conduct, because the ceremonies in which a *mwenye mlunga* had to participate were all of heathen descent and not in keeping with the dignity and profession of the missionary. But, on the way from Kisambwa to the mission itself, the veteran missionary explained to Melchior that Europe would never have been Christianized if the preachers of that age would have disdained the use of pagan customs. "There is no doubt that there are certain things that cannot be endorsed, but, as the enthusiastic mlunga next to me asks, how are we supposed to combat them when we do not even know them and have nothing to say about them?" (Melchior 1950: 182).

Father Bukkems was convinced that his membership of the society of *wenye mlunga* gave him the knowledge and power to influence the affairs of the Waluguru of Tegetero in a much more profound manner than his predecessors and colleagues. On Easter Monday, 1949, the day of his initiation as Mzee Mwogera, he noted in the mission diary that it is "a ceremony worth participating in – if only to have a penetrating look into the refined social system of the blacks, but even more because of the influence which the Father gets through being regarded and revered just like any other elder in this country".[2] Bukkems thought, as did many missionaries, anthropologists and colonial administrators before and after him, that he had privileged access to knowledge of his "others" – pagan Waluguru – and consequently, that this knowledge was not biased by his practical interest in converting them. These objective

---

[1] A *mwenye mlunga* (kil.) is literally an "owner of spirit emblems", someone who has been initiated into one of two ranks of the men and women of influence in a specific valley. During fieldwork, I commonly used Swahili, but most Waluguru are completely bilingual in Swahili and Kiluguru; if their Kiliguru origin (kil.) is not indicated, Bantu words used in the text are Swahili. All translations, including from the French and Dutch, are mine.
[2] TD 18.4.49 (for abbreviations and notes on archival sources, see appendix A).

representations of others were a prerequisite for a "better" relation-ship, producing both more effective, and more legitimate, power of the one over the other.

However, during my fieldwork in the Uluguru mountains in 1989–90, Mzee Magoma Mwanamtali, successor to the *mwenye mlunga* who installed Bukkems, told me that the Father only got a "reception rank" (*cheo cha kukabidhiwa*). The Luguru elders of Tegetero staged the reception to honour Bukkems, but the cocktail they served was a peculiarly mixed one. Bukkems received the turban, sash and bangle, the ceremonial axe and most probably the three-legged chair which are all covered by the name *milunga*, and the occasion was accompanied by lavish amounts of ceremonial beer. But the ceremony was held during the day; there is no evi-dence that Bukkems underwent the seven-day death and rebirthing process that belongs to the initiation and that reaches its climax in the passing on of secret knowledge to the initiand on the night before "coming out" (kil. *mlao*). Mzee Magoma told me that Bukkems was never shown the leaves of power that form the core of the *wenye mlunga*'s secrets. Moreover, no *milunga* can be entrusted to a single man, because his wife is installed at the same time: an insurmountable obstacle for a Catholic priest.[3]

One might conclude from this that Bukkems' rank was, indeed, a masquerade. This suggests a reversed, ideological concep-tion of power and knowledge, in which power limits knowledge and transforms it into its own image; as Nietzsche said, *Macht verdummt*. It is based on the argument that those who have a vested interest in controlling and changing others are often not capable of understanding them fully. Representations of the objects of the gaze of power will be false to the extent that they mirror the projects in which the powers that be are engaged. This ideological

---

[3] Moreover, "Mwogera" is not a matrilineal or *lukolo* name, but derives from the father's lineage (kil. *mtala*). Waluguru trace lineage membership through the mother; the child is never a member of the father's lineage. A *mwenye mlunga* receives a *lukolo*, not a *mtala* name on initiation. "Mwogera", by the way, means "white" (FN: Mzee Magoma Mwanamtali, Tegetero, 16.1.90, Mzee Petri Mloka, Kiswira, 14.8.89; TD 18.1.49).

conception criticizes ethnographic representations by the powerful for being tainted by their material interests. Both the objectivist and the ideological conception, therefore, assume a direct correspondence between the legitimacy of a colonial intervention and the authenticity of the knowledge of "others" it produces. Indeed, struggles over the authenticity of ethnographic knowledge have always been part of colonial discourse. Even though, in the twentieth century, missionaries have been portrayed as the paradigm of colonial ethnocentrism,[4] all missionaries had to form a conception of what it was that they wanted to convert people from (Van der Veer 1995), and missionary interests and perceptions played a formative role in the emergence of anthropology (Pels 1990a, 1995).

However, I feel that Father Bukkems' *milunga* raise doubts about the centrality of such debates on cultural authenticity in our current attempts to understand the strategies and tactics of a missionary encounter – or, for that matter, any other colonial intervention. At the very least, Bukkems' involvement in Luguru initiation set him off from his *confrères*, which warns us against drawing overly homogeneous pictures of the missionaries' projects, culture or interests. Moreover, most participants in the process were themselves uncertain about the cultural authenticity of the ceremony and the Father's *milunga*, and we are only left with the conviction that the ceremony was actually organized and that Bukkems received objects which he thought were spirit emblems. This suggests that in the practice of missionary interaction, the truth and falsity of *representations* of ethnic difference may have been subordinate to the immediate necessity to *present* oneself to the other. This book concentrates on, and tries to assess the relative weight of, the latter dimension in colonial interaction.

Whereas the ceremony that Bukkems was presented with seems to have been an innovation by the elders of Tegetero, adapted to Bukkems' "otherness", it is likely that the whole sequence of events was caused by the emergence of a set of practical concerns which Bukkems shared with Waluguru. Bukkems' background in rural Dutch Brabant may partly explain why he was widely known

---

[4] See the references in note 10.

as "the farmer of Tegetero" (Melchior 1950: 183). He was not unique in his willingness to participate in and advise on agriculture and the keeping of livestock, even though few of his colleagues shared his preference for millet and maize above canons and bad customs. With chickens running through the mission house and fleas jumping on the visiting Bishop's purple stockings, Bukkems' style of life was in many ways less influenced by the boundaries of hygiene that many of his colleagues drew around them. Not long before the ceremony took place, he usurped an office of the local landholder by claiming to have successfully prayed for rain, which fell abundantly on the Christians while the rest of Tegetero went without it. One of his colleagues told me that Bukkems had a strong belief in the presence of the devil and therefore could appreciate Waluguru when they suspected evil spirits (*pepo mbaya*) in some place or person. Moreover, Bukkems liked native beer.

If Bukkems presented himself to the people of Tegetero in ways that led them to make him a present of their own, the exchange drew both parties into a power-play along fault lines that neither party anticipated. Shortly after the visit of Melchior, Bukkems went on leave to Europe, but on his return to Tegetero in 1951, he resigned some months after arrival. Although the full circumstances are not altogether clear (Bukkems made a habit of baffling or antagonizing his *confrères*, and Bishop Hilhorst in particular), it seems that his resignation was caused by the African teachers of the mission school, who protested to the Bishop that Bukkems was attending ceremonies in which they were not allowed to participate. By his attendance he lent respect to positions of power which threatened their own. His example could induce converts to participate in pagan ritual and revive Christians' waning respect for traditional authority, especially in Tegetero, where the majority of *wenye mlunga* were either pagan or Muslim.[5]

In such a case, the "ethnic" authenticity of the representations of these events is itself being debated: while Bukkems believed that his initiation was genuine Luguru and the native

---

[5] IPAC 10a: 642. For the conflict between traditional power holders and mission teachers, see chapter five.

mission teachers acted as if it was genuine, Mzee Magoma and his elders were apparently not giving Bukkems the full traditional *mlunga* treat. Bukkems' colleagues were divided about the question whether his new rank was "true Luguru" or not, and even if it was, most would not have supported his participation in it. Dr. Melchior took Bukkems' "Luguru" authority seriously, despite the fact that he found his attire a "masquerade". In other words, a focus on the representations of these events leads us into an "epistemic murk" typical of colonial situations (Taussig 1987: 120). Whereas Bukkems' initiation as such may have been unique, its "unfixing of signifiers" is a much more general aspect of colonial processes (Comaroff and Comaroff 1991: 18). Colonizers and colonized may try to construct their world in terms of dichotomous oppositions, but in colonial practice such clarity is an exception (Stoler and Cooper 1997: 8).

But what would "unfixing" the signifiers of cultural boundaries mean? There is little reason to doubt that Bukkems received the *milunga*, that feasts of honour were held to celebrate them and that a conflict over the proper conduct of missionaries ensued among both Waluguru and missionaries. To answer the question, it seems less relevant to ponder the issue of the "authenticity" of Bukkems' *milunga* than to follow, in detail, the exchange of objects, the enacting of rituals of power, and the conduct of debates about them among all participants in the process. These practices brought about a crisis in the relationships between Bukkems, his colleagues, his teachers, and other Waluguru of Tegetero. In this book, I want to keep away from the discussion about cultural authenticity (which until recently dominated and dichotomized the study of mission in Africa), and concentrate on some of these microphysical processes of colonial contact, in order to assess both their historical role and their possible impact on our thinking about colonial contact.

Father Bukkems' initiation points out a possible direction in which the examination of such processes may go. In his remarks to Dr. Melchior, he indicated that the project of conversion hardly needed legitimation by ethnography, since there was "no doubt" about the necessity of combating indigenous customs. In his diary entry, he ranked the *practical* social power which his initiation as *mwenye mlunga* might give, above the knowledge of the Luguru social system it promised to yield. Jean and John Comaroff have suggested that the change of *mind* implied by the notion of "conversion" may be less important for our understanding of the mutual tactics of missionary and Africans than their practical involvement in ritual (1991: 249). Indeed, Father Bukkems' initiation displaced, at least temporarily, the necessarily one-way traffic of conversion by the two-way involvement of both parties in ritual action. Bukkems was not the only one: the issue is, in the Catholic Church, as old as the rites controversy triggered by the work of the Jesuits in Asia from the sixteenth century onwards (Minamiki 1985). The case of Father Bukkems suggests that in the study of Roman Catholic missionary practice, the metaphor of "initiation" may often be more useful than that of "conversion", because it shifts our attention from an individual change of mind to a inequal yet reciprocal relationship.

Moreover, a focus on initiation and its accompanying discipline shifts our attention from changes of mind to transformations of bodies. Recent studies of initiation stress that the body does what cannot be expressed by participants or observers. Initiations work at least in part through the production of a "knowledge of the body" that materially mediates and determines communication without recourse to discourse (Jackson 1983; cf. also Bourdieu 1977; Comaroff 1985; De Boeck 1995). To paraphrase Victor Turner, the liminal subject of a rite of passage may be structurally "invisible" because it no longer represents an accepted category of society and culture (1967: 95), but that does not make the initiand *physically* "invisible". Ritual liminality is materially mediated by physical forms that have ceased to "stand for" any specifiable meaning. As in the study of material culture, such material mediations "exist as a physically concrete form independent of any individual's mental image of it" and this form is not just the *tabula rasa* of an arbitrary signifier but determining to a certain degree (Miller 1987: 98–9). Likewise, in the case of missions, we should be aware, first of all, that a mission is a movement of bodies to the mission area and into the church (see chapters two and three). In historical anthropology, we are presently ill-equipped to think about such material mediations of colonial contact, and this introduction attempts to indicate where such thinking could start.

Of course, by saying we should concentrate on the material mediations, or microphysics, of colonial contact I am not trying to deny the constitutive role of representations of self and other or us and them, and of the symbolic orders that they construe as a "home" opposed to a place abroad. If I may seem to exaggerate a physicalist or materialist reading of my sources, this is, as Arjun Appadurai noted in the context of the study of material culture, an epistemological "fetishism" meant as a "corrective to the tendency to excessively sociologize" or culturalize material transactions (Appadurai 1986: 5). Below, I will try to show how many students of missions in Africa let themselves be trapped in the dichotomous images of colonialism that are the result of such excessive sociologizing and culturalizing, and try to explain why a "tactile" metaphor of knowledge production may help us to keep away from them. I think this corrective is needed for two reasons, one that is specific to this study of the Uluguru missions, while the other pertains to the level of general theorizing about the study of colonial situations.

First, I want to bring out the indeterminacy and uncertainty of the whole process to the participants themselves. If Father Bukkems could not anticipate what was going to be the result of the way in which he presented himself to the people of Tegetero, how could Bishop Hilhorst be expected to predict and control his church-building at a far more ambitious level of operation? The diversity of possible responses by Waluguru is brought out by the available choice between the ritual cooptation of one of the mission's representatives (Father Bukkems), and the decision to join the developing national organisation of education represented by the mission teachers. A focus on the microphysics of these interactions brings out the extent to which *strategic* calculation from sets of sociocultural standards by both parties was superseded, in practice, by the *tactical* negotiation of often contradictory possibilities, in a process of trial-and-error (such as the giving and receiving of the *milunga* in Father Bukkems' case).[6] Above, I used the term

---

[6] For the distinction between strategy and tactic, see De Certeau (1984: xix, 36–7).

"to present" (oneself to an other), and indeed, both missionaries and Waluguru often described the process in terms of a *gift*: a "sacrifice" given by the missionary, a gift (of revelation) received by Waluguru. Indeed, a gift implies a lack of anticipation (of the nature and quality of the presentation by the receiver), a relation of inequality (between giver and receiver), and – and this is aggravated when it occurs at the crossroads of several sociocultural routines – uncertainty about the timing and calculation of appropriate presentation and return (Bourdieu 1977: 4–8).

Put in a more general way, including the material mediation of communication in the analysis comes closer to the perception of the process by its participants, because it brings out the problems of fixing these mediations as signifiers that unambiguously "stand for" some cultural content. This brings me to my second motive to stress the microphysics of colonial contact. While, on the one hand, some argue that colonial contact leads to an "unfixing" of signifiers (Comaroff and Comaroff 1991: 18), on the other, others say that the whole distinction of signifier and signified is part of the strategies of European colonialism – that it is, in fact, situated at its core (Mitchell 1991). While I admire Timothy Mitchell's attempt to show the centrality of a discourse of representation in European colonial strategies, and agree (as will be apparent from the conclusion of this book) that it is important for an understanding of its operation, it is clearly not sufficient to understand the operation of colonial society. Everyday European understandings of what representation is like are themselves "unfixed" in the process of colonization, because they are transferred to new contexts, where they are used to transform routines that cannot be measured in the same terms. Edward Said has argued that a representation is based on the absence of what is to be re-presented (1978: 21; Fabian 1990b). Although this absence, as Mitchell argues, creates an appearance of order that hides its author(s) and authority, an absence can neither explain nor describe the historical and social circumstances and the microphysics through which these mechanisms were made effective by Europeans or resisted by the colonized, or vice versa (Hirschkind 1991; Pels 1994, 1996). Therefore, despite its evident contribution to a critical analysis of colonial discourse, the immunity of the study of discourses of colonial representation to historical contingency and material change makes it necessary to explore alternative epistemologies that give us a better feel of the specificities of colonial contact. The rest of this introduction tries to open up one such alternative. In order to do so, I will first concentrate on the effects of a specific instance of the European discourse of representation – ethnography – on anthropologists' writings about missionaries, particularly in Africa. Next, I hope to show how we might move from ethnography towards alternative conceptualizations of colonial contact. Lastly, I hope to indicate how these epistemological alternatives – all urging a microphysics of colonial contact – relate to the study of religious phenomena, and "conversion" and "initiation" in particular.

THE MISSION OF ETHNOGRAPHY: ETHNIC WHOLES AND COLONIAL DUALITIES

During the largest part of its history, it was the mission of ethnography to deny colonial contact. As we have seen, ethnographic representation usually involved a judgment of cultural authenticity, and this was its main contribution to the maintenance of the Manichean dichotomies of colonial ideology. Before we enter into the specific consequences of this historical fact, let me clarify my use of "mission" and "ethnography" and briefly sketch the relationships between the two.

One needs to avoid two common connotations of "mission". Firstly, a mission is not necessarily religious: bombers fly missions, French bureaucrats are *en mission*; United States officials are sent on a mission to the Netherlands to find out how badly drug-traffic is handled by the Dutch authorities.[7] Anthropologists can be on a mission, too: the concept was applied to the funding of anthropological research in Thailand by the US Department of Defense, meant to aid a policy of "stability" – that is, the repression of factions hostile to US interests (Wolf and Jorgensen 1970). This implies, secondly, that "mission" does not primarily signify the

---

[7] Example from *NRC-Handelsblad*, 11.8.87.

bringing of knowledge (or bombs), but also its gathering and taking away (Pels 1990a: 78–9). Mission implies the perception of the *lack* of something among the people to whom it is directed: a lack of control of drug-traffic in Holland, a lack of "stability" in Thailand, and in the case of Christian missions, the lack of the knowledge of the Gospel and the institution of the Church. The pivot of mission is the strategy of moving "out there" to rectify that lack.

A missionary perspective was a staple of European travellers' diets. In the early modern period, conquest and mission were rarely thought as separate endeavours, and post-crusade Christianity seems to have given Europeans a far more acute sense of cultural segregation than many of the people encountered felt towards Europeans.[8] Ethnography emerged in the late eighteenth century in the guise of a "manners-and-customs" genre which produced ethnic difference "without an explicit anchoring either in an observing self or in a particular encounter in which *contact* with the Other takes place" (Pratt 1985: 121, emphasis mine), and by this "denial of coevalness" (Fabian 1983a) ethnographers created a positive essentialization of the Other's "nature" that tended to replace the negative characterizations of early modern missionizing perspectives (Thomas 1994: 71). During the resurgence of Christian missionary inspiration in the early nineteenth century, ethnography was added to missionary activity as something indispensable for the proper incorporation of pagans in the modern world. Yet, a tension often existed between the missionary and ethnographic parts of colonial projects: missionary interests, for instance, criticized the reification of the Indian "other" by orientalism, for creating an obstacle to conversion. This criticism provided the context, in Britain and India, for the popularizing of the concept of "ethnology", which arose within the tension between the definition of ethnic essences and the disruption of them by universal measures of "improvement" (Pels 1995).

"Ethnology" was a universal science that could subsume ethnic differences under overarching spatio-temporal schemes, whether Christian or scientific, and it accomodated to missionizing

---

[8] See, for example, the essays of Lockhart, Reid and Da Silva in Schwartz (1994).

by creating the image of the Other as a "past" in terms of a discourse on origins or traditions, the base line from which someone
had to be converted (Pels 1995; Thomas 1992: 373; Van der Veer
1995). But contrary to many members of the colonial administration, Christian missionaries had little interest in recreating the
whole "original" constitution of the tribe of ethnic group in order
to graft colonial rule on it. The primary interest of missionaries was
to convert individuals, and classifications of ethnic essences could
be both means to that end and obstacles in its way. In some cases,
missionaries contributed to the definition of ethnicities by identifying the part of the population at which proselytizing could most
profitably be directed (Dirks 1995). In others, they actively produced those ethnicities by the necessity of classifying and recording
a language in which proselytizing could proceed (Vail 1989: 11–12).
But the practical goal of conversion directed their ethnography at
the splitting up of ethnic wholes, by identifying those customs that
could, and those that could not, be adopted by a Christian. In other
words, for many missionaries ethnography was a way to separate
out "customs" rather than an essentialization of an ethnic whole
(Pels 1994; Thomas 1992).

In the nineteenth century, this "selective" goal of ethno-
graphizing was shared by many colonial administrators and anthropologists (see Tylor 1873, II: 453). Ethnology was inspired by
missionary interests, and friendly cooperation between anthropologists and missionaries was the rule rather than an exception
(Ackerman 1987: 8, 122, 153; Müller 1873; Pels 1995). Even where
missionaries, anthropologists and administrators did not share a
Christian ideal, the civilizing mission of secular "welfare" retained
much of its rhetoric (Mitchell n.d.; Viswanathan 1989). Because the
early attempts towards professionalization of anthropologists were
primarily directed at funding by the colonial establishment, they
initially stressed that they could serve missionaries and administrators with their general knowledge, rather than with local ethnographic expertise, an expertise missionaries were still supposed to
share (Hocart 1914; Rivers 1920; Smith 1924; Temple 1914).

Even though, in the twentieth century, development work
retained this missionary dimension, professional anthropology

started to set itself off from missionary interests. This was not just because Malinowski developed a "hatred of missionaries" (1967: 31) and passed his suspicions on to his pupils (Firth 1936: 49; Powdermaker 1966: 43; Stocking 1991), but also because the development of fieldwork expertise and the claim to professional authority based on the brokerage of *local* "native points of view" made missionaries into rivals of anthropologists, rather than sources of their ethnography or clients of their general expertise (Pels 1990a). Malinowski and Radcliffe-Brown were involved in several skirmishes with missionaries like Wilhelm Schmidt, H. P. Junod and Diedrich Westermann about the formers' new claims to ethnographic authority (Brandewie 1983a: 111–6; 1983b, 1990; Junod 1935; Tomas 1991; Westermann 1931). In practice, this anthropological *dédain* of missionary activity was often hard to sustain: Malinowski's attempts to expand the number of professional fieldworkers were realized by a missionary (J. H. Oldham) who put him up as the most promising candidate for Rockefeller funding (Stocking 1985) and this cooperation may have led Malinowski to soften his judgments (Malinowski 1935b). This ambiguity between criticism of missionary activities and the necessity for practical cooperation[9] may partly explain why anthropologists preferred to keep silent about missionaries between 1930 and 1960 (Van der Geest and Kirby 1992).

This silence should not obscure, however, that a shift was taking place in the relationships between anthropologists and missionaries. Rockefeller funding enabled Malinowski to emancipate anthropology from the patronage of the colonial establishment, and allowed for a reformulation of the profession as a "pure" academic endeavour. This reduced, for academic anthropologists, the tension between the ethnographic project and the practical exigencies of the civilizing mission: the latter was no longer structurally and practically allied to the former. Building their academic identity on professional ethnography, anthropologists "inclined to introduce into the object the principles of [their] relation to the object", in

---

[9] In the sense of both academic cooperation at home and practical support of anthropologists by missionaries in the field.

other words, to constitute practical activity from an academic point of view "as an *object of observation and analysis, a representation*" (Bourdieu 1977: 2, emphases in original). "Ethnography" became the "map" of a whole culture, which professional anthropologists could (refuse to) deal out to "practical men" engaged with its administration and development, whether in Christian, political or economic terms. Henceforth, anthropologists would assess missionary or any other "amateur" ethnographic activity in the context of this academic, intellectualist discourse. In recent years, the meaning of "ethnography" has shifted again, from the idea of the description of an ethnic whole to a "fieldwork" method for which the description of ethnic wholes is something to avoid rather than to practice (more about that below).

Particularly in the more politicized relations between "First", "Second" and "Third World" countries in the period of decolonization, the missionary desire for conversion was interpreted as the opposite of the respect for other cultures that was associated with "ethnography". Many anthropologists argued the idea of an essential difference between missionaries and anthropologists. Missionaries, they said, come to teach, while anthropologists come to learn; in other words, the essential characteristic of the missionary was that he *imposes* his culture upon others.[10] It was challenged by scholars who did not see that this opposition was necessary, and who argued that anthropologists and missionaries had a lot in common and that the former are excessively prejudiced against the latter.[11] The implicit parameter of these discussions was the holist

---

[10] See Abbink 1985, 1990; Beidelman 1982: 5–6, 17 n. 34; Brown 1944: 217; Delfendahl 1981; Fields 1982a; Hughes 1978; Hvalkof and Aaby 1981; La Fontaine 1985: 21. This is partly because the lack of studies of late and postcolonial societies has perpetuated Victorian or Edwardian images of missionaries among anthropologists and historians (Etherington 1983: 129). This gap is being filled (see Arbuckle 1978; Hezel 1978; Huber 1988; Ngokwey 1978; Schieffelin 1981; Shapiro 1981).

[11] See Brandewie 1983a; Forster 1986; Hiebert 1978a, 1978b; Luzbetak 1961; Nida 1959, 1966; Stipe 1980; Thomas 1989: 70–73, Van der Geest 1990; see also the essays of Droogers, Trouwborst and Van Beek in Bonsen *et al.* 1990 and the majority of essays in Salamone and Whiteman 1983.

concept of culture, which identified missionaries as belonging to a dominating, Christian one, and anthropologists as the brokers of the culture threatened by it.

These discussions were, until recently, rarely based on empirical studies of the process of missionization. However, they stimulated interest in it, and this may be the reason why many recent anthropological studies of missions "at the grassroots" are characterized by a similar holist reification of missionary and indigenous culture.[12] Beidelman's studies portray missionaries as being caught in their own institution (which he modelled upon bureaucracy) or as "prisoner[s] of [their] own concepts" (1974: 246). As a result, colonial contact can only be conceived in terms of "inconsistencies" (1974: 246) or "contradictions" (1981, 1982: 60–71) between the ordered institution or world view and the world itself. In other words, the analysis could not grasp the dialectical relation which was established between missionaries and Africans: Beidelman's perspective could account for misunderstanding between them, but not explain why this was a *working* misunderstanding" (Wyllie 1976: 202, emphasis mine). This view retained the functionalist and colonialist tendency to analyze change as the breakdown of traditional structures ("detribalization" – see, for instance, the essays of Middleton and Bates in Harlow and Chilver 1965). The analysis did not provide means with which to understand the creation of new relations between missionary and African, and Africans remained largely out of the picture.

Beidelman's ironic treatment of missionaries ("they do not do what they say they do") is characteristic of the anthropological stereotype of the misfit between missionary representations and colonial reality (Comaroff and Comaroff 1992: 36; Fernandez 1964; Rigby 1981). A recent analysis of the functioning of these kind of tropes in colonial discourse shows that missionary world views were not that naive, but does not bring the contact of missionaries and indigenous people into perspective (see Huber 1988, and

---

[12] In the following overview, I have left out the few contributions of sociologists (Heise 1967; Park 1944), the work of Karen Fields (1982a, 1982a, 1985) excepted.

my critique, Pels 1990b). Many such interpretive (or structuralist – see Corbey 1989a, 1989b; Corbey and Melssen 1990) studies of missionary discourse do not seem to be able to escape the closure that the postulate of systematic relationships of symbols and narratives brings with it (Comaroff and Comaroff 1991: 16), and of course, this postulate was, until recently, the core of most ethnography in a "symbolic" vein. Although biographical treatments of missionary careers produce much suggestive material about colonial contact and ethnography (Clifford 1982; Forster 1989), their focus on individual and often exceptionally sensitive missionary ethnographers is misleading on the missionary side, and tends to reify the "other".

Whereas ethnographies of missionaries tend to isolate them from their contact with, and influence on, Africans, ethnographies of African responses to missions often leave out the colonizer. African Christian movements, for instance, have been a focus of interest for quite some time (see Fabian 1979, Fernandez 1978), but mostly for the light they could throw on "authentic" indigenous expressions of Christianity (cf. Etherington 1983: 122). The concept of "movement" often functioned as a surrogate for "tribe" or "culture" (Fabian 1981: 112). Even in one of the most brilliant studies of a Christian-inspired independent movement to date, Fernandez' *Bwiti* (1982), the full impact of colonial contact is not taken into account (Vansina 1984: 230). Studies of orthodox mission Christians are still scarce (Fabian 1971: 165; Meyer 1992, note 7; but see Colson 1970), which partly explains the enduring appeal of the idea that they are simply the victims of missionary imposition (Meyer 1992: 98).[13]

This reification of the African side of colonial contact accounts for the popularity of the "conversion" theory put forward by Horton (1971). Horton treats cosmological beliefs of Africans as independent variables (Ranger and Kimambo 1972: 9–10).[14]

---

[13] Isolated studies of missions and the movements they spawned can exist between the covers of one book: Mary Huber's account of cargo cults in the Sepik area (1988: 107 ff.) is as divorced from her account of Sepik mission practice as the study of African religious movements was from African missions.

[14] Cf. Thomas' remarks about Sahlins' culturalist history of Hawaii (1989: 111).

This fostered the conviction that missions, perhaps, did nothing for Africans that Africans could not do for themselves (witness the independent churches – Etherington 1983: 121). Thus, Horton (1971: 104) and others tended to agree with Wole Soyinka's idea that the colonial factor was a mere "catalytic incident" (quoted in Prins 1980: 15). From such a perspective, colonial contact appears at best as the meeting of "two unrelated structures of belief" (Isichei 1970: 212) and it is not surprising that such a lack of relation also entails a lack of acknowledgment for the impact of "white power" (Ifeka-Möller 1974). Horton's essay is not, strictly speaking, about conversion (as a process), but about its intellectual conditions as they pertain within "traditional" or "modern" cosmologies. The concepts of the intellectualist perspective "fail to explain just *how* changed social circumstances or individuals' needs come to be matched by ideational changes" (Peel 1990: 339, emphasis in original).[15]

The tendency of ethnography to ignore the "epistemological priority of interaction" by the creation of "two opposed ideal types" (Peel 1990: 339) may be fruitfully countered by historicizing "ethnography" and "culture" as necessary *parts of* colonial projects (Dirks 1992; Thomas 1994). But historiography is not an easy way out: like ethnography, historians' conceptions of historical agency often had the same effect of reifying one side of the colonial encounter. Histories written by missionary scholars often reify the role of Western Churches as agents of change (for a recent example, see Sahlberg 1986). Roland Oliver's pioneering study of East African missions (1952) had little to say about African initiatives.[16]

---

[15] Horton's Popperian terminology also imports Western concepts to understand African ones, with ethnocentric implications (see Fernandez 1978: 220–2). Here, however, my aim is first of all to show how Horton's analysis tends to bracket out the *presence* of missionaries. I deal further with the concept of "conversion" below (pp. 22 ff.).

[16] I have no room for a full overview of historical work on African missions, but will regularly refer to it (aided by Etherington 1983) in order to show the convergence of anthropological and historical problems in the study of the colonial encounter, and criticize the so-called lack of theoretical sophistication of historians (Beidelman 1974: 237, also criticized by Etherington 1977: 31). Much more nuanced views can be found in Cohn (1987), Comaroff and Comaroff (1992: 17), Dirks (1992) and Thomas (1989, 1994).

What appeared in anthropology as a way of understanding colonial relationships from the point of view of native cosmologies, was, for a later generation of nationalist historians, a way of affirming African initiative.[17] The nationalist history of the 1960s turned the tables on the missionary: instead of being an important historical factor (as in Oliver 1952), he now was presented as a mere conveyor of the political projects of the colonial powers (see the literature cited by Etherington, 1983: 117). Christianity became the "ritual aspect of European colonialism" (Welbourn 1971: 310). In this way, the missionary lost much of his status as an independent agent in African history. Conversely, the historical study of African religion shifted from active European agents ("all too easy" to describe historically – Ranger and Kimambo 1972: 2–3) to the symbolic and ritual systems that encompassed African responses to them (see the references to Horton [1971] and Swantz [1986; first published 1970] in Ranger and Kimambo 1972). Etherington remarked that while the study of African religion had grown to impressive proportions, the missionary had largely disappeared from it (1983: 122).

Thus, the shift to African initiative in historiography showed a tendency to take over the anthropological reification of culture. It either ignored the missionary altogether, or reinforced the dichotomy of cultures by interpreting colonial contact predominantly in terms of Western imposition and African resistance (Linden and Linden 1974; Schoffeleers and Linden 1972; Strayer 1973). The tendency to reify one "culture" by ethnography contributed, at a more encompassing level of analysis, to seeing historical process in terms of colonial dualities, and the making of colonial society in terms of two distinct cultural and social entities standing in a relationship of opposition and conflict. This tendency towards dualism was itself a legacy of colonial discourse

---

[17] For East Africa, see Kimambo and Temu (1969), Temu (1972). The movement attempted to restore historical initiative to Africans, initially by focussing on the pre-colonial period (Kimambo 1969; Ogot 1967; Roberts 1968) or by drawing attention to Africans' modernizing agency (Iliffe 1973; Ochieng 1972). For an overview of African historiography, see Jewsewiecki and Newbury (1986).

(Cooper 1992: 210), and had only been reinforced by the advent of professional ethnography. One of the possible responses to this situation was what has been termed a "historiographic revolution" (Marks, cited in Comaroff and Comaroff 1991: 8): the study of longer-term processes of colonial conquest and rule from a political economy perspective, focussing on the articulation of different modes of production with each other. In East African history, the approach became popular among scholars dissatisfied with the "preoccupation with politics" (Kimambo 1991: xii; see also Sheriff 1987) of African nationalist perspectives. But whereas Marxist analysis has been crucial in foregrounding the material mediations of colonial contact through the exchange of objects and labour, and the concept of "articulation" promised advances in the study of how capitalism and the commodity form became more prominent in African societies, it seemed that the concept of "mode of production" again reified colonial contact (Comaroff 1985: 154).

In many studies that employed the concept of "mode of production", the missionary fared as badly as before. Etherington (1983: 130) remarks upon the total neglect of missionaries in histories of underdevelopment (McCracken [1977] excepted[18]). In one of the most comprehensive overviews of the relevance of a political economy perspective to global history, mission and missionaries are not even mentioned in the index (Wolf 1982: 491), despite the fact that missionaries had an enormous impact on the way in which indigenous people were integrated in colonial and global economies (Comaroff 1985; Fabian 1983b: 169). It is significant that one of the more ethnographically detailed analysis of missions from a political economy perspective shows how the majority of Masai were *not* converted (Rigby 1981). By emphasizing the integration of ideology in a mode of production, the analysis went no further than the statement that occasional conversions were a "result of

---

[18] McCracken shows how missionaries instituted wage labour and commodity exchange, but ignores the importance of, for instance, missionary education for the colonial economy (cf. Fabian 1983b: 171) and the *cultural* impact of the "commodity form" (see Comaroff and Comaroff 1991: 23; and chapter five and seven below).

historical circumstances" and the reiteration of the thesis of a "flagrant contradiction" between the behaviour of missionaries and their professed values (1981: 115, 122).

These conclusions resemble Beidelman's, and confirm the suspicion that Marxist analyses, by postulating an integrated *whole* by means of the concept of "mode of production", can reintroduce functionalist biases towards history and change into a discourse that was meant to overcome it (cf. Eves' critique of Godelier, 1991: 112).[19] In short, they again tend to reduce colonial contact to a meeting of coherent wholes (now "modes of production" instead of "tribes" or "cultures") and reproduce a dualistic view of colonial society. Thus, a number of different approaches towards the history of missions and African Christianity reproduce the colonial mission of ethnography: the attempt to bring a certain classificatory order (in terms of establishing the existence of cultural wholes like "tribes", "religious movements", "modes of production" or coherent groups of historical agents) to colonial situations that apparently – and I would add, often actually – lack such coherence. Yet, the recent changes in the notion of ethnography that I already mentioned above signal attempts to explore different epistemological possibilities, and some of these may help us to go beyond the dichotomous images of colonial situations that until recently held the field.

TOWARDS AN EPISTEMOLOGY OF COLONIAL CONTACT

In a sense, the tension within a missionary project between the practice of converting or improving "others" and the necessity to classify them as "other" is parallelled, in twentieth-century ethnography, by the tension between the necessity of intimate (field) contact with people and the work of representing them in

---

[19] Conversely, the historian's bias towards historical agency leads him to impute "capitalist" motives to the bureaucrats of the colonial administration, and to ignore the material mediations of capitalist relations of production by missionary education (see Kimambo 1991 and my critique of that volume, Pels 1992b).

writing. The awareness of that tension is a fairly recent development: while from Tylor to the early Malinowski, ethnography was
taken to be an exercise in classification, that is, an ascription of cultural traits to ethnic wholes (Malinowski 1911: 25; Tylor 1873, I: 7),
in the latter part of the twentieth century it is increasingly taken to
also encompass "the facticity of first-hand experience" (Comaroff
and Comaroff 1992: 8) and the practice of fieldwork as such
(Hammersley and Atkinson 1983). This tension between the classifying "eye" and the observing "I" was present in ethnography from
its colonial beginnings (Pratt 1985), but this elementary condition
of *textual* authority should not obscure that fieldwork entails many
activities that are not "ethnographic" and that the description of
cultural wholes should be distinguished from fieldwork practice
(cf. Thomas 1991b: note 3).[20] The subsumption of fieldwork under
ethnography was made possible by the fiction of ethnographic
holism. From a theoretical assumption about adequate classification, holism became not just a descriptive convention, but also
a "method" (Firth 1968: 320), that is, a research strategy, despite the
fact that in the practice of research, "social wholes cannot be directly
perceived by a single human observer" (Thornton 1988: 288).

Here, I do not want to take issue with the uses of "ethnography" in present-day social science (but see Pels and Salemink
1994: 16–7) except by noting that the present, encompassing notion
of "ethnography" has created an awareness of a number of different
epistemological possibilities. In fact, recent critiques of ethnography started from the observation that the production of textual
authority in ethnography needs to be distinguished from the production of knowledge in the fieldwork encounter (Clifford 1983;
Pratt 1985: 121). Anthropology defined its object through a denial
of contact between anthropologist and "others", through a textual
production of distance between them which was reified in concepts
like "culture" and elaborated in theories that "circumvented" or
"preempted" time and history (Fabian 1983a; Thomas 1991a: 3).

---

[20] Even in his charter of modern fieldwork practice, Malinowski was careful to
distinguish "ethnographic" from "archaeological" or "zoological fieldwork"
(1922: 24).

Ethnography as the textual production of ethnic wholes foregrounds a *visualist* epistemology that constitutes knowledge as
reflecting or representing its object, not as a product of interacting
with it. It thereby denies some of the epistemological possibilities
that enabled it to produce this knowledge in the first place. In fact,
the "denial of coevalness" with the people with whom ethnographers make knowledge (Fabian 1983a: 31) can be compared to the
denial of contact, charted in the previous section, between missionaries and the Africans with whom they made African Christianity.

Both denials of shared history seem to have a common epistemological background, one that goes back upon the visualist
conception of ethnographic representation contained within eigh-
teenth- and nineteenth-century practices of statistics, naturalist
expeditions and questionnaires (Pels and Salemink 1994: 6–9). This
"survey" model of ethnic classification was, in the twentieth century,
incorporated into fieldwork methodology by the dominance (especially in Anglo-Saxon anthropology) of the doctrine of cultural
holism. This further reinforced a politics of perception based on a
visualist sensory regime of "observation", while emotive or tactile
conceptions of privileged mediation and production of knowledge (like "sympathy", "tact" or physical experiment) disappeared
from the language of anthropological research.[21] As Johannes
Fabian has argued, "visualism" contributes much to the rhetorical
creation of temporal and spatial distance between observer and
observed, and thus to the reification of the dichotomy between self
and other. This suggests that, to improve our understanding of
colonial contact, we may profitably ask what other epistemological
possibilities are relevant to the politics of perception of ethnographic fieldwork.[22]

---

[21] For the visualist survey model, see Malinowski's definition of ethnographic
fieldwork as based on a "complete survey" of "tribal life" and his insistence on
"mental charts" and "synoptic tables" (1922: 11, 13, 14). For the emotive and
tactile conceptions of research mediation, see Temple (1914), Haddon (1921),
Kuklick (1991: 199).
[22] The notion of a "politics of perception" in anthropological fieldwork is
further explored in Van Dijk and Pels (1996).

Criticizing ethnographic rhetoric from his understanding of fieldwork practice, Johannes Fabian has argued that for anthropological research, conversation – the dialectics of aural and oral perception – may provide a better starting-point for epistemological reflection than perception through vision (1983a: 119; 1990a: 4). The model of conversation foregrounds turn-taking in speech and a coeval experience of time between interlocutors, and thereby brings time, change in initiative and participation in interaction back to epistemological reflection. These are all issues that are crucial for an understanding of colonial contact. Jean and John Comaroff, by stressing a "long conversation" going on between colonizers and colonized (1991: 11; also, Gray 1990: 75), have shown that such a shift in epistemological attention makes missionary-African contact central to the understanding of colonial history. They divorce "culture" from the "binary world map or axis of typological difference" (1992: 32) that is, from the fundamental assumption of ethnographic holism. They understand "culture" as a far wider repertoire of signifiers-in-action, and emphasize the dimension of power by focussing on the ideological contest and the mutual construction of "mute" hegemony among missionaries and Africans (1991: 19–27). They stress this epistemological dimension of colonial contact by emphasizing that consciousness should not only be taken as content, but also as form, as "modes of knowing" (1991: 29), and have early on explored the extent to which these modes of knowing are materially mediated, in particular through the body (Comaroff 1985).

I want to try to take these seminal insights one step further. Although "conversation" is an epistemologically rich metaphor, one may question whether it extends to the way people communicate non-verbally. Jean and John Comaroff argue that ideology invites argument, while hegemony is "mute" and finds its "natural habitat" in the human body (1992: 29, 40). This would imply that many patterns of hegemony are communicated at the level of the body, that is, *not* articulate, argumentative or conversational. The complementarity of, and difference between, articulate linguistic exchange and "mute" corporeal communication can be best brought out by zooming in on one of the most excellent essays devoted to the former.[23] Vicente Rafael has argued that Spanish missionaries' attempts to conquer the Philippines through conversion was predicated on the linguistic exchange (the "conversation") of translation. Translation through the contextualizing categories of Spanish Christian thought turned the Tagalog language into a derivative of Latin and Castilian and structured confessional discourse "in such a way that the convert's narrative of sin was filled with the syntax of Christian wishfulness" (1992: 70). Yet, this structure of power in Spanish translations does not explain the readiness of Tagalogs to receive Christianity. Rafael shows how certain Spanish signifiers were emptied of their content, shifting the pronunciation of a name like "JesusMaria" from an expression of submission to a charm that defends against evil (1992: 74). Moreover, he argues that Tagalog turned the missionary translation of "soul" (loob) from a sign of submission to the missionary into one of reciprocity with him (1992: 83). Thus, the unfixing of verbal signifiers in the process of conversation created the space for a contest of meanings in which power remained negotiable. But Rafael also argues that the "shocking" gift of signs by Spanish missionaries – more a gesture than a linguistic sign – drove Tagalog to return it by participating in a confession ritual. Although the Tagalog responses "subverted the entire *conceptual* apparatus of confession" (1992: 85, my emphasis), it may not have subverted the physical discipline of confession, that individualized the body of the penitent by putting it at the disposal of the confessor until the latter's absolution was given. This indicates that a "mute" microphysics of ritual may generate a different power relationship, parallel and not reducible to the articulate exchange and unfixing of verbal signifiers.[24]

---

[23] Other useful approaches to (post-) colonial contact through conceptions of linguistic exchange employ concepts like "translation" (Meyer 1992, 1995; Rafael 1988), "rhetoric" and "reciprocity" (Schieffelin 1981), "dialogue" (Schoffeleers 1975, 1982, 1988), "pidginization" (Fabian 1978: 317; Pels 1996) or "creolization" (Hannerz 1987). For a critique of "dialogue", see note 26.

[24] Of course, Rafael's seventeenth-century sources may not allow explicit conclusions about the microphysics of such linguistic performance. The example is not meant as a critique of, but as a thought-experiment with, Rafael's argument.

The example may well be compared with Father Bukkems' initiation, in which the microphysics of the ways in which Bukkems and the elders of Tegetero presented themselves to each other generated a power-play that escaped the verbal signifiers of a "genuine" or "faked" Luguru initiation. In order to systematically address this layering of the contact situation in explicitly articulated but unfixed signifiers and a "mute" microphysics that also contributed to the generation of power relationships, I feel that another extension of our awareness of epistemological possibilities, like the one suggested by Fabian and the Comaroffs, is called for.[25] If an epistemology of "conversation" criticizes the dominance of the sense of vision in anthropological epistemology by invoking the oral/aural senses as a counterpoint, this implies a broadening of our *aesthetics* (in the Aristotelian sense of the word), that is, of our study of the material process of mediation of knowledge through the senses (Eagleton 1990: 13). In order to appreciate the microphysics of colonial contact, I feel that it is necessary to extend our aesthetics one step further, to the root of the word con*tact*: tactility, the sense of touch (cf. Taussig 1991).

As in the case of Fabian's switch to the aural/oral, the sense of touch is important not because of its literal meaning, but because it points to a further improvement of a dialectical concept of communication (Fabian 1983a: 119). While a focus on aural perception and oral expression may still tempt us to reduce the analysis of colonial contact to "dialogue",[26] an awareness of tactile communication foregrounds the way in which both verbal exchange and

---

[25] So does Fabian (1991: 398–9; see also 1983a: 108). Sanjek's attack on Fabian's "narrow" epistemological metaphors (1992: 619), therefore, is misconceived. The Comaroffs use sensory registers more eclectically than Fabian. They seem to shift from "conversation" to metaphors of vision (e.g. the "chain of consciousness" from "unseen" to "seen"; 1991: 29) especially when trying to subordinate "contingency" to "historical structure" in a kind of retrospective panopticon: "What might *once* have seemed eventful and contingent *now* (i.e. from our present/pp) looks to have been part of a more regular pattern..." (1991: 18, emphases mine).

[26] A reduction criticized by, among others, Comaroff and Comaroff (1992: 10–1), Fabian (1991) and Said (1989).

other forms of communication are *materially mediated*. Perception through touch happens when our body comes into immediate contact with other matters. As I indicated above in discussing Rafael's example, the power relationships negotiated in the process of verbal exchange need to be set next to the way in which, in linguistic performance, the bodies of speakers are brought in touch with each other. Other perceptual processes, however, also have tactile dimensions: Walter Benjamin has pointed this out for vision, when he wrote that Dada, film, photography and architecture provoke a kind of "distracted" perception which acquires a "tactile quality" (quoted in Taussig 1991: 148–9).[27] Aural perception also acquires tactility through sound: think of the different touch of sound waves on the eardrum of a whispered, as compared to a shouted, message. As Taussig has argued, an intellectualist point of view (he calls it the "contemplative" mode) often ignores the importance of such tactile mediation in social processes (1991).[28]

Secondly, tactile perception is impossible without *movement*. For matters to come into touch, they have to move towards each other. Thus, the sense of touch, like the turn-taking of the oral and aural senses, implies a *temporal* mode of perception. The extent to which contact implies movement, however, has hardly been acknowledged in studies of colonial society. Even where anthropologists acknowledge that missionaries had to *move to* the societies where they wanted to do their proselytizing, the preconditions for this move and the changes which these movements embody have only recently become a subject of study (Clifford 1992; Comaroff and Comaroff 1991: ch. 5; Fabian 1985; see chapter two). The same goes for the movements of Africans to and into the churches (see chapter three). Although we may not always be able

---

[27] Vision, therefore, is much more multifaceted than the "visualism" that Fabian criticizes (see Van Dijk and Pels 1996).

[28] Note 21 gives references to earlier anthropology, in which the head measuring and biceps pinching of physical anthropology combined with notions of "tact" in attitude, to give more tactile dimensions to research; the Torres Straits expedition even had a separate researcher for the natives' "tactile sensibility" (Quiggin 1942: 101).

to say what these movements *mean*, they often *embody* the historical changes that so many anthropological concepts do not seem to be able to grasp.

Tactility also highlights the extent to which *material processes of communication can be both indeterminate and determining*. The touch is indeterminate: it is not directly apparent from the act itself what it represents. The touch is also determining, a presentation that makes a physical difference (depending, for instance, on whether it is a blow or a caress). Similarly, a building is indeterminate to the extent that, though the people using it need not be aware of the principles that went into its construction, yet its physical structure at least partly determines their movements and perception: the building materially mediates the different processes of signification of its production and consumption. The same goes for the making of a photograph and its perception by someone else unconnected to its production process, or the production of a sound and the way it is inserted into a process of signification by a listener. Essentially, this is an argument against the reduction of matter to meaning, of material culture to linguistic conceptions of signification (Miller 1987). A plea for tactility, therefore, is a safeguard against the Geertzian reification of meaning (Scholte 1986). It suggests that we should not let the "thick description" of webs of significance (Geertz 1973) efface the "thin description" of the events, objects and performances that (partly) escape these webs of significance.

The latter argument connects up with a last, maybe obvious, but very important point: that tactility is impossible without perceiver and perceived being *co-present*. Co-presence or coevalness is a trait which both tactile and oral/aural perception share, but it distinguishes them at the same time. Co-presence is not merely a condition for communication, it *is* communication: it points out the possibility that communication is actually achieved without recourse to discourse. This connects up with the argument made by several scholars that *bodily mimesis and positioning* is one of the most important carriers of cultural – and, I would add, cross-cultural – continuity (Bourdieu 1977; Comaroff 1985; Foucault 1979; Jackson 1983). Father Bukkems' experiences illustrate this point: trouble started not because he was given a native rank (disputable in any case), but because he had been present at a ritual performance and mimed – through dress and greetings and attending beer-feasts – the fact that he had. In other words, it was not the paradoxical discourse on Bukkems' rank, but co-presence and bodily mimesis which triggered the sequence of power struggles in Tegetero. However, bodily mimesis and positioning is only a part of the microphysics mediating the interactions between missionary and African: in the following chapters I will add, among others things, the placement of photographs in missionary journals, buildings and their use, the exchange of objects, labour and money, dance and discipline.

I should emphasize that my stress on tactility does not imply a claim to ontological *priority*. Even if, in the following chapters, I may seem to emphasize the material mediations of the contact between Holy Ghost Fathers and Waluguru at the expense of their theological contests, this is often more the result of the Roman Catholic Church's own preoccupation with ritual action, and not a theoretical choice that opposes an ideational superstructure to a material base. I have emphasized the epistemological layering of colonial contact to bring out that the contest among missionaries and Waluguru over ways to re-present self and other was both reinforced, and offset by the way they had to present themselves to each other, *and vice versa*. If the material mediations of discipline and initiation, production and exchange could trigger the "unfixing" or ground the "fixing" of a number of floating signifiers, the repertoire of representations of both missionaries and Africans were also crucial for the timing, placing and material form of the ways in which they got in touch with each other.

Before turning to the consequences of this perspective for our understanding of missionization, it is necessary to caution against some unwanted consequences of the identification of hegemony with "mute" tactile communication and both with a "non-agentive" mode of power (Comaroff and Comaroff 1992: 28). As Jean and John Comaroff write elsewhere, the human body can become a zone of social struggle (1992: 40), implying that even mute communication takes place in a partly "agentive" mode, even if it does not have the articulate and argumentative dimension of ideological struggle. It is necessary to caution against this identification of tactile communication with a nonagentive hegemony, because it might lead to the anthropological stereotype of missionaries who consciously fight for conversion, but remained unconscious of the messages they conveyed in practice (Beidelman 1982; Comaroff and Comaroff 1992: 36). As I hope the following pages show, missionaries and African could consciously engage in struggles even if these rarely reached the level of articulate reflection. In fact, this is what Michel Foucault referred to when he wrote that the model for "microphysics" was a kind of "perpetual battle" (1979: 26). In battle, when the planning of strategies has given way to tactical physical engagement, it is gut reaction rather than reflection that determines the combatants' moves.

CONVERSION, INITIATION, RELIGION AND DISCIPLINE

What consequences does this view of a dialectic of verbal and tactile communication have for our conception of the religious change that missionaries wanted to effect and Africans were meant to undergo? I have already concluded from the example of Father Bukkems that conversion usually denotes a one-way mental process, the terms of which were dictated by the missionary, but that initiation seemed to be something of a more reciprocal and social nature: a process in which initiands put their bodies at the disposal of the initiators and are (in)vested with some of their powers in return. Indeed, Waluguru often talked of the coming of Christianity in terms of the "gift" of religion by the missionaries, a term that suggests the possibility, even the obligation, of reciprocity by an appropriate return. When Waluguru talked of "eating" baptism (kula matema; chapter six) – their early interpretation of the rite that, for the missionaries, marked their conversion – the change of allegiance that it implied was looked upon with the caution Waluguru reserve for the potent magic of initiated elders. As I argue in chapter three, the success of Christianity in Uluguru in the 1930s is better understood as a novel and alternative initiation into adulthood. This reinforces the doubts about the utility of the term conversion that have already been voiced by Jean and John Comaroff (1991: 250). "Conversion", taken as a change of mind (Horton 1971, 1975; Peel 1977), may indeed only be the projected change missionaries were taught to engineer, not the actual change that their activities helped to engender.

In contrast, initiation was far more common than the unique experience of Father Bukkems may suggest. Incorporation into the Catholic Church occurred partly through forms of initiation. The missionaries themselves had, of course, undergone a severe initiation into the spirituality of the Congregation during their noviciate (chapter two). In Uluguru, the sacraments of baptism and marriage, and the ordination of African priests were usually accompanied by ceremonies and rhythms that Waluguru had used earlier to mark their own initiatiory practices (chapter three). In other words, whereas the question of the meaning of conversion for Waluguru leads immediately to doubts about the extent to which it was a genuine change of mind or not, and thus seems to lead into a realm of epistemic murk that also accompanied the question of the authenticity of Father Bukkems' "Luguru" rank, there seems to be little doubt that the religious change that occurred when Waluguru became Catholic involved the microphysics of bodily positioning and transformation that belongs to initiation.

I also think "initiation" is a more useful concept around which to organize a history of Luguru Christianity because of some of the epistemological assumptions that cling to the notion of "conversion". Conversion is a change of mind, and as such primarily knowable as a representation of self after the fact, within the context of a technology of self-control by the already converted. Notions of conversion, therefore, cut up the process of change by means of a dichotomy of before and after. Of course, initiation also implies such a dichotomy, but presents it in a more gradual way, as something akin to training and disciplining. It is a process of ceremonial transformation of self to which initiands knowingly submit themselves even if its consequences are not apparent beforehand, while for the initiator, it works as a technology of domination.

For the convert, the *telos* of the process is already clear, but for the initiand, the process is only known by the expectation of a future improvement through the powers with which he or she is invested. The historical specificity of this concept of conversion becomes clear once it is acknowledged that the present meaning of the word arose in the context of seventeenth-century Protestant Christianity (Van der Veer 1995), and in particular, in the context of a theological development towards an idea of religion as a privatized, individual kind of belief for which the idea of religious *training* – including initiation – had become marginal (Asad 1993: 53–4).

This theological development has had profound consequences for the anthropology of religion. Anthropological views of "religion" have been notoriously inept in the face of change and movement. To the extent that most theories of religion start from either the intellectualist (Tylorian) assumption that religion is a system of ideas for making sense of the world, or from the functionalist (Durkheimian) one that religion is a way of expressing social coherence, they are incapable of overcoming the reifications of culture or social structure criticized above – in fact, one might well presume they have contributed to the (re)formulation of these reifications. Goody's critique of definitions of religion in terms of the dichotomies of sacred and profane, or supernatural and natural, still holds: no such definition of religion can escape the fact that these dichotomies are projections of the observer which cannot be universalized on the level of native points of view (1961: 160). Talal Asad has argued that this is precisely because in Christian history, a concept of religion evolved that defines it as a symbolic order, a belief system either individually or collectively held – religion as a state of mind rather than practical knowledge (1993: 47 and *passim*).

Hence the ubiquitous tendency in anthropology to define initiation as the expression or representation of a social order, instead of a condensed physical transformation that aims to enable a person to function as a member of society (the idea of initiation as enabling rather than expressive and ordering practice is further elaborated in chapter four). In contrast, Talal Asad brings out the importance of tactile communication for religious training and initiation by focussing on the role of the infliction of physical pain in making medieval monastic discipline take effect (1993: 83 ff.). Pain, as all tactile communication, is not a representation and cannot be decoded: it neither expresses nor refers, but is the physical transformation itself. This is how I understand initiation, and also how I interpret Foucault's notion of "microphysics", as indicating the way in which disciplinary power is "more dependent on bodies and what they do" (Foucault, quoted in Hirschkind 1991: 283) than on the categories in which it is represented. In the following study of religious change, therefore, initiation and discipline occupy much more attention than the representations of conversion. While the process of religious transformation is in full swing, such represen-tations are murky and unstable, and their excessive instability pro-vokes a sense of crisis among people. But the crisis as such is set in motion by a microphysics of contact, in particular by the inter-action of Luguru initiation and Christian and educational discipline.

It might be that in stressing such knowledge of the body, I am reinstating a classic "missionary position".[29] Indeed, Talal Asad quotes the medieval theologian Hugh of St. Victor's remark that sacraments have been instituted "on account of humilitation, on account of instruction, on account of exercise" – a programme directed at the transformation of religious subjects that is very different from the Protestant tendency to see sacraments as symbols standing for something else (1993: 78). The Roman Catholic Church has, up to now, never completely relinquished this "materi-alist" view of the sacraments, and this may partly account for the emphasis that this book puts on initiation, ritual and magic shared among missionaries and Africans, rather than the more rigid repre-sentations of conversion that many Protestant missions asked from their African members (even among the neighbours of the Waluguru, see Beidelman 1982). But such a dose of Catholicism may be healthy for a scholarly tradition that is, as Asad has shown, still heavily indebted to the development of Protestant theology. Perhaps the debt is such that even my own representations of the process cannot completely convey the indeterminacy and poly-valence of the continuity, in the development of Luguru Christianity,

---

[29] As suggested in a discussion of this chapter by Prabhu Mohapatra.

between Christian discipline and Luguru initiations. This way of formulating the continuity already indicates that the words with which I need to express this microphysics do not escape restating the dichotomies I try to avoid. Very often, my only solution to this dilemma was to resort to paradoxy – in itself, a classical rhetorical strategy of Catholic theology[30] – by, for instance, choosing oxymorons for titles (like "*Kizungu* Rhythms", chapter three, or "White Magic", chapter six) or wavering in description between calling something a *ngoma* or a "school" (chapters three and five). Yet, I do not think that the result boils down to a conversation between two European Christian traditions only: this book is the product of contact with a Christianity that, even at the time when the white missionary was its main officiant, was also distinctively *African*.

CONTACTING THE PAST

The African Christianity studied in this book was the product of interactions between the inhabitants of the Uluguru Mountains, in Eastern Tanganyika (see map one) and Dutch Holy Ghost Fathers in the late colonial period, from about 1930 to Tanganyikan Independence, 1961. The people who in the course of the colonial encounter were identified as "Waluguru" or "people of the mountains" (Iliffe 1979: 8–9) seem to have been composed of groups of migrants arriving from all points of the compass in the late eighteenth and early nineteenth century (Mzuanda 1958: 7–8). Threatened by war or famine, they lost or left behind what cattle they owned and settled down as agriculturalists on the fertile slopes of the well-watered mountains. In this book, I will concentrate on the Waluguru of the Eastern slopes, where regular rainfall safeguards harvests against the recurrent droughts of the Eastern Tanzanian climate.[31]

---

[30] See Colie 1966; Horton 1970, 1973; Skorupski 1975.

[31] Although there are many points of similarity, there are sufficient differences between the well-watered, fertile Eastern slopes with their history of regular contacts with the Swahili coast and the drier Western slopes. For the recent history of West Uluguru, see Van Donge (1993).

The Congregation of the Holy Ghost has been one of the largest Roman Catholic congregations engaged in "foreign missions" since it merged with Francis Libermann's Congregation of the Holy Heart of Maria in 1848 under the latter's leadership. It was the first to build a Christian church on the East African mainland, at Bagamoyo. From Bagamoyo, Alsatian Holy Ghost missionaries founded the first stations on the slopes of the Uluguru mountains. Operating from the three Uluguru "mother"-stations, Morogoro (founded 1884), Matombo (1897) and Mgeta (1905), the Alsatian Fathers and Brothers slowly acquired a following, but mass baptisms of Waluguru occurred only after the arrival of the first Dutch missionaries and shortly before the Vicariate was assigned to the Dutch province of the Holy Ghost Fathers in 1933.[32]

In other words, the following history of the Eastern Uluguru missions is not neatly periodized. For some of the transformations which characterize the development of Luguru Christianity in the late colonial period, we have to go back to the beginning of this century or the end of the last to pick up the thread (see chapters three and five). For others, we have to move into post-independence history (chapter six). A watershed in the political field is 1925, the introduction of Indirect Rule to Uluguru (see Pels 1996). Ecclesiastically speaking, it is 1933, the assignment of the Vicariate of Bagamoyo to the Dutch Holy Ghost Fathers (chapter two). But for Waluguru, an important transformation seems to occur somewhere in between (chapter three). Not that periodization is very important for this study, as I do not attempt to describe chronological sequences and their demarcation in detail, but try to point out microphysical relationships that were relevant throughout the colonial period and beyond, although some are more important during the earlier phases of contact and others at a later stage.[33]

---

[32] See chapter three. Relevant aspects of Catholic culture and the Holy Ghost congregation in Holland are dealt with in chapter two. For the early history of the Vicariate of Bagamoyo, see Hertlein (1976, 1983), Kieran (1969, 1971), Sahlberg (1986); for the Congregation of the Holy Ghost in general, Koren (1983).

[33] A chronology of the most salient historical events is provided in appendix B.

Most of the chapters are written on the basis of material from fieldwork, interviewing and archival research done for a Ph.D. in anthropology. The material was dispersed over three countries, turned out to be sufficient for two books, but had to be dealt with in the time and with the funding available for only one.[34] Such a schedule necessitated choices in both research and writing up, and this book obviously presents only a specific slice of a much more multi-sided process.[35] But apart from an acknowledgment of the necessary constraints under which any historian or anthropologist labours, the choices made in research and its representation raise the more profound methodological problem of how one has contacted the past. In other words, is the epistemology of colonial contact I tried to sketch above also applicable to my own research? How did I get "in touch" with the past I shall try to evoke in this book?

At first sight, a tactile relation with the past seems impossible. Collingwood has argued that only reflective thought, a representation that is conscious of itself as a representation, can be the subject-matter of history (1961: 308). The referent of this representation is absent, our approach to it barred by time. Of course, Vicente Rafael's work is a good example of how one can access this past by reading existing documents against the grain, guided by the conviction that historical sources are traces of a contest of meanings, debates that not even the most powerful hegemony can erase. This possibility is enhanced when one can critically juxtapose

---

[34] In 1989 and 1990, I spent seventeen months in Tanzania, twelve in Uluguru and the remaining five in archives in Dar es Salaam. Interviewing Dutch missionaries and British administrators and consulting archives in Holland and the United Kingdom took another eight months.

[35] The most glaring gap in my account is the omission of the influence of the (mainly German) Sisters of the Precious Blood as the missions' housekeepers, teachers and, most important, nurses on Luguru life. I started to be interested in their work much too late and found no opportunity to study their diaries or interview the Sisters with the rigor required (despite the help of Sister Carel in Morogoro and Sister Canisiana in Germany, for which I am grateful). I address the political history of Uluguru in a separate paper (1996) and will elaborate it into a volume on the recent political history of Uluguru.

different sources, something which I have tried to do with setting interviews with missionaries against interviews with Waluguru, and both against the written sources produced in the period of which I write. This effectually builds on and extends traditions of historical source-criticism, even though, in colonial history in general and through the work of the Subaltern Studies collective in particular, we know now that much work still can and needs be done, and this introduction points in a direction in which such work might develop further. This kind of reinterpretation often seems to be the limit of historiography: a critical rereading of the written representations that were either produced in or after the period under study, or of the representations one has recorded oneself as oral history or tradition.

I feel, however, that for this study in particular, and for historical anthropologists in general, this is a too narrow conception of the activity of historiography. Scholars as diverse as Walter Benjamin and Johan Huizinga have speculated about the possibility of an immediate historical experience, a "shock" of recognition (Benjamin 1977: 260) or a "historical contact" (Huizinga, quoted in Ankersmit 1993: 11) in which the historian has a sensation of the immediate presence of the past. Of course, Collingwood also argued that the past needs to become contemporaneous to be known, through the performance of an act of recognition (1961: 284). But the metaphors of "shock" and "contact" employed by Benjamin and Huizinga suggest, contrary to Collingwood, that this can happen without the mediation of representation, by a physical or tactile action of the past on the knower. I am not sure whether such seemingly mystical notions can be, or need be, defended philosophically (but see Ankersmit 1993; Taussig 1993: 39–40). I do think, however, that such contact with the past, and the concomitant abolition of temporal distance, is a feature of all historical research.

Most obviously, we have immediate contact with the past through the materials stored in archives: the sense of authenticity of a document or publication – of its having been produced in the period under study – is not only constructed through source-criticism, but also conveyed by our handling of these palpably "old" materials while we are moving through the appropriate archival settings. Of course, this is not a foolproof "method": I am not sure whether I could have discovered the "inauthenticity" of a well-faked minute, produced in the 1970s, but slipped among His Excellency the Governor's correspondence of the 1930s in an archive. But this in itself shows the importance of such tactile "proof", for the most certain way of deciding such a question would be to subject the material to a further handling, by, for instance, chemical analysis. Moreover, it also shows that the physical setting of an archive may in itself convince us of the presence of the past, even though the past contained in it may be faked. As I indicated above, all tactile communication is indeterminate, and we cannot expect immediate contact with the past to be any the less foolproof than other interpretive activities.

I also indicated, however, that tactile communication is determining, and I feel the same can be said about our contact with the past. This determination occurs not so much at the moment of demonstrable proof or methodical exposition, but through the hunch that prefigures hypothesis.[36] In my own case, it was usually such a hypothesis that was at the back of the attempt to group certain matters under a specific chapter heading, and eventually contributed to the kind of approach outlined in this introduction. The hunch at the back of the hypothesis, however, was very often a direct result of fieldwork experience, not in the sense of being there and "seeing for oneself" – a claim that, especially in the case of historical research, is limited – but in the sense of being taken up in the history of the place one happens to be in.

I was, for instance, addressed by many Waluguru as *Baba*, "Father", despite my age. As this was also the title bestowed on the missionaries, I was disconcerted with this and tried to escape the classification, until I realized that this form of address set me off in a positive sense from the more distanced *Bwana* ("Sir") applied to other white men. The missionaries were "Fathers" not just because of their religious status, but also because of their far greater intimacy

---

[36] Thus, one might say that contact with the past determines what Charles Saunders Peirce called the process of abduction (see Eco and Sebeok 1983).

with Waluguru, an intimacy I was thought to share. Thus, at the same time that I realized how I was being situated in Luguru history, I discovered a classification that, at a later stage, came to inform much of my work (especially in my comparisons of missionaries and colonial administrators; see Pels 1994). Before becoming *Baba*, however, it had been rumoured that I was the *mumiani*, the white vampire who draws African blood for medicine, who first appeared on the Luguru scene in the 1930s in the guise of white men engaging African wage labour for mysterious purposes (see Pels 1992a and pp. 269 ff.). Didn't I also engage African labour, even if only by employing my research guide, and wasn't my purpose – gathering history – as mysterious? The rumour passed, but not the impression it made on me. This way of being engaged in Luguru history led, among other things, to the emphasis I put on wage labour as a critical mediation of colonial society in this book (chapters three and six).

Similar instances of contact with a history made present informed the writing of the following chapters. Chapter two owes much to the recognition of the role of exotic adventure and of adaptation to Luguru society in the life of the missionaries. This recognition was partly possible because their sense of adventure was often produced by the books I also read as a child, and because we shared the experience of adapting to Luguru society by the necessity of daily contact with Waluguru in order to work, learn a language, and move through the mountains. These hunches ran counter to much of the received wisdom about missionaries among anthropologists, particularly where they stereotyped missionaries as being in complete thrall to the conversion story and totally subject to monastic discipline. Instead, I became increasingly convinced that these forms of ideological and institutional closure had built-in tendencies to break their bounds and prepare the missionary for the unexpected, tendencies that appear once one contemplates the Catholic idea of sacrifice, the use of exotic images in mission propaganda, and the tension between monastic life and professional ministry in missionary practice in Holland. These tendencies were exacerbated by the exigencies of building and maintaining the mission stations in the Uluguru mountains. One might say that the maintenance of the mission implied the maintenance of contact with (potential) converts, which again implied the maintenance of many of the contradictions that threatened the integrity of the mission.

The hunch that went into the composition of chapters three and four, both about *ngoma* or initiation, is summarized in the introduction to chapter three: the "coming out" of Mama Mkoba from her mourning period as a widow. It made me realize that *ngoma* was an institution for effecting a change in the rhythm of life, and that the other meanings of the word – rhythm, drum, dance – ought therefore to be taken seriously (chapter three). I had, of course, participated in many dances already, but all of them surrounding female initiation (chapter four). The men's *ngoma* had disappeared, it seemed, in the face of Christianity, but the women's held on. As may be expected from the preceding arguments, this historical problem – the contemporary presence of female, and absence of male initiation – became increasingly important for this book. These initiations condensed a microphysics of colonial contact that attuned Waluguru to new administrative, wage labour, cash cropping and trade routines of colonial society. Whereas the initiations struck a tenuous balance of power between generations of Waluguru, these balances remained tenuous because they were adapted by each new generation to novel possibilities in colonial society, with results reverberating into the domestic sphere.

From the beginning of this century onwards, the boys' *ngoma* was primarily attuned to the opportunities offered by novel forms of work in colonial society and changed in relation to it, until it disappeared in the late 1960s. In chapter three, I try to show that such a change can be described analogous to the change of musical patterns. Whereas anthropologists often tend to think of music as a kind of "superstructural" phenomenon not actually engaged in the substance of historical change, Charles Keil has argued that we can learn from the appeal of music, and rhythm in particular, that historical change can best be studied "at its very point of creation, if we attend closely to the discrepancies that enhance participation and the contexts that generate these discrepancies" (1987: 281). The Luguru "discrepancy" that mostly enhanced participation in the modern world and Christianity was the male *ngoma*, an institution that attuned the boys to European work rhythms. But while European rhythms were incorporated in *ngoma*, Luguru rhythms of the latter were increasingly incorporated in Christianity, leading to a folklorization of Luguru music on the one hand, and to the superseding of the male rite of passage on the other. These continuities can be charted through missionary statistics, recording the movement of Luguru bodies in and out of the Church. It shows that, like the missionary institution, *ngoma* tried to reproduce itself by engaging with "other" routines that at the same time continued to threaten its integrity. Unlike the Church, however, the male *ngoma* could not be maintained as an institution in the face of these contradictions.

But if historical changes of male initiation can be best described in terms of the shifts of musical patterns, for the female *ngoma* a model of struggle is more appropriate. Chapter four charts how endemic this struggle was in the case of Luguru women, who suffered more from colonial innovations and therefore resisted them more. Here, *ngoma* as an institution survived because it served a purpose as an opposition movement. The chapter shows how the discipline that the missionaries tried to impose upon church members, and women in particular, largely failed because the material mediations of this discipline were not accepted. Discipline remained "legal", so to speak, and did not provide sufficient material advantages to restructure the domestic sphere to such an extent that the dominance of elder women over girls was eroded, as it did in relation to the dominance of elder men over the careers of the boys.

Discipline did become material enough in one of the biggest assets of the Uluguru missions: the school. In its description in chapter five, my extension of a Foucauldian microphysics becomes most evident. Much has been written about colonial education, but this has generally concentrated on missionary and administrative curricula, on the African desire for education and the resulting "struggle for the school" (Anderson 1970). By concentrating on the material mediations of the school – the fact that to have a school, one needs a plot, a building, pupils and a teacher – I show how missionaries had to adapt to local relations of power, and how this balance of power had to adapt to the educational discipline which the colonial state imposed through the missionaries, not always with the latters' whole-hearted support. Through this analysis, *ngoma* and school are linked: if the former provided the context for the creation of the latter, the latter was the context of the gradual disappearance of the former (that is, as male initiation). Moreover, it charts the way in which forms of individual discipline prefigured a commodification of knowledge that turned Christianity more and more into a "finite province of meaning" (Schutz, quoted in Olivier de Sardan 1992: 11), losing much of its relevance for daily life in the face of the secular magic of colonial education.

State intervention in education secularized the school in a way that that many missionaries regretted. A similar compartmentalization of spiritual and secular characterizes the missionary intervention in the fields of Luguru magic. Chapter six starts from the observation that, since the late colonial period, anthropologists have usually subsumed "magic" under the study of witchcraft. The witchcraft paradigm, however, stresses a system of belief, and this is not very useful in the study of a situation like Uluguru, where missionaries made magic even though they did not share Luguru beliefs in it. I take up a more pragmatic alternative theory of magical acts formulated by Malinowski (1935a: 213–252). By concentrating on these material mediations of magic, I try to show how missionaries, their battle against "superstition" notwithstanding, were intimately engaged in the magical field (cf. Fields' argument about administrators, 1982b). This chapter stands out from the rest in the sense that it does not deal with the direct action on bodies characteristic of initiation and discipline, but with action on (social and individual) bodies at a distance. The language of magic is a language about the protection, healing or destruction of bodies, and it therefore deals with the (lack of) integrity of these bodies and the (lack of) contacts that can both enhance or threaten this integrity. This chapter is therefore about a debate, rather than the material mediations of that debate, and closer to a "conversational" rather than a "tactile" analysis.

To some extent, the chapter about magic parallels the analysis in the conclusion, since it partly deals with Luguru imaginations of and magical intervention in colonial contact. The conclusion does the same for missionary imaginations of and interventions in colonial contact, which I trace through the ethnographies they wrote of Uluguru (see also Pels 1994). I try to show that while the missionaries tried to produce Waluguru as self-responsible individual Christians, what their intervention achieved was a further penetration of Luguru society by commodity forms, "objects, persons, or elements of persons" that have been "placed in a context in which they have exchange value and can be alienated" (Thomas 1991a: 39). Commodification, therefore, is not a feature of modernity only (Appadurai 1986). Waluguru were not disturbed by commodities as objects of exchange, since they had a history of long-distance trade (Thomas 1991a: 4; see also Kimambo 1991: 38 ff.). In Uluguru, the historical trajectory of modernity was determined, among other things, by the suspicion of Waluguru towards the commodification of the human body, expressed in terms of slavery or witchcraft. Many Waluguru were disturbed by the sale of *labour power*, used as they were to the exchange of labour in relations of production organized by a discourse of kinship and descent, a discourse that protected the integrity of both social and individual bodies.

Especially chapters three, four and six show how wage labour at the plantations or in government service implied relations of production based on discipline that severed Luguru workers from the social body in which they had been initiated. Not only Waluguru, but also the missionaries, were suspicious of its effects on Luguru society and therefore often opposed this form of disciplinary power. However, missionaries also tried to produce "individuals" or "souls" whose identity was thought to be completely determined by the specific regime of discipline to which they were subjected. This conclusion endorses that of others about the way in which missions prepared Africans for participation in a capitalist world economy (Comaroff 1985; Fabian 1983b), but it should not downplay the historical importance of the tensions of empire (Cooper and Stoler 1989). The missionaries' colonizing strategies were not, as Mitchell (1991) sometimes seems to suggest, completely taken up within a discourse of representation. They also saw their work in terms of a politics of "presence" rather than of representation, and the mission should not be interpreted as a total and coherent institution (*pace* Beidelman 1982) but as a makeshift of sometimes contradictory strategies and uncertain outcomes.

One outcome was regretted by the missionaries themselves: the fact that their probably most important strategy – the system of education – was set up in such a way that it was more and more dominated by the state (and eventually, after independence, handed over completely). This secularization was also experienced by Waluguru, but for them it already started with the arrival of the missionaries. This set in motion a process which, through commodification processes and the consequent shift of authority in spiritual and secular matters to experts from outside the mountains, amounted to a decrease in the capacity of Waluguru to provide their own revelations of how the world was constituted. Because the practice of revelation was closely tied to the capacity to protect social and individual bodies, loss of control over it heightened Waluguru's sense of crisis. The missionaries, too, regretted to see that the integrity of families and individuals which their doctrines promoted could not be sufficiently upheld. To paraphrase Stanley Diamond (1974: 93), the mission was the work of men in crisis trying to convert a people in crisis, and this book tries to describe this work's material mediations.

CHAPTER TWO

The Mission as Movement, or: Creating and Crossing the Boundaries of "Home" and "Mission"

As indicated in the introduction, the pivot of a mission is the strategy of moving "out there" to rectify a lack perceived from the centre. This perception of a lack draws boundaries between self and other, "here" and "there", but the mission is meant to move across these boundaries. This chapter outlines the consequences of this institutionalized transgression of boundaries for the maintenance of the Dutch Holy Ghost Fathers' mission to Eastern Uluguru. The mission was not merely a movement towards the place where it had to rectify the lack of the Gospel and the Church, it was also a religious movement at "home" attuned to an other place, the "mission". Johannes Fabian has argued that, to understand religious movements, one ought to refuse "fixation on the integrating, stabilizing, soothing functions of religion" for this tends to reduce them to attempts to "reestablish a measure of social order" (1981: 112–3). In line with this, one should not see the Holy Ghost Fathers' mission as just a part of the reestablishment of the Roman Catholic Church within the Dutch nation-state, or as the agent of the reproduction of European religious or educational institutions in Uluguru. The mission, as a religious movement, did not merely reproduce or salvage a past, it also imagined a future for its participants. It did this partly by setting the boundaries of self and other along a temporal axis that kept the self at its future end. However, this future was, as all futures, uncertain: although Divine Grace assured success in the end, it was not clear when and through what means it would be achieved. The mission, therefore, put itself at risk where it imaginatively fashioned this future for itself.

Maybe this is just an extreme example of the boundary work that any institution needs for its maintenance, but the picture is rather different from previous studies that described a mission as a "total" and "greedy" institution (Beidelman 1982: 21); an institution that – being "displaced" to the mission field (Huber 1988: 200) – actually belongs at "home". Instead, a study of the mission both at "home" and "abroad" shows how instable these categories already were at "home". "Home" and "mission" are examples of the Manichean categories with which colonizers tried to stabilize their messy practice (Stoler and Cooper 1997: 8). They cover up this essential instability of the mission, the "tensions of empire" that it had to negotiate already at "home", and the fact that the mission was – literally – more a movement than a stable institution resident at some unambiguously definable "home". It is this movement which this chapter tries to outline.

At "home", the tensions of empire appear once we acknowledge that the mission created boundaries between self and other that were far more complex than the simple dichotomy of Christian and heathen would suggest. In the first part of this chapter, I try to show that the ways of drawing these boundaries did not merely reinforce, but also contradict each other, and that these tensions could be condensed in a number of highly ambiguous signs. The in religious terms most central of these signs was the concept of "sacrifice", a notion that simultaneously set up, and straddled, boundaries between the missionary's maternal home, his new home in the Congregation's seminary and monasteries, and the home he would have to make for himself in "the mission" abroad. Another set of signs, equally indeterminate, provided a kind of "worldly" counterpoint to this religious notion of sacrifice: the different forms in which the dis- and attractions of the exotic were presented in mission propaganda and adventure stories. Although adventure stories could be subordinated under the manifestly religious signs of sacrifice and martyrdom, the exotic was less easily controlled when presented in the form of exotic photographs and drawings, which allowed a positive, "tactile" distraction from the negative stereotypes common to the missionaries' stories of (the necessity of) conversion. Comparable tensions characterized the boundaries

which were set up at the Congregation's minor and major seminar-
ies. These boundaries, meant to protect a recruit's vocation from
"the world", fostered both a monastic and a professional disposition, dispositions that, as I hope to show in the second part of this
chapter, could come to stand in a relationship of contradiction.[1]

In the second part of this chapter, I try to show how these
tensions in missionary thought and practice were transformed by
movement to the mission area and daily contact with (future) converts. On the spiritual side of mission work, monastic discipline,
propagated from the Bishop's headquarters, came in conflict with
the "bush" missionaries' practical autonomy, their professional dedication to ministry and their direct contacts with Africans. But the
mission also had to be materially reproduced, and this necessitated
adaptations to African routines – in acquiring language competence,
in maintaining the economy of the mission, in expanding the mission's reach to new areas and new converts. The attractions of the
exotic were transformed, by some missionaries, into painstaking
ethnography (see Pels 1994b and the conclusion). "Sacrifice" and
discipline also underwent substantial changes when applied in the
Uluguru missions. The necessity of localizing a European monastic
institution in daily contact with Luguru life, therefore, "africanized"
it even where its European personnel had no intention to do so, and
even when formal power remained in its hands.

THE "SACRIFICE" OF DUTCH
CATHOLICS FOR THE MISSIONS

When the French Fathers of the Congregation of the Holy
Ghost settled down in the former hotel "De Roos" in Weert in 1904
(see map 1), they were late arrivals. The fervour of Dutch
Catholicism after the restoration of the diocesan hierarchy in 1853
created fertile ground for foreign missionary congregations and
orders, whether they were fleeing from governments hostile to the

---

[1] I should add that this does not amount to a "thick description" of Dutch
Catholic missionary fervour. For that, another Ph.D. research would be needed.

MAP 1   *The Congregation of the Holy Ghost in the Netherlands*
1: Weert, minor seminary (1904)   *5: Rhenen (1947)*
2: Baarle-Nassau, education of brothers *6: Berg en Dal, museum (1950)*
(1913)   *7: Halfweg, procura (1950)*
3: Gemert, major seminary (1914)   *8: Hattem (1957)*
4: Gennep, noviciate (1924)

Vatican (like the Society of the Divine Word, established in Holland
in 1875, and the missionaries of the Sacred Heart in 1882) or were
looking for opportunities to expand (like the White Fathers in
1889, Mill Hill in 1890 and the Society for African Missions in
1892). These circumstances produced one of the most important

Dutch religious movements of the twentieth century: the "Grand Mission Hour" (*'t Groote Missieuur*) of Dutch Catholicism. The financial effort of Dutch Catholics for the missions was estimated at seven million guilders during the Depression year of 1931; in 1930, Dutch Catholics could claim to have produced ten per cent of all Catholic missionaries in the world, from a population comprising only one per cent of all Catholics (Coleman 1978: 2; Roes 1974: 16, 37, 39). This momentum lasted at least until 1953, when the Dutch made up only two per cent of all Catholics, yet produced eleven per cent of all missionaries (Mulders 1953: 200). The history of the Dutch Holy Ghost Fathers reflects these developments: when the French founders of the Dutch province arrived in 1904, the missionary was, to many Dutch Catholics, still an ambiguous figure. After the First World War, the Congregation rose on the waves of missionary romanticism, and its Dutch province was officially established in 1931 at the height of the "Grand Mission Hour". It reached its peak in property and manpower in the 1950s. After that, its rapid decline mirrored the fate of most Catholic institutions in the Netherlands.

While the tight organization, strong dogmatism and impressive *élan* of Dutch Catholic culture have often been noted (Van Doorn 1958: 196), few social scientists have paid attention to the contribution made to it by the missionary effort (Roes 1974). Studies of Dutch Catholic culture between the wars are scarce, because most scholars concentrate on the second half of the nineteenth century, the period of emancipation of Dutch Catholics from the hegemonic Protestant culture (Bax 1983, 1989; Meurkens 1985, 1989; Romijn 1989; Van den Brink 1991), or focus on the "revolutionary" period after the Second World War, when groups of Dutch Catholics rebelled against the control exerted by the Vatican and the seeming unity of Catholicism in Holland was shattered (Akkerman and Stuurman 1985; Bax 1984, 1985, 1986, Coleman 1978, Goddijn 1973). Although interesting studies of mission folklore have been done by scholars allied to Catholic institutions (Dirkse 1983; *Kunst met een Missie* 1988; Roes 1974), they are largely ignored by social scientists who describe the history of Dutch Catholicism. The social background of Dutch missionaries has hardly been studied, let alone measured in terms of differences in participation along class and gender lines, of the contribution by different regions, by towns or rural areas or by different orders and congregations.[2] The student of Dutch Catholic missions cannot fall back on a corpus of studies which locate this movement in its socio-cultural context. Any generalization about the construction of the "vocation" (roeping) or call of God that led a young boy to join the Congregation of the Holy Ghost, therefore, is bound to remain provisional.

Catholic popular culture was in part the result of a succesful civilizing offensive by the elite (Bax 1984, 1985, 1986; Meurkens 1985, 1989), and the transformation of the missionary into a popular hero after the First World War cemented the Catholic "pillar" (zuil) at a time when it seemed to lose its coherence (Roes 1974: 42, 161). The initiative towards "mission-action" taken during the War was taken up and carried further by a tight cooperation between diocesan and monastic clergy under the leadership of the Dutch Cardinal Van Rossum, who was the secretary of the Congregatio de Propaganda Fide from 1918 to 1932, and therefore head of all the missionary activity of the Roman Catholic Church. Bishops and parish priests set up, in each parish, the Papal mission associations through which donations for the mission flowed to the Vatican (Roes 1974: 141).[3] Parish priests were told that "in a parish which has not given the church a missionary or mission-sister in

---

[2] This accounts for the tendency to generalize about Dutch Catholicism in terms of findings from the South (Brabant and Limburg), while little is known of the considerable contribution by Catholic communities in the North, the province of Friesland and the city of Amsterdam in particular.

[3] It is therefore wrong to characterize the early half of twentieth-century Dutch Catholicism in terms of the triumph of a diocesan regime over its permanent rival, the monastic clergy (Bax 1983, 1989). Monastic clergy expanded through the channels and on the initiative of diocesan authorities (Romijn 1989: 139) and particularly through vocations for the missions. The "Mission-union of priests" (Priestermissiebond), founded on the request of the Vatican in 1919 to follow up on a 1916 Dutch initiative, united all diocesan clergy to work for the mission's monastic clergy, who were not supposed to be a member (De Reeper 1955; Roes 1974: 21, 23).

years, the current of life slows down and the true Catholic disposition is weakened" (quoted in Roes 1974: 141). Propaganda for the
missions spread through exhibitions, journals and movies; "sewing
circles" produced religious garments for missionaries; *zelatrices*
"begged" for Papal mission associations or particular Congregations; and the processions of the Holy Infancy (one of the Papal
associations) excited many a child's fantasy.[4] The missionary was
one of Holland's most popular heroes between the two World Wars.

While the Catholic elite's organization was impressive, it
does not fully explain the appeal of "mission-action" among large
sections of the Catholic population. In rural North Brabant, rising
birthrates, the commercialization and resulting scarcity of land, and
unemployment certainly pushed youngsters into religious orders
(Bax 1989: 32; Roes 1974: 46; Van den Brink 1991). However, one
can doubt whether the same explanation applies to wealthy farmers
in Friesland or the Haarlemmermeer, or relatively well-to-do shop-
keepers in Amsterdam. A monastic career was certainly highly
valued by Catholic parents (Bax 1989: 33), but many also felt it as a
"sacrifice" of their child to the Church. We have to pay more attention to the mediations of a vocation through Catholic mission folklore to see how the elite's civilizing offensive, or the promise of
economic advancement, were popularly motivated.

The missionaries I interviewed listed a number of motives.
Some told of their fascination with the cloth itself: the habit of the
Dominicans, or the blue jabot of the Holy Ghost Fathers. Others,
maybe through having been an altarboy, were drawn by the mysteries of Catholic liturgy and the privileged role of the priests. Some
only stated their desire for monastic life and said they developed
their love for the missions at the seminary of the Holy Ghost

---

[4] In 1927, there were 75 sewing circles in the Netherlands, almost half of
which in the diocese of Den Bosch (Roes 1974: 28). It was not only charity,
but also the challenge of producing highly skilled needlework that attracted
participants (VPRO). The elite often felt it should apologize for "begging",
especially by tracing it to Biblical sources ("St. Paul was the first beggar for the
missions" – BHG 34 [1938]: 68, see also Van den Eerenbeemt 1953: 51–62). The
Holy Ghost Fathers, too, saw their publishing work as "not just ordinary begging, but a stylish propaganda fitting our priestly dignity" (OO 15 [1950]: 22).

Fathers, where they ended up because it was the cheapest or most accessible Congregation available.[5] Most frequently, however, it was the mixture of attractions of missionary work itself that appealed to a young boy, and some of these attractions – like exotic adventure – were regarded with suspicion by the Catholic elite. One missionary related how, five years old, he watched a movie showing a missionary on horseback approaching the hut of the magician where a girl was tied to a pole. He took out his knife, cut the rope, placed the girl behind him on his horse and rode away. The young boy watching this movie thought: "that's what I want, too" and told his family he wanted to become a missionary. The missionaries I interviewed often linked this "Lone Ranger"-type of missionary image to the figure of Old Shatterhand, the Christian hero of the immensely popular series of books by the German Karl May which related the adventures of the former and his noble Indian friend Winnetou in the Wild West.[6] To the Catholic leadership, the Protestant Old Shatterhand was suspect, and a host of titles like "Ranger-bishop" (Vencken n.d.), "Drums of Krukru" (Van der Kooy n.d.) and "To the Strange Countries" (Zuure n.d.) were produced to show that Catholic missions were themselves adventurous, even beyond what Old Shatterhand had to offer (Roes 1974: 44).

Martyrdom, and the death of the Dutch Bishop Hamer during the Boxer rising in China in particular, could link the popular culture of missionary adventure to "sacrifice" (*offer*), the dominant symbol of the elite to promote contributions to the missions by the Catholic population (Roes 1974: 154).[7] Martyrdom was a heroism of negation applicable to all missionaries: saying goodbye to one's family in order to move to the mission was just such a negation,

---

[5] IPAC 12a: 032, 17a: 000; KMM 514/1a: 000.
[6] The "Lone-Ranger" story was recorded in a radio-programme of the *Vrijzinnig Protestantse Radio-Omroep* on Dutch missionary enthusiasm (VPRO: *Het Spoor Terug*, 20-11-1990), available on cassette; permission to quote from this programme is hereby gratefully acknowledged. On Old Shatterhand: IPAC 1a: 074, 9a: 117, 17a: 110.
[7] Holy Ghost missionaries only mentioned Mgr. Hamer (VPRO; IPAC 9a: 000; KMM 447/1a: 000, 591/1a: 030). Other popular martyrs were Damian the leper, Peerke Donders and Felix Westerwoudt (Roes 1974: 40).

a sacrifice of "all that I am and possess".[8] The central image behind this notion of sacrifice was, of course, the redemption of mankind through the self-sacrifice of Christ on the Cross, an act that each Catholic family could emulate by sacrificing one of its children for the redemption of those people whom the historical Christ did not have the opportunity to reach. For Holy Ghost missionaries, the sacrifice was clearly gendered: it was the loss of their mother, whose own sacrifice was mirrored by the figure of the mother Maria. Thus, sacrifice for the missions defined one of the missionary's "homes" as primarily maternal, and emphasized that he should abandon this identity. It shows that at this "home", the mission intervened as deeply into the domestic sphere as it did among Africans (see chapter four).

A boy's vocation could be a real sacrifice for his parents when he was their only son (and therefore heir of the family name), or because his father needed him at the farm or in his business. Paying for their son's upkeep at the seminary was also a sacrifice, and even when parents received help from the Congregation or its allied parish priests, they had to pay something "because of the sacrifice they need to make for the greatest bliss that can ever befall them and their child".[9] Parents were exhorted to give their "best children" and some, at least, prayed that this cup would pass from them (Roes 1974: 43). Many mothers went to great lengths to give their son the expensive golden chalice, used when saying Mass, on the occasion of his ordination.[10] In fact, *all* "mission-action", whether sewing, begging, donating, or subscribing to a mission journal, could be interpreted as sacrifice.

To appreciate what Dutch Catholics thought to gain from the act of sacrifice, one has to acknowledge its *paradoxy*. A sacrifice mediates between human and non-human worlds through abnegation

---

[8] A line from the popular poem *The Missionary* by A. van Duinkerken (quoted in Roes 1974: 50; also VPRO).

[9] The quote is from the Dutch Holy Ghost Fathers' Provincial Superior, Vogel (Missievereeniging Roermond 1939: 211). Other examples in the text are from IPAC 2a: 000, 3a: 000, 6a: 000, 9a: 096, 17a: 075.

[10] IPAC 17a: 075.

of something "human", and thereby simultaneously establishes interpenetration of and distance between the two worlds (Hubert and Mauss 1964: 99), conjunction and disjunction (De Heusch 1985: 207, 213). A sacrifice entails both abnegation and selfishness (Hubert and Mauss 1964: 100), both an unselfish gift (without a predetermined return) and an exchange with a clear profit motive (a bribe or the payment of a debt; see Van Baal 1981: 217; De Heusch 1985: 204). Christian elites have, for several centuries, tried to combat the profit-motive of sacrifice, as it was associated with the give-and-take of magic (Thomas 1971; see also chapter six), but in everyday Dutch Catholicism such reciprocal expectations were common. Each issue of the Holy Ghost Fathers' journal, the *Bode van de Heilige Geest* ("Holy Ghost Messenger") lists masses said by priests after payment by the supplicant for the passing of an exam, the curing of an illness, or "blessing in business". The Pope promised an indulgence (*aflaat*) for special prayers for missionary vocations in 1957, when the decline of the missionary movement became visible (AC/WvA, 1957: 5). The sacrifice of a son to the missions promised at least spiritual benefits through self-sacralization, or privileged access to an intermediary with the supernatural. This paradoxy – the oscillation between unconditional surrender of "all that I am and possess" and the profits gained in return – allowed for the expression of the divergent interests of the religious leadership and the Catholic population by one and the same symbol.[11]

The strong Dutch Catholic "fighting spirit" of the 1950s was, therefore, less the result of an after-effect or defense of Catholic emancipation (Van Doorn 1958: 197–8) as of the missionary fervour sustained by, among other things, the symbolic practice of sacrifice. The mobilizing potential of "sacrifice" lay not just in

---

[11] "Sacrifice" played a similar role in most large social movements in early twentieth-century Europe, communism and fascism in particular (Gabriel van den Brink, personal communication). Further research into the emancipation of Dutch Catholics, with its simultaneous betterment of lower class Catholics and promotion of new class differences (Bax and Nieuwenhuis 1982) may uncover its relevance beyond the mission sphere.

the ambiguity of unconditional surrender and reciprocity, but also in the paradox that it simultaneously created and crossed boundaries that were crucial for the making of Catholic, especially missionary, identities. The sacrifice of parents defined "home" and mission house as distinct entities, while this boundary was breached, and would continue to be negotiated, by the transfer of their son to the latter. The missionary learnt to see himself as a sacrifice to God, creating yet crossing a boundary between secular and sacred, that also helped to construct the relationship of the (future) missionary with his superiors, who were closer to God than he was. Most important, it was also a sacrifice *for others* – among Dutch Holy Ghost missionaries, usually for Africans – that articulated the identity of the mission and Congregation as a whole. In a sense, it posited Catholicism as a "home" against the outside world of the not yet converted, but also urged the missionary to cross that boundary in the interests of expanding that identity, and making the globe into that home. Contrary to stereotype, however, that story, the story of conversion, did not completely dominate the image of "others" maintained by mission folklore in the Netherlands. If the boundaries between self and other that were articulated and transgressed by sacrifice were already polyvalent, signifying devotion, adventure and self-interest in turn, the use of exoticism in missionary propaganda further complicated them.

CONVERSION AND MISSIONARY EXOTICISM, 1931–1957

The *Brousse*! It is a magnificent, a wonderful word, because it comprises wildness in its entirety. (Caption to a jungle photograph, AC 50 [1954]: back cover).

The processions of the Holy Infancy, the Papal mission-association collecting donations for the conversion of heathen children, were supreme moments of many a Catholic childhood. Some dressed as little brides, others as Chinese or Africans, but most preferred to go as nuns or priests. Often, after the procession, everyone would go to a mission movie to watch the "blackies without clothes" (*zwartjes zonder kleertjes aan*), thus coupling the attractions of the cloth to its absence among "heathens". To some boys, the fight against material poverty was as attractive as that against its spiritual counterpart, and this shows that within the "narrative structure" (Corbey and Melssen 1990: 21) or "order of knowledge" (Mudimbe 1988) of the conversion story, several forms of negative stereotyping of "others" could be transposed on each other.[12] Yet, this seemingly transparent structure of an Other who lacks something, as opposed to a Christian who is fulfilled, is disrupted by the presence, through mimesis, of Chinese and Africans, showing that at least to some children, the "heathen" possessed sufficient attractions to become like him, if only for a while. These exotic attractions were often not mediated by narrative, but by objects, photographs and other icons, which provided a "tactile distraction" from the conversion story (Taussig 1991). In this way, missionary propaganda structurally incorporated a positive image of otherness in its repertoire – in its own interests, for as one of the editors of the Holy Ghost Fathers' propaganda journal once put it, the journal was both "pulpit and collecting-bag" (AC 48 [1952]: front cover) and exoticism helped to fill the latter.

This is not to deny that the negative images of the conversion story dominated the textual representations of Africans between the covers of the *Holy Ghost Messenger*. In the 1930s, the propagandists often relied on Father Michael Witte's "begging"-letters (*bedelbrieven*) from East Africa that unfolded a narrative of salvation through the opposition of "peace, love, God's light" and "pagan fear, ignorance and hate". In one of his stories, the latter was personified by a chief-cum-sorcerer who, in the course of the tale, gets converted by the appearance in his dreams of a martyred nun. Thus, Divine intervention, mediated by the heroic sacrifice of the nun, inexorably led to the transformation of negative blackness into white Christianity. Negative stereotype either fixed on the incontinence of Africans – too much movement in dance, too much noise

---

[12] VPRO; IPAC 1a: 119, 18a: 055.

in drumming, too much appetite for food and sex – or on their "superstition" (*bijgeloof*), the first usually caused by their lack of self-control, and the second by the missionaries' professional rival, the medicine-man (see chapter six). Both were, of course, caused by the whisperings of the devil, and a future missionary may have felt a thrill of adventure when faced with the prospect of fighting this formidable opponent.[13]

Africans were usually *zwartjes* ("blackies"; the diminutive suffix showing missionary paternalism), but it is crucial to realize that such racism was neither single nor monolithic (Goldberg 1990: xiii) and that shifts in meaning, inversions and positive evaluations were possible. Defending missionary romanticism in the late 1940s, the Congregation's journal editor argued that *zwartjes* meant people who were spiritually and materially poor, thus attempting to shift a racial signifier to religious and material differences. Racial hierarchies could be inverted by insisting that Europeans were less religious than Africans, who were more like the early Christians. For missionaries, racial differences could never be absolute, because "conversion" implied assumptions of human similarity. Such assumptions surfaced most explicitly in stories about the devotion of converted Africans, but also appeared in African critiques of the Europeans' "devastating wars" or in the ubiquitous assertions that African childrens' play or African women's desire for fashion were "just like home". Moreover, assertions of human difference could also be made in a neutral, or even positive, mode. The missionaries' selective ethnography could, indeed, single out sorcery or dancing to inspire the reader with horror or revulsion (and some excitement, too), but might as well present African storytelling, food and foodways, or hunting simply as an object of curiosity.[14]

---

[13] On Father Witte and his career, see De Jong (1974) and chapter five; his story of the converted chief is in BHG 44 (1948): 74; on dancing, BHG 43 (1947): 121; on deviltry and incontinence, BHG 45 (1949): 56, 46 (1950): 161, 47 (1951): 79; on lack of self-control, BHG 46 (1950): 265.

[14] *Zwartjes*, BHG 46/10 (1950): inside cover; Africans more religious than Europeans, BHG 43 (1947): 68; Africans more like early Christians, BHG 38–42 (1946): 146; stories of African devotion, BHG 33 (1937): 155, 43 (1947): 153, AC 49/12 (1952): 7; critiques of European wars, BHG 47 (1951): 26–7,

As its editor indicated, the missionaries' propaganda journal was not just a means of preaching, but also of making money through providing its public with information about Africa, information that, in the 1930s and 1940s, few other publications in the Netherlands printed in similar quantities. Of course, the *Holy Ghost Messenger* informed its reader primarily about the Holy Ghost Fathers' establishment in the Netherlands, and the seminary where many of the readers had sent their sons in particular. Each issue of the journal carried sermons to the reader. These articles were more or less evenly balanced with articles providing news from abroad – and as the title of the successor to the *Holy Ghost Messenger, Africa Christo,* indicates, mostly from Africa. Among these latter articles, news from the missions, the successes and failures of the work of conversion in particular, predominate: only about one-third of them present plain exoticism through stories about wild animals and ethnography. One cannot appreciate the role of such exoticism, however, by focusing on the content of the missionaries' representations only. Its form, in particular the way in which Africa was presented to the home public by material culture, photographs and drawings, was also important, as is witnessed by the huge success of the mission exhibition in creating the heroic image of the missionary (Roes 1974: 42).

A striking feature of the mission exhibition, and one which enabled it, like the mission journals, to become a mass medium, was its mobility (Coombes 1994: 178). Exhibitions were set up in a way that allowed them to be held in different parts of the country, thus contributing to the rapid spread of images and knowledge about congregations and orders that was itself a practical precondition of the missionary movement. Exhibitions were organized by the "Associated Missionaries" (*Vereenigde Missionarissen,* founded in

---

AC 50 (1954): 10; "neutral" ethnography can be found in BHG 43 (1947): 72, 44 (1948): 12, 25, 35, AC 49/5 (1953): 7; especially interesting is the series on "native religion" written by a Cameroonian seminarian, in which everything but black magic is presented in positive terms: BHG 27 (1931): 226, 257, 279; the missionaries' ethnography is discussed in detail in Pels (1994b) and in the conclusion.

1920), which in 1923 had already held forty of them in different towns all over the Netherlands, an average of ten a year (Roes 1974: 27). People flocked to them in great numbers and they were an important source of income for the missionaries. Each Congregation or Order had its stand where it displayed curiosa from the missions, the more elaborate, the more exciting (see plate 1). A Father (Sisters and Brothers were not allowed to speak or put up their own stand) would wait for an opportunity to start his "tall tales", using the artefacts exhibited as illustration. The Holy Ghost Fathers often deplored the mediocrity of their African artefacts as compared to the cultural wealth brought from the Dutch Indies by their colleagues from other Congregations, but according to their propagandist, their stuff "illustrate[d] admirably the battle against heathendom" (OO 8 [1948]: 132). This shows how necessary the

PLATE 1   *The Holy Ghost Fathers' stand at a Dutch mission exhibition (from BHG 28 [1932]: 6). Antelope horns present the exotic in animal form, but fetishes, masks and other artefacts predominate. The association of otherness with animality was less common in mission propaganda than in other colonial discourses (cf. Corbey 1988). The map in the middle shows the Congregation's missions, in Latin America and – mostly – Africa*

missionaries found the objects for their performance at the exhibition. When, in 1957, a new and more functionalist design of the exhibitions completely focused on the conversion story, and dispensed with "unnecessary" curiosa, the missionaries were quick to smuggle them back in (see plate 2a and 2b, and Pels 1989). Moreover, it shows that the calabashes, statues, and masks (see plate 1) could not become "illustrations" of conversion without a story that transformed them into magical gourds, fetishes or witch-doctor's clothes. Like the photographs in the propaganda journal, the objects did not symbolize conversion by themselves: it had to be added by a caption or a commentator (see plate 3).

The role of the exotic in missionary propaganda cannot be understood without taking account of this relative autonomy of exotic icons from the narrative of conversion. There are three types of exotic – mostly African – images (photographs, drawings) presented in the *Holy Ghost Messenger*: representations of *landscape* that can be expected to produce a touristic kind of yearning to be "there" (the most common image being the palm tree, see plates 8c and 8d); of *animals*, the wilder the better, giving a sense of adventure that was reinforced by the missionaries "tall tales" about lions and snakes during the exhibitions (see plate 1); and of the *human other* whose difference was primarily marked by a dark skin and curly hair. The fact that the latter could produce the whole gamut of exotic thrills – horror, pity, astonishment, curiosity, admiration – shows that such objects or photographs are not simply "visual" or "pictorial narratives" (Corbey 1988: 75; 1989a). Their polyvalence indicates that the icons communicate meanings in a way that cannot be captured in a single narrative structure, and that an explicit link to the conversion story had to be made in order to have them "illustrate" it. It is, however, not just a question of different – narrative and iconic – levels in a single act of communication: it is clear that the missionaries used the narrative and the iconic as different acts of communication, because a majority of exotic images in the *Holy Ghost Messenger* are used on their own, not linked to an accompanying text (see also Thomas 1992: 371–2).

This is evident with the journal's eyecatchers, the covers, which, up to 1957, carried predominantly exotic images without a

PLATE 2a–b   *The AMATE exhibition of 1957 was a new functionalist design, emphasizing a conversion story of linear progress in a modernizing Africa (see also plate 9). However, the designers were unable to control the exhibition for long: the missionaries smuggled the curiosities by which they told their stories back in: in one of the pictures, the curtain is even sagging under their weight*

PLATE 3   *A page from the* Holy Ghost Messenger *(BHG 47 [1951]: 166), show-*
ing how photographs were used in isolation: printed within the context of
an article on the Holy Ghost missions to the Amazon, these photograph
needed a caption: "1. The King of Oussoye; one can hardly judge from
his looks that he is also head-magician and grand-feticheur of the area
2. A burial-ground of fetishes in Oussoye. Father Govers has already.
found scores of these huts. 3. A hut of fetishes, that accomodates pigs' jaws
and palm-wine pots, apart from other, here unnamable, objects"

PLATE 4   *A cover of Africa Christo (48/3 [1952]), an example of exotic*
imagery not directly associated with wildness or deviltry

KABAA.

K bladerde enkele dagen terug in de oude tijdschriften en vond in een Bode van 1925 „Voor de arme Kabaa-School" zooveel van St. Nicolaas, zooveel van Amsterdam, zooveel van Weert..... en ik kreeg er tranen van in de oogen. Wat zouden diezelfde weldoeners zeggen, als ze eens in nieuwKabaa konden rondkijken, waarvan de enkele plaatjes hierbij maar een heel zwak idee geven.

Het is een prachtschool geworden, een „eerste klas" als ge wilt, maar voor een héél groot deel dank zij de giftjes en gaafjes van 1925, toen alles en allen nog behuisd waren in een rijtje leemen hutten onder grasbedekking. Toen heb 'k den klap gewaagd: alles opgemonterd met geld, dat 'k nog niet had, maar vast vertrouwde dat zou komen — en 't is gekomen. Schuld! wat een akelig woord, maar ik maakte ze voor Gods eer en met een stellig vertrouwen op de Voorzienigheid. Toen konden de protestantsche Regeeringsinspecteurs niet veel meer afkeuren, moesten ze helpen — en ze hebben geholpen, op de shilling voor shilling-basis, d.i. voor iedere shilling, die ik kreeg, moest ik er een bij zoeken. Wat een werk,

met telkens het schuldspook voor de deur. Maar toen heeft het College van Weert geholpen en het „Zanzibar-Comité" van Amsterdam. Hoezeer te pas, hoe providentieel! God zal 't hun beloonen: ik kan alleen een woordje van dank stamelen, als 'k opzie van m'n werk en 200 vroolijke jongens rond me zie stoeien met een hemel van reinheid weerkaatsend in hun oog. En in plaats van alleen te worstelen, heb 'k een uitstekenden Pater-assistent en twee onbetaalbare Broeders aan m'n zijde. Onlangs waren we met de openbare examens weer bovenaan — want al hebben de jongens de helft der gebouwen welhaast op hun rekening, er gaat geen oogenblik verloren en als er gestudeerd wordt, nu dan wordt er gestudeerd, dat de einden er haast afvliegen. Want daarachter het hoogste motief: de eere Gods en de eer der Katholieke Kerk door de eer der Katholieke School.

Nog is alles niet gedaan hier: over de helft der gebouwen is nog „voorloopig"; het komende jaar moet 'k weer een school met drie klassen erbij bouwen en drie nieuwe slaapzalen. Voor de kerk kan 'k geen cent van de Regeering krijgen en toch is ze te klein en te arm vooral: in zandsteenen opgetrokken, in de zon gedroogd. Ik zal weer een sprong moeten wagen in de armen der Voorzienigheid. En ik

PLATE 5   *A page from the* Holy Ghost Messenger *(BHG 27 [1931]: 64–5) showing the use of a "conversion" vignette to head an article about Father Michael Witte's Kabaa school in Kenya (see chapter 5)*

"De Geest des Heeren heeft heel de aarde vervuld...."

PLATE 6   *"Spiritus" vignette, used to head "sermon" genre articles (in BHG 27 [1931])*

64

PLATE 7   *"Student scribbles", recurring rubric vignette of news supposedly written by a student of the minor seminary. Note the cigarette, a misleading mark of jocularity since smoking was severely restricted in seminary life*

PLATE 8a–e   *Exotic vignettes, used throughout the journal to head diverse kinds of articles: (a) "Through Africa"; (b) "From below the equatorial sun"; (c) "Where palm trees rustle"; (d) "Under Africa's waving palms"; (e) "From Far and Away"*

visible relationship to an evaluating story up to 1957 (see plate 4 and Pels 1989). Counting the occurrence of photographs between the covers of the journal, one discovers that this presentation of images without an accompanying text is normal procedure, and that the exotic photographs that are not accompanied by a story or caption form a significant counterpoint to the stories of conversion in the journal. Not only do images from Africa, both of the mission and of the exotic, predominate, while half of the photographs from the African missions illustrate a text printed next to it, less than one-tenth of the exotic images illustrates a text.[15] Only rarely, an exotic photograph is linked to judgments of civilization and backwardness by an accompanying caption, identifying "superstition" (see plate 3). This is also the case with the vignettes that regularly accompany an article: "conversion" vignettes head articles about mission work (see plate 5) and articles about the home base have their fixed vignette (plates 6 and 7) belonging to the text. Exotic vignettes, however, predominate (plate 8), and these usually accompany texts that do not deal with anything exotic. Thus, images structurally presented "others" without an obvious reference to what should, or should not, be the goal of mission work. What was normally kept distant in print was made present through pictures.

One might argue, because of their predominance, that the conversion stories contextualized the pictures – that the "before and after story" of conversion, even when discontinuous in its presentation with the images, provided a "master caption" that set each exotic picture at a temporal distance in the past, and images of mission work in the present and future (Thomas 1992: 372–3). This would, however, conflate the different registers of communication and fail to distinguish the way in which they were used by missionary propaganda from the ways in which they might have been perceived by its consumers. The fact that the missionaries used their

---

[15] In the 1936 volume, for instance, 35 out of a total of 68 photographs are exotic, while only three of them illustrate a text printed on the same page; of 27 photographs of the African mission, 11 do not illustrate a text; and of the six photographs from home, only 2 do not illustrate a text.

journal as both pulpit and collecting-bag is significant for the interpretation of this discontinuity between narrative and iconic messages, because it shows the missionaries were aware of the different
effects these messages produced and the different goals they could
serve. In fact, the crisis of the missionary movement in the late
1950s provoked criticism of the commercial use of exoticism, for
being "hypocritical" and not in keeping with the elevated goals of
missionary work (Pels 1989). But while on the side of the producers
of missionary propaganda, a certain hierarchy of perception – of
narrative above iconic – accompanied the hierarchy of conversion
versus exoticism, there is no evidence that the same hierarchy was
always perceived by its consumers: for many readers, and for children in particular, the pictures may have contextualized the stories.
While the explicit *reading* of the missionaries' texts put across a
story of conversion (with all the ideological and paradoxical effects
noted above), the *viewing* of the pages implied a kind of "distracted", "tactile" perception of others (Taussig 1991). This presentation
of otherness may not have been spelled out consciously by its consumers, but – given the enormous success of the mission exhibitions – must have had a popular appeal, and may have transformed
the combativeness and piety of the conversion story into something
more romantic, more amenable to the fantasies of young boys
inspired by the example of a hero like Old Shatterhand. Like sacrifice, missionary exoticism drew on ambiguous mediations of otherness – the supernatural Other in the former case, the non-Western
other in the latter. But unlike sacrifice, exoticism seems to have
catered for a far broader range of popular demand than just the religious (see also Coombes 1994: 174).

NEW HOME, NEW IDENTITY: MONASTIC
DISCIPLINE AND SEMINARY CURRICULUM

In the 1930s, many congregations were at large harvesting
new recruits and the Holy Ghost missionaries had to work hard to
get their share. The Holy Ghost Fathers' *roepingenboer* (literally
"vocations-farmer") toured the country to look for new candidates.
Often, the local parish priest, family relationships, or the low

educational demands and cost of the Congregation, made a boy decide to enter the minor seminary in Weert.[16] The minor seminary was equivalent to secondary education, but was also meant to transform the "simple thought" of going to the missions into an "obstinate decision" (as a propaganda line of the White Fathers put it).[17] In the seclusion of this predominantly religious atmosphere, the boys were taught a missionary sense of service, and were subjected to monastic discipline. Although Bertus – the fictive writer of the Holy Ghost Messenger's *Weerter Studentenkrabbels* ("Student-scribbles from Weert") – was sometimes supposed to dream of feeding monkeys (BHG 33 [1937]: 78), in reality he had to work, and work hard.

Weert was the French Holy Ghost Fathers' first acquisition. After settling down in Hotel "De Roos" in 1904, they managed, with the support of the local diocesan college, to expand their facilities and to start a minor seminary of their own in 1906. In 1913, a plot on the Belgian border, in Baarle-Nassau (see map 2), became a separate house for the education of religious Brothers,[18] while the first students of major seminary level in the Netherlands started their philosophy-studies in Gemert, in a castle owned by Jesuits, in 1914. Weert soon became too small and three classes were transferred to Gemert in 1920, when the last Jesuit left the castle. Novices[19] were first accomodated in Paris, but when the noviciate

---

[16] BHG 34 (1938): 6. Poullart des Places, first founder of the congregation in 1703, intended his association for the benefit of poor candidates for the priesthood. The missionary element was later added by its second founder, Francis Libermann, but the first element was never forgotten. Some parish priests (like Father De Graaf of the Amsterdam parish of St. Vincentius, IPAC 9a: 070) preferred these "simple" priests and supported candidates from their parish financially.

[17] June 1951 (VPRO). Not all reached this "obstinate decision" (see below), and these drop-outs may indicate that the minor seminary sometimes served as a substitute for the secondary education which children from lower class families could not afford.

[18] "Brothers" were members of the Congregation who were not ordained as priests and took care of most menial work.

[19] The noviciate was the probation year between minor and major seminary during which students were prepared for their official membership of the congregation (see below).

became too much of a burden on the mother-house, it was moved to Gennep, where a house was acquired in 1924. In 1928, the castle in Gemert became the property of the Holy Ghost Fathers, who therefore started their own province in 1931 with four houses (*Jubileum-uitgave* 1929). Four other, smaller houses were acquired after the Second World War (AC/WvA (1957): 7–11; see map 2).

Bertus arrived, clean linen and all, in a monastery: its walls and regime separated the young boys from the outside world. Morning and evening prayers, Mass, and religious conferences framed, defended and nourished the boys' vocations. The student could not expect luxurious surroundings. Many commented on the poverty of the minor seminary and to a student like Alfons Loogman, coming from the relatively well-to-do Jesuits to devote himself to the missions with the Holy Ghost Fathers, the latters' simple ways were quite a shock. Many of Bertus' classmates were severely homesick in their first year. The religious retreat at the beginning of each school year marked their separation from home and not seldom some boys cried themselves to sleep at night.[20] But during the days, not much time was left to think: the boys were moved from dormitory to chapel, chapel to class, class to refectory and back again like the hands of the clock.

A description from 1949 brings out the regimentation of seminary life: at 5.40 a.m. the bell rang, and at six o'clock all said morning prayers in the study, followed by a ten minutes' sermon (*meditatie*) by the supervising Father. Mass at 6.20, after which they did the beds. Then half an hour of study until breakfast (which was usually eaten in silence, while someone read from the Bible or another book; only on Sundays and Feastdays were they allowed to talk). After breakfast they had some time off (*recreatie*), in which most did their obligatory manual work: peeling potatoes, sweeping and dusting the dormitories and classrooms. The lessons started at 8.45, four lessons in the morning (with only short breaks outside) followed by another 20 minutes of study. They said the rosary (*rozenhoedje*) and had lunch, after which they were allowed an hour

---

[20] IPAC 12a: 065; KMM 710/1a: 008, 514/1a: 000, 827/1a: 091; OO 72 (1961): 12.

off. Then again two lessons and study; on Tuesdays an hour's study was followed by sports or a long walk in rows under the surveillance of a Father, while on Thursdays singing lessons replaced the hour of study. At half past five, the long evening study started, for at least two hours, usually followed by a long sermon (*conferentie*). Dinner at eight, half an hour's *recreatie*, evening prayers at nine and then to bed (BHG 45 [1949]: 15). And this every day except Sunday (when there were no lessons), every week, with only the holidays spent at home.

Bertus was kept under thorough surveillance, by the teacher during class hours, by another Father on the playing field, in the study, during walks and in the dormitory. The tables in the refectory were chaired by a "chef" and "underchef" from one of the higher classes; the younger boys were arranged in a row and each year, a boy would shift a little closer to the chair of the table president. *Recreatie* would take place inside the monastery: outside, the boys had to line up for their (as one missionary recalled, "extremely boring") walks. A boy who put his hands in his pockets could be punished. The missionaries I interviewed recall that most of the time they were preoccupied with their studies; intellectually speaking, they attended a normal secondary school, except for the three days' obligatory conversation in French introduced by the French Fathers. (This was changed when the Dutch Fathers more and more took the complete education of candidates for the priesthood in their hands.) As one missionary said euphemistically: "there was not much time for your own personality".[21] In fact, it was a physical discipline directed at creating a new, malleable personality, docile towards superiors and physically conditioned for strenuous mission work.

To the physical regime the Fathers added forms of psychological closure. The new arrivals would band together, united by being distinguished from the higher classes at the dinner-table and on the playing field. This banding together softened the experience of discipline and, as one Father recalls, they would tell each other that discipline and hard work would not last forever and that they

---

[21] MS v/d Poel 1990a,b; AC 54 (1958): 33; BHG 38-42 (1946): 81; IPAC 12a: 065, 17a: 132, 18a: 084.

would all get through in the end. However, many boys did not get through, and their former classmates were never told what happened to them. "What did he do wrong?" was the question the boys asked themselves when one of their classmates did not return after a holiday.[22] Of course, he might not have done anything wrong except finding out that he could not adjust to seminary discipline or could not manage his studies, but the boys were not told the reason – that is, not until the regime was softened in the late 1950s. The question shows the uncertainty which characterized the boys' relationship with the outside, including the world of those who disciplined them. The smallest irregularity, like saying goodnight to someone when the dormitory was supposed to be completely silent, could be suspected by the surveillants. One former transgressor recalls being interrogated like a prisoner of war, with a lamp in his eyes and his Father Superior in the shade.[23] One might suspect that such harshness was intentional, especially because at the same time, the prefect of studies was a "fatherly" and accessible person loved by the boys. Both surrender to personal uncertainty and devotion to superiors were central to missionary discipline.

If the "bonding" of classmates created an internal resistance against the excesses of regimentation, the regime itself also had built-in transgressions, most adequately symbolized by the smoking of cigarettes. Significantly, the vignette of the *Weerter Studentenkrabbels* in 1931 (plate 7) shows a student smoking, framed by sport implements and books. It is a mark of the jocularity characterizing the "student-news" genre of the Holy Ghost Messenger, in which "Bertus" generally only wrote about the sports events, the visit of Santa Claus or the tall tale of one of the visiting missionaries. Smoking, however, was only possible when the surveillant gave explicit permission.[24] Generally, the boys would band together in the case of minor infractions of the rules and refrain

---

[22] IPAC 1a: 166, 17a: 132.

[23] IPAC 17a: 132.

[24] Bertus wrote: "*Ja, opsteken!* (yes, light it!), one called out. Afterwards, it turned out that no permission had been given; of course, I regretted that, but the cigarette was finished" (BHG 43 [1947]: 62).

from betraying a classmate to the Fathers. But the same solidarity kept a check on those who were inclined to be more than their mates, reinforcing the emphasis on humility which also character-ized the Fathers' education.[25]

Missionary work was not a regular feature of the curriculum. Before 1925, life at the seminary was completely devoted to studies punctuated by sports and manual labour. Mission stories would occasionally feature in a *conferentie* by a missionary back from Africa; in later years, the boys could enjoy a mission movie. In 1925, the mission club of St. Paul was founded: all students were a member and consequently engaged to do mission work during the holidays; senior boys were appointed chairman and treasurer. The mission club printed small books or bought mission almanachs to sell to people at home. In this way they supported their own mis-sions while at the same time, "mission fire" was kept burning in their hearts (Jubileumblad SPM 1950). A big map of Africa showed all the missions where Holy Ghost Fathers from the Netherlands were working. Some boys would study architectural drawing in their spare time because it could be useful in the missions; but, as one missionary put it, they remained "bald frogs" (*kale kikkers*), that is, largely ignorant of circumstances in Africa and in the missions.

However, just as one moved closer to the position of the table "chef" each year, class by class the possibility of actually going to the missions approached. Some started to shave as soon as the first downy hair appeared on their cheeks, to approximate the "tough beards" that were thought to identify the true bush-missionary (Van der Geest 1988). The boys sang – during walks, I imagine – their own song: "Africa fairest on earth" (*Afrika 't schoonst op aard*).[26] In general, most boys remained extremely con-scious of their goal – the missions – and their desires were fueled by

---

[25] IPAC 1a: 166; MS. v. d. Poel 1990a.

[26] "Bald frogs", IPAC 2a: 125; tough beards, KMM 514/1a: 000; the song is another example of paradoxy: the continent which is often pictured as being in the grip of the devil is now "fairest on earth". In the source quoted, however, is it used ironically (BHG 43 [1947]: 52).

the occasional tall tale of a passing missionary and, last but not least, the longing of their teachers, who themselves had wanted to go to Africa but were kept in Holland to teach at the seminary.

The biggest hurdle still in the way was the "Big Crossing" (*Grote Oversteek*): the noviciate, in which the boys, 18 years old, had to undergo a rite of passage which was both the epitome of monastic discipline and their initiation into the Congregation. The noviciate taught the initiand the characteristic spirituality of the Congregation, and by making its future member "more conscious of [his] own insufficiency, weakness and impotence" turn him into "a more tractable and meritorious instrument in the hands of God" (AC/WvA [1957]: 15). For a year, novices had to endure the strictest discipline, and those who weathered the storm would come out satisfied that they had survived the worst. The noviciate would start – predictably – with handing in all the cigarettes the students still possessed (OO 17 [1951]: 16). It was largely conducted in silence, preventing the sociability that was so important at the minor seminary. The novices had to perform any and all menial tasks which the novice-master could think of, and sometimes, practice "humility" when, for instance, the Father Superior soiled his feet on purpose to dirty the floor which one of the novices had just mopped.[27] The uncertainty and dependency characteristic of seminary discipline was continued in the noviciate, but now the students were taught not to seek support in their peer group, but in an individual relationship with God, to prepare for the confrontation with the troubles and disappointments of lonely mission work.

The physical discipline of the Brothers' noviciate in Baarle-Nassau was perhaps even more severe. As one Brother explained it, future priests could be humiliated both intellectually and physically, but novice Brothers (who usually had not spent six years at the seminary) had not only been "in the world" much longer, but were also expected to be less amenable to more intellectual forms of disciplining. The Brother who displayed too much piety was mocked behind his back by the novice-master. The former seminary student who had failed his exams was taught not to put on airs among the

---

[27] MS v. d. Poel 1990a: 2.

Brothers: he was told to take the best saw and start to cut trees, while the saw he got was, of course, as blunt as a baseball bat. Independent individual decisions could be publicly punished.[28] This "sweeping away of the sense of independence", as one Brother called it, was useful in the missions when the Brother sometimes had to obey eccentric Superiors.

Generally, the status of the religious Brothers was low. They could not perform the ritual functions of the priests and were mostly engaged in manual work. Not very long ago, the priests who inhabited the "Fathers' corridor" in the castle in Gemert protested indignantly when their bursar (*Econoom*) wanted to house some Brothers in empty rooms on the corridor. The bursar himself – a Brother back from Tanzania since 1970 – was tolerated because he needed to use the safe, which was placed in the bursar's room on the "Fathers' corridor".[29] Brothers were justified in complaining that the Dutch province's internal bulletin hardly published anything about them (OO 19 [1951]: 26). (However, we will see that the status difference was never felt or practised as strongly in the missions.) The high standards of dedication and the severity of the Brother's noviciate were even maintained in the 1950s, when the number of vocations had decreased and was nearing its sharp and final decline. More than a quarter of the candidates that enrolled between June 1945 and August 1949 (12 out of 45) left the *postulaat* (a year of training before entering the noviciate) before becoming a novice. Of the remainder, one-third consisted of sent-down seminarians (OO 11 [1949]: 185).

If discipline in Baarle-Nassau was severe, in 1949 at least, surveillance seems to have been less ubiquitous. The candidates were thought to have already developed their own sense of duty (OO 11 [1949]: 186). Six hours of every day were devoted to manual work, a little less for novices. During the week, the novices spent two hours on singing lessons, and twelve on studying monastic

---

[28] IPAC 9a: 539–656. In one case, a Brother had to wear a horse's halter around his neck for a week after having driven a cart along a road which the Superior had told him not to take.
[29] KMM 111/1a: 157.

rules, the history of the Congregation, religion, liturgy and the New Testament. Postulants would spend six hours a week in the classroom, studying religion, history of the missions, biblical history and etiquette (*wellevendheid*). In their spare time, they kept up their professional knowledge, or studied languages (OO 11 [1949]: 185). Postulants and novices would not be allowed to indulge in their own preferences. They had to submit to all sorts of domestic and gardening work in order to show aptitude, dedication and "holy indifference" to their own wishes (OO 11 [1949]: 186). The postulate and noviciate did not train the candidate in a specific trade; if a trade had to be learned, it should be done in the three years after taking the first vows. Several Brothers, however, especially during the 1930s and 1940s, were consciously trained as jack-of-all-trades, because they were generally more useful in the missions, where the nature of the skills required could not easily be determined beforehand.[30]

For future priests, the noviciate led to the higher studies of the major seminary and the learning of their profession proper: philosophy in the first two years, theology (Dogma, Morals, Scripture and Church Law) in the next, while language training, at least before the Second World War, would be obligatory in the form of one day of French and another of German conversation. Again, year by year the *fraters* (the title for students who had received the habit but had not yet been ordained) could see their missionary adventure draw closer: the tonsure after the first year of philosophy, and the making of the permanent vows of obedience, poverty and chastity marked steps towards ordination and the *divisio apostolorum*, the day when they would get their appointments for the missions or at home. The generation of Fathers who went to the missions before the Second World War describe the major seminary in terms of this expectation: they talk of their philosophy and theology as a process of intellectual ripening and of increasing clarity about their task. Members of the post-war generation, however,

---

[30] One brother had a protracted battle with the authorities who wanted him to become a carpenter while he preferred gardening; despite being the most stubborn of candidates, he had to submit in the end (IPAC 3a: 077); on jack-of-all-trades, IPAC 9b: 111, AC/WvA (1957): 19.

often remark upon its inadequacy and the lack of preparation for their specifically *missionary* tasks. To them, what they learned as "missiology" was "just a bit of theology".[31]

This divergence can, of course, largely be explained by the fact that the post-war generation looks back upon their work through the filter of the experience of the Africanization of their diocese in the 1960s and 1970s, and the upheavals surrounding the Second Vatican Council, especially in the Netherlands. Nevertheless, it is not just a judgment *ex posteriori*. The first group of pre-war students did their theology studies in Belgium, at the University of Leuven, where in the first three decades of this century missiologists like Pierre Charles SJ were effecting a paradigm shift in missiological theory (see Masson 1978). The theories of mission expounded by catholic missiological pioneers like Joseph Schmidlin (see Müller 1980) focussed on *conversion* as the primary aim of mission work, a "saving of souls" which was also a main feature of the popular view of mission work. Charles and his *confrères* shifted the emphasis of theory (in accordance with Papal letters) to the *planting* of the church as the prime goal. The first group of Dutch Holy Ghost Fathers in East Tanganyika, future Bishop Bernard Hilhorst foremost among them, experienced this exciting atmosphere personally,[32] and as we shall see, Hilhorst put some *plantatio* theory into practice.

However, the authority of Pierre Charles was at that time still eclipsed by that of Schmidlin and conversion remained the students' main goal. The next group of pre-war students went through the major seminary in Gemert, where the popular atmosphere of the "ceaseless hunt for souls" was more in tune with the "conversion"-missiology of Schmidlin than the "planting" of the Church propagated by Charles (BHG 34 (1938): 48, Missievereeniging Hoeven 1924: 51 ff).[33] The actual debate between the followers

---

[31] IPAC 2a: 141, 8a: 031, 17a: 198; KMM 708/1a: 045.

[32] OO 33 (1955): 23, KMM 710/1a: 060.

[33] One missionary recalls his dismay when, as a young boy, he heard of mass conversions in Cameroon; he was afraid there would be no work left for him when he would finally be ready for the missions (VPRO).

of Schmidlin and Charles left Dutch missionary circles largely unperturbed (Roes 1974: 155), until such time as the post-war world order demanded the adoption of Charles' ideas (Van den Eeerenbeemt 1953: 15; Freitag 1953: 689 ff.). The lack of appeal of the ideas of Charles may partly have been caused by the fact that Charles and his followers played down the popular heroism of the missionary: they argued against the value of martyrdom and praised virtues of cross-cultural understanding, accommodation to native points of view, and, consequently, of detachment from European bias (Roes 1974: 47–9). The critique of martyrdom, in particular, made *plantatio* theory less easy to fuse with the image of sacrifice for the soul of the Other.

The students ordained shortly before or during the war received additional education in the war years because they were not able to leave for Africa, and this entailed the type of subjects promoted by Charles: implantation missiology, ethnology, Swahili. The Holy Ghost Fathers' missiologist, Loffeld, and two ethnologists, one professional (Dr. Vroklage SVD, later the first professor of ethnology at the University of Nijmegen), and one amateur (Father de Rooij CSSp, who had worked in Uluguru) gave lessons to the students. Therefore, the generation of missionaries sent out shortly after the war had been made conscious of the possibility that their education did not fully prepare them for the work which they were going to do. This feeling of the inadequacy of missionary training was to increase. According to one Father, students who had tasted another, much more open way of life during the war (when the seminary had to close down because of the German occupation) started to resist the old regime in the 1950s. Ironically, "missiology" began to flourish in the Netherlands at a time when missionaries started to doubt the "monopoly on the Faith" of Europeans and to contemplate the "adaptation" (*aanpassing*) of Christianity and the eventual withdrawal of the European missionary from the African scene.[34]

---

[34] Wartime additional education, IPAC 17a: 198, KMM 708/1a: 055, 447/2a: 000; resisting the old regime, IPAC 14a: 185; adaptation, OO 33 (1955): 23, Freitag 1953: 68; though missiologists widely discussed adaptation (Donatus 1949; Gregorius 1955; Van den Bercken 1952), my other sources (BHG, AC

After the war, the Grand Mission Hour went into its dying minutes. There were recurrent problems with monastic discipline, both among missionaries returning from Africa, among novices and among the students of the major seminary. Students challenged the old theology by new missiological ideas, and even the tightening of monastic closure could not prevent the increase of drop-outs after 1956. The minor seminary had to adapt quickly to the government's secular standards of teaching in order to retain students, which also implied admitting the "worldly" influence of hired, qualified teachers. It could not withstand the secularization of secondary education and was closed down in the 1960s. "Mission action" found little response among Dutch youth, and mission propaganda lost the exotic market to a large number of rival publications. Initially, propagandists tried to turn the tide by a more aggressive tone, that now included communism among satanic evils.[35] Around 1957, however, mission propaganda increasingly shifted to a "Christian anti-colonialism" that included criticism of South-African apartheid and employed a non-exotic imagery closer to that of the promotion of development aid and the secular mission of the Peace Corps Volunteers (see plate 9 and Pels 1989). Although the missionary activity of Dutch catholics did not cease, the religious movement

---

and OO) rarely did. A missiology chair was established at the Catholic University of Nijmegen in 1930, but the discussion only started to flourish when a journal and an institute for missiology were started shortly after 1945 (Mulders 1955).

[35] On monastic discipline, OO 4 (1947): 58, 5 (1947): 74, 8 (1947): 22, 14 (1950): 3, 25 (1953): 3, 33 (1955): 2, 35 (1955): 3, 37 (1956): 3; theology and curriculum, IPAC 14a: 185, 315–440; OO 15 (1950): 16, 38 (1956): 3, 33 (1955): 7, 54 (1960): 8, 57 (1960): 11; closure, OO 48 (1958): 6; drop-outs, OO 41 (1957): 3; decline of minor seminary: OO 10 (1947): 164; 21 (1952): 17; 41 (1957): 8; 42 (1957): 7; 44 (1957): 2, 15; 61 (1961): 14; AC/WVA (1957); IPAC 18a: 132; decline of mission action: OO 9 (1948): 146; 12 (1949): 205; 25 (1953): 19; BHG 46/1 (1950): inside cover; BHG 47/6 & 7 (1951): inside cover; AC 48/1–2 (1952): 2; rival exotic publications were a.o. Julien (1940, 1949) and Melchior (1950, 1957); the new aggressiveness is apparent from the *Holy Ghost Messenger*'s early 1950s editorials, called the "editorial battle-axe" (*de strijdbijl der redactie*).

PLATE 9   *A cover of* Africa Christo *(56 [1960]), showing an example of the images of African Christianity that became prominent after 1955. On the covers of the journal before 1955, a different skin colour was usually reinforced by other markers of difference (see plate 4), but here, human universality within the church is emphasized. Other photographs in this style would show African workers in a factory, reading newspapers, or African priests baptizing children (see plate 2a)*

centered around sacrifices for the salvation of exotic African souls was at its end by the time that decolonization transformed the mission in Africa.

TO THE MISSIONS

Before we turn to that African part of the missionary movement, it may be useful to consider at what image of the mission we have arrived. It is not, as Mary Huber argues, an institution that is "displaced" to the mission field and that therefore needs a "structure" of ironic self-representation to cope with the consequent instabilities (1988: 200–8). Huber bases these conclusions mostly on the analysis of a mission propaganda journal without setting this source in the context of the "home" base where it has, in the last analysis, been produced (Ranger 1987: 183; Pels 1990b: 111). An analysis of this "home" base shows how instable the mission was even before the move to Africa had been made – that it was, in fact, a movement *within* Dutch Catholicism before it could become a movement *to* Africa. The missionaries were, so to speak, always on the move: from maternal home to seminary, from seminary, through the noviciate, to the Congregation, from the Congregation, through ordination and travel, to the mission area. In order to picture that movement to themselves, missionaries did not have to ironically "cope with" an instability inflicted upon them, but paradoxically account for the reasons why they actively created and sought out such instability. Paradoxical conceptions of sacrifice and the exotic could manage that movement; seminary and monastic discipline tried to inure the boys to its uncertainties. In the end, the missionaries were not so much "displaced" as engaged in making a new place – for themselves, for their families, for their *confrères*, for future African converts.

Nor are we dealing simply with a "total" or "greedy" institution, as Thomas Beidelman suggests (1982: 21). Although the mission certainly demanded the full allegiance of its members, the necessity of constant movement across its boundaries implied that it could not do so by monastic discipline and closure only. In fact, "mission" in the canonical sense (*missio canonica*, or investing a person with the juridical authority to teach religion) includes both the *sacras missiones* for the conversion of sinners and the confirmation of the just, and the *missiones externas* for the spreading of the faith among unbelievers and heretics (Mulders 1950: 14–5). "Mission" is usually reserved for the latter, but the inclusion of ministry shows that the *professional* work of a parish priest formally belongs to it. In fact, the education of missionaries embodied this institutionalized duality: the missionary always remained a member of a monastic, total institution, but was at the same time a religious professional combining a certain technical competence, taught to him at the major seminary, with the ideal of putting this competence at the service of – future – Christians (cf. Wilensky 1964: 138; see also Pels 1990a). In Africa, the mission was both a transplanted European monastery and a diocese in the making, and we shall see that this tension between monastic closure and professional ministry was constant in the Uluguru missions.

But if the mission was an institutionalized form of movement, this does not mean it was sufficiently flexible to make a place for the Catholic Church in Uluguru without adapting itself to local routines. Even if such localization was primarily directed by the missionaries (Huber 1988: 203), the boundaries of monastic closure, the strategies of professional ministry, and the self-image of the missionary as someone sacrificing himself for the conversion of the African heathen underwent substantial changes under the influence of the confrontation with (future) Luguru converts. Such adaptation became necessary immediately after the Holy Ghost Fathers had first ventured into Uluguru, with the intention of setting up a Christian village near Morogoro modelled on the physically bounded monastic institution. In 1882, they bought land from local lineage heads in order to "acquire material as well as spiritual boundaries sufficiently strong to ward off non-Catholics and other unwanted folk" (BHG 29 [1933]: 4). In Christian villages built on French Utopian models, the converts (usually ex-slaves brought from the coast) would, under strict surveillance, create an example that, the Fathers hoped, would attract new converts from the surrounding tribes (Kieran 1971). This *kitumwa* ("slavery") strategy (Sahlberg

1986: 47) entailed setting up a total institution that tried to keep its inside pure by controlling communications with the outside. The villages did not attract a promising number of converts from the surroundings, and even failed to keep out "Satan and some of his stooges" (BHG 29 [1933]: 4). The strategy was abandoned around 1885 and the mission began to rely exclusively on outschools supervised by catechists recruited, initially, from the missionaries' orphanages and later, from the first Luguru converts (Nolan 1972: 3). The Fathers increasingly supervised the catechists, rather than the converts, and as the catechist became the main agent for converting Waluguru, the missionary fell back on his other role of ministring to the needs of the already converted. It was to this professional role that a new recruit, arriving forty years later, in what had then become Tanganyika Territory, first had to adapt himself.

PROFESSIONAL COMPETENCE, OR: LEARNING HOW TO TALK

The young missionary's desire to sacrifice himself for the conversion of Africans and his expectations of exotic adventure were not immediately realized on stepping ashore in Dar es Salaam. For some time, he would still move within the confines of the missionary institution: first, being welcomed by the White Fathers in Dar es Salaam, and next, sent to the Holy Ghost Fathers' Bagamoyo or Morogoro mission. There, the young recruit could be appointed – to his intense regret – to teach at the minor seminary or the Teacher Training College. Parish work in Morogoro Town was not up to his standards either, because there was "no missionary work in it": it was mere ministry. "True" missionizing was converting people, opening schools, and going on *safari* into the farther reaches of the mountains. This "youthful dream of yesterday" only became reality, for most missionaries, when they could start a new mission on their own, but often it did not come true at all.[36] Few,

---

[36] KMM 708/1a: 240; IPAC 2a: 392, 7a: 531, 582; BHG 32 (1936): 51–3.

however, would be denied a period of training in one of the bigger "bush" stations.

Of the bush stations in Uluguru, only Mgeta or Matombo could be reached, before the 1950s, by car (see map 2). The gravel roads were (and are) often bad, and sometimes impassable, during the rains, especially from April to June. From Matombo or Mgeta the other missions had to be approached *per pedes apostolorum*. Usually, carriers from the mission of destination would come to collect the loads of the missionary from somewhere along the road and bring them up. He himself would have to climb up on his own (although he was occasionally carried across a river), and to many of the fresh arrivals the experience must have been as exhilarating as mine when I first ventured on a long *safari* through the mountains. However, it was often as tiresome as it was exhilarating, especially during the rainy season, or when the missionary was not yet used to the marching speed of Waluguru, which enables them to cover up to 50 kilometers a day on a regular journey.

On arrival at his destination, the first task of the new missionary was to learn yet another language. Apart from the French, German, Latin and Greek he had to master at home, and the English that was necessary to communicate with the British authorities and to teach at the Teacher Training School, the missionary had to learn the language with which to minister to the needs of African Christians. This was mostly Swahili, although during the 1920s and 1930s, many Waluguru did not yet speak it and one had to master Kiluguru or use an interpreter.[37] This was reflected in an interpenetration of languages in missionary speech and writing, with up to four languages used in one sentence. Swahili words like *safari* (journey), *baraza* (council meeting), *shamba* (field), *kiwanja* (plot), *mchumba* (unmarried partner), *mali* (property or brideprice), and *shauri* (issue of debate) were commonly used. Swahili verbs usually appeared in the infinitive, designating a specific activity of Waluguru (like *kuhamia ndege*, chasing away the birds from the fields, a word

---

[37] Others working outside Uluguru had to master one of several of the other languages spoken in the Vicariate: Kinguru, Kizaramo, Kikwere, even the complex Kisandawe.

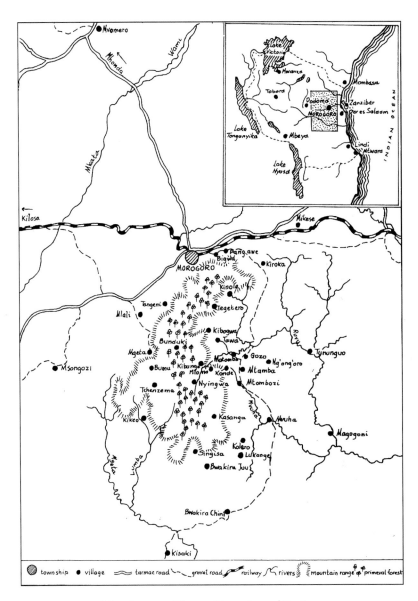

MAP 2   *Uluguru Mountains and Environs*

that carried meaning for the missionaries because this seasonal activity kept children away from the mission school). A very few verbs were "Dutchified", designating activities which missionaries asked Africans to engage in (*liemeren* from *kulima*, clearing the field or road; *piemeren* from *kupima*, measuring, in this case examining an African's knowledge of the catechism before he or she could receive the sacraments).[38] On the one hand, this language-switching can be interpreted in terms of power: the predominance of nouns in texts of explorers and missionaries "on the road" may signify an author's claim to authority and mastery of his subject matter (Fabian 1985: 42). However, we are here also dealing with a situation of "settling in", in which the use of Swahili words is an act of location, of making oneself at home by displaying the linguistic competence required in that place.

The young Father taught himself Swahili grammar in the morning, aided by books written by one of the Congregation's veterans (Sacleux, Loogman or De Rooij), and practised with children or students of the seminary in the afternoon. He could start reading the Latin Mass immediately, and administer sacraments if he restricted himself to the Latin *rituale*, or its Swahili equivalent after it became available in 1958/9. His linguistic knowledge was tested after several months by his first Swahili sermon, which, most missionaries recall, gave the faithful an amusing Sunday. After some six months (four for fast learners, eight for the slow) the young priest received, after an exam, the "jurisdiction" that professionally qualified him to administer sacraments in the Vicariate without prior permission of his Superior. For a new Brother, language learning was often more frustrating. Because his expertise was always too urgently needed, he was often dumped at a workshop or building site and left to his own devices and despair. According to one

---

[38] In the 1920s and 1930s, the mission diaries alternate French and Swahili. After 1940, most missionaries switched from French to their native Dutch (MD 24.5.41, SD 25.11.42, TuD 4.7.41) before it was officially allowed in 1948 (SD 9.11.48, KD 1.11.48, TD March '49). In some diaries, English was used to enable African priests to read them (TuD 1.9.46, MD 9.8.44). Examples of *piemeren* and *liemeren* in KD 16.10.56, SD 7.6.50.

Brother, they learned faster than the Fathers in this way, but also less "deep", that is, with less grammatical knowledge, and the Brothers' *boerentaal* ("farmers' language") was sometimes easier to understand for ordinary Waluguru than the Fathers' polished Swahili. Another Brother had already mastered Swahili and two other local languages after 18 months, a competence which most Fathers never attained. The standardized Swahili learned by the Fathers was not necessarily superior to the Brothers' "learning from the bottom".[39]

There were, of course, Fathers who invested more energy in language learning, especially in the years before the Second World War, when Swahili study material was scarce and many local languages still unrecorded. These experts usually started their studies when residing far from the centre of the Vicariate, in a city like Mombasa, or in remote mountain parishes like Tegetero and Singiza. Only a few Fathers spoke fluent Kiluguru; others used interpreters when they thought their Swahili was not sufficiently understood. Interestingly, African languages were most neglected in the Vicariate's centre itself: both Bishop Hilhorst and his Irish predecessor, Wilson, are said never to have mastered Swahili completely. Both came from a non-missionary background to Bagamoyo and apparently did not have the time or inclination to learn the language as thoroughly as their priests. Hilhorst had some of his speeches delivered by his bursar and he decided on difficult marriage-disputes with the help of the Swahili scholar, Father Loogman. It suggests that the Bishop had insufficient time and professional contacts with Africans to make fluent Swahili conversation a necessity.[40]

---

[39] On Fathers' language, KMM 77.710: 3l; IPAC 1a: 658, 2a: 234, 5a: 319, 12a: 201, 13b: 394, 15a: 308, 17a: 397; MtD 15.1.59, SD 26.2.58, 3.7.46, 14.3.62; BHG 29/4: 54; on Brothers' language, IPAC 3a: 269–353, IPAC 9b: 127–200, KMM 591/1a: 138; the difference between the Fathers' and Brothers' Swahili may also be the result of the fact that the Fathers learned, through the influence of expert Father Loogman, coastal Swahili, and not the local dialect influenced by Kiluguru or another local language.

[40] IPAC 11b: 120; KMM 514/1a: 035, 708/1a: 130, 710/1a: 260; SD 15.3.35, 28.7.40, 21.10.40; Hilhorst's successor, Van Elswijk, had worked in the diocese and spoke fluent Swahili.

Learning a language implies cultural training. In order to hear confession or marry people, the Father had to be able to translate dictionary meanings into pragmatic ones. One had, for example, to learn both the synonyms and meanings of *kupiga bao* ("to hit the board", divination; see chapter six) in order to understand it when it was confessed, and to decide upon the appropriate penance. In the case of marriage, a Father had to know about *mali* ("property", but here: brideprice; see chapter four), and the customs and parties involved in its exchange. Instruction of newlyweds in appropriate conduct implied mastery of covert turns of phrase accompanying both Luguru and missionary talk of sex. This learning process was determined by the Father Superior of the mission, whose informal instruction during recreation, at lunch or in the evenings taught the newcomer his working knowledge of Luguru custom and the standard ways of coping with problems or novel experiences. Before the Second World War, most Dutch Fathers took their cue from their Alsatian superiors, and passed on their knowledge to their successors in the same way. Few would try to find out things for themselves, and it was only during the 1960s that the generation of 1946 (already different because of their war experience in Holland) started to doubt existing attitudes towards Luguru customs, and marriage in particular (see chapter four).[41]

It has to be emphasized that a concept of Luguru "culture" hardly figured in the missionaries' comprehension of the situation. As I show elsewhere (Pels 1994b and the conclusion), the missionaries' ethnographic texts were selective, picking out customs and practices that could be endorsed or should be combated, without putting them in the context of a "tribal" or "ethnic" whole. Their experiences of

---

[41] On independent inquiry, IPAC 12a: 270; another Father compared tales about the perversities of initiation to the character of his pupils who had undergone it, and found the former wanting; he thought that most of his colleagues were uncertain about their knowledge of Luguru routines but failed to check this knowledge with Africans: IPAC 8a: 175, 248–275; on the post-war generation, IPAC 1b: 000, 8a: 175, 12a: 445, 15a: 273, 352, 17a: 469; after 1945, jurisdiction for confession or marriage was granted by headquarters (IPAC 5a: 155), but before, examination was often left to the Superior of the mission (KMM 77.710: 4).

difference were framed in terms of isolable Luguru "customs" or generalized African "mentality", and these were not necessarily connected. For most, their knowledge was practical, and generalizations about *la mentalité incompréhensible de nos chers noirs* usually occur in the mission diaries at moments of adversity, when in some way or another the expectations or normal practices of the missionary are frustrated by Waluguru. *Routine* ways of acting differently – missionary accomodations to and adoptions of Luguru practices – were not classified as "different". On the contrary, this immersion in African ways of life was often the way in which missionaries expressed how they felt at home and how they loved the country and its inhabitants.[42]

CLOSURE AND CONTROL AT THE MISSION STATION'S BOUNDARIES

Of course, the missionaries' "immersion" in Africa did not mean that their racism disappeared, only that it materialized differently: usually, on the physical boundaries of the mission compound. Big stations like Matombo or Mgeta were often economically self-sufficient communities led by an all-male European staff that set itself off from its surroundings by an architecturally enclosed space, like a monastery. Yet, the maintenance of these boundaries hardly ever met the standards of monastic discipline as they were envisaged from the Bishop's House in Morogoro: contact with Waluguru demanded schedules and kinds of work which were not easy to combine with monastic life. A new recruit would continue to practise at one of these stations under the supervision of the Father Superior, who usually stayed at the mission to deal with the ministry of nearby places, while his assistants went on *safari* to the distant outschools. The Superior was assisted by an experienced

---

[42] For expressions of otherness in times of adversity, KD Feb./March 39, KD 7.2.40, KD 15.4.41, SD 2.11.40, IPAC 9b: 526, IPAC 17b: 276; returned missionaries said they "left their heart in Africa" because they had "poured themselves out into the people". Some cried on departure; those who had left Africa expressed a strong desire to go back: BHG 28/2 (1932): 39, 28/9 (1932): 199, 32/1 (1936): 5; KMM 43/1a: 442, 447/2a: 398, IPAC 6b: 23; SD 15.8.56.

Father as bursar. The (German, later African) Sisters at the mission had a separate community, but their Mother Superior was subject to the Father Superior of the mission. Messages from Fathers to Sisters and *vice versa* were supposed to pass through Father and Mother Superior only. The Sisters took care of the mission school, dispensary, and kitchen and did not have as much freedom as the Fathers to leave the mission compound. Their work never brought them on *safari*, except between their headquarters in Morogoro and the mission. They could not easily mingle with Fathers and Brothers; "boys", domestic servants from nearby Luguru settlements, cleaned the Fathers' rooms.

The mission was set apart from the African life surrounding it by the site and buildings of the mission. Usually built on a hill, they stood out from the landscape, presenting a front which must have seemed as imposing to Waluguru as Catholic liturgy itself (see plate 10). An elaborate garden, and clumps of trees providing shade, timber or oranges distinguished the hill from the surrounding fields which had been cleared for cultivation. The missionaries stuck to a European diet as much as possible, and vegetable gardens and a *basse-cour* for poultry and cattle were common in the more developed stations. For one "bush" missionary the big mission of

PLATE 10   *Matombo mission in the 1950s*

Matombo was *Ulaya*, Swahili for "Europe". The Dutch missionaries also contrasted their "cosiness" (*gezelligheid*) with the "dour" Alsatian and "schoolmasterish" Irish Holy Ghost Fathers, and the "arrogant" English administrators. Dutch identity was ritually affirmed on the fifth of December by the typically Dutch feast of *Sinterklaas* (in which the missionaries let the Sisters, German or African, share).[43]

The Bishop and the Congregation's inspectors tried to create even more forbidding boundaries. In 1937, Bishop Hilhorst issued a new *Directory* prescribing mission life that went far beyond one of his predecessors' statement that the regulations of the Congregation's houses in Europe should be followed (Vogt 1909: 5). Hilhorst carefully outlined a regime and timetable, and observations on how to implement it (Hilhorst 1937: 1–2), but although the missionaries were sufficiently disciplined to implement it when time allowed, especially on *safari* this regime was hard to follow. One missionary gave up morning meditation because Waluguru came to confess at that time; another said that in the mission, you had "all eternity". The Brothers often adopted the daily work rhythm of Africans and continued from breakfast (6.30 a.m.) until 3.00 p.m. (when Waluguru went home to eat) before having lunch, after which serious work ceased. In other words, the Bishop lost much of his grip on that most important of disciplinary methods: the regimentation of time and rhythm of work (Foucault 1979: 149, 157–9).[44]

Of course, the hierarchy was not very happy with this development, and Hilhorst seems to have been more succesful than his predecessors in restoring a measure of discipline. The *Livre des visites* of Matombo mission shows how long the Alsatian Fathers ignored their Superiors' demands to implement religious discipline in the community. Despite occasional improvements, complaints about the lack of discipline recur until the appointment of the first

---

[43] On Matombo as *Ulaya*, KD 3.6.41; on Dutch culture, KMM 43/1a: 071, 710/1a: 078, IPAC 13a: 000; KD 6.12.50, SD 5.12.50, 5.12.57.
[44] On time, KMM 710/1a: 102, 77.710: 11; on work rhythm, KMM 514/1a: 280, 591/1a: 225, 710/1a: 102.

Dutch Superior in 1940. Hilhorst called Matombo *la communauté des impossibilités*, referring to the arguments employed by its Fathers and Brothers that full discipline was impossible to maintain. Although Hilhorst managed to restore order for some time, in 1957 a more indulgent inspector had already conceded that because of the work it was not always possible to keep to the rule.[45]

The physical closure of a monastery was even more difficult to establish (Hilhorst 1937: 5). By 1928, the inspectors were finally satisfied that Africans, women in particular, were no longer admitted on the first floor of the Fathers' house, but complaints about "invasions" of Africans in the central courtyard recur until 1942, when after seven years of futile exhortations, Hilhorst ordered to keep Africans out of the compound and have them come to the verandah up front. In 1955, Hilhorst's successor Van Elswijk even wanted to keep the Africans out of the offices on the verandah except for private discussions. Similarly, Hilhorst forbade travelling "not connected with ministry, business or health" (Hilhorst 1937: 5), but many Fathers at lonely outposts took any excuse to visit nearby *confrères*. Up to 1940, Hilhorst also had much difficulty in having the missionaries keep regular accounts, diaries and statistics. After 1940, the only recurring complaint was that the monthly "chapter" was not held. In the chapter, Father Superior coordinated and inspected mission work, which must have been a practically superfluous performance of hierarchy in a situation where all community members breakfasted, lunched, dined and relaxed together every day.[46]

The relationship between Brothers and Fathers was much more equal in the missions than in the Netherlands, for the commensality of the mission station abolished the careful distinctions maintained in Dutch houses. Friendships between Fathers and

---

[45] MP, Livre des Visites: 17.9.08, 14.7.12, 12.10.28, 16.8.35, 24.11.36, 6.11.40, 8.2.57; Cahier des chapitres: Stam to De Vries, 13.11.40.

[46] On physical closure, MP, Livre des visites: 17.9.08, 16.10.11, 14.7.12, 11.8.13, 3.2.21, 12.10.28, Cahier des chapitres: 19.8.35, 17.11.40, Hilhorst to v.d. Eeden 9.10.42, ibidem 5.11.42, 1.2.55; on monthly chapter, MP, Livre des visites: 22.6.09, 20.10.15, 24.11.35, 14.10.41, 16.10.51, 29.8.53, 8.8.55.

Brothers developed more easily, and although a kind of solidarity between Brothers remained, they were also divided over the different missions and only saw each other once a year at the annual retreat. This increase in respectability was also the result of the enormous value of their work for the mission, a value that made some of them answerable only to Hilhorst, bypassing the Father Superior's wishes, and brushing off the orders that newly arrived Fathers tried to give them. Nevertheless, the Brothers remained a subordinate category: during the election of a new Bishop in 1954, they were not allowed to vote. Only from the late 1950s onwards, this subordination was gradually lessened. Sisters were in a still more subordinate position: independent as far as their spiritual life was concerned, they completely relied on the Father Superior for supplies and equipment and would have a hard time when he neglected their requirements. In 1952, the Sisters were granted more financial responsibility, but real independence was only acquired by the German Sisters in the 1960s, while African Sisters remained, in most respects, dependent on the Father Superior.[47]

Hilhorst also tried to reinforce the closure of a mission by re-iterating the necessity of observing the vows of poverty, chastity and obedience (with the latter as "principal virtue", Hilhorst 1937: 9), insisting upon "fraternal charity" between the missionaries, and safeguarding this internal unity by reserving the duty to receive visitors to Superiors (Hilhorst 1937: 2). A Father should not broadcast his troubles before strangers, and obtaining information from natives about other Fathers, Brothers and missions was "simply detestable" (Hilhorst 1937: 4). Hilhorst was colour conscious, and warned his missionaries against creating "in the minds of the natives any criticism or suspicion towards our Confreres or other

---

[47] On election, IPAC 10a: 129, 144, 166; the election itself, however, already showed the increasing tendency of Rome to consider the wishes of those lower in the hierarchy; on the Sisters' position, MP, Cahier des chapitres: 14.12.35; Contract Sisters of the Precious Blood: 1932 Agreement, p. 3; 1952 Agreement.

Europeans" (Hilhorst 1937: 19). In practice, such European solidarity was not always forthcoming, for the Alsatian Brother Simon made a habit of releasing tax defaulters rounded up by a British administrator, and some Fathers criticized the implementation of a British soil conservation scheme in front of Waluguru in the 1950s. But the principle was generally accepted: one Father took care not to carry his own luggage like an African after his motorbike broke down on the road, and also kept his dignity by not following an African hunt although his feet itched to do so. Similarly, a Brother argued that "descending" in order to "act like a black" did not please the African. One should remain an object to be admired, not out of haughtiness, but because "the European has to be a European".[48] To Hilhorst, it was necessary to impress the native "by exterior things" and "not to lose prestige" (Hilhorst 1937: 12, 18). The directive echoed assumptions about how Africans should be approached shared by most other colonialists.

EXPANSION AND EXCHANGE ACROSS THE MISSION'S BOUNDARIES

If the Bishop had to work to keep the boundaries of the missions clear, he could not but further blur them by promoting the expansion of the mission's sphere of operation and the increase in contact with Waluguru which it necessitated. At the same time, the biggest reward that Hilhorst had in store for a missionary who had toed his line was to ask him to open a new station. For Father Vermunt, his "youthful dream" came true in 1936. After having worked under Father Hürth in Mgeta for some years, he received a chit from Hilhorst telling him to open a new station at Kikeo. After a walk of two days he presented himself at the house of the local headman and put up his tent at his new "home". They chose a hill site and had the schoolchildren clear the plot guided by the catechists. When Vermunt wanted to mark the plot, the headman objected. Vermunt took care not to give him reason to complain and

---

[48] IPAC 4a: 101, 17b: 591–694, KMM 591/1a: 138; BHG 28 (1932): 43, 116.

left, with the intention to return when a provisional dwelling would have been erected by the Christians (BHG 32/4 [1936]: 51–3).

After 1900, all new missions had been built on the foundations laid by catechists and schoolchildren. Once a wattle-and daub building, *style nègre*, had been erected, a Brother could start a garden and improve the buildings further. But a plot, building and labour could not be had for nothing: any expansion involved a missionary in local power relationships with traditional "big men" (*wakubwa*) and British-appointed Native Authorities. Christians and catechists would feel backed up by the power of a resident priest, but non-Christian headmen could also gamble for presents, employment advantages, and other benefits. As Father Vermunt's case shows, they were very conscious of their rights and opportunities and manipulated them to get most out of it.[49]

In the 1930s, there was little opposition to the expansion of the mission by Waluguru. While the foundation of Matombo mission in 1897 was followed by an attack by the people of Lusangalala, opponents of the Singiza mission in the 1930s merely killed the fish which the Brother had just set out in a pool: a threat, but nothing more. Opponents of the mission could appeal to the Native Authorities, who would be backed up by the British administration: they prevented, for instance, the acquisition of the old German fort in Kisaki, meant to extend the mission's influence among the Muslims of the Kisaki plains. Missionaries distrusted Muslim Native Authorities and *vice versa*, and the former preferred to have Catholics appointed to these posts. The mission cherished Catholic subchiefs like Martini Kimanga of Mgeta (1930–5) and Matias Bambarawe of Matombo (1926–46), helped them with gathering tax

---

[49] The foundation of Singiza created possibilities for earning cash through work on the mission building; the Brother started a bricklaying school; the Father increased the number of catechists, expanding the sources of income and power for some members of the community (KMM 77.710: 11–2, 14–5); in 1936, the headman of Kasanga, Chegulo, threatened to back out when the missionaries could not decide upon a plot for the new mission, invoked higher authorities, then became friendly again and managed to obtain a present of 6 shillings before he organized the lease of the plots concerned: KD 18.10.36, 26.10.36.

and allowed Bambarawe considerable leeway with his "ancestor worship" (*tambiko*; see chapter six). Despite the missionary suspicion of Islam, there were few actual conflicts with Muslims in Uluguru. In 1933, there was a brawl at Matombo mission called the *vita ya machupa* (the Bottles War, after the weapons employed), but it was provoked by the personal intransigence of the Father Superior and the stubbornness of the Muslims, rather than by a history of mutual opposition.[50] Only in a predominantly Muslim area like Tegetero, resistance against Christian expansion was endemic (see chapter five).

The earlier missions were built on land bought from Waluguru, but after Governor Cameron declared the Uluguru mountains closed to all non-native settlement in 1930, the missionaries could only get land on lease, and even then, should not ask for much if they wanted the District Commissioner's approval (ten acres was normal). Administrators often doubted whether missionary expansion was in the interests of Waluguru, but rarely refused a request, because it was always supported by Luguru Christians. Only once, fears of overpopulation in the 1950s led the administration to refuse a lease in Kibungo, but a petition by Kibungo Christians to a visiting United Nations commission reversed that decision (Alexander 1990). Relations with the British authorities were minimal, except in the field of education (see chapter five). The Bishop was an honorary member of the British "Morogoro Club", but never came there. One of the missionaries in Morogoro was visiting justice of the prison. For the rest, the parties

---

[50] One informant claimed the Matombo Superior got the DC to falsify an election in the late 1940s in favour of a Catholic and at the expense of a Muslim candidate, but other informants deny this. On Matombo, Singiza and Kisaki, MD 21.9.1897, SD 15.7.32; TNA 61/29/B/279: Application for Kasanga and Kisaki missions, 9.4.36; DC's Report on Kisaki, 29.8.39; on Kimanga: BHG 28/12 (1932): 271, 29/4 (1933): 64); on Bambarawe: Rhodes House Library: Bagshawe diary, 1.1.30; on the 1946 election: FN 148, 173; MD 20.01.47; TNA 31347: Juma Mzee to CS, 27.3.47; on attitudes to islam: BHG 28/11 (1932): 249, 274–7, IPAC 4a: 059–101, 7b: 046, KD 8.2.57; on *vita ya machupa*: TNA 21715, MD 5.7.33–2.11.33, 5.6.35, 23.6.35, IPAC 12b: 022, FN: Mzee Daudi Maduga, Kiswira, 14.12.89.

kept out of each other's way as much as possible. Hilhorst wrote: "Good and friendly relations with the civil authorities are necessary for our work" (Hilhorst 1937: 43).[51]

From the moment of his arrival in 1934, Hilhorst embarked on a programme of expansion in the whole Vicariate. In Uluguru, he immediately sent one of the Dutch veterans to open Tegetero mission (1934); next, Kikeo and Kasanga (1936), followed by Tangeni (1937), Msongozi (1938), and the thwarted attempt at Kisaki (1939). The war brought this effort to a halt, because Hilhorst had to send several Fathers to Kenya to replace Italian missionaries who had been interned, and because new recruits were not able to leave Holland. After the arrival of 23 new Fathers in 1946, he tried to make up for lost time: Matombo spawned Mtombozi and Tawa (1949), and later Kibungo (1955), while several new stations were founded from Mgeta in Western Uluguru. Some new stations were founded to block the progress of Islam (Kisaki; maybe Tegetero, too); another, to stop the Protestant Church Missionary Society (Taragwe, far to the West in Ukaguru).[52] But, as a rule, a new mission was founded where the density of Christians produced demands that the Fathers of a large mother-mission like Matombo could no longer meet.

In other words, the missionaries moved in *after* the need for their presence had been established among Waluguru by catechists. The development of this need in the 1930s and 1940s is the subject of the following chapters, but it should be noted that before that time, other forms of bringing Waluguru into the orbit of the mission, such as baptism in return for a piece of cloth or food, had been employed. Hilhorst and his missionaries wanted to put a stop to those "absolutely wrong" practices, but some relationships of exchange, like labour power for money, or small presents for a

---

[51] Lease registrations in TNA 61/29, B and C files; on relations with British: IPAC 2b: 195, 12b: 150, 628, 14a: 000, IPAC 17b: 591–694, KMM 708/1b: 262, MS Van der Poel, 5; two exceptions to such amiability were attributed to administrators being freemasons, or to their warnings to missionaries not to attack indigenous customs (KMM 514/1a: 035).

[52] KMM 708/1a: 137, 316; MS Van der Poel, 6.

headman's support, could not be avoided. One missionary acknowledged that small gifts to children, or donations of salt, were still the "little tricks that had nothing to do with religion and yet influenced it". Moreover, charity (*caritas*) urged the missionaries to provide free medical care or to help a leper-colony with food.[53]

Some missionaries expressed their doubts about *caritas*, arguing that Africans did not understand the concept. There are indications that *caritas* led some Waluguru to interpret the wealth of Rome (*mali ya Roma*) as a reservoir from which everyone could draw at liberty. The idea of a charitable gift without necessary return was difficult to reconcile with the expectations of people used to relations established by gift-*exchange*. Waluguru tried to draw the missionaries into these relations of exchange, and although some Fathers thought the gifts of eggs, chicken or vegetables which they received on trek or on arrival at a new mission were just tokens of appreciation (which was true to some extent), others clearly saw that the gift to a Father also implied an expectation of return.[54] Moreover, for Waluguru the Fathers' spiritual powers were the most important counter-gift that they could get, even though the Fathers themselves did not want to conflate the latter with gifts that were "not religious" (see chapter six).

The Alsatian and Irish predecessors of Hilhorst used another form of "persuasion" that did not fit the latter's view of Church-building. Violence, in the form of beatings, was a common occurence until Hilhorst "absolutely" prohibited its use (Hilhorst 1937: 19). Many missionaries did not agree with the prohibition of corporal punishment, and Hilhorst had to threaten with immediate suspension from duties if it occurred. Hilhorst apparently based his decision first of all on the fact that the civil authorities forbade its use by others than themselves. Beatings (*viboko*) were applied on other occasions than official punishment, seldom out of mere anger,

---

[53] On baptism as exchange: KMM 710/1a: 260, 514/1a: 035, IPAC 12a: 201, FN: Mzee Petri Mloka, Kiswira, 14.12.89; on gifts and charity: KD 25.2.41, BHG 28 (1932): 213, 28 (1932): 272, 29 (1933): 15, KMM 77.710: 17.
[54] Doubts about charity, BHG 28 (1932): 272, KD 24.5.54; interpreting Luguru gifts, KMM 77.710: 5, BHG 29 (1933): 14.

sometimes to "beat up a marriage".[55] Most often, however, the missionaries thought *viboko* were indispensable for getting reluctant children into school and administering punishments decided upon by a mission *baraza*. While beatings for not attending school were tolerated by the British authorities, they reserved the right to punish adults for themselves.

Although the use of *viboko* seems a completely one-sided affair, there is a communicative side to it (see Blok 1991: 190). Many catechists felt that force (*nguvu*) was necessary to support their prestige. Many missionaries were convinced that a kind of toughness was part of the African way of life; they related stories of how the Africans themselves asked for *viboko*. One of them interpreted the beatings as an African way of accounting, or paying a debt which the public judgment of a *baraza* had decided upon. After punishment, the misdeed for which it was meted out should never be mentioned again: after all, the debt was paid (in this it resembled the penance given after confession, see the last section of this chapter). The Father who mentioned the misdeed after it had been punished was committing a great injustice, or so the missionary thought Waluguru thought. Whatever the true situation may have been, Hilhorst suppressed *viboko*; after 1945, no complaints of the missionaries about their lack of *nguvu* are recorded. However, it was only when *Uhuru* or independence was approaching that some Waluguru dared to hit back.[56]

In sum, Hilhorst's way of "planting the Church", implied not just a physical expansion by means of mission stations, but also the extension of a practice of ministry modelled on the diocesan

---

[55] *Kiboko* (hippopotamus) also referred to a whip of the animal's hide. However, the plural *viboko* was mostly used, and referred to beatings with a small cane. The English "beating up a marriage" fails to put the Dutch pun across: *een huwelijk in elkaar slaan* can also mean "to beat together" or "nail up" a marriage and referred to the use of *viboko* to force a quarreling couple to live together again; BHG 32 (1936): 140, IPAC 9b: 326, KD 30.5.46.

[56] On 'African' toughness: KD 8.9.42, SD 19.11.40; IPAC 1b: 000, 9b: 226, KMM 591/1a: 138; on corporal punishment: IPAC 9b: 326–526; on hitting back: IPAC 12a: 693.

regime in Holland. "Non-religious" exchanges practised earlier (of gifts or blows) had to be rooted out. The Church in Uluguru had to become self-sufficient, and Waluguru were to earn the ministry of their priests by their own sacrifices (*sadaka*) – the small donations of money collected during Sunday Mass and at specific holidays. Hilhorst wanted Waluguru to learn that a Church did not live by worldly exchange, but by religious sacrifice. Hilhorst's successor tried to introduce the *sadaka* systematically, but Waluguru were hard to convince of its necessity (after all, *mali ya Roma* was plentiful and they had nothing). To this day, the diocese of Morogoro is crippled without donations from Europe.[57]

"Sacrifice" also served to legitimate the budget cuts which Hilhorst wanted his missionaries to make, and he was convinced that a mission founded with pain would be a mission blessed and that no religious work could flourish without sacrifice. He impressed upon his missionaries that they should be "good" – meaning the denial of selfishness and self-love and a consciousness of one's own insignificance. Such humility may at times have been harder to maintain towards authorities (when "giving oneself away" meant being obedient to Hilhorst) than towards Africans. Given the suspicion which the European's powers could arouse among Africans, the missionaries held that they would only be accepted when they gave themselves freely and were always ready when someone was in need. Such "giving oneself" was, indeed, a prime example of the missionaries' professional sense of service, and it was institutionalized in the sick-call, the occasion when a priest would go, even in the middle of the night, to attend to the welfare of someone in danger of death. He sometimes brought medical help, but was called in to do his religious duties: confession and extreme unction for a Christian, confession and baptism if someone wanted to be converted before dying. These calls came from all directions and often led to forced marches of eight to ten hours. The missionaries were bound by canon law to answer these calls.[58]

---

[57] KMM 710/1b: 216, IPAC 10b: 135; BHG 30 (1934): 104, 31 (1935): 13; KD 4.9.44; school fees posed a similar problem (see chapter five).

[58] On "goodness", IPAC 8b: 180, BHG 31/4 (1927): 49–51; on giving and acceptance, KMM 111/1a: 045, 447/2a: 254, IPAC 3b: 341–409, 5b: 555; from

MAINTAINING THE MISSION: BUILDING, ECONOMY AND TRAVEL

If both Hilhorst and his missionaries tried to keep their work sacred by disallowing "non-religious" exchanges and importing their idea of sacrifice, the material maintenance of the mission made for a blurring of the boundaries between sacred and secular. There was an institutionalized distinction between spiritual and secular work, for building, farming and housekeeping ought ideally to be left to the Brothers and Sisters, who, lacking the ritual prerogatives of a priest, did not contribute much to the former. But there were never enough Brothers available (cf. Huber 1988: 71), and, as we have seen, the Fathers had to negotiate about land, and sometimes build the Church and house themselves (with the help of the Christians); they had to raise money for daily subsistence, building material, and catechists' and workers' wages, to supervise their employees, and this all led to a blurring of occupational boundaries (Huber 1988: 48) that made a consistent distinction between sacred and secular a practical impossibility (but see Beidelman 1982). Moreover, God himself was implicated in the worldly maintenance of the mission: any material benefit a mission received could be taken as a sign of Grace, while all kinds of work could, by interpreting them as sacrifice, be sacralized. At the same time, the contacts with Waluguru necessary for the maintenance of the mission "africanized" the mission from the bottom up.

Poor missions were subsidized by headquarters, but that was only possible when the bigger missions produced a surplus. Hilhorst therefore urged every missionary to make his mission self-sufficient. The bigger missions had started their own enterprises: a carpentry workshop in Matombo and Mhonda, cotton growing in Mandera, vegetables in Mgeta. Father Bukkems, the "farmer of Tegetero", maintained his mission by raising poultry and cattle, and many missions engaged in small-scale coffee- and maize-trade.

1942, it was no longer obligatory to answer sick-calls more than a two-hour walk away (KMM 43/1a: 166), but the practice continued. The task became less arduous the more missions were founded.

Sometimes, the missionaries accepted a government assignment to build a bridge or resthouse, for which they would be paid. Farming activities which generated a surplus were organized by a Brother, but its distribution was often the Fathers' job: Father Bukkems in Tegetero, and his colleagues in Mgeta, had to find markets for their eggs, cattle and (European) vegetables and organize its transport.[59]

Generally, however, the Brothers organized African employees' activities, and they were often closer to some of their Luguru co-workers than Fathers to their catechists. A Brother who supervised the work in the carpentry shop, for instance, would be there the whole day, and as I noted above, share much time and talk with Africans. When their linguistic competence sufficed, they had access to gossip and rumours in a way that the Father's more elevated status prohibited. This proximity, which at times resulted in tenuous friendships, gave the Brother the opportunity to engage in informal spiritual work. One of them related how he would preach at work about how to live a good life when a subject raised by his workers gave him the opportunity. At times, he would join his workers in the pit where they treaded cement or mud for bricks, not because it was necessary, but because he could show them in this way that disdain of manual work did not befit a true Christian.[60] In this way, close working contacts produced an interpenetration of spiritual and secular work that some of the missionaries' formal distinctions kept apart.

At the same time, the Brother's work incorporated African routines into the mission's functioning. One of the Brothers, for instance, relied largely on a core group of Vidunda workers[61] who followed him to every new job, and organized his relations with local workers at a new building site. This system of recruitment usually allowed him to finish his job on time, for he never lacked personnel. When in need of more workers, the Brother asked his

---

[59] KMM 710/1b: 155, 77.710: 16, IPAC 2a: 392, BHG 28/7 (1932): 161, 29/1 (1933): 16.
[60] His *confrères* would jokingly say he was merely "earning a dime", referring to his workers' wages, IPAC 9b: 200, 300.
[61] Uvidunda is a mountainous area south-west of Uluguru.

Wavidunda whether they knew someone who could help, and they would recruit through their own family relationships. Conversely, the workers would use their relationship with "our Brother" (*mfolea wetu*) to help their relatives to a job. The method of recruiting through relatives was probably used by most Brothers. Another Brother took care, in the case of a fatal accident during work, to compensate the family for the loss of a life in a typically Luguru way.[62] In chapter seven we will see how a Brother practised Luguru magical routines to support his work.

Because the Brothers lacked the spiritual authority of the Fathers, they relied on other ways of establishing authority. This could both reinforce and blur cultural boundaries. One Brother told me he would never show Africans that he was ignorant of certain aspects of the work process. He tried to learn them in secret or from other Brothers in order not to damage the image of the superior white man. Another related how his arrival at Matombo mission triggered a drawn-out contest between him and several of the Luguru Catholic leaders, until he had proven himself, in terms of Luguru conceptions of authority, to be a big man (*mkubwa*) and not just a *kijana* (young man). Similar though less intense struggles seem to have taken place every time that a Brother at a mission was replaced by another one.

The mission would also be integrated in local systems of exchange. A mission with a pig-sty exchanged maize-bran (used as fodder) for salt. The payment of rent (*ngoto*) for the use of a piece of mission-land was simply adopted from the relationship between a Luguru landholder and the occupants of his land who were not members of his lineage. Other forms of exchange reinforced the way in which Waluguru were drawn into a money-economy. Some missions, for instance, would maintain a shop which enabled the

---

[62] The Brother with the Vidunda workers also blurred distinctions by not distinguishing between Muslims and Christians: as long as they were good men, he worked with them (IPAC 9b: 300). The accident mentioned was not due to negligence by the missionaries, according to the British court that judged it, but the Brother concerned preferred to use a Luguru concept of guilt (IPAC 13b: 324).

Christians to buy cloth, oil and other necessities (to prevent them from going to the Muslim Indian trader).[63]

The most important form of exchange was, however, that of African labour for money. When local Christians were no longer willing to provide labour "for free", that is, in exchange for the spiritual power the missionary would bring into their midst, the missionary had to pay. The carpentry shops, cotton fields and vegetable gardens all needed African labour ("for a dime", as noted above) to deliver their products. In remoter areas, this was the only way for Waluguru to earn tax money without going to the plantations near Morogoro and Kisaki. This again combined the material with the spiritual: by providing employment, the missionaries prevented Waluguru from moving to the plantations and being exposed to the nefarious influences of civilization, while the spiritual benefits they usually expected from "work" were not lost. If employment was the carrot, the Fathers also tried the stick of refusing sacraments to prevent Christians from going to the plantations, but here, Hilhorst intervened: such a blurring of spiritual and secular went too far.[64] However, this intertwining of relations between spiritual leader and followers and employer and wage-earners gave missionary wage-labour its specific identity (see p. 275).

This blurring of boundaries between spiritual and material at the grassroots was implicitly acknowledged by the attempts at headquarters to keep spiritual values uppermost. A decree from the Vatican in 1951, stating that "any kind of pursuit of profit and money, even if for the mission or Congregation, is unbefitting the religious and should be avoided", forced Hilhorst to consider the legitimacy of, among other things, the carpentry workshops of Matombo and Mhonda. The decree was circumvented by the argument that the workshops produced for the missions and were at the same time a vocational school. As long as the sale to strangers remained an "exception", the sizeable income turned over to the Vicariate could be ignored. When the discovery of gold near

---

[63] On struggle for authority, IPAC 3b: 000, 10a: 073; other exchanges, KMM 514/1a: 035.
[64] KD 10.12.39, 16.4.40, SD 8.9.36, 15.7.41, 4.4.54, KMM 710/1b: 000, 77.710: 16, MP, Decreta et Documenta: Theological Conference, 19.8.49.

Matombo in 1934 created a similar problem, the argument was that, if the Brother of the mission did not occupy all possible claims in the mission's own area, large numbers of European goldiggers would come to pollute the spiritual life of Luguru Christians. The enterprise proved profitable, and near the end of the year 120 workers were employed on the mission's claims. In 1935, Hilhorst prohibited prospecting outside the mission area, but when the war prevented European donations to reach the mission, it was started again in 1940. The Alsatian Brother Simon developed gold-fever, but had to stop the work after some small successes and a long series of disappointments in October 1942.[65]

A last instance of material work necessary for maintaining the spiritual mission was the *safari*. The missionary felt he could not exert his influence without his personal presence; therefore, he had to travel, and mostly on foot. Because many of the outschools were far away from the mission, the missionary spent long days walking through the mountains from school to school, accompanied only by a few carriers and a cook (*mpishi boy*). At times they would bring along a tent, but more often the Father would sleep in the school or in one of the houses of the Christians. What he did in these centres of proselytization is outlined in the next section; here, it must be pointed out that on *safari*, the Father was often closer to Africans than at the mission itself (see plate 11). This proximity is well evoked by Father Guffens when, in order to record for posterity some of the beauties and hardships of the work, he described a *safari* of more than two weeks in the Tununguo diary. One entry in particular brings out this proximity to Waluguru, and the enjoyment of the Father: after having distributed cigarettes to enable his carriers to *kukumbuka* (recall the experiences of the day), he writes:

> *Bado kuvuta, kucheza* (still some smoking and dancing/pp) and finally they push their callous footsoles together at the fire and fall asleep. Now and again one of them mutters in his sleep;

---

[65] On prohibition of commerce, MP, Decreta et Documenta: Hilhorst to Superiors, 6.3.51; the Matombo workshop provided the Vicariate with 10,000 shillings in 1942, and 15,000 in 1943 and 1944, MD 8.8.44; on gold, MD 7/8.2.34, 29.5.34, 7.11.34, 24.7.40, 14.9.41, 2.8.42; MP, Livre des Visites: 9.10.42; FN: Th. Winkelmolen, Morogoro, 28.11.89.

PLATE 11   *Father Flapper and his* mpishi-boy *on* safari *(ca. 1950). The Father reads his breviary, the boy does school work. Photo courtesy of Father Flapper*

> another stirs up the fire. I, too, always sleep in the free air, *kiwanjani* (in the field/pp) or under the *baraza* of a house. Fresh air, fresh sleep.

Fathers enjoyed listening to camp-fire stories, and although they all found these foot-journeys the toughest part of their job, many comments show that it was not the worst. One of the Brothers thought the Fathers' proximity to Africans during *safari*, shared in a context different from the usual spiritual work, was similar to his experiences of companionship at the building-site.[66]

MAINTAINING CHRISTIANS: THE SACRAMENTS

If the reproduction of the mission blurred the boundaries between spiritual and material, administering sacraments was the

---

[66] Guffens in TuD 20.7.42; plate 11 shows this proximity of father and *mpishi boy*, although the chair accentuates their differences; TuD 5.8.42; BHG 32/4 (1936): 58, 30/9 (1934): 136–8; IPAC 9b: 576, 10b: 135; KMM 43/1a: 166.

most important way in which they could be reinforced. But even the sacraments contained institutionalized ways to cope with transgressions, a Catholic "to forgive and forget" that distinguished the Church from the rigid boundaries set up by the neighbouring Protestant missions in Ukaguru (Beidelman 1982: 88). The sacraments (baptism, confirmation, communion, confession, extreme unction, ordination and marriage) were always both markers of the Church's boundaries and ways to cross them. Baptism was taken as conversion, while the administration and refusal of communion and marriage in particular marked proper conduct and was used to force those whose were baptized to do things which – the missionaries thought – Christians ought to do. Sometimes the missionaries tried to get Christians to build a church for free by refusing to come, read Mass and administer the sacraments; they tried to prevent visits to travelling medicine-men, concubinage, or attending ancestral sacrifices or traditional initiation by refusing communion (see chapters three, four and six).

The Fathers did not have the right to excommunicate someone (a privilege of the Bishop), but Hilhorst allowed his priests to refuse absolution after confession to prevent blasphemy (that is, not confessing every sin), and without absolution, one could not obtain the other sacraments. To the chagrin of some of his missionaries, Hilhorst disallowed the non-religious application of this kind of refusal of sacraments to, for instance, children who played truant from the mission school or to their parents. It was particularly often applied in the field of Christian marriage, for the building of Christian families was so fundamental to mission work that Church law (enforced by refusing sacraments) was observed most strictly in that sphere (see chapter four).[67]

As some missionaries explained it to me, Church law, inspired by the Ten Commandments, was based on "natural law", which should be distinguished from the disciplinary laws of the

---

[67] MP, Decreta et Documenta: Hilhorst to Superiors, 16.6.48, Theological Conference, 9.9.48; Casus Matrimonii: passim; KMM 710/1a: 260; IPAC 11b: 100; FN: Mzee Petri Mloka, Kiswira, 5.2.90, Th. Winkelmolen, Morogoro, 12.8.90.

church itself. These disciplinary laws (like the injunction not to eat meat on Friday) were often thought to be incompatible with the circumstances in Uluguru and ignored (although some took them seriously enough to ask the Bishop whether ants and grubs should also be included in the category "meat"). The canons based on "natural" law, however, were generally observed (but see below). Some Fathers later complained that they had been forced to preach an ethnocentric Church law rather than the universality of the Gospel. At the time, "accomodation" (if any) was only applied to ritual and religious art.[68]

But the Fathers could exert a measure of professional independence in the administration of sacraments and the interpretation of Church law. Baptism, for instance, could as a rule only be administered after the candidate had shown sufficient knowledge of the Faith *and* could be expected to continue to lead a Christian life afterwards.[69] One Father took the latter injunction seriously: he seldom baptized people who knew their catechism but could not be expected to lead a Christian life after the rite. His colleagues disapproved, but the Bishop left the decision to the Fathers' discretion. The successor to this scrupulous Father was more lenient: he immediately baptized all who had been refused the sacrament before, and even allowed marriages between full (cross-) cousins – the preferential marriage for most Waluguru – despite the fact that it was legally classified as incest (see also chapter five).[70] Similar leniency was possible with disciplinary laws, and the possibility, and necessity, of interpreting legal rules before applying them must also have allowed for many a silent transgression.[71]

---

[68] IPAC 7a: 013, 619, 15a: 446; MP, Th. Winkelmolen, Morogoro, 12.8.90; KMM 710/1a: 166, 2a: 097, 43/1b: 235; AC 53 (1957): 23.

[69] Of course, this did not apply to baptism *in periculo mortis* (in danger of death) or of babies; the stricture was particularly relevant to missions where many adults and grown-up children had to be baptized.

[70] Again, there are codified possibilities for dispensation, but in the case of first cousin marriage, these had to be given by the Vatican (as was done in many royal marriages in European history).

[71] IPAC 11a: 546-655, 17b: 350; KMM 708/1a: 408, 447/2a: 362. On interpretation of marriage law, IPAC 14b: 656.

Ritual accomodation to Luguru routines allowed for still more creativity. The Alsatian Fathers of Matombo persuaded Christian Waluguru to give up the worship of their ancestral spirits (which violated the First Commandment) and to replace the sacrifice for the spirit of the deceased (*tambiko*) on the last of the forty days of mourning, by the planting of a cross on the grave and the preparation of a "beer of the cross" (*pombe ya msalaba*). In Matombo, a general *pombe ya msalaba* was held on the second of November, All Souls' Day, but because it was less prevalent in other mountain parishes, this seems to have been a local initiative of the Matombo Fathers.[72] The Luguru custom of wearing a bracelet (*bangili*) to distinguish someone with an ancestral name (*jina*; received during a healing ceremony or upon accession to *mlunga* rank) was also seen as a violation of the First Commandment (see Bombwe 1983 and chapter six). Because it also supported traditional authority, with which the mission had no quarrel, one Father tried to replace it by a Christian medal, thus preserving the distinction of a *wenye mlunga* while dropping the rite of *kutawala jina* ("to rule the name"). The "name" illustrates the diversity of the missionaries' improvisations: while, as we have seen, Father Bukkems adopted a *jina* himself, the Father mentioned above tried to find some kind of replacement; yet others simply removed the *bangili* from a Christian's wrist, whether they depended on the local authority marked by it or not. Lastly, there was a Father who only found out what the *bangili* meant after forty years in Africa.[73]

One sacrament epitomized the combination of transgression of Church law, accomodation to Luguru routines and the marking of the Church's boundaries: confession. Confession and absolution allowed for the simultaneous accomodation to and condemnation

---

[72] IPAC 5b: 265; MD 2.11.53, 2.11.54; FN, 253; in some other missions, All Saint's Day (Nov. 1st) often accomodated the veneration of Luguru ancestors.
[73] On *pombe ya msalaba*, IPAC 5b: 265; MD 2.11.53, 2.11.54; FN, 253; in some other missions, All Saint's Day accomodated the veneration of Luguru ancestors; on *jina*, see introduction and KMM 43/1b: 193; IPAC 12a: 404, 445, 6b: 372. The variability of attitudes towards customs to which the missionaries were opposed also comes out in chapters three, four and six.

of a visit to a diviner, a forbidden dance, or an ancestral ceremony. It was much sought after by Waluguru and tallied with their routines during divination, where transgressions of norms could be confessed in the idiom of spirits and magic (chapter six and Parkin 1985: 241). At major Catholic feasts, the Fathers faced seemingly interminable lines of people who wanted to be absolved of their sins. The Fathers themselves saw confession as a cleaning job (*grote schoonmaak*, NL. "spring-cleaning", or *kupiga deki*, Sw. "dusting off*") by which many sins and violations of Church law could be washed off. There were few transgressions that could not, after the appropriate penance, be forgiven. Absolution was refused only to a "public sinner", someone whose *vie mauvaise* was common knowledge and whose punishment was necessary for "external discipline". The *cheti ya paska* (chit obtained when absolved at the Easter confession) became the mark of the true, practising Christian adhering to this discipline (see chapter three).[74]

However, Christian confession differed profoundly from Luguru divination in the way in which power relationships were enacted, and particularly in realizing public discipline through a private, individual ritual. In one case, a Father allowed an important headman to take a second wife (after his partner in Catholic marriage had left him) if they would not live or come together publicly, thus keeping the sin a "private" one that could be confessed and absolved time and again. Instead of the confession during Luguru divination, directly addressed to the audience present, this afflicted individual was only responsible to his confessor, and his individualization could be used to privately and secretly safeguard public conformity. The Christian confession was "at the heart of the procedures of individualization by power" (Foucault 1980: 59) and achieved this individualization by a microphysics of isolating confessor and penitent in a "private" consultation. This disciplinary procedure was not accepted by Waluguru without negotiation or struggle: the Fathers were unnerved when the children of a penitent

---

[74] BHG 32 (1936): 6; KD 13.9.54, 15.3.56; MP, Decreta et Documenta: Hilhorst to Superiors, 16.6.48, Theological Conference, 9.9.48, 19.8.49.

who only understood Kiluguru shouted the Swahili translation of her words through the window. Moreover, confession became an "arduous" job when people came but kept silent about their sins or their failure to fulfil Christian duties.[75] In fact, a whole apparatus of informers was necessary to guarantee that a Father would not be cheated during the confessional.

That brings us to the last subject of this section: the extent to which Waluguru were themselves involved in the spiritual maintenance of the church. The catechists' energy and authority were, as we have seen, indispensable to the missionaries as source of information and enforcement of church discipline (see also chapter five). Although he had a veto in all matters, the Father relied on Waluguru for many disciplinary decisions. Christians who had gone astray were usually judged by a form of lay action which the Fathers had adopted from African routines: the mission *baraza* or council meeting, which often incorporated Luguru-style public confession. This *baraza* often arrived at a decision through the discussions of Waluguru, while the Father merely approved the result, and the British administration (whose own council meetings were far more authoritarian – see Pels 1996) tolerated them as a kind of adjunct to the native courts, in cases where tradition (*mila*) did not completely apply because some of the litigants were Christian. This usually concerned marriage problems between Catholics, decided upon by a discussion between the local headmen, teachers and catechists. Similarly, lay action committees like the *Legio Mariae* served to implicate "good Christians" in the work of maintaining the Church, and although some Fathers suspected that enthusiasm for them was dampened by the fact that lay action functioned as a "squealing-system", especially the supervisors (*wasimamizi*) of the remoter parishes were praised by the missionaries for their work in keeping the faithful faithful.[76]

The peak of indigenous involvement in maintaining the Church was, of course, when a Mluguru became a member of the

---

[75] SD 29.3.53; KMM 43/2a: 025, IPAC 1b: 044, 7a: 139.
[76] KMM 111/2a: 080, 710/1b: 039; IPAC 12b: 306, 17a: 583; MD Oct.'40.

clergy himself. Although the education of African priests had already begun under Bishop Wilson[77], it was Hilhorst who was most determined to realize this aspect of the "planting of the Church". A seminary was started in Ilonga and moved to Bagamoyo to be put under the stern direction of Father Witte (see De Jong 1974), who was succeeded by the Swahili scholar, Loogman. During the war, the first candidates for the priesthood did their probation year in one of the parishes and in 1942, the first African priest said Mass in Mgeta. The ceremony drew large numbers of Waluguru, who sometimes travelled all the way from Matombo to Mgeta on foot. Shortly afterwards, the first Mluguru priest was ordained and especially after the war the seminary produced a steady flow of African priests.[78]

Hilhorst also tried to start an African Sisters' convent and an indigenous congregation of Brothers. While the former was – despite the mistrust of many parents (see chapter four) – a resounding success, the latter failed miserably. The diary of Tununguo, the mission where the "Servants of the Lord" (*Watumishi wa Rabbi*) were settled in 1943, shows how the number of African Brothers fluctuated. The initial group of thirty candidates and professed Brothers did not grow: only twenty-two were left in 1947. Even the seniors among them went away: they had "no vocation", felt they would be "happier in marriage" or were sent away because of "bad conduct". Although the number again increased slightly in the next two years, in 1949 the Father Superior complained that it would probably take years "before a negro can be found with a true religious state of mind". Shortly afterwards, an African Brother at the point of making his perpetual vows was sent away because he complained about monastic life and his vow of poverty, and the absence of trousers (instead of shorts), shoes and good food in particular. The *Watumishi wa Rabbi* were disbanded not long afterwards.[79]

---

[77] With difficulties: the missionaries went to Matombo with Wasagara and Wagogo seminarians to show that the latter had not been killed at the seminary and to convince Waluguru that there was no danger in sending their own boys (MD 4.10.26).

[78] SD 2.12.39, 11.9.43, 12.1.44, 9.8.44.

[79] TuD 10.2.43, 23.12.46, 8.4.47, dec. 47, 15.7.48, 8.3.49, 9.8.49, 28.8.49; KMM 710/2a: 018.

Such problems were not limited to the indigenous Brothers. Despite the fact that for many Dutch missionaries, the choice of their career was a significant social advancement, they tended to think of it in terms of surrender, "sacrifice" and of being humble "servants" of the Lord. But for Waluguru, the Catholic priest was, first of all, a new and attractive power in their midst. Through the African priests, they would be able to partake of that power themselves. In other words, the African priests came from a society which looked upon the priest as a big man (*mkubwa*), not as an inferior (*mdogo*) or servant (*mtumishi*). The examples for the African priests were the rulers of the mission compounds, not – as for the missionaries – the martyrs of the faith. This did not lead to much friction under Hilhorst, who was so proud of his African priests that a Dutch missionary once complained that he should "paint himself black" to escape the Bishop's wrath. Hilhorst was careful not to discriminate and even appointed African priests as the first Superiors of the new missions of Mtombozi and Tawa. Although Matombo Christians suspected that their African priests were not always treated justly, and some cultural frictions occurred, mutual relationships at Matombo mission seem to have been respectful, even cordial.[80] After Bishop Van Elswijk succeeded Hilhorst in 1954, however, doubts about African priests' abilities grew and segregation became stronger (because, one Father said, Van Elswijk tended to obey the wishes of his Dutch personnel). Missions started under an African Superior once more reverted to

---

[80] On *mkubwa* and *mdogo*, FN: A. Nyawale, Morogoro, 1.2.90, Th. Winkelmolen, Morogoro, 5.2.90. A Matombo rumour says a Dutch Father insulted his African colleague and was severely punished by Hilhorst, but the two went, in good friendship, to Rome shortly after the incident which triggered the rumour. If the rumour was untrue, it shows that Matombo Christians were conscious of the possibility of discrimination (IPAC 13a: 319–510; MD 12.4.50; FN i, 30, 173). On good relations between missionaries and African priests, MD 13.3.44, June '45, 3.10.46, 8.1.47, 2.8.49, 10.8.49, KD 8.6.54, 3.10.59, SD 7.3.56, MtD 16.2.59; FN 173; on their conflicts, KD 29.10.55; IPAC 5b: 030–156, 6b: 440, 13a: 319–510, 17b: 123–241; KMM 111/1a: 318, 708/1a: 408, 710/1b: 315; FN: Th. Winkelmolen, Morogoro, 6.11.89, 2.2.90.

Dutch rule, and the 1960s found most missions still in Dutch hands. Under the influence of Tanganyikan independence, and after the first African Bishop was appointed in 1967, tension mounted until it broke out in a nasty conflict which reversed the situation and led many missionaries to resign and return to Holland. But that is part of another story and will not be dealt with further.

CONCLUSION

In the introduction, I have argued that an epistemology of colonial contact should include an awareness of the extent to which participants have to *move towards each other* in order to get in touch. This chapter was meant to bring out this dimension of the mission as movement, particularly in the way in which it simultaneously defined and transgressed, practically realized and moved across, its boundaries. In order to produce the enormous amount of resources and manpower needed to move to Africa, the missionary movement in Holland employed conceptions of sacrifice and exoticism, the push of duty and the pull of desire. It disciplined the acquired recruits in an institution that, while still at "home", was already set apart to orient its subjects to the missions. When these dispositions were subsequently moved to Africa, they were transformed by this move. The ambiguities of "sacrifice" within Dutch Catholic folklore were exacerbated by the attempt to make ordinary Waluguru or African Brothers and priests adopt similar attitudes. Many of the exotic reifications of "otherness" lost relevance in the mission area, to be replaced by the practical knowledge needed for ministry, the occasional racism of despair, or the unquestioned acceptance of Luguru routines as "normal" parts of the mission. Discipline was also modified by moving to the missions, mapping the tension between monastic and professional dispositions on to the struggle between the mission headquarters' centralizing discipline and the autonomy of stations in the "bush", and reducing the hierarchy between priests and Brothers. Most important was, however, that in order to survive in Uluguru, the mission had to "Africanize" long before this became a dominant refrain of Catholic missiology, and we have seen that the Catholic Church had a surprising number of institutionalized ways of responding to that situation. However, the African element of the Christianity that the mission produced has not been dealt with in this chapter, except in passing. The success of the Holy Ghost Fathers' mission can, I feel, only be explained because Waluguru also had an institution that, like the mission, created and crossed the boundaries of their society. It will be the subject of the following chapter.

CHAPTER THREE

Kizungu Rhythms: Luguru Christianity as *Ngoma*

In the 1930s, shortly before the arrival of Bishop Hilhorst, Christianity swept the whole non-Muslim area of Uluguru, with hundreds of people being baptized every year. One missionary reported home that conversion for political protection, gifts, medals, or employment, was largely a thing of the past; conversion out of conviction was now the rule. Some Fathers pondered, in awe, the mysterious workings of Grace. It was, one of them recalls, as if Waluguru were prepared for it.[1] In this chapter, I will explore the extent to which Waluguru were, indeed, prepared for Christianity by an institutionalization of changes in the rhythm of life – by what they themselves call *ngoma*.

Ngoma, in Swahili, is "dance", "drum" or "rhythm", and among Waluguru, it also denotes some of their rites of passage. Contrary to John Janzen, I do not take *ngoma* to be a musical "symbol" which "defines" healing institutions (1991: 291). Although there are many uses of *ngoma* among Waluguru that indicate its healing potential, the term is not a mere analogy or metaphor for something else: *ngoma*, in all its senses, means the embodied – danced, drummed, or otherwise performed – change in the rhythm of life that metonymically connects different states of being within Luguru society and beyond it.[2] The initiation is therefore not just

---

[1] KMM 710/1a: 166; BHG 28 (1932): 132, 269; IPAC 2a: 478.

[2] Although Janzen acknowledges the relevance of *ngoma* to African constructions of political communities and rites of passage, his overview unduly emphasizes more or less marginal "cults" or "drums of affliction" that "resist co-optation by the nation-state" (1992: 177). His emphasis on "discourses of healing" does not take account of the way in which the drum could *embody* state power in, for instance, the interlacustrine kingdoms of East Africa, or the way in which Luguru rhythms embodied the transition to different states of being within and beyond Luguru society.

an institution that reinforces the legitimacy of Luguru systems of authority (cf. La Fontaine 1985: 17), but also a moving pattern that can include alternatives and counterpoints to these systems of authority in its movement, and by including them, can change itself.

I was brought to this interpretation of *ngoma* by two hunches. The first occurred when Mama Adriani, widow of Mzee Mloka, my late adopted father, finished her mourning period. The elder who guided the proceedings had removed the signs of mourning and buried them in the bush, together with small shavings of Mama's hair, and Mama had changed from the white mourning cloth into her normal, brightly-coloured *kanga*. When she was ceremonially returned by her husband's lineage to representatives of her father's lineage, the leading elder said: *Ngoma imekwisha sasa* ("the *ngoma* has finished now"). This made me realize that here, *ngoma* did not refer to a drum, nor a dance, nor a specific rhythm, but was more correctly translated as "rite of passage", in this case, Mama's transition from married woman to widow. Moreover, it dawned on me that only the ceremonies associated with a change in someone's rhythm of *life* (initiation, marriage, becoming a mother, being widowed) were called *ngoma*. Those that dealt with coming into life, dying, and with the ancestors were not. Waluguru associated, like Rodney Needham (1967), percussion with transition, but only transitions from one phase of life to another were associated with an ongoing *rhythm*.

If the first hunch led me to recognize the importance of *ngoma* for Luguru consciousness, the second led to an interpretation that went beyond it. It entailed the realization that it was possible to draw up certain clusters of events in Luguru history, by which one could associate a specific political crisis in Uluguru with the cleansing work of a travelling medicine-hunter (*mganga*; see chapter six), and with the establishment of a new form of male initiation into the political constellation that had emerged after the crisis. The first cluster to emerge was the crisis of Luguru relationships with the German authorities, that led to their – limited – participation in the Maji-Maji rebellion under the guidance of a medicine hunter in the early years of this century (see Iliffe 1967). This crisis seemed to be partly resolved by the introduction of a circumcision *ngoma* called *jando*, which I interpret here as a Luguru adaptation to German, and later British, wage labour relationships. The second cluster was formed by the introduction of Indirect Rule in Uluguru in 1925, followed by the work of the medicine hunter Ngoja bin Kimeta in 1926, and the mass conversions of Waluguru to Christianity around 1929. This cluster was the source of the idea that Waluguru related to Christianity as if it was a *ngoma*. The third cluster, which I shall not discuss in detail here, was the sequence of a violent intrusion of late colonial agricultural campaigns in the 1950s, followed by the cleansing work of a medicine hunter called Nguvumali and the mushrooming of membership of the Tanganyika African National Union in Uluguru from 1955 onwards (see chapter six).

An important feature of successive *ngoma* is that a new one never completely displaced previous ones. Pre-German *ngoma* endured even when *jando* was securely established, and *jando* was not wiped out by Christianity, despite strenuous efforts by the missionaries. This piling up of different institutionalizations of changes in the rhythm of life characterized both male and female Luguru initiation, but the dynamic of the boys' *ngoma* was more attuned to changes in colonial society, and I shall concentrate on that dynamic in this chapter. The boys were directly involved in the opportunities for work and accumulation that colonial wage labour and cash cropping offered, and it was through them that elders in Luguru society experienced the need to adapt their *ngoma* to these novel rhythms of work, or found that Christianity was a viable alternative to these adaptations.

The importance of treating Christianity, for Waluguru, as a *kizungu* rhythm (or a "white" *ngoma*), lies in the way in which it shows how the adoption of a European institution was mediated by an African one. John Chernoff has argued that many African communities are "not held together by ideas, by cognitive symbols or by emotional conformity" but by a musical performance that establishes community "through the interaction of individual rhythms and the people who embody them" (1991: 1095). The relevance of this participatory potential of the rhythmic medium to the way Africans related to colonialism is brought out by A. M. Jones' analysis of a rhythm called *mganda*. Each drum, taking its cue from a beat of the preceding one, beats its own sequence and time (to which the rhythm of the song adds another). Thus, while "[a] band-master can beat time to a military band and keep all the instruments in time, no bandmaster could beat time for *sefa* (the introductory rhythm of *mganda*/pp) for his beating would only coincide with one out of the three drums" (Jones 1945: 184).[3] Yet, the give-and-take of the drummers' rhythmic interaction achieves a "wonderfully clever imitation" of the military march rhythm (Jones 1945: 184), creating a copy of colonial regimentation through a medium foreign to it. This is why we should take the "rhythm" element of the *ngoma* metaphor seriously, for it attunes us to a mediation of European forms that goes far beyond direct imitation.

I already indicated that rhythm is not merely a useful metaphor for colonial contact, it at the same time metonymically relates social forms coming into contact. Since Karl Bücher, scholars have recognized the importance of rhythm for the regulation of work, that is, for the material embodiment of a political economy (Bücher 1902). Bücher taught Malinowski that, for calling some-thing "economic", one should also attend to the structuration of time by ceremonial acts and magical incantation (see, for instance, Malinowski 1912). Although ethnomusicologists have stressed sim-ilar points (see Chernoff 1979, 1991; Keil 1979, 1987), it has only recently been highlighted again how important rhythmic structura-tion is for the interaction of different political economies in colo-nial Africa (Cooper 1992). In an independent African Church, the

---

[3] The majority of analyses by Europeans reintroduces an imaginary regimen-tation into African rhythm (by the 'biggest drum', by motor behavior, or a mys-terious 'metronome sense'; see Merriam 1959: 76–85). Jones' "crossing of the beats", however, indicates a rhythmic ordering through interlocution or "conver-sation" (Chernoff 1979: 55). The opposition between models of the "conversa-tion" of musical performance and the "regimentation" by a conductor or musical score, appears in anthropological theory when we compare Gregory Bateson's attempt to think of the "pattern that connects" as "a dance of interacting parts" (Bateson 1979: 13–4) with Claude Lévi-Strauss' argument that music's "first articulation" is the "hierarchical structure of the scale" (1975: 16, 22).

dance and the drum can be seen as the "drill of the troops of the theocracy" that defies "the physical regimentation of the workplace" (Comaroff 1985: 248). Such forms of opposition go back upon a history of rhythmic structuration, in which missionaries very often – and in retrospect, not without reason – opposed the alternative bodily discipline provided by *ngoma* and its cognates. But in the Luguru boys' *ngoma*, the vertical axis of discipline – the control of the boys' labour by Luguru elders – not only opposed, but continually interacted with a horizontal one – the young men's attempts to gain power by subjecting themselves to colonial labour regimes. It is within this tension that Christianity could become a "white" (*kizungu*) rhythm.

NGOMA AND THE INITIATION OF LUGURU BOYS

The most exhaustive demonstration of the importance of *ngoma* for colonial contact has been given by Terence Ranger. His *Dance and Society in Eastern Africa* (1975) tells the fascinating story of the *Beni ngoma*, which derived its surface appearance from the European military brass band. From the 1890s until the middle of this century, *Beni* spread in the wake of colonial power in various guises from the East African coast to the mainland of what is now Kenya, Tanzania, Zambia and Malawi. Ranger argues that it was not a mere adoption of the forms of absolute power: such parroting occurred only under conditions of severe discipline, in particular in the freed slave settlements of the missionaries on the East African coast (1975: 9).[4] Instead, *Beni* came to Mombasa and Lamu through Zanzibar and not from the Kenyan Coast where the missionary settlements were (1975: 21). Like the military march forms of Jones' analysis of the *mganda* rhythm – which was, in fact, an offshoot of

---

[4] By this argument, Ranger tried to escape from the accusation by Magubane (1971) that some social scientists (like Mitchell 1956) emphasized African colonial "fashion" to prove that acculturation consisted of parroting of white prestige forms. Below, I show that he was not completely successful.

Beni (Hartwig 1969: 56; Mitchell 1956) – *Beni* was "made use of" in another medium: the competition between the two moieties in which the towns of Lamu and Mombasa were traditionally divided (1975: 15, 18). Similarly, on the Tanganyikan coast and in the towns in the interior it was made to fit the performance of a distinction between elite and commoners prevalent there (1975: 40).

Despite this innovative analysis of *Beni* in coastal societies, however, Ranger still speaks of its appearance elsewhere in terms of "false consciousness" or mere "carnival" (1975: 104–5), or as a direct imitation of prestigious forms "to express the essence of colonialism" (1975: 244). This may be the result of his concentration on a *specific* fashion in the hope that it will exemplify the movement of fashion in general. But just as the study of a Western type of dress or musical genre does not necessarily produce understanding of the movements of commodities in the marketplace of fashion, so the study of the diffusion of *Beni* does not necessarily produce understanding of the movements of *ngoma*. In following the traces of *Beni* in Eastern Africa, Ranger is seduced into writing as if these traces somehow retained a link with the original produced in Mombasa and Lamu.[5] From one of the case studies cited by Ranger, however, it becomes clear that *Beni* is not a sufficient focus for understanding *ngoma*, because colonial relationships (and "cash crops and Christianity" in particular) in Ukerebe produced a "deluge" of different *ngoma* long before *Beni* arrived (Hartwig 1969: 46, 52, 56).

This was the result of the loss of control over *ngoma* by traditional elders, who could not contain the initiatives of modern youths tapping new power resources available in colonial society (1969: 46, 51). Given that one commentator has argued that the "prime function" of the Luguru boys' *ngoma* was to "curb rebellion of youths against elders" (Brain 1980a: 370), it might be useful to think of *ngoma* in the rural areas in terms of patterns of intergenerational power interwoven with patterns of new colonial relationships.

---

[5] Yet he has to conclude that in the rural areas "it [is] difficult to see Beni history in any one district as part of a coherent development of dance and musical forms" (1975: 112).

This would explain why the Luguru boys' initiation changed at every significant intervention of the colonial world: it was their contact with the outside world of the towns and coast, through colonial railworks, armies, schools and plantations, through selling cash crops, and through their involvement in the nationalist party that produced the potential for generational conflict. In the colonial situation, young Luguru men had opportunities to tap new sources of power which elder men and women and the girls lacked.[6]

All *ngoma* incorporate *tambiko*, sacrifice to and reconciliation with the ancestors (see chapter six). Because the ancestors give the elders their power, *tambiko* is always a reconciliation with the elders at the same time. In each *ngoma* there is a moment where the initiand passes from the liminal phase and has to be reconciled with social routines. This reintegration, however, did not just encompass the boundaries between ancestors and elders on the one hand, and the younger generation on the other: the more the younger generation was influenced by relations with an outside world and the career possibilities it offered, the more the *ngoma* had to reconcile outside influences with Luguru patterns of authority. Because the nature of the initiands – the boys – changed under the influence of colonial society, the nature of this reconciliation had to change, too. While lineage relations remained in force, they had to incorporate new types of *persona* (social masks) and adapt their ritual accordingly. Thus, the adoption of signifiers of the European presence in Luguru *ngoma* was not so much a colonization of Luguru imaginations as an attempt to *embody* and survive the effects of this presence.[7] Although the history of Luguru *ngoma* shows that this

---

[6] A close tie to the lineage implied a close tie to the land. Lineage elders (members of the group of *wenye mlunga*) were not allowed to travel away from their land for longer than a week. Daughters were thought to be more close to the lineage than sons and thus were more likely to take care of the land when men travelled to work elsewhere (see Van Donge 1993: 65–7).

[7] Thus, it was "an active mode of coping, not just passive imitation" of the European influence (Fabian 1990a: 56). Healing *ngoma*, and spirit possession in particular, can be similarly characterized (cf. Kramer 1987; see also Ranger 1975: 47). The conception of ritual as embodiment of societal possibilities is further elaborated below (chapter four).

process was often a conscious one, the necessity of *tambiko* and of keeping clan authority intact implied that the reconciliation had to pass off as eternal and unchanging. Therefore, we often have to rely on other than oral sources – archival, statistical – to demonstrate the significant moments of this pattern of innovation.

The adaptability of Luguru *ngoma* is displayed by the proliferation of names for ritual practices and their accompanying rhythms which predate the first major colonial intervention. Sometimes these names refer to different moments in the ritual process: thus, *lungu* refers to the bundle of medicine carried by the initiands to the village on the day of coming out, medicines which played an important role throughout the passage. *Kitawa* refers to the shouting of abuse which accompanied this coming out, while *ng'ula* or *kukula* – derived from a Kiluguru root which means "growing" – often refers to the ceremony as a whole (like *lwindi* or *mwangazi*). The use of certain medicines and rhythms suggests that some of the ceremonies were only practised by Waluguru who were in daily contact with the people of the plains. Other ceremonies, like *sae* or *kong'ongo* are said to be typical of the higher mountain range and deemed to be "original" Luguru (and therefore accompanied by *mbeta* or *mkenge*: Luguru rhythms).[8] Whatever the case may be, most commentators stress that *sae* proceedings were later incorporated into the richer ceremonial of the *ng'ula/lwindi/lusona* and *jando* ceremonies. The multitude of names shows that these

---

[8] Before the introduction of *jando* (circumcision), Waluguru say they engaged their sons in *sae*, *kong'ongo*, *lusona*, *lungu*, *kitawa*, *kigoma*, *kikami*, *mwangazi*, *lwindi* or *ng'ula*, and these ceremonies were accompanied by different rhythms beaten on different drums: *mbeta*, *mkenge*, *chatu*, *ndengela*, *mkwaju* or *mganda* (the list is not exhaustive). The use of medicines which cannot be obtained higher up in the mountains (such as *mpingu*, ebony) suggests that the *ng'ula* and *lwindi* ceremonies were more related to the plains; often, *mganda* or *mkwaju* rhythms, said to come from the Wakutu and Wazaramo who live in the Eastern plains, accompanied *ng'ula*. The "dirty" (sexually explicit, magically profuse) nature of the *ng'ula/lwindi/lusona* ceremonies may well have led missionary commentators, defending Luguru "purity", to describe the other ceremonies (*sae* and *kong'ong'o*) as "original tradition" (Mzuanda 1958: 95; MSS. Vermunt, 3.1).

"original" Luguru ceremonies were acts of location that were far more specific than *jando* (circumcision), which retained the same name while it spread throughout the mountain area and other parts of Tanganyika after the turn of the century (see Cory 1947, 1948).

Given the diversity of the ceremonies associated with the words *lwindi*, *ng'ula*, and *lusona*, it is impossible to sketch a uniform picture of Luguru initiations before the coming of *jando*. Moreover, the conception of *ngoma* advanced here makes this an enterprise of doubtful value. Often, the ceremonies are said to have other than Luguru origins: *lusona* is supposed to come from Ukwere (between Dar es Salaam and Morogoro), *lwindi* from Usagara (in the West, beyond Kilosa). *Lwindi*, however, is also called *kikami*, suggesting an origin in the Ukami plains between Uluguru and Ukwere. Because Wakami were taken to be the same tribe as Waluguru by British administrators, this lends support to the claim made by Wazaramo (on the coast near Dar es Salaam) that *ng'ula* (which in many respects is identical to *lwindi*) is originally a Luguru *ngoma*. If *ngoma* is indeed an activity in which communications with the world outside the lineage are incorporated in order to adjust to new influences brought by the younger generation, it comes as no surprise that it is hard to ascribe a *ngoma* to a specific "tribal tradition" (as many anthropologists do): their ties to territory or cultural background cannot but be diverse. It is interesting to speculate upon the way in which Luguru generations have adjusted their initiation activities to the people with whom they communicated after their arrival in the mountains in the beginning of the nineteenth century. Hunting, in cooperation or competition with plains peoples, may have been one of the most important activities which produced interlocal contact, and thus, new forms of *ngoma*.[9] Lack of detailed evidence compels us to leave it at that.

Both *lwindi*, *ng'ula* and *lusona* were ceremonies in which the initiand was taken to the bush to be initiated in lineage histories and

---

[9] Cf. Hartwig 1969: 42–5. Like Hartwig, Caplan shows how a *ngoma* can be identified because it retains the language of the area from which it was introduced: on Mafia Island, this was Kingindo for *jando* and Kizaramo for the girls' initiation (1976: 30).

proper forms of conduct. Someone who had passed through *sae*[10] no longer had to pass through one of the other ceremonies. The initiation usually entailed removing the boy from the women's realm: the boy was said to be dead during *lwindi* and the word referred to a pot symbolizing the vagina. In this way, the *ngoma* provided a new birth into the realm of men. In *ng'ula*, the boy's hairs were plaited like a woman's, symbolizing his subjected status and his femininity, which had to be removed before coming out. The boy, by dying, entered the land of the spirits (*kuzimu*). These acts of entering and leaving the spirit-land were always accompanied by sacrifice to and reconciliation with the ancestors (*tambiko*), symbolized by repeating an act seven times: seven times up and down above the hole where the medicine called *lungu* was put; seven times eating and spitting out of food when reentering the normal world. The period in spirit-land was characterized by acts common to an inverted world: walking through the wilds, walking at night, abusing one's elders, putting excrement all over the house.[11]

The ceremonies were, like their successor *jando*, meant for boys who had reached the age of discretion, and could be taught to distinguish "between good and bad". They taught proper sexual behavior towards one's future wife, and proper deference towards elders, parents and generally everyone superior. The teaching was often harsh and usually proceeded by means of riddles (*mizungu*), sung or chanted, which the pupils were meant to memorize under the threat of being penalized. Only when they learnt the riddles and their meaning by heart were they allowed to leave the camp. Sexual knowledge was taught through symbolic examples, with the use of objects created with sticks of the ebony (*mpingu*) and the *mkole* tree. Several riddles emphasized the boy's proper behaviour towards his mother: henceforth, he had to keep his distance from her. After a stay in the bush or in a camp close to home the initiand (*mwali*)

---

[10] In Kiluguru, called *ingoma ye saye*, or *kumbi lye chikahenga*, "camp of the ancestors" (Mawinza 1963: 19).

[11] FN: Andre Averini, Kiswira, 4.10.89; Mzee Stefani Sabini Matiasi, Gubi, 10.10.89; Mama Mkoba, Kiswira, 17.9.90; Mzee Alois Mkoba, Morogoro, 7.11.90.

would "come out" under great rejoicing. Apart from some "cleaning up" work, in which the powerful remains of the medicine would be disposed of by the initiands and their teachers, the boys had now finished the transition to full members of male society. In Matombo, *ng'ula/lwindi* disappeared in the early 1950s, shortly after a big expert (*fundi*) of the ceremony had died.[12] By that time, however, it had already been overlaid by two successors: *jando* and Christianity.

JANDO: THE FIRST MODERN *NGOMA*

Jando – circumcision – was introduced in the Uluguru mountains at the beginning of this century, and most sources agree that it came from Usagara. According to Mzee Mloka, circumcision was brought to Matombo by a Mluguru who had lived in Bagamoyo and Kilosa for a while, where he became impressed by the cosmetic beauty (*urembo*) of the Arab's circumcized penis. He therefore brought the practice to Uluguru, along with a *ngoma* called *ndenge* (I could not find out whether this was a drum, a rhythm, a ritual, or all three together). Most Catholic priests insisted that Muslims introduced circumcision to Uluguru in order to counter the work of the missionaries. The British administrator E. E. Hutchins disagreed, because *jando* was introduced at an age (ten to fifteen years) at which an ordinary Muslim would already have been circumcized for eight years or so.[13]

---

[12] The *mkole* tree is also crucial to the girls' initiation and is associated with growth and fertility (see chapter four). In Kiluguru, the bush camp was called *kiwalani*; the camp closer to home, *kiponera* or *seto*; it is not clear in which sequence these camps were occupied (FN: Mama Mkoba, Kiswira, 17.9.90, Mzee Alois Mkoba, Morogoro, 7.11.90).

[13] FN: Mzee Petri Mloka, Kiswira, 28.1.90; TNA MF 19, MDB: "The Waluguru", by Father v.d. Kimmenade, MSS. Vermunt 3.1: "Nyando 1" (but see Mzuanda 1958: 133); TNA MF 19, MDB: "Notes on the Waluguru and Wakami", by E. Hutchins. Brain is also sceptical about the "muslim origin" interpretation, but is then seduced – against all other sources – into believing that *jando* was somehow more ancient than *ng'ula* (1980a: 374). Cory says *jando* is the result of "Islamic missionary work" but agrees that it is a "good example of the way in which Bantu institutions sometimes react to foreign influences" (1947: 160).

The history of the introduction of circumcision in Uluguru shows that, on the whole, Hutchins was right, even though Islam played a role in the process. The Matombo Fathers noted in January 1904 that in some areas under their missionizing influence, Islam was on the move. The note is important, in the sense that it shows how the rival creed was already spreading before the introduction of circumcision in the Matombo area. In August 1905, news of unrest reached the mission: stories of a medicine hunter (*mganga*) who urged people not to pay their tax (except to him) and proclaimed the end of the world, show that the Maji Maji revolt had by that time reached Kisaki and Kasanga on the Southeastern slopes of Uluguru. Headmen in the Matombo area came to assure the Fathers that they were still willing to pay their tax and would not revolt. The German-appointed headman (*jumbe*) of the Western (Mgeta) area, however, who was the son of the lineage head, magician and "big man" Mbago, came to Mvuha to bring his tax to the leader of the movement. A first skirmish of insurgents with German troops near Kisaki coincided with the first mention of circumcision in the Matombo diary, at Tawa, September the 4th, 1905.[14] For the missionaries it meant apostasy, not remarkable in the case of the old Christian headman of Tawa (who had already taken several wives anyway), but threatening when it was committed by two Christians in Mbagalala (near Gozo) and even worse, by one of their carpenters, Franz Josef.

The reports about circumcision ceased for a while. Mbago was arrested and died in jail in Morogoro. The Maji Maji warriors were driven south to Mahenge, and Mbago's son was arrested and executed. The *mganga* suffered the same fate, having been arrested and brought to Morogoro by a Christian (who got the post of *jumbe* of Mvuha as a reward). Two years later, many Christians were having themselves circumcized. Many Christian headmen were

---

[14] MD Jan. '04, Aug. 05, 4.9.05. The mention of a *mganga* near Mvuha suggests that this was an assistant of Kinjekitile, the medicine hunter and prophet who triggered the Maji Maji rising. The assistant probably used the shrine of the spirit (*mzimu*) of Kolero, which was related to Kinjekitile's spirit Bokero, to increase the latter's following (Gwassa 1972).

taking several wives and the number of catechumens decreased in their areas, only the higher slopes excepted. Despite his promise, the *Bezirksamtmann* did not replace these *jumbes apostats*. Again, in November 1909, *le diable de circoncision* haunts the missionaries' fields.[15] Given such a chronology, it is tempting to interpret circumcision as a Muslim-inspired symbolic resistance against European power which replaced the actual physical resistance of the Maji Maji war. But interpreted in such a way, *jando* becomes, like some instances of Ranger's *Beni*, a "false consciousness"; a weak response to power. Its only positive aspect is a kind of collective psychotherapy.

That interpretation would only be based on a part of *jando* history in Uluguru. Father Vermunt reported that *jando* was introduced to the Mgeta area in 1915, a full ten years after the arrest of Mbago and coinciding with a large increase in the number of Christians. In Singiza, circumcision only made headway in the 1930s, while in Kasanga, closest to the Maji Maji prophet's influence, circumcision was spreading only in 1942. In both cases it coincided with the increase of Christians after the foundation of both missions in 1931 and 1937, respectively, although in the case of Kasanga, Islam was on the increase, too.[16] Moreover, the early reports in the Matombo diary – although they mention "apostasy" from Christianity – never state that circumcision meant conversion to Islam at the same time. In fact, the *jumbes apostats* who were circumcized in 1907 are still referred to as *jumbes chrétiens* in 1908. Apparently, the relationship between circumcision and religious creed was less direct than some missionaries thought.

Before we can say more about the reasons for the adoption of *jando*, it is necessary to look at the *ngoma* itself as it was reported to have taken place in the 1940s and 1950s. *Jando* incorporated most of the previous Luguru initiations: someone who had passed through the latter still had to pass through the former but

---

[15] MD 25.10.05 (arrest Mbago), 2.11.05 (death Mbago), 10.12.05 (soldiers to Mahenge), 15.1.06 (hanging of *mganga*), 20.4.06 (hanging of Mwanambago), MD Apr.–Jun. 07, Aug. 08, 25.11.09 (new circumcisions).

[16] MSS. Vermunt 3.1, "Nyando 1"; BG 1923–4: 321; FN, Th. Winkelmolen, Morogoro, Dec. '89; KD 29.9.41, 17.8.42.

not the other way around. The circumcision was added to Luguru routines. It was done early in the morning, during the cold months, so that the boys' bodies were not yet completely awake and the blood would not run fast. After the operation, the circumcizer (*ng'ariba*) was treated to a feast in the village, while the boys were kept in a camp in the bush by the *showari* (the one to hold the boy during circumcision) and the *kungwi* (the boy's dresser). In the camp, lessons in sexuality and proper conduct would be held until the wounds had healed and the boys could go *kugongola*: show themselves in the village, covered by black cloth so that no one could recognize them, and ask for food. I have no evidence that this was accompanied by *ng'ula*-like rituals of inversion (abuse, the spreading of excrement), but that absence may have been due to the missionaries' presence in Matombo. Shortly afterwards, there was the feast of *mwogo*, the first bath after circumcision, accompanied by a sumptuous meal of rice and goat. The boys could then go home until the coming out ceremony (*mlao*) had been prepared. Three days before "coming out", the boys returned to the bush camp. There, they received their last lessons. The night before *mlao*, the Ndengela drum was beaten in the village for the *tambiko ya ngoma*[17]:

> [drumbeat] *Kimbamizungu gona* (7x)
> [drumbeat] *Banguzi gona* (7x)
> [drumbeat] *Chete gona* (7x), etcetera

Thus, the names of the Lords of the Dance (*wafalme wa ngoma*), or Head Circumcizers (*mang'ariba wakuu*), the organizers of *jando* in Matombo, were recited and they were urged to "sleep in peace" (*gona*, kil.). The position of head circumcizer was, like a lineage headmanship, something which was passed on from one generation to the other. Kimbamizungu ("The Riddle Singer") was the last of the head circumcizers to have any real authority: when he arrived

---

[17] Thus, this was a *tambiko*, reconciliation with ancestors, not *ngoma* or rhythm (see chapter six): before each incantation, the *Ndengela* was only beaten once (see note 40).

at a coming out ceremony in the 1940s, he could take all the beer, money and food he wanted, and no one would get something without his consent.[18] His successor was uninfluential; *jando*, moreover, was slowly dying out: circumcision is now mostly done in hospital.

The next morning, after a last exam, the boys received a Muslim name when they left the camp (by stepping over the body of one of the camp attendants, Mzuanda 1958: 139). They burned the camp, all their camp clothes, shavings and other attributes except the new clothes they were wearing now: a white *kanzu* (the Muslim dress), white cap (*kofia*) or preferably (if their father could afford it) a red fez. Singing, they would return to the village:

Keakea Keakea	K.A.R. K.A.R. K.A.R. K.A.R.
Kwetu kuna limba	We have a *limba*
la kiwanja pembe	of the horn-field
Kianja alongole eeh eeh	Kianja went ahead eeh eeh

Kianja ("He who started") was the camp-name of the first boy to be circumcized (he is followed by *Fumbi*, then *Fumbi-Gogo*, *Fumbi la mbele*, etcetera until the last, *Kifunga-Limba*, "to close the *limba*", Mzuanda 1958: 134). The "horn-field" was the camp itself: the *pembe* (horn) stood for the penis. The *limba* was the point just beyond the entrance of the camp where someone hads to show, by identifying certain medicines and symbolic objects, that he had been circumcized: it therefore stood for the secret knowledge of the initiated.[19] Most important is, however, the mention of the K.A.R.: the abbreviation of "King's African Rifles", the British

---

[18] FN: Mzee Petri Mloka, Kiswira, 28.1.90. Knowledge of circumcision was not necessarily passed on along lineage lines frequently, the father taught his son, contrary to matrilineal routines.

[19] My field guide said that *limba* was the camp (FN: Thomas Martiniani, Kiswira, 3.10.89); Mzuanda, however, makes clear that it is the *mtego* or trap which people not initiated into the meaning of the medicines and metaphorical (mostly sexual) objects that lie underneath it dare not pass; secrets which Father Mzuanda could only summarize under the names *ushirikina na matusi* (superstition and abuse; 1958: 137).

battalions of African soldiers in the First World War. The son of a wealthy man would, on coming out, wear the red fez of the Briton's soldier. Apparently, the *jando* camp could be likened to conscription in the British army.

This is not the only reference to the British. When the boys returned from the camp singing *keakea* and still covered by cloth, they circled the *ndengela* drum seven times and entered a house. After taking a meal together with their dressers, they reappeared to circle the drum another three times and then laid off their cloth. Then they danced, one after the other, in the order of their circumcision. When they reentered the house after that, the women sang:[20]

Ndole Ndole Mwanangu, aiééé	I see I see my child, aiééé
Mgeretsa katenda	The Englishman did it
	(brought the ngoma/pp)

A curious mix of possibilities: a ngoma with Muslim names and clothing, brought to Matombo at a time when the Southeastern peoples of Tanganyika rose against the Germans, is associated in the 1940s and 1950s with the experience of Africans conscripted in the British Army.

These articulations of an "outside world" become even more muddled when we see that Cory's paper about *jando* (which is at least partly based on the knowledge of Luguru informants: Cory 1947: 159) does not mention European colonial powers, but abounds with references to the Swahili coast. Of course, the facts that the language of *jando* is Swahili (even in Uluguru, where many of the riddles were not sung in Kiluguru but in Swahili) and that the initiated get Muslim names, point to this crucial influence of Swahili culture.[21] Cory's rendering of *jando* is important in the

---

[20] The interpretation that the Englishman brought the *ngoma* was given by an informant (FN, Mzee Petri Mloka, 28.1.90), who also insisted that the initiands sang the song. The text of the song, however, supports Mzuanda's assertion that the women sang it (1958: 139).

[21] See appendix D for some of Cory's material on *jando* and the coast. It was a Mluguru from Bagamoyo, one of the centres of Swahili culture, who brought *jando* to Matombo. In Ukerebe, it was *Beni* which introduced the Swahili language into the local *ngoma* practices (Hartwig 1969: 56), but among Mafia Island Waswahili, *jando* retained its language of origin, Kingindo (Caplan 1976: 30).

sense that it shows that the *didactic* songs he recorded show no reference whatsoever to outside influences (the Swahili coast in particular). They taught proper sexual behaviour, the appropriate distance taken from the women's and especially the mother's world, and respect for superiors (1948: 93) and can therefore be said to mark the intergenerational axis of power within the initiation. In contrast, songs marking the contact with the world outside the camp, all used the metaphor of a journey to the coast. Take this story, which served to explain the meaning of two figurines used as *limba*, that is, as the marker of the initiates' secret knowledge:

> One doll represented a *mshenzi* ("bush nigger") with a load on his head who was supposed to be on a journey to the coast looking for work. The other doll was supposed to be a coastal man on a journey from the coast inland. The coastal man asks the *mshenzi* what he is carrying. The "bush nigger" answers *nyamafu* (that is the name given to the carcase of an animal which has not been killed according to Islamic rites). The doll representing the coastal man is then made to jump up and down and says: "If you go to the coast with this load, you will be expelled; on the coast everybody is a Mohamedan. Throw away your load and take one like mine which is not so heavy." It is a *msala* (a praying mat). Now the "bush nigger" doll dances up and down pulled by the strings (Cory 1947: 165).

The heavy load referred to the "extra luggage" of the *mshenzi*'s prepuce. Once he drops that, he will not be expelled. It is tempting to associate it with sexual contact with women on the coast, who will expel an uncircumcized man (see chapter four and Appendix D).[22] Another of Cory's songs, sung by the women this time, associates *jando* with "going into war" (1948: 85). It is significant that Luguru women also, in a sense, sung about the war when associating their circumcized sons with K.A.R. soldiers.

Cory was even more enchanted by the magic of the name *jando* than Ranger was with *Beni*. He thought that because among

---

[22] The association of sexual prowess with power in general through the concept of *moto* (fire, heat) is, as among Bemba (Richards 1956: 35), common among Waluguru; moreover, *pembe* refers to both penis and powerful magic (see p. 269).

all different tribes there was something called *jando*, there must have been one "correct sequence" in the ceremonies and one "authentic text" for every song (1947: 159; 1948: 83). Luguru *jando*, however, departed in many respects from the sequence recorded by Cory, and in particular by including *mlao*, which is completely absent from Cory's account. Cory's assertion that "[i]t was not possible for me to find the general rule for the rhythm of the songs" (1948: 92) seems to hide the fact that there was no "general rule", for the ways of life of the different ethnic groups in Tanganyika Territory were affected by different sequences of historical experiences mediated by different rhythms. Instead, we can suppose that *jando* spread through Tanganyika because it could be intertwined, on the one hand, with existing intergenerational balances of power, expressed in songs and dances that celebrate respect for elders, and on the other, with a number of different experiences of an "outside" colonial rule that young men had, or were expected, to undergo. Just as Tanganyika Territory *Beni* quickly changed its orientation from German to British power after World War One (Ranger 1975: 56), just so *jando* in Matombo seems to have rapidly incorporated the experience of the British army and its conscription policies.[23] These adaptations of *jando* show that this *ngoma* was both a metaphor for colonial contact, and a way of mediating this contact by initiating young boys into its secrets and adapting them to its rhythms of work – the rhythm of wage labour in particular.

The latter interpretation – of *jando* as a "wage labour" *ngoma* – is reinforced when we return to the events of the first decade of this century. Recall that by 1907, after the defeat of the Maji Maji warriors, circumcision was making headway among Eastern Waluguru. In 1906, Mkuyuni and Kinole people moved to the plains near the new railway (while holding on to their plots at home). The railway stretch from Dar to Morogoro was opened in October 1907 and work continued on the line from Morogoro to the Western part of

---

[23] This is not surprising, given that the victory of the British was particularly visible on the Eastern Uluguru slopes, along which they chased the Germans to Kisaki and beyond, making a number of Waluguru the victim of either conscription or gunfire (MD Sep. '16, 27.12.17).

Deutsch Ost Afrika. In 1909, the Matombo Fathers complain that many young boys leave school for the railway works. Not only are the wages so high that the Fathers cannot compete with them,

> le contact quotidien de nos chrétiens avec les noirs arabisants de la côte a produit des effets désastreux: la circoncision et d'autres usages musulmans se sont introduits; quelques chrétiens sont retournés à la polygamie, d'autres ont apostasié, et enfin le travail d'évangelisation est devenu beaucoup plus difficile.[24]

This reinforces the suggestion that *jando* was not a cultural reaction to the military defeat of the Maji Maji warriors: on the contrary, its early introduction in Matombo may have been related to the fact that Matombo Waluguru did *not* participate in Maji Maji. The coming of *jando* to Matombo coincided with the participation of Waluguru in the German railway works, where they met the example of fairly powerful Africans – most of them from the Swahili coast – working in the employ of the German authorities. This experience was incorporated by the adoption of a new *ngoma*, that adjusted Luguru boys to the prominence of Africans who were their employers in the colonial communities formed in the hinterland. The adaptation went both ways: Iliffe records the fact that Waluguru took a prominent place in the dances held at the Kaiser's birthday (1979: 238), which inaugurated a folklorization of "tribal" identity through *ngoma* that would continue throughout the twentieth century. The conscription of Waluguru into the German and British carrier corps during the War was another form of "initiation" of the younger generation into secrets which the Luguru elders did not know and which provoked them to change their *ngoma*. *Jando*, therefore, adapted Luguru initiation practice to a

---

[24] TNA MF 19 MDB: E. E. Hutchins, "Notes on the Waluguru and Wakami", 1929; MD 3.10.07, 2.08.09. The ambivalence of Luguru attitudes towards railway work ("fear", MD 10.7.09, 19.2.10) or "indifference", MD 28.10.09) may be attributed to the fact that whereas young men profited from it, to elders and women it was a liability (see note 6 and chapter four). I thank Henny Blokland for giving me the quote, from *Annales de la Congrégation du St. Esprit* 25/8 (1909): 228.

world in which young men were liable to go out of the mountains to sell their labour, at railworks and plantations and in the army.[25]

MISSIONARY SOUNDS AND SENSIBILITIES

The missionaries were not at all happy with the coming of *jando*, which they associated with Islamic competition and polygamy. Moreover, the drive towards town (Morogoro in particular) drew young men from their influence, destroyed marriages, and exposed Waluguru to the material attractions of colonial society (BHG 29 [1933]: 5–6). If *jando* partly incorporated that influence and thus gave it a place in Luguru practice, the struggle of missionaries against Luguru rhythms no longer appears as mere ethnocentrism, fed by a desire to arbitrarily impose a Christian aesthetic. Instead, this aesthetic may turn out to be a strategic and reasonable response to a rival pattern of social control. It is therefore worth while to examine the missionaries' own musical preferences.

Many missionaries were irritated by the sound of the drum. Some of them asked people to stop the noise (*kelele*) when they had to sleep anywhere near a dance while travelling. Others were provoked to confiscate drums (especially when they were beaten during Sunday Mass) or even to destroy them. As one French Holy Ghost Father put it, the beat of the drum is attractive to the African because he is a child, and children love noise.

> For centuries impervious to the inquiries of the spirit, the pleasures of knowledge and the attractions of civilized life, [the negro] claims a place for his body and senses in the least material of his enjoyments: clamour in company and organized rhythm are to him almost as enticing as a banquet or drinking-bout.[26]

---

[25] It may not have been *jando* only which effected this adaptation, as the following Luguru *kigoma* song suggests: "Two days nothing happens/the third day nothing happens/I work on my monthly labour card" (Cory 1937: 63; Cory fails to give the original text, but in Swahili the last line would probably read *ninafanya kazi kibaruani*). The monthly labour card was employed by both German and British, both official and private employers.

[26] BHG 29 (1933): 41; SD 2.10.43; FN: Fr. Th. Winkelmolen, Morogoro, 7–12.12.89.

The quote clearly shows the missionary preference for a music of the spirit, at odds with the embodied rhythm of the dance. But despite the revulsion felt by some of the missionaries, drumming played an important part on many Christian occasions: the reception of the Bishop or of a new Father, or a Father's farewell-party; the ordination of an African priest; first communion or marriage, all were framed by the rhythm of the drums. Moreover, the success of Christianity after 1928 seems to have convinced the Dutch Fathers that it was not the music, nor circumcision as such which made *jando* – or any other *ngoma* – objectionable. Although *jando* practice was forbidden, the Fathers themselves organized circumcision, taking care that it was done early, and thus preventing its association with a puberty ritual.[27] In this way, the missionaries tried to pull Luguru initiation practices apart.

Despite this early form of "accomodation" to indigenous routines, the association of rhythm with bodily movement and ecstasy continued to raise missionary suspicions. Although judgments became less severe in the decades after 1930, dancing not associated with Christian ritual remained a sure sign that something was wrong. The Dutch missionaries never went as far as the Alsatian Brother Simon, who fired his (empty) gun at a women's *ngoma* because it was "obscene". Still, dancing was often equated with sexual licence. A Christian who had been seen at a Luguru *ngoma* could be accused before the mission council of a *peccatum publicum* and penalized.[28] Because sexual instruction was central to both male and female initiation, and because the missionaries

---

[27] SD 12.8.35, 9.7.40, 29.8.49, KD 26.10.52, 17.8.43, TD 25.8.54; MP, Decreta et Documenta, Theological Conference Morogoro, 9.9.48; in 1942, *jando* seems to have been less associated with Islam: Father Vermeulen called circumcision an *affaire impure*, not a Muslim practice (KD 17.87.42).

[28] On sexual licence and forbidden ngoma, KMM 111/1b: 054, 514/1a: 035; IPAC 12b: 380, BHG 46 (1950): 134, AC 55 (1959) 17; for a dissenting voice, TNA MF 19, MDB: Fr. v. d. Kimmenade "The Waluguru"; Brother Simon was accused, and acquitted, probably because his gun was loaded with salt (MD 3.11.12). Among the Dutch Fathers, however, there is a story of another Brother in the Belgian Congo who accidentally killed a woman because *his* gun was loaded with ball.

associated sexual education not supervised by themselves with licentiousness, their combative attitude was reasonable, given their preconceptions. Just as a Luguru initiation defined and thereby appropriated sexuality for a specific gender category, just so did the missionaries try to appropriate sexuality, or any other element of *ngoma*, to Christian strategies. They did not aim at the wanton destruction of all *ngoma* practice: instead, they selectively incorporated its "good" aspects, while opposing what they thought was "obscene" (and their wrath fell more on the female than on the male dance; see the next chapter).

Moreover, they took special care to introduce music which fitted the elevated sensibility of the true servants of the Lord. Every parish had to have its choir; the missionaries, and later their catechists and organists, trained the Christians in Gregorian chants. The *Liber Usualis* (the book of Catholic liturgy) and the conductor, the sweet but hierarchical tonal harmonies and the bell tolling the Angelus had to displace and subordinate the drummer and his "conversation" with his co-players. Luguru Christians took this up with enthusiasm, and the descriptions which the missionaries give of Christmas celebrations praise the Africans for remembering and singing harmoniously (if a little loud) ten out of the twelve Masses. The Luguru choir, which "gave what it had", compared favourably with the "rodent squeak" of the average Dutch Catholic.[29] The time when the missionaries started to appreciate the complexity of African rhythms (which, according to a trained musician among them, were so complex as to "defy notation") and incorporate them into liturgical practice was still far off, but Waluguru and their neighbours do not seem to have been less enthusiastic about Gregorian chant. Moreover, although the priest would not participate in a dance, Mluguru and missionary shared songs: on Christmas Eve, for instance, the missionaries would be among the Christians (who had come to the church from far away during daylight) and chat, joke, and, above all, sing until midnight mass.[30]

---

[29] BHG 28 (1932): 11, 29 (1933): 13; KMM 43/1b: 253, 111/2a: 139; compare this to Evans-Pritchard: "Natives always sing the hymns out of tune" (1928: 449).
[30] BHG 27 (1931): 45, 28 (1932): 9, AC 55 (1959): 17; KMM 43/1b: 235, 708/1b: 000; MD 25.12.66.

Thus, the missionaries had other forms of musical participation to offer besides the occasional drumming. In Christian practice, both the drums of joy, the togetherness of singing and the beat of the choirmaster had their place, although the latter took precedence. At the same time, however, the missionaries fought a running battle with the "obscenities" and "superstitions'" of Luguru initiation. Even when they were revolted by the physical ecstasy which they associated with Luguru rhythmic performance, they selectively appropriated it to Christian initiations. Could it be that, in the heat of battle, they overlooked that Waluguru did not share their exclusiveness and desire for Christian "spiritual" purity, and that Waluguru interpreted Christianity as a new *ngoma* to be added to existing ones? To answer that question we must locate – "temporalize" is a better word – Luguru conversions to Christianity in their historical context.

CASH CROPS, CHRISTIANITY AND INDIRECT RULE

The Morogoro District Annual Report of 1920–1 records that only eight out of the fifty-six planters in the District imported labour during that year. After six years and the introduction of Indirect Rule, the situation was changed: complaints about labour abound and the estates (mainly sisal) had to recruit people from as far away as the Eastern Congo and Nyasaland. In 1929, the Fatemi Estate even took the unprecedented step of trying to *attract* instead of *contract* labourers, because many Waluguru did not respect the terms on which they were recruited. The Public Works Department could only avoid delays in the execution of works because it was supplied with a suitable number of tax defaulters and prison convict labour. Thus, the problems with imposing a novel rhythm of work, outlined by Fred Cooper for Mombasa harbour (1992), were, in Uluguru, aggravated after the introduction of Indirect Rule.[31]

---

[31] TNA: 1733/4: Morogoro District Ann. Rep. 1920–1; TNA 11676/I: Ann. Rep. Eastern Province, 1927; TNA 11676/III: Ann. Rep. Eastern Province, 1929.

Shortly before labour shortage became a problem for employers in Morogoro, the authorities had to restrict food sale after a bad harvest in order to conserve native food reserves. If cash cropping started in this, for Waluguru slightly self-destructive, way, it soon turned into a more profitable venture. In 1926, millet (*mtama*) became a cash crop; in 1928, native cotton growing (on the new "indirect" rulers' commands) took off with a harvest of 3,197 tons (as compared to 945 tons in 1927), while in the same year, 7,500 coffee seedlings were distributed by the government. The new economy immediately had its impact on the availability of land, judging from the fact that in 1928, the mountains were thought to be so congested that the government had to close them temporarily for non-native settlement.[32] The 1930s saw the further innovation of cash cropping in Eastern Uluguru through the growing of peas and beans for the Dar es Salaam market (Mlahagwa 1974: 23), while the inhabitants of the Mgeta area started to follow the example of the missionaries in supplying the Morogoro market with European vegetables.[33]

Some years before this take-off of cash cropping, District Commissioner Hutchins wrote:

> The Christian Missionary cannot hold his own in Morogoro against Islam nor are the methods adopted by the younger missionaries (Dutch and Irish/pp) calculated to advance their cause. We have been able to assist them by placing Christian Akidas (native officials before Indirect Rule/pp) in Christian areas in three cases, but we have not been overwhelmed with

---

[32] The measure was made permanent by Governor Cameron in 1930 (TNA 1733/13: Morogoro District Ann. Rep., 1925; TNA MF 19 MDB: "Notes on the Waluguru and Wakami", E. E. Hutchins; TNA 11676/II: Ann. Rep. Eastern Province, 1928; TNA 18913: Cameron to CS Jardine, 13.5.30; Land Development Survey, Uluguru Moutains, by F. J. Bagshawe 1930).

[33] Thus, it was not the presence of the urban markets which introduced cash cropping (as Mlahagwa suggests, 1974: 23), but the presence of money earned elsewhere which developed an internal *mtama*-market. The market was internal because millet was almost exclusively used in the production of beer for (indeed!) *ngoma* and *tambiko*. Cotton, coffee, peas and beans for the Morogoro and Dar es Salaam markets were introduced a few years later.

gratitude for this concession. It is possible that some day these missionaries will realise the fallacy of attempting to combine commercial and religious aspirations. Proselytism is too often combined with demands for labour at inferior wages. ...No traces of organised Islamic propaganda have been observed.[34]

This was 1923, only five years before Christian participation by Waluguru started to rise spectacularly. Although the Matombo mission diary does not mention an increase in Islam, it noted the lack of enthusiasm for the schools, and the statistics of the mission show that the growth of the number of Christians slackened and the number of baptisms even fell in 1923 (see fig. 1).[35] Contrary to stereotype, therefore, government support and the provision of labour opportunities by the mission did *not* enhance the popularity of Christianity before 1928. After that, however, the number of candidates for baptism (*catechumens*, those who followed the four-year course of catechetical instruction) rose spectacularly, while the number of practising Christians (measured by Easter communions) also started to rise after having been stationary since at least 1924. The growing number of catechumens in 1928–9 is reflected in the comparatively sharp increase in the total number of Christians after 1933: because the catechumenate took approximately four years, most of them had by that time been baptized (fig. 1).

---

[34] TNA 1733/12: Morogoro District Ann. Rep., 1923.

[35] It is surprising how little use has been made of mission statistics in assessing *cultural* change in Africa (as distinct from quantitative developments), by, for instance, comparing different types of baptism recorded. The Holy Ghost Fathers, like any other Catholic mission, were required to produce a *status animarum* ("state of souls") every first of July, and these data allow for year-to-year comparisons of the fluctuation of participation in Christianity with other events. These data must be available throughout Africa, even where – as in my case – they are incomplete and have to be reconstructed from various sources. The graphs I use here are based on the statistics in the diocesan archive in Morogoro (1940–9; 1956–62), supplemented with sources listed which each diagram. Where data are lacking, the year is not indicated on the lower X-axis. "Easter communions" indicate *practising* Christians, in contrast to registered Catholics. "Catechumens" are candidates for baptism. If the legenda lists Y2 behind one of the categories of data, the numbers are given on the right hand vertical axis. If not otherwise indicated, the vertical axes give absolute numbers.

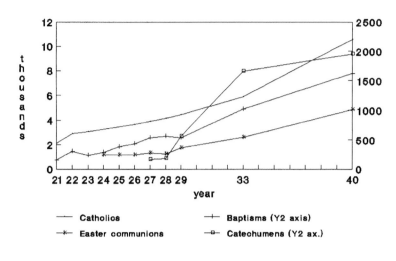

Sources: BG 29 (1923-4): 320-1,
33 (1927-8): 99-100; BHG 29 (1933):
168, 180; MD 1.7.27, 1.7.28, 1.7.29.

FIGURE 1   *Matombo Parish, 1921–1940*

This spectacular rise in the number of Christians therefore coincides with the successful introduction of cash crops since 1926. At first sight, this seems an evident explanation. After all, didn't the native cotton growers see that non-native growers got a 30 per cent higher price for their crops because they entered into a written contract with prospective buyers and were therefore less vulnerable to price fluctuations when supply was high?[36] Where could the necessary trading skills – reading, writing and arithmetic – be learned except in the missionaries' schools? But the mission schools, teaching the four subjects of the three R's and the catechism, had already been in operation for a while (see chapter five). Why didn't the Eastern Waluguru flock to them in 1926, 1927 or early 1928? In this and the following section, I want to suggest that the intervening variable was the successful introduction of Indirect Rule, which, like the Maji Maji war in 1905–6, provoked a tremendous upheaval in the political economy of Eastern Uluguru. Indirect Rule was prepared in 1925 and implemented in 1926, but due to the weak

---

[36] TNA 11676/II, Ann. Rep. Eastern Province, 1928.

health of the old sultan of South Uluguru, the new form of administration only started to make an impact on Eastern Waluguru in
1928, when his nephew, Kingalu Mwanarubela, succeeded him.[37]
Significantly, his first job was to help the Agricultural Officer in
getting people to improve their crops.

Elsewhere, I have argued that Indirect Rule in Uluguru created
a "pidgin" of Luguru political discourse in the form of an administrative ethnography that elevated certain traditional headmen above
others, and made a hierarchy of chiefships and subchiefships out of
a formerly fluid rivalry between "big persons" (*wakubwa*) operating
from different power bases in the mountains (Pels 1996). The newly
appointed "sultan" of South Uluguru thus took precedence over his
rivals, whom before he had had to approach which much caution,
magical protection, and placatory gestures, and such political
reshuffling was replicated at all the lower levels of Luguru politics.
The Mbago who was hanged after becoming involved with the medicine hunter and prophet leading the Maji Maji rebellion, had been
such a "big man", and his successor was now subordinated by
British decree to someone who used to be his equal. Thus, the
introduction of Indirect Rule upset the political balances pertaining
in Uluguru. The difference with the upheavals around and after the
Maji Maji rebellion, which, as we have seen, led to an emphasis on
wage labour in German employ, was that power was now once more
predicated on the control of land – needed for cash cropping – by
reinvented "traditional" claims which the British felt they had to
recognize in order to be able to appoint "Native Authorities".

The implementation of Indirect Rule in Uluguru was immediately followed by the arrival of a travelling medicine hunter,
Ngoja bin Kimeta (see Lee 1976). He came to Uluguru in the last
months of 1926, after the new Native Authorities had been installed
by the British. Ngoja's father was said to have been a leader in the
Maji Maji rebellion and the authorities feared a recurrence of
African protest. Ngoja was put under house-arrest in Dar es Salaam

---

[37] The first incumbent of the South Uluguru chiefship was Kingalu 10
(Mwanamfuko). For an account of Luguru discourses of power, and their
"pidginization" by Indirect Rule, see Pels (1996).

in December, but his agents probably continued their practice in his absence.[38] Ngoja, unlike the Maji Maji prophet Kinjekitile, did not add anti-colonial prophecy to his work of cleansing villages and individuals of evil medicines. The coming of Ngoja right after the implementation of Indirect Rule can be compared to the arrival of the next "witchcraft eradication" movement in Uluguru, that of Nguvumali (in 1958), which followed immediately upon the rise to power of TANU members (in 1956–7) in the wake of the upheavals created by the Uluguru Land Usage Scheme (in 1950–5). That supports the idea, advanced by David Parkin (1968), that "witchraft eradication" is above all an attempt to modify medicine as a source of power. Related to Uluguru, it would imply that a "witchcraft eradicator" is called in when changes in power relationships have created an imbalance between the possession of medicine (*dawa*) and the possession of a position of power. By eradicating medicine, witchcraft which harms a newly found or imposed order is avoided.[39]

But if the headmen who threw in their lot with the Germans, instead of the Maji Maji prophet, felt they could use *jando* to attune their young men to this new constellation of power, how did the new order established by Indirect Rule respond? I want to suggest that, when it became clear that the new Native Authorities had settled down and the disruptive potential of the medicines of previous powerholders had been neutralized, Christianity provided the obvious alternative. *Jando*, based on the contact with the outside world through migrant labour or war service, could not sufficiently accomodate to this change. *Ngoma* practice now had to adapt to a situation where power was first of all based on *local* factors: on lineage authority reified by British administrative ethnography and on authority over land which gave an advantage in the production of cash crops. While *jando* incorporated global powers that had settled in towns and plantations, now the possibilities of a career were once more localized on Luguru land itself.

---

[38] TNA 11676/I: Ann. Rep. Eastern Province, 1927, which also mentions witchcleansing after Ngoja's arrest; TNA 12333 for Ngoja in general, and TNA 12333: Acting PC Eastern Province to CS, 16.3.27, for Ngoja's father.

[39] I deal further with the "witchcraft eradication" literature in chapter six, pp. 263 ff.

Where were these global powers more localized in Eastern Uluguru than in the imposing mission buildings of Matombo, surrounded by large tracts of mission land, bought from Waluguru and even rented out according to Luguru "traditional" custom? Given the fact that a neo-traditional office holder was told by his British superiors that literacy would become a necessary requirement for holding office, what was more logical than to send his future successor to the mission school to be initiated in its powerful mysteries? Now that the younger generation looked to the production of cash crops for improving one's life, the promise of the technological skills and spiritual powers of the school, and the proof of these powers given by the local missionaries themselves, became the most fitting model for modern success. Moreover, if one was not in a lineage which commanded a Native Authority position and large tracts of land, the career of a teacher or catechist (*mwalimu*) was the most immediate means of upward mobility (see chapter five).

THE MEDIATION OF LUGURU CHRISTIANITY BY *NGOMA*

The previous discussion should in itself be sufficient to show that there is reason to treat Luguru enthusiasm for Christianity as comparable to their adoption of *jando*, and *ngoma* as a useful metaphor for the sudden acceptance of Christian baptism. But I would also like to show that Luguru responses to Christianity were mediated by the routines of *ngoma* practice; that the initiation into Christianity of Waluguru conformed in many respects to existing *ngoma* routines. Christian "initiations" in Uluguru – baptism, first communion, marriage, taking the vows, ordination – were (and are) always accompanied by drums playing Luguru rhythms; the initiand was (and is) called *mwali*, just like the initiands in both male and female initiations. However, that would be only a superficial correspondence if there was no evidence that, in 1928, Eastern Luguru Christianity underwent a fundamental *qualitative* change. As indicated in the introduction to this essay, *ngoma* is related to a change in the rhythm of *life*: it is not used for the ceremonies surrounding birth, and although a drum (the Ndengela) is used to announce death and burial, it does not beat an ongoing rhythm.[40] Christianity, however, like *tambiko*, referred to both death and life: its ritual articulated birth and death as much as changes in the rhythm of life (first communion, confirmation, marriage). The Matombo statistics show that until 1933 most baptisms were *in periculo mortis*, in danger of death. Usually, the missionary would be called by a catechist to come to the village to baptize a mortally ill pagan who felt the need for the extra safeguard of the Father's blessing (which might well have been interpreted by Waluguru as a cure to which one only resorted in the last instance). From 1933 to 1940, however, the number of baptisms *extra periculo mortis* – conversions for life, one might call them – rises steeply above the number of conversions at death (see fig. 2). This is, of course, the result of the baptism of

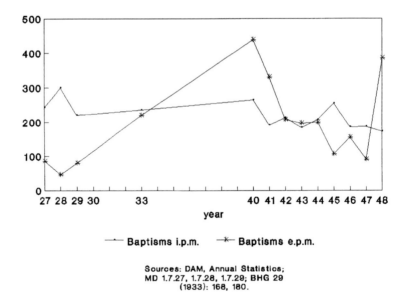

Sources: DAM, Annual Statistics;
MD 1.7.27, 1.7.28, 1.7.29; BHG 29
(1933): 168, 180.

FIGURE 2   *Matombo, baptisms, 1927–48*

---

[40] On the contrary: at death, one beats *mzunguli*, which begins with several slow and hard beats which peter out in fast and soft patters (Dum! Dum! Dum Dum dum dumdumdumdum ....). It only begins in order to stop moving. It is closer to *tambiko* than to *ngoma* (see note 17).

large numbers of catechumens who came to the mission in 1928–9 (fig. 1). While the majority of adult converts to Christianity in 1927–8 adopted it for a better hereafter, or for a cure that could no longer be expected otherwise, in 1928–9 the trend is reversed until in 1940, the majority accepted baptism for a better life in the here and now. (The reasons for the sharp drop in the war years shown by fig. 2 will be discussed below.) In other words, while before 1928 conversion to Christianity was mainly relevant to Eastern Waluguru because of its role in (preventing) the passage to an after-life, from 1928, the majority of (future) converts was motivated by its this-worldly relevance, suggesting that through the Christian *ngoma*, one could become attuned to the rhythms of an indirectly ruled, cash cropping world.

That some Waluguru actually looked upon Christianity as *ngoma* is suggested by the fact that young men and women who already paid tax or had become an initiand (*mwali*) – that is, had already (almost) passed into adulthood – refused to attend the school or be baptized.[41] (Interestingly, the *Mkenge* rhythm was also called *Shilingi Mbili*, referring to the 2/- tax marking a young man's adulthood.) If Christianity was seen as a kind of new initiation into adulthood, then adults should not bother about it. Moreover, the "bush" form of the mission school, which preceded its formalization by government intervention, resembled the initiation camp in its patterns of authority, teaching modes and form of discipline (see chapter five). The missionaries, too, were anxious about the "initiatory" interpretation of Christian baptism, as is evident from their worries about whether someone would lead a Christian life after the rite (see p. 106 ff.). As in Europe, a number of Luguru Christians failed to practise their religion after baptism (as is shown by the difference between Easter communions and the number of nominal, that is, baptized, Christians – see fig. 3). But this difference between practising and nominal Christians increased after 1958, when the presence of the Tanganyika African National Union seduced an increasing number of youngsters to join another

---

[41] SD 19.11.40, TuD 17.4.25.

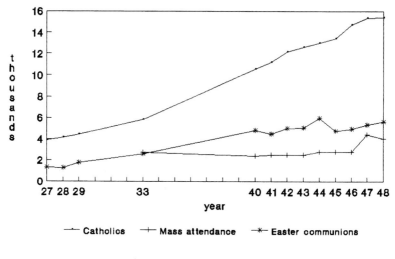

FIGURE 3   *Matombo parish, 1927–48*

community of initiates and neglect the weekly observance of Catholic duties (fig. 5). If we combine the idea of Christianity as *ngoma* – a Western institution interpreted by Waluguru as an initiation into a different rhythm of Luguru life – with the intertwined effects of Indirect Rule and cash crops, we have a powerful perspective with which to interpret the mission's statistics, and thus, to write the history of Christianity in Uluguru in the late colonial period.

For such an interpretation, one needs to watch closely the variability of the direct indicators of Christian "life" (baptisms *extra periculo mortis* and marriages), for these show the development of Luguru Christianity much more clearly than other variables can. We see, for instance, that both the number of baptisms e.p.m. and the number of Catholic marriages drops sharply in 1941 and again in 1945 (fig. 2, fig. 4). Although Waluguru never remarked on this period as being of particular importance in their history, it is significant that the war years were characterized by two different attempts by the British government to move Waluguru from the mountains – that is, from the land and the localizations of power of

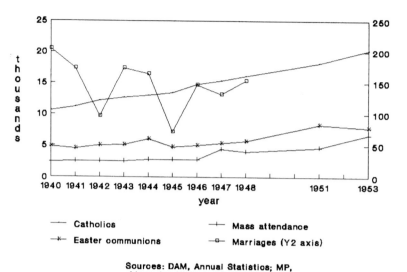

Sources: DAM, Annual Statistics; MP,
Livre des Visites; BG 1956: 434 ff.

FIGURE 4   *Matombo District, 1940–53. (incl. parishes split off since 1949)*

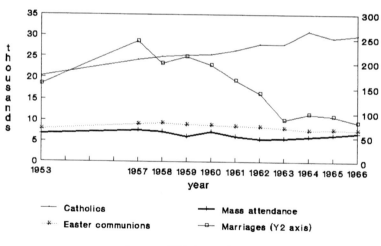

Sources: DAM, Annual Statistics;
BG 1956: 434 ff.; MP, Livre des
Visites.

FIGURE 5   *Matombo District, 1953–66. (incl. parishes split off since 1949)*

Indirect Rule – first, to make them grow cotton in the plains on the East, and second, to recruit them into war work. It is especially the first which seems to have created the biggest pressure on Matombo Waluguru. The Increased Production Campaigns initiated by the Depression were stepped up because of the war effort which Tanganyikan peasants had to make for the British markets. Before the war, in 1935–6, the authorities attempted to move Waluguru to the plains to plant cotton, a policy "part way between encouragement and exhortation with a bias against the tax defaulter". The policy was characterized by excessive pressure of the agricultural staff, compulsion and "misguided prosecution" by Native Authorities (and this despite the fact that the object was not prosecution but "self-improvement" of Waluguru). The policy led to the nearly complete failure of the cotton crop due to lack of disease control.[42]

Thus, when the Matombo missionaries were told by the British to stimulate the growth of cotton and buy it from Waluguru in January 1941, they hesitated, because they understood Luguru doubts about its profitability. Although there is no evidence for 1941 that cotton measures were coupled with an effort to move Waluguru from the mountains to the plains, for 1944 there is. Moreover, throughout the war years, the British conscripted Waluguru for army work (some, in Matombo, accepting it for the high wages, others, in Kasanga, even hiding themselves from the British officer who came to show a war propaganda film in Mtamba). The period could have given Waluguru the impression that power, money and work were once more to be obtained by migration out of the mountains instead of being mediated by the locally entrenched representatives of that power. Although we have no data showing an increase in participation in *jando* (the *ngoma* of migrant labour), it is significant that in places like Kasanga, where fear of war recruitment was acute, this was the time when *jando* was first introduced. Some ten years before, the simultaneous introduction of *jando* and

---

[42] TNA 11676/V: Ann. Rep. Eastern Province, 1932; TNA 11676/VI: Ann. Rep. Eastern Province, 1933; TNA MF 19 MDB: "Cotton Planting Propaganda", J. F. De S. Lewis-Barned, 26.9.60; Mlahagwa (1974: 23–4).

Christianity in the Singiza region, and the struggle between Luguru factions supporting either *jando* or Christianity, coincided with large-scale labour migration to the Kisaki plantations *and* an increase in power of the Native Authorities (who promoted the mission schools).[43]

This interpretation is reinforced by the developments around the Uluguru Land Usage Scheme (ULUS) in the 1950s. When ULUS was planned in the late 1940s, its primary objective was to stop erosion in order to reduce the flash floods of the Ruvu river that damaged the economically important rice and cotton crops of the people living near the Ruvu delta. During its implementation, however, the emphasis shifted to the terracing of the steeper Uluguru slopes (partly because Waluguru showed no inclination to move to the plains to alleviate population pressure on the land higher up the mountains). The terracing work was extremely heavy and a nuisance (as most Waluguru recall). It further boosted the local power of the Native Authorities, who acted as overseers of the terracing work, and was directed at the improvement of Luguru agriculture and cash cropping in particular. The Kinole and Mtamba strikes of July 1955 put an end to terracing and created fertile ground for the spectacular rise to popularity of the independence movement led by the Tanganyika African National Union (TANU) in Uluguru in 1956–7. The emphasis of ULUS shifted to a kind of social development programme (road building, schools, women's organizations) and the original objectives of countering Ruvu floods and soil erosion were either forgotten or dropped completely. The medicine hunter Nguvumali came to mop up puddles of power left after the floods of government intervention and TANU popularity swept Luguru politics into the channel of African

---

[43] MD Jan. 41, 28.8.41, KD 12.8.42, SD 4.9.34, TD 21.6.41; TNA MF 19, MDB, "Cotton Planting Propaganda", J. F. De S. Lewis-Barned, 26.9.60; IPAC 12b: 084–180. The fact that a similar project in 1920–1, coupling migration to cotton planting and its subsequent failure (MD 13.8.20, 4.10.20, 8.8.21, UDSM: Cory Paper 430), did *not* lead to a significant decrease in Christian participation (fig. 1) reinforces the interpretation of 1930s Christianity as *ngoma*.

nationalism. At the time, Waluguru were no longer inclined to put money into the *sadaka ya kueneza dini* (contributions to mission work); instead, they paid for Nguvumali's cleansing medicine (*usembe*).[44]

In other words, the Christian *ngoma* seems to have held its own as long as the local representatives of global power, responsible for the implementation of ULUS, could maintain their position. The sequence suggests that membership of TANU, headed by Julius Nyerere, was regarded as a kind of new, alternative *ngoma*. If so, it was a *ngoma* which deprived Luguru elders of their local control over initiation. The educated African elite of TANU showed that schooling, rather than initiation, provided career opportunities and suggested that the legitimacy of local power holders – the Native Authorities, discredited already by their association with ULUS – had come to an end. In fact, I believe that TANU was the end of *ngoma* (as a dynamic balance between the generations) and the beginning of a period in which youngsters could no longer be sufficiently controlled by elders in Luguru society (except, perhaps, through the threat of lethal magic; see chapter six).

Unfortunately, the data fail to show the precise fluctuations of Matombo Christianity in those crucial years: 1949–1950, when the effort to move Waluguru to the plains was revived;[45] and 1954–56, when Eastern Waluguru rose in protest against ULUS terracing work. The graphs *do* show, however, that the number of adherents of the Christian ngoma in Matombo continued to grow until 1957, when marriages reached a peak (fig. 5). Apparently, the introduction of ULUS made no difference to participation in the Christian ngoma up to 1957 (neither the interviews with missionaries nor the mission diaries gave me reason to doubt that conclusion), but when ULUS shifted to a social development scheme that

---

[44] On ULUS, TNA MF 19, MDB: "Notes on ULUS", by A. H. Savile and P. C. Duff; also Brain (1979), Young and Fosbrooke (1960), and Temple (1972). I hope to elaborate on their accounts in another book. On Nguvumali, see chapter six.

[45] TNA MF 19, MDB: "Cotton Planting Propaganda", by J. F. De S. Lewis-Barned, 26.9.60.

stressed mobility (through roads and schooling) rather than the control of land and crops, and TANU emphasized that the road to power led out of the mountains, Christianity lost much of its relevance. The drop in the number of marriages after 1957 (fig. 5) shows that the elders could no longer compel their children to marry in the church.[46] When, in 1961, TANU politics had emphasized that lineage power through the Native Authorities was to be abolished, the number of baptisms *extra periculo mortis* drops below the number of baptisms *in periculo mortis* for the first time since 1957, and perhaps – but here data are lacking – since 1948 (fig. 6).

The correspondence between Christianity and *jando* as modern *ngoma* can also be gleaned from the fact that the head circumcizer (*mwinzi* or *ng'ariba mkuu*) was likened to a bishop. Where

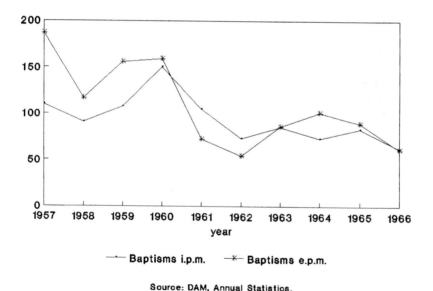

Source: DAM, Annual Statistics.

FIGURE 6   *Matombo, baptisms, 1957–66. (incl. parishes split off since 1949)*

---

[46] It was this interpretation, put before me by Father Theodor Winkelmolen and Jan Kees van Donge, that developed into the analysis of mission statistics presented in this chapter.

Christianity was strong, as in Mgeta, circumcision was abolished "voluntarily" indicating that the Christian *ngoma* seemed a sufficient replacement. Where Islam was strong, however, circumcision held its place: muslim boys could, of course, never gain prominence in Christian circles, and needed to remain attuned to their own religious community. In the predominantly Muslim environment of Tegetero mission, mission school attendance and conversion to Christianity were highest in the 1930s and shortly after World War Two, but the opposition against (predominantly Christian) Native Authorities surfaced regularly in between, which culminated in making the area the heartland of opposition to ULUS and support for TANU in the 1950s. The patterns of conversion and *ngoma* differed from place to place in other respects: in Kasanga, for instance, just as *jando* did not become popular until the war years, Christianity took off only after the war. While the foundation of the parish in 1937 must have created an initial enthusiasm, still, in 1938, people in the outschools did not "follow the religion" but were eager to be baptized when in danger of death; marriages were rare. When the Kasanga Waluguru saw themselves threatened by war recruitment, *jando* was introduced while Christian conversion declined (see figs. 7 and 8).[47] It was only during the ULUS period, when government intervention through the Native Authorities first started to bother the people of Kasanga, that Christianity really took off, only to be stopped in its tracks by the rise of TANU (fig. 7).

It is important to repeat that in the preceding pages, I have mainly described the history of the young men's initiation. The women had their own dance. The female initiand passed into adulthood through a sequence of acts which centred on the domestic sphere (even if they were not limited to it), and were therefore less directly related to experiences of the world outside Uluguru. On the one hand, the elder women who organized the female *ngoma* must have looked favourably on Christianity, for it promised a relief from the threat of migrating husbands setting up households outside the mountains, in their place of work. At the same time, the patriarchal inclinations of the missionaries tended to reduce the power

---

[47] KD 25.11.38, 19.2.39, 17.8.42.

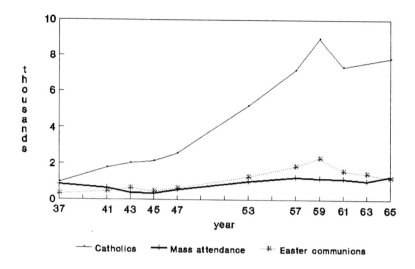

Sources: DAM, Annual Statistics; KD,
30.7.37.

FIGURE 7   *Kasanga parish, 1937–65*

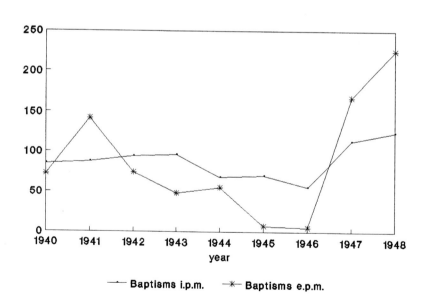

Source: DAM, Annual Statistics.

FIGURE 8   *Kasanga, baptisms, 1940–48*

of women in Luguru society. The girls' *ngoma* was a form of resistance against those aspects of Christianity that reduced the women's power base, and it was therefore maintained with much more vigour than the *ng'ula/lwindi* or *jando ngoma*, even when girls also attended the mission schools and were baptized (see the next chapter). It may be for that reason that the participation of girls in Christian training was always less than that of the boys. Sixty-three per cent of the pupils of the Matombo schools in 1928 were boys, while males only made up forty-seven per cent of the total Luguru population at the time. At the same time, several men (and only men) from Matombo formed the first *association pieuse* and pledged, among other things, to keep away from everything *ya ngoma*.[48] The Matombo statistics show that girls were a relative minority at school (fig. 9). This imbalance was redressed at the time that Christianity lost much of its appeal to youngsters (fig. 10).

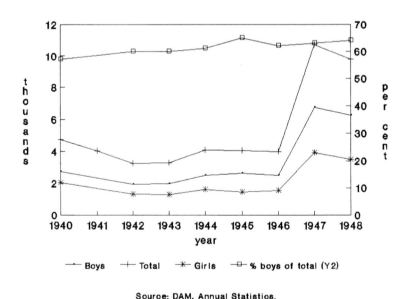

Source: DAM, Annual Statistics.

FIGURE 9   *Matombo, schools, 1940–48*

[48] TD Dec. '34. MD Oct. '28, 30.12.28; TNA MF 15 MDB: Native District Census 1928.

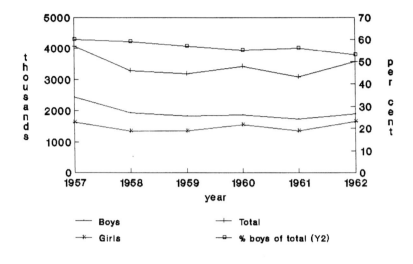

Source: DAM, Annual Statistics.

FIGURE 10   *Matombo, schools, 1957–62. (incl. parishes split off in 1949)*

CONCLUSION

Let me stress that in the preceding pages, I have not tried to completely identify Luguru Christianity with *ngoma*. Even if my interpretation holds, it still leaves out the agency of the missionaries and many other aspects of Luguru interpretations of Christianity. I have tried to show that, just as *mganda* "imitated" the military march by grafting it on a rhythmic pattern completely different from military discipline, just so Christianity was carried into Luguru society by being grafted on their *ngoma* patterns. Taking seriously the Luguru understanding of *ngoma* as both rhythm and initiation, I have tried to show the creative potential of Luguru initiation in combining the reproduction of the balance of power between the generations with a way of adapting to, and incorporating, novel forms of the exchange of labour and the control of land. This creativity and adaptability of *ngoma* prepared Waluguru for the acceptance of Christianity after a novel localization of power within the mountains had made previous adaptations, and *jando* in particular, less viable. Thus, *ngoma* served both as a metaphor for a change in the rhythm of life, and as a mediation of novel rhythms of work introduced by the colonial economy. Like the Catholic mission, *ngoma* was a mobile pattern that mediated between different structures of power and signification, part of a microphysics of colonial contact that cannot be reduced to one or either of these structures. Like the Dutch mission, *ngoma* defined a "home" while simultaneously pointing in a direction away from it.

But if Waluguru were prepared for Christianity by *ngoma*, Christianity was also a major cause of the crisis in the balance of power between Luguru generations which led to the disappearance of *ngoma* as male initiation. The mission incorporated Waluguru, as priests, as lay members of the Church, and as pupils and teachers, to exert the disciplinary power of the state and the Roman Church through the school (see chapter five). The male *ngoma* attuned Luguru boys to colonial power, but in the process, it was contextualized by it. That does not mean that we can reduce *ngoma* to a magical mimesis, based on an illusory hope to influence the future which did not materialize. The marked improvements that reading, writing and arithmetic brought to the control of land and the cash crop market, and that the catechist's and teacher's careers brought to one's functioning in colonial society, show how reasonable the decision was to be initiated in Christianity. If the young men were, given their position in the lineage relations of production, the ones most likely to use such colonial advantages for their individual benefit, elders could only try to incorporate their experience as something integral to the rhythm of Luguru life.

With Christianity, Waluguru incorporated a Trojan horse. Luguru *ngoma* became so attuned to the mimesis of global power that it lost the capacity to locally reproduce it. If it is true that African nationalism succeeded Christianity as *ngoma*, it was also too global, directed by powers located outside of the Luguru mountains, to function as a local balance of power between generations (see the conclusion). This process of reduction of the Luguru elders' ability to control their youngsters' careers plunged Luguru society in a crisis marked by the loss of the capacity to be its own source of valuation of work and life (see Van Donge 1993). The male *ngoma* disappeared, and its rhythms became a folklorized and commercialized "Luguru tradition". Luguru drummers were now called up to play their rhythms before a TANU audience for money. This commodification process of *ngoma* had been inaugurated by the Kaiser's feast and the missionaries, and produced some of the best and most popular music of Tanzania in the 1970s. But these "rhythms of home" were played outside the mountains, in the dance-halls of Morogoro and Dar es Salaam.[49]

---

[49] SD 3.10.48. Luguru rhythms fed popular bands like Morogoro Jazz and Super Volcano in the 1970s. Their descendant, the Dar es Salaam-based Mlimani Park Orchestra, still plays the danceable and complex *ingoma ya ukae* (kil.): "the rhythm of home".

CHAPTER FOUR

Luguru Woman or Lawful Wife: *Mwali*, Marriage and the Mission

In the 1932 *Holy Ghost Messenger*, Father Retera described an encounter with a British administrator during a *safari* in the Nguru Mountains, north of Morogoro. The official was accompanied by his "skinny, adventurous wife" who was carried up the mountain in an improvised palanquin by four Africans. Father Retera was enraptured:

> If one encounters such a procession on the most difficult and impassable roads of Africa, one has to accept, without more ado, the thesis that husband and wife are one! And, of course, it is also a powerful example for our blacks, who, instead of carrying their wives, burden them like pack-donkeys, and follow them five steps behind, dignified, walking-stick in hand. (BHG 28 [1932]: 136)

Apart from ignoring that, in this case, it was not exactly the husband who carried a burden, Father Retera also invoked the stereotype image of the African woman as pack-donkey. According to most missionaries, African women were treated like "property" and had to do all the work while men lazed under a tree. African women were perceived as "slaves" or "chattel" to be exchanged for a goat or money. A good Christian, on the contrary, should not buy but love his wife. African women would, the missionaries supposed, be "emancipated" by the mission.[1]

The society of the celibate missionaries was even more male-focussed than that of colonial administrators (Hammond and Jablow, quoted in Wipper 1972: 144; Callaway 1987). We therefore have reason to suspect the terms on which the missionary emancipation of women was to be realized (Hafkin and Bay 1976b: 2–4).

---

[1] BHG 43 (1947): 21, 44 (1948): 69, 118, 46 (1950): 46, 88, 47 (1951): 97; IPAC 9b: 200; KMM 43/1a: 299.

Compared to the active Luguru women whom we will meet in this chapter, the administrator's wife, passively seated, seems an icon of European sexism. Her status as "wife", appendix of "man", was less independent than that of her Luguru "sisters" (Sacks 1982: 110). As sisters and mothers of the lineage, Luguru women could count on support independent of their marital relationships. Moreover, they could tap important sources of power in relations of production and reproduction, and wielded considerable authority in lineage affairs.

The missionaries noted that opposition to their work in Uluguru was strongest on the part of the women. Especially elder women were suspected for their conservatism and their refusal to modify their customs and use modern medicines.[2] This antagonism between missionaries and Luguru women was rarely a debate about differing cultural valuations of gender, implicit in the use of concepts like "wife" *versus* "sister". Many Luguru and missionary ideals of proper relations between the sexes corresponded (the major exception being Luguru "trial marriage", see below). Neither did the missionaries attack the division of labour between men and women except when complaining about the laziness of Luguru men. The main sources of female power in Uluguru – tenant rights, crop ownership, political position – were outside the missionary sphere of operation and rarely endangered by their interference. Instead, the struggle was over *ngoma*: the transformation of girls into female adults by Luguru women, and the women's resistance to the missionaries' attempt to usurp control over this transformation by the legal form of Catholic marriage.

Unlike the boys' *ng'ula* or *jando*, female initiation survived colonial rule, because it gave women the possibility to counter the instabilities created by the growing independence from lineage relations of production of young men earning cash. That meant that the missionaries' opposition to female initiation was directed against the ways in which the women tried to alleviate the pressures which the colonial economy exerted upon them. Moreover, Catholic marriage law individualized both spouses, to the advantage

---

[2] IPAC 5b: 350; KD 27.2.48, MD 19.6.27, SD 28.7.40.

of the man – who became more independent from the claims of his lineage to his earnings – and to the detriment of the woman, whose power crucially depended on the multiplicity of social roles (*both* "wife" *and* "mother" *and* "sister") embodied during initiation. The women, therefore, retained part of their initiatory microphysics to counter the threat, and an analysis of their practices of bodily transformation will better enable us to understand why the mission's interference was experienced as threatening.[3]

MALE AND FEMALE POWER IN ULUGURU

To the missionaries, the terms "matrilineal" and "matriarchal" designated the power of the mother's brother (*mjomba*; kil. *mkolo*), not that of the female members of the lineage. They took the father to be the ruler of the household and the mother's brother of the lineage.[4] However, they were not in a good position to judge the influence which Luguru women exerted upon their environment. The missionaries came from a predominantly male realm and created Luguru Christianity in its image. Up to the 1950s, all catechists and teachers were men. The position of the catechist was in many ways comparable to that of a clan head except that it lacked the latter's female counterpart (see below, chapter five, and Pels 1996). When Father Schaegelen instituted the first organization for lay action in Matombo, it consisted of men only. In the larger Christian communities, an older overseer (*msimamizi*) was appointed to assist the teacher (often a young man) in his work, usher his Christians to church on Sunday, and, most

---

[3] Henrietta Moore points out the defects of accounts which treat gender only in terms of cultural constructions or reduce it to social roles, but her solution (that both are mediated by the competing claims of men and women in specific strategic situations) fails to show *why* gender stereotypes "have a perfect material reality" (1988: 38). This material reality may, I feel, be grasped through the microphysics of bodily seclusion and transformation advanced in this chapter.

[4] This position was also popular among anthropologists (Fox 1967: 99; La Fontaine 1985: 172; Schneider 1961: 6–7), but has, like the thesis of universal male dominance which it supports, been challenged (Poewe 1981).

importantly, watch over the Christian life of his community. His main task was to report to the Father on broken marriages and concubinage. (One Father called the organizations of lay action a "squealing-system".) From this group of overseers, about four councillors *(watu wa shauri)* were appointed as assessors of the mission *baraza*.[5]

The *baraza* therefore only consisted of elder men, and its discussions were usually limited to who could marry whom and the amount of brideprice *(mali)* that was to be transacted between the father and mother's brother of the boy and those of the girl. Transactions about a plot for a church or school were also restricted to male society: the missionaries talked to the big man of the area and the male occupants of the plot; their women (who probably contributed informally to the decision) remained out of the picture. Like British administrators, therefore, the missionaries did not exaggerate male power in Uluguru out of mere Western prejudice, but because they fashioned the "empirical" proof for their convictions during the ethnographic occasions that they constructed with Waluguru to discuss Luguru patterns of authority (Pels 1994).

Former colonial administrators argued that the formal power of Luguru women was limited to the selection of new candidates for the lineage headmanship after the death of an incumbent (Brain 1978: 177; Young and Fosbrooke 1960: 53). Like them, I first assumed that the formal participation of women in lineage politics was incidental, that female power (if any) was informal and domestic, that the first answer to the question "who rules this area?" was also the only one possible, and that this answer consisted of the genealogy of male clanheads, the only formal expression of authority in the lineage. When, therefore, Mzee Lwango (the Konde valley landholder) told me that we hadn't finished our talk (of several months back) about his valley's leaders, I was surprised and said as much. "We haven't done the mothers", he remonstrated. He showed me that each clan-head could not only name all his male

---

[5] MP, Catholic Action: "Rapport Organisation Action Catholique", by Fr. Schaegelen, 28.1.36; KMM 710/1b: 039.

predecessors, but also recite the full list of their mothers, the nominal sisters of those whom they succeeded in office.[6]

This showed that women did, indeed, possess formal positions of authority: each lineage had a presiding *mama* (or *bibi*, grandmother) who was responsible for storing the goods paid as land rent (*ngoto*) by those who were guests on lineage land. She and her direct advisors did not only appoint the successor to the lineage head (just like the lineage head could appoint the successor to the *mama*), but were also able to depose him when his conduct threatened the functioning of the community. Two successors to the name of Bambarawe, the landholder of Matombo, were deposed by the women of the Matombo lineage of the Watonga clan in the 1950s, because of their alcoholism, womanizing, and wanton sale of lineage land. The women could not find suitable successors and have not conferred the name on anyone since.[7] Similarly, the *mama* of the Wabunga of Kibungo took away the name of Chewe and its spirit emblems (*milunga*) from the incumbent since he, too, disgraced the position of lineage head. When the women of the clan had grievances or objected to measures taken by the clan leaders, they gathered at the *mama's* house and discussed matters. The *mama* could then take up the matter with the clan leader and inform him of the women's wishes.[8] Thus, in some respects, Luguru patterns of authority were a kind of "dual-sex political system" (Okonjo 1976).

A *mwenye mlunga* could not get a name and spirit emblems if he was not married and his wife not as respected as he himself; the

---

[6] FN, Mzee Lwango Mwanamsangule, Konde, 18.9.90. This contact with the past (see introduction, p. 33 ff.) became possible because Mzee Lwango accepted me as a relative after my participation in the funeral of one of his relatives, which was the direct cause of his invitation to tell me more.

[7] Finding successors to lineage names was, and is, complicated by the fact that lineage heads not only have to be competent and married to an equally competent woman, but also have to agree not to leave the area for longer than a week on end, a condition that few of the members of the younger, migrant generation are prepared to accept.

[8] UDSM, Cory Paper 159, "Propositions for a reform of the Uluguru Councils", 1956; FN, Mzee Petri Mloka, Kiswira, 24.12.89; Mama Mkoba, Kiswira, 1.10.90, Mzee Mkombo, Mtamba, 8.2.90.

choice of the successor of a lineage head also depended on the character and capabilities of his spouse. Spirit emblems were bestowed on the couple, not only on the man. Some women even refused to get *milunga* through their husband and insisted on a separate ceremony and a separate name, which they duly got. During a beer-feast, the male *mwenye mlunga* would get the first drink, but no lower-ranked participant should try to touch the beer before the women of *mlunga* rank had had their fill. Smaller disputes were and are settled before lineage leaders (including the women) with women and men participating freely in the discussion. It was only in the larger gatherings that the women sat apart and kept silent. On the single occasion that I was able to witness myself, one of the male elders put the women's point of view before the audience and a compromise was reached.[9]

Husband and wife would add their own plots to the means of production of the household. Although land was the property of the lineage or clan, sons and daughters had an inalienable right to use a field and a plot for building their house (which influenced patterns of residence; see below). If the couple worked on a plot together, they had an equal right to the crop: on divorce, the crop would be divided between them, as would the building materials of the house. If a spouse worked on a plot alone (depending on his or her own lineage for the extra labour), he or she was the owner of the crop (Young and Fosbrooke 1960: 58–61). Father Scheerder reported that when a marriage contract was made, the newlyweds took half of their possessions to the new house, while the other half was kept by the mothers of the couple (Scheerder and Tastevin 1950: 267). On divorce, the children, as members of her lineage, remained with the mother.

The husband's tasks were cutting wood in the forest and bringing it to the house for building or firewood, bringing the harvested crops to the house, providing the household, and especially his wife, with clothes, and producing furniture and other implements.

---

[9] Under the Ujamaa regime, dealing with disputes became the task of the "head of ten houses" (*mjumbe*) who would take the matter higher up, to the Reconciliation Council or Village Chairman if he was unable to solve it. In Matombo, however, the lineage council still resolves most of its own disputes (including marriage troubles), although some clan disputes and all rows between non-relatives appear before the *mjumbe*.

The woman had to take care of the babies, prepare food (including pounding the meal and fetching water) and make beer at feasts. Especially beer-making was (and still is) an important economic asset: through the promise of *pombe*, extra labour was attracted for clearing large tracts of land or building a house. Beer making and the organization of a sufficient amount of millet for its production gave the women control over the parts of the production process on which the position of big men relied (see also Clark, quoted in Strobel 1982: 111).

Fetching firewood close to the house, sweeping the house and its surroundings, bringing hot washing water for the husband, taking care of storage in the granary (where the woman alone may enter), making pottery and going to the market (to sell her pottery and crops or to buy food with her husband's money), were also among a woman's tasks. (Interestingly enough, Father Scheerder notes that the husband meets the wife on her return from the market to relieve her of her burden [Scheerder and Tastevin 1950: 268] – so much for the "pack-donkey".) Thus, we see that the domestic division of labour associates the man with the bush (cutting wood) and the outside world (getting clothes), while the woman is associated with the house, the market and local communities of labour. Husband and wife cultivated the land together, although clearing the bush was more of a man's job.

Both the bush and the outside world were regarded with suspicion by Waluguru. The bush was thought to be the province of wild animals, witches and the white vampire called *mumiani* (see chapter six). The outside world was associated with foreign powers that could rob a Luguru community of one of its members if it resisted their demands.[10] Men – youngsters in particular – were

---

[10] Summing up the attempts of a Kingalu to procure slaves for the Zanzibar market, the hangings of Mwanambago and Shenekambi by the Germans, the disappearance of two men who rebelled against British compulsory road work, and the death of John Mahenge in the ULUS riots, Mzee Pius Wendelin writes that "we can say that on each occasion of disturbance someone is bound to disappear or die" (Wendelini 1990: 52). This is one of the reasons why many Waluguru hesitated to send their children to the schools of Morogoro and Mhonda – see ch. 5 and below.

closer to this wild world, which contained both attractive benefits and terrible dangers. The boys' *ngoma* took place in the bush, while the female initiand was kept in the house. The boys could go out to trade in Bagamoyo or work for the white man, but the girls, future mothers of lineage children, should be kept behind. Therefore, when this wild world attracted more and more young men with its promise of economic and political power, this was likely to reverberate on the position of women in Luguru society. Again, the change was mediated by *ngoma*, but, as we shall see, it was one step removed from colonial society: female initiation was largely connected to it indirectly, through the men.

FEMALE INITIATION, MALE DOMINANCE AND PRACTICAL MIMESIS

Words (...) limit the range of choices and render difficult or impossible (...) the relations which the language of the body suggests (Bourdieu 1977: 120).

Given the amount of literature on women in Sub-Saharan Africa inspired by feminist scholarship, it is surprising that so little has been written by feminist anthropologists about female initiation.[11] Jean La Fontaine explains this (cf. Mauss 1973: 80) by the relative scarcity of these rites, but that is partly because she excludes individual puberty rites, based on "natural" changes, from initiation *per sé*, which she defines as collective and based on "social" changes to maturity (1985: 14, 163).[12] Brown, using a broader definition, shows that female initiation and puberty rites are widespread

---

[11] On African women, see Hafkin and Bay 1976a; Hay and Wright 1982; Obbo 1981; Oppong 1983; Poewe 1981; Robertson and Berger 1986; Sacks 1982; Strobel 1982; Wipper 1972. Moore's (1988) index does not list "initiation" or "puberty rite". Those who do pay attention to initiation often cannot decide between judging it as male oppression or as female solidarity (Strobel 1982: 127).

[12] I show below that the transformations of the Luguru female initiand are not merely "natural" nor "individual" (but rather "dividual": Marriot, quoted in Strathern 1988: 348). More important, however, is that La Fontaine's perspective seems to obscure that initiation is *always* social (as well as natural).

throughout Sub-Saharan Africa, the Americas and parts of Oceania (1963: 839). Perhaps the lack of elaborated studies of female initiation is the result of the fact that these rituals, especially because of their association with genital mutilation, were taken as obvious supports of male dominance (Hafkin and Bay 1976b: 9–10). There are three reasons why this should be criticized as an *over*emphasis on male dominance.

First of all, many interpretations of female initiation seem to be inspired by the supposition that non-Western women *must* be more oppressed than European "wives" (cf. Hafkin and Bay 1976b: 2). This seems to be a colonialist legacy: (former) administrators commenting on African female initiations feel the need to emphasize the *absence* of clitoridectomy (District Commissioner Hutchins; White 1953: 15)[13] – implying that is exceptional and that genital mutilation is normal in female initiation. But whereas explanations of female initiation as caused by male envy of female procreative capacities (Bettelheim 1954) are usually based on genital mutilation rites only, such ceremonies themselves are "extremely rare" (Brown 1963: 837). The "male envy" hypothesis has also been applied to Luguru female initiation, but there is no evidence that the rite was actually meant "to prevent women gaining a dominant position" and "to invoke the authority of the male ancestors through the elder women" (Brain 1978: 186). If the ceremony in Uluguru was such a violent disciplining of women by men, it is curious that the latter played no directing part in the initiation at all. Brain gives no evidence that the ancestors invoked were, indeed, all male, and as we have seen, a *tambiko* might well include the female lineage ancestors.

A second way of overemphasizing male domination in female initiation is through functionalist analyses that assume that it contributes to the maintenance of social order and *mutatis mutandis* of local structures of power that privilege men (La Fontaine 1985: 179; Godelier 1986: 50; for a critique of the latter, see Eves 1991). As we have seen in the case of the boys' *ngoma*, ritual can also

---

[13] TNA MF 19, Morogoro District Book, "Notes on the Waluguru and Wakami", E. E. Hutchins, 1929; C. M. N. White was a Rhodesian official before he joined the Rhodes-Livingstone Institute.

mediate the contradictions between the dominance of elder men over boys within Luguru society, and the independence from lineage power that the boys were offered through novel colonial work opportunities. I argue below that such contradictions appear in female initiation as a tension between young men's independence and young women's dependence on lineage support. But such colonial intervention or antagonism of interest between the sexes has hardly been described in female initiation. Audrey Richards, although she said the absence of 40% to 60% of the men at the mines was reflected in the Bemba *chisungu*, did not incorporate this extraction of labour and income in her analysis (1956: 28, 75, n.1, 103). Given that the mission prohibited *chisungu* thirty years before Richards witnessed it (1956: 139), and that the women mimicked the mission school's drill during the rite (1956: 68), it is strange that Richards largely ignored the mission's influence and changes in *chisungu* performance. Richards argued there was no "sex hostility" in *chisungu* (1956: 159), but during the rite, the young man in European clothes is at least regarded as a mixed blessing (1956: 210). All these themes were played out in the Luguru female *mwali* rite, and they suggest, if not hostility, at least antagonism of interests between the sexes, based on both labour migration and the presence of the mission. This antagonism appears in initiation, because initiation maintains *both* social contradictions *and* social order.

Lastly, male dominance is often overemphasized because accounts of female initiation tend to stress obedience to the (future) husband (La Fontaine 1982: xxxiii), which, however, is often *not* the primary relation of authority enacted in female initiation ritual. In *chisungu*, the husband's access to his bride is mediated by the mistress of the ceremony and can only be obtained through gifts to her (1956: 100). The senior women control both the labour of their daughters and of their sons-in-law, which shows that the authority of elder women is more important than that of the future husband.[14] Moreover, if female initiation in a patrilineal society like the Pokot communicates to the girls "not only the power and authority of

---

[14] But cf. La Fontaine (1982: xxv, xxxiii); see also Strobel's ambivalence (1982: 127).

senior women but the general sense of power which Pokot women appear to feel" (Meyerhoff, quoted in La Fontaine 1985: 170), what about a society under the sway of matrilineal ideology (which, some argue, refutes the thesis of universal male dominance – Poewe, 1981)? As we will see, during the *mwali* rite, the Luguru initiand's expected obedience to the husband is very much qualified and made conditional to the well-being of the woman and her household.

The overemphasis on male dominance is mostly caused by the tendency in anthropology to regard ritual as a symbolic expression of extant power relationships. In the introduction, I referred to Talal Asad's argument that the development of Protestantism eliminated the dimension of religious training and discipline from the definition of religion (p. 30 ff.). As a result, ritual was no longer regarded as apt performance, a discipline with merit in its own right, but as a set of symbols that had to be decoded, whose real meaning lay elsewhere, in the social order to which it referred (Asad 1993: 60–62). In such a conception, initiation ritual is reduced to the conservative function of maintaining the "principles" that "govern" social structure (Turner 1967: 50, 54) or the ideological function of hiding the reality of power for the oppressed (Bloch 1987), a view in which initiands are treated as patients, rather than disciplined agents (Asad 1993: 167). By mapping power relations directly on ritual, the *mediation* through the trained, disciplined and initiated body is ignored: the body is treated as a mere "effect of semiotic causes" or a neutral "vehicle for the expression of a reified social rationality" (Jackson 1983: 329). However, the training, disciplining and initiation of the body does not only graft "symbols" on some kind of natural *tabula rasa*, as if the body was a mere "instrument" (Mauss 1973: 75) or "simple piece of wood" (Van Gennep 1960: 72); it changes the body into a different subject (Comaroff 1985: 7–8).

Power relationships transform bodies, but in the process are transformed by bodies into a "microphysics" of power (Foucault 1979: 139). Given that the body can do what cannot be expressed (Jackson 1983: 334–5), ritual often enacts, rather than (mis)represents, social relations and helps to internalize them by producing a condensed embodied knowledge of their operation

(De Boeck 1995). The inversions characteristic of rituals of rebellion, for instance, are not merely expressions of desires repressed in normal life (Gluckman 1963), but also a practical mimesis of the habitus of the powerful, a reproduction of the other in oneself (Jackson 1983: 336). The term "habitus", therefore, does not refer to a structure of *limits* but to a repertoire of *possibilities* or dispositions, something that enables, rather than restricts, social behavior.[15] This repertoire, embodied by practical mimesis, cannot be fully grasped by consciousness (Bourdieu 1977: 94), which is the reason why many events in an initiation ritual cannot be explained by the participants (Jackson 1983; for an example, Richards, 1956: 52–110). Such practical mimesis is both natural and cultural:

> Just as ... natural mimicry has survival value for a species, so it may be supposed that the survival of Kuranko society depends on the creation of responsible adults through initiatory ordeals as much as it depends upon the physical birth of children. To create adults requires a concerted application of information from *throughout the environment* ... (Jackson 1983: 335, emphasis in original).

Luguru female initiation was triggered by the girl's first menstruation and transformed her body cosmetically and magically to fit lineage patterns of authority and exchange (which, of course, everyday socializing also impressed upon the girl both before and after initiation). The male initiand was, after the introduction of *jando*, circumcized in order to mimic his new (sexual) relationship to the female realm and place him in connection with wider patterns of social relationships (including, as we have seen, the colonial world). The body, therefore, was treated as a crossroads of nature and culture, of bodily and social routines and capacities that could be condensed in *ngoma*. In other words, female initiation may mimick male dominance, but never at the expense of existing patterns of female authority. Initiation aims at apt performance, and therefore at the creation of an indeterminate, "dividual" body (Marriott, quoted by Strathern 1988: 348) that can relate to different, and at

---

[15] The term "habitus" was coined by Mauss (1973: 73) and elaborated by Bourdieu (1977).

times mutually contradicting, patterns of natural and social production and reproduction. As we shall see, this "dividuality" could come in sharp conflict with the "individual" body which the legal discipline of the missionaries' marriage policies tried to produce.

MWALI AND MARRIAGE IN THE 1930s

The Luguru female *mwali* passed into womanhood in three stages: seclusion after her first menstruation (*kufungwa*), instruction (*mkoleni* or *galigali*, kil.), and "coming out" (*mlao*, kil.). Before the 1950s, the sequence included engagement (*kuchumbiwa*)[16] before the initiation proper, and ended with marriage (after *mlao*). I will deal with the rite as I believe it existed when Christianity was most popular, in the 1930s and 1940s. The future husband, after first meeting the girl and getting approval for the match from both sets of parents, sent his envoy (usually an elder brother) to the girl's parents with the opening gift (*kifungo*). The girl and her lineage would then be officially consulted by her father and when nobody raised objections, the boy, carrying a new hoe, went to stay with his future in-laws. He was supposed to further his suit by demonstrating his capacity for agricultural work on a field that would be given to the new couple after their official marriage. The girl was responsible for his food during this "trial-marriage". In the 1930s, this arrangement was common everywhere in Eastern Uluguru, although in Matombo, the boy and girl were said not to sleep together, while in Kasanga and Singiza they supposedly did.[17] This all took place before the girl's first menstruation.

After her first period, the girl went into seclusion (*kufungwa*), meant to transform the girl's body into an object of adult desire: a

---

[16] Literally, "to be roommated", from *mchumba*, fiancé(e) or "the person of the room".

[17] An arrangement reflecting the greater influence of the mission in Matombo; Scheerder and Tastevin (1950: 263–4), Wendelini (1990: 10–12); TNA MF 19, MDB: "The Waluguru", by Fr. v. d. Kimmenade 1937, and "Notes on the Waluguru and Wakami", by E. Hutchins 1929; MP, Reports Diaconal Meetings Matombo, 27.1.43.

pale, fat and beautiful woman who could charm potential suitors and raise brideprice payments (as one woman told me: *Si ndio biashara?* – "It's business, isn't it?"). After her first menstruation, the girl was kept inside and fed on food containing a lot of fat and sugars. She had to rub herself with the maize chaff so the old skin would peel off, and wasn't allowed to wash, cut her hair or go out into the sun (so her new skin remained slightly pale – the whiter, the better). It must have been an ordeal, although the women who went through the confinement shrug it off with a laugh. The girl had to use a small bed (*usaga*, kil.), about four feet long, requiring her to sleep with her legs folded.[18] She had to stay in the central, darkest and most smoke-filled room of the house, the kitchen (*jiko*; see plate 12) of her father's sister (*shangazi*) or elder sister (*dada*). During her stay there, men could not enter the kitchen, for it had become an initiation "camp" (*kumbi*). Whether the girl was allowed to have companions (fellow-initiands, or an uninitiated girl as attendant [*kisepi*, kil.]) depended on the mistress of the ceremony (*mhunga mkulu*, kil.), her maternal grandmother or the female leader of the lineage. Apart from the *mhunga mkulu*, there would be a main officiant (*mhunga*, usually her mother's younger sister), a second officiant (*mnandi*, kil.), and a guardian to keep her in her house (*mjandigu*, kil.).[19]

Although sources differ, most of my informants agree that the maximum confinement was about a year, since a girl entered the *kumbi* when she first menstruated and "came out" after the next harvest in August or September.[20] Whatever the duration of seclusion, its results were painful and unhealthy. Those whom the missionaries persuaded to send their *mwali* to church on Sunday, saw them

---

[18] I could get no explanation for the *usaga*. The foetal position, however, suggests a rebirth into adult society after the girl's symbolic death by entry of the spirit-realm (*kuzimu*).

[19] Mzuanda (1958: 119–22); FN: Mama Mkoba, Kiswira, 9–11.9.89, 18.11.89, 1.10.90; Thomas Martiniani, Kiswira, 5.10.89; Mama Camillus, Kiswira, 1.10.90; Mama Mkoba and Petronilla Bunga, Kiswira, 26.10.90. Brain mentions no *mjandigu* and says the *mhunga* is from the girl's, and the *mnandi* from her father's or future in-laws' lineage (1978: 180–1).

[20] Mluanda (1971: 62), Scheerder and Tastevin (1950: 262), Schlieben (1941: 143); AC 48 (1952): 7; TNA MF 19, MDB: "The Waluguru", by

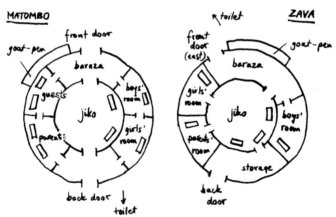

PLATE 12   *A traditional round house in Zava under construction (photograph by author, 1990). The floor-plan of houses in Zava and the houses that used to be built in Matombo was slightly different, probably to shut out the cold mountain breezes of Zava by changing the position of the doors*

Fr. v.d. Kimmenade; MP, Reports Diaconal Meetings Matombo, 30.1.47; FN: Mama Scola, Kiswira, 8.10.89, Mama Mkoba, Kiswira, 17.11.89, 26.10.90. DC Hutchins thought confinement could last two years: TNA MF 19, MDB: "Notes on the Waluguru and Wakami" (ca. 1926); Mzuanda (whose church opposed confinement) that it lasted three years in the past, and was reduced to a year in 1950s (Mzuanda 1958: 120).

suffer. Some girls only managed the climb to the mission by crawl-
ing on all fours, crying all the way. The missionaries thought they
were treated like "animals". The women I interviewed, however,
generally made light of it. They agreed seclusion was unhealthy, but
described it jokingly as something temporary, a phase one had to go
through.[21]

Kufungwa subjected the girl, through the authority of elder
women, to the lineage in general. She was removed from her
mother's house under the leadership of one of the senior women of
the lineage. Her beauty (*urembo*) on "coming out" should further
the lineage by increasing the brideprice (*mali*). Relations with lineage ancestors were newly cemented because seclusion, apart from
beautifying the girl, also put the girl in the realm of the spirits (*kuzimu*), just like the boys in their bush-*kumbi*. Seclusion transformed
the girl from a child, connected to the lineage through her mother,
into an embodiment of the lineage itself. She was now subjected to
the authority of her *mhunga mkulu* rather than that of her mother:
it was the former who received complaints if the girl misbehaved
towards her husband, and who applied corrective measures. As
senior midwife of her *mwali*, she exerted considerable control over
reproduction, which included infanticide in the case of "evil" birth
or *kigego* – children whose upper teeth came first, who were born in
an abnormal way (like twins), or whose mother died in childbirth
(see Mauss 1973: 79).[22] Seclusion in the kitchen-space can therefore
be seen as a thorough "domestication", in the most literal sense of
the word, of the girl by the lineage.

At least on the lower slopes of the mountains, the girl was
taken to the *mkole* tree some time after midnight on a day at the
end of the seclusion period. She was still in the spirit-world, so all
who accompanied her had to wear black cloth (*kaniki*) to please its
inhabitants. The *mwali* was freshly anointed with castor-oil, the
(bad) smell of which was also meant to appease spirits. Near the

---

[21] Seclusion is (nearly) abolished, so one cannot ask Luguru girls how *kufungwa*
feels. Some confined girls deserted to the mission (see p. 186). Swantz also
noted ambivalence among Zaramo girls (1986: 197–8, 401).

[22] SD 2.6.52. In Matombo, one of a pair of twins was poisoned as late as 1960.

tree, a small lean-to (*kichanja*, sw.; *ulalo*, kil.) was built, on which the main officiant sat down with the girl on her lap. The second officiant passed seven times underneath the lean-to while all sang to the spirits to rest quietly, thus reconciling them (*tambiko*) while returning the girl to the everyday world. According to Mzuanda, a future sister-in-law undressed and climbed the tree to pick leaves with her mouth (see Richards 1956: 71–2), which she passed on to the, also naked, second officiant, who distributed them to the others. The girl was sat, undressed, under the tree, and the white cloth given her at first menstruation was taken from her by the main officiant and given to the girl's keeper for secret disposal. Then followed songs which the Catholic Father Mzuanda described as "very dirty" (*chafu sana*).

The songs and other lessons taught cleanliness and discretion while washing, menstruating or having sex, and while the women sang in celebration of fertility,[23] the pubic hair of the *mwali* was shaven (some say pulled out) and collected together with the menstrual cloth. (Some men suppose that these "dangerous" things were used to make magic guaranteeing the girl's obedience to the elder women.) If the girl was betrothed, her future sister-in-law would hand her a bow adorned with white beads, acceptance of which showed the girl's agreement with the choice of her fiancé. In that case, the sister-in-law would sing *Mke! Mke! Mke!* (A woman! A woman! A woman!) under great rejoicing of the rest – including the fiancé and his relatives, who had carried her to the tree and were kept waiting nearby on the road. (If the *mwali* refused, they would quietly sneak home.) Then, the girl was brought back to the house, partly on the backs of her second officiant and sister-in-law. At home, a contest of strength was held, the women inside trying to hold the door against those pushing against it from the outside. The result would show whether the man or the woman would have the upper hand in future household relationships.

---

[23] *A-oh Chandile/Chandile tombo/Tombo dikema ugali/ugali dikema mafutsi.* The latter two sentences of this song mean: the breast gives food/food gives (grows/pp) pubic hair (I could not get an interpretation of *Chandile*). The *mkole* tree is also a fertility symbol (cf. Swantz 1986: 397).

The lessons (*galigali*, kil.), which the women nowadays regard as absolutely essential for the girl's "coming out", brideprice and marriage, continued inside. Sexual instruction proceeded by means of artefacts, or – according to Catholic men – by life-size simulation or even the act itself (Scheerder and Tastevin 1950: 263). The women denied that the *galigali* songs were "dirty", but the following songs show why some men, and most missionaries, felt the need to condemn their contents and advice:

Mke mchekecha	Woman twist your hips
mke mchekecha	woman twist your hips
neyemara pfayage	if I have finished his [thing]
katema digogo digwa matsi	and the log is cut and floats on the water
pfanitenda?	what do I do?
ah-ah ukae kuna	ah-ah there are strangers at
wageni chinyara	home, how shameful
ukae ng'aina mwana	at home there is no child
mkeme bibi kumgunda	call *bibi* from the field
tsede fiji fidogodogo	let her bring a bit of rice-porridge
mtende mkurusimba	to treat Big Lion with
mkurusimba hajaji mkimbi	Big Lion doesn't eat *mkimbi*
ah-ah ukae kuna	ah-ah there are strangers at
wageni chinyara	home, how shameful

The first five sentences refer to the woman's sexual role and her doubts about what to do afterwards; the question "what do I do?" can be answered by the lessons of how to wipe the man clean after having had intercourse.[24] *Ukae kuna wageni chinyara* may be a warning that women should not have extramarital sex – so far, nothing objectionable to Luguru men (although the missionaries

---

[24] My (male) research guide translated *neyemara pfayage* not as "if I have satisfied him" (as the next reference to the "cut" and "floating log" would suggest), but as "if I have finished his property", which might mean "taken his presents". This interpretation by means of the economic side of sex, although not implausible (see the next song), may be an example of the suspicion of Luguru men towards female sexuality.

might have suspected the enjoyment of sex here, and not without justification). But "at home there is no child" may refer to the husband's impotence, in which case a woman seeking to reproduce her lineage with another man will not be severely judged. The last sentences suggest that *bibi* (grandmother) may be asked for help during a secret liaison, and that the man ("Big Lion") should have strong food after sex (*mkimbi*, cassava-pudding, is heavy on starch but without nutritious value, so Waluguru say). The following song takes the warnings about secrets liaisons a step further:

Ghwe mlembe migodi ya mno	You *mlembe* up in the tree
kogoga wanu wajinga	you catch the stupid people
Mmale wangu kokaa Mlogolo	my husband is in Morogoro
Mmale wangu kokaa Mlogolo	my husband is in Morogoro
Kinyambo nafasi utse	Kinyambo come there is room
wase ukae yangu	lie down in my house
uleke kulonga	don't talk to me
mwanufana kohirika	my mother-in-law will hear
uleke kulonga	don't talk to me
mwanufana kohirika	my mother-in-law will hear
imwali ulonga na nani	mwali, who are you talking to?
nae, silonga na munu	I'm not talking to someone
nalonga na mbwa limkano	I spoke to a rat
umalitsa mahindi yangu	who is eating my maize
imwali mbona konitsunguluta	mwali, why try to confuse me?
imwali mbona konitsunguluta	mwali, why try to confuse me?
chungilile ng'anda chooni	What have you brought inside?

The warning is so obvious that it is almost unnecessary to add that the *mlembe* or honey-guide is a small bird (*Indicator Indicator* – Brain 1980b: 125) which can guide a famished hunter to a honeycomb but, according to Waluguru, can also lead him into great danger in the bush.[25] The song told the girl to beware when she wants to invite a boyfriend into the house when her husband is in Morogoro. ("Mlogolo" was the name of the town at the time when labour migration started; the word is now no longer used except in songs

---

[25] Cf. MSS Vermunt 6.0: "Uganga. Malaguzi. Omen".

like this.) Moreover, the mention of the mother-in-law at home shows that the girl married virilocally, a practice specific to the Eastern Uluguru area where, up to the 1950s, labour migration was most prevalent (this will be further elaborated below).

In this way, the girl was made a woman: her female identity was produced by a combination of domestic, reproductive and sexual "techniques of the body" (Mauss 1973: 80, 84; on sexual mimesis, see also Jackson 1983: 335). At the same time, the lessons show that some of the *products* of this body disposition – food, sexual pleasure – could be commodified in order to protect the household against the wrong influences of the outside world – of "Mlogolo's" attractions to potentially migrant husbands. Like the *jando* songs in the boys' *ngoma*, the *galigali* lessons introduced sexuality as an important mediation of the outside world. But whereas for the men, bodily adaption – circumcision – was necessary to have access to sexual pleasure, for the women, sexual pleasure itself needed to be instrumentalized and alienated in order to engage with the outside world. Their body was not, like the men's, directly modified to fit the outside world, but rather commodified in order to enter into exchange with the men embodying that outside world. Compared to that of the men, the power of women over that outside world was, therefore, indirect. The other side of the coin was, of course, that the women, by producing offspring for the lineage, had access to a source of power within Luguru society that was denied to the men – even to the extent of marginalizing men who were infertile.

If the girl did not have a fiancé, *mkoleni/galigali* was immediately followed by "coming out" (*mlao*) the next afternoon. (If she was betrothed, the fiancé had to come in the morning and cleave a piece of *mhalaka* wood tied up with some medicines with an axe, as a sign of potency – failure to hit it precisely in the middle produced abusive comments from the *mhunga mkulu*. Beer was poured on both axe and wood to symbolize menstrual blood and semen, after which the boy and girl were instructed in marriage matters [Mzuanda 1958: 127–8].) After all these months, the girl was washed, dressed up and taken to a crossroads close to her parental home. A good father would have arranged lavish drinking, drumming and dancing, and when this reached a peak, the girl was carried by her future brother-in-law (or another strong man) into the melée (*kunemwa*, kil.). Eyes closed, she showed off her dancing skills, her left hand waving a fly-whisk (to chase away demons), her right a beer-spoon (*upawa*; see plate 13). Her carrier had a hard job when the girls were still fat and heavy, and my female informants would recount with some retrospective delight the fear and danger of falling. "Coming out" allowed the father to show his wealth: his daughter's *kanga* cloth, the large amounts of beer for the participants. The mother shouted out her pride: *Ndole mwanangu kakanoga!*, "Look how beautiful my child is!" (Scheerder and Tastevin 1950: 262). To this day, *mlao* is the most popular feast throughout Eastern Uluguru.

Yet it was also time for business: shortly after coming out, the girl was to be married, so brideprice discussions needed to be brought to a (temporary) conclusion. After agreeing to and paying

PLATE 13   *A* mwali *dancing at her coming-out* (mlao) *in 1989 (photograph taken by the author at Nige village near Gozo). Notice that, instead of the* upawa *or beer-spoon of the 1930s, the girl carries, next to the fly-whisk of a wildebeest tail that can whisk away lingering spirits and demons, a brand-new folded* kanga

the brideprice, a ceremony of the exchange of blood between the couple, or between two witnesses, made them into *ndugu*, relatives (Wendelini 1990: 10–12; Father G. Bombwe, personal communication). Now, they could build the house in which they would live as husband and wife. After 1945, however, more and more girls were not betrothed before or during their initiation: my female informants stressed that in those cases, the beauty of the girl was also meant to charm potential suitors into laying the opening gift (*kifungo*) at her feet during the *mlao* feast itself – another measure of the way in which cash provided the younger men with increasing independence from the choices of lineage elders.

MARRIAGE AND CASH

James Brain notes, on the basis of his research in the 1960s, that Luguru marriages were unstable and frequently ended in divorce, because of a "fairly generalized pattern" in which initially uxorilocal marriage was followed by virilocal residence after the birth of the first child. When children grew up and returned to the lineage land to which they had first degree – in this case, matrilineal – tenant rights their mother often followed them and the couple was effectively separated (1969: 126). Brain also notes that divorce was most frequent in the plains areas, where a greater degree of mobility and contact with urban centers was possible because of better communications (1969: 128). Virilocal residence, however, had only become a "generalized pattern" during the twenty years before Brain's fieldwork, and an analysis of the contacts with the non-Luguru world is needed to explain this shift.

An ideal Luguru marriage is with a cross-cousin, stable, and uxorilocal (Brain 1969: 126). Throughout all initiation ceremonies (including the installation of a *mwenye mlunga*), stability, peace, restraint and fidelity between spouses are stressed.[26] For a girl, marrying her mother's brother's son implied that she would have

---

[26] Amongst each other, however, men would whisper that the taboo on extra-marital sex should not be taken too seriously; cf. the *ngoma* songs in this chapter and appendix F.

first-degree tenant rights from her *lukolo* or mother's lineage, while her husband held them from his *mtala* or father's lineage. If a girl married her father's sister's son, her *mtala* rights derived from the same lineage as that of her husband. In both cases, the fragmentation of lineage land was countered, but most effectively when residence was uxorilocal. Uxorilocality was widely affirmed for both West and East Uluguru in the late 1920s and early 1930s.[27] Thus, cross-cousin marriage, uxorilocal residence and marriage stability mutually reinforced each other. The complex shows that the relations between lineages remained the major economic background of marriage long after the introduction of a cash economy. In his notes gathered during the 1930s, Father Scheerder still found it necessary to add the equivalent *in natura* of the brideprice of forty to sixty shillings (Scheerder and Tastevin 1950: 263). Post-World War Two accounts only give the amount in cash.

In 1952, however, the situation on the Eastern slopes had changed drastically: while in the West, uxorilocal marriage was still the rule and most people lived on land to which they had first degree *lukolo* rights, in the areas close to the gravel road from Morogoro to Kisaki (Mtamba, Mkuyuni, Madamu) and the railroad (Mikese) things had changed:

Locality	Viri/Uxori-local	1st/2nd degree land rights
Mgeta area (from census)	29%/71%	95%/5%
Mgeta area (tax register)	23%/77%	97%/3%
Matombo, Konde valley	45%/55%	93%/7%
Matombo, Mtamba area	70%/30%	26%/74%
Mkuyuni, Kinole	80%/20%	69%/36%
Mkuyuni, Madamu	85%/15%	11%/89%
Mkuyuni, Mkuyuni	88%/12%	27%/73%
Mkuyuni, Rudewa	74%/22%	56%/44%
Mikese	93%/7%	9%/91%

(Source: TNA 26/328, "Luguru Land and Lineages", H. Fosbrooke 1954.)

---

[27] Scheerder and Tastevin (1950: 263–4); TNA MF 19, MDB, "The Waluguru" by Fr. v. d. Kimmenade 1937; TNA MF 19, MDB, "Notes on the Waluguru and Wakami", by E. E. Hutchins 1929.

In the East, virilocal residence went together with a high proportion of squatters (people who, lacking tenant rights, had to pay land rent [*ngoto*] to the landholding lineage). The lineage heads in the sparsely populated plains close to the road, however, needed extra labour and therefore waived the paying of *ngoto* to facilitate the settling of new members of the community.[28] These were the areas to which young men migrated whose position in lineage politics prevented them from profiting from the cash-crop economy in their home area (Young and Fosbrooke 1960: 63). A third pattern, in Konde, Kinole and Rudewa, shows a tendency towards virilocal marriage combined with first degree *mtala* rights, and may be explained by the capacity of these fertile valleys to produce profit by cash crops for both an official landholder and his sons, something that was impossible in the drier Mgeta area.

While increasing virilocal settlement induced by the lure of cash cropping implied an increasing dependence of the household on the husband, cash worked to deteriorate women's positions in other ways. One of the main factors was that a boy no longer had to rely exclusively on lineage support for a marriage contract. Acquiring and preserving land rights became less necessary when wages from migrant labour could provide the brideprice. This had its effects on marriage stability:

> [T]he old people did not practice divorce, they had several wives but one only was regarded as the real (sic) and as a matter of fact they never departed (sic) from the real wife. What is actually being done by modern external influences is something of a divorce. The husband sends his wife simply away, asks his dowry (sic) back and if this is done publicly the divorce is a fact.[29]

The husband could never have asked "his" brideprice back when it was largely produced by his father and the senior members of his lineage, and he could only offer his labour in return. Now that his labour had acquired an independent and individual monetary value, realized by the sale of cash crops or wage labour, and

---

[28] TNA 26/328: "Luguru Land and Lineages", H. Fosbrooke 1954, p. 5.
[29] MP, Casus Matrimonii: "Enquiry into African Marriage", not dated (probably around 1940; English original).

divorced from lineage relationships, divorce from his wife also became a more individual choice.

Yet another way in which cash eroded female power was through making millet into the first cash crop in Uluguru (see p. 138), which removed most women from the production of the basic beer-crop, and made them dependent on the financial assets of their husbands for the vital task of organizing labour and redistributing wealth through beer-parties. Moreover, while the requirement to pay tax put an extra burden on the man's shoulders (for only the male head of the household was supposed to pay tax), it also drove him to go out and earn money elsewhere. Teachers, carpenters and other labourers of the mission were away from the house and fields during a large part of the day, increasing the burden of work for the women (even if the possibility of buying millet absolved them from growing it themselves). For the women's small retail trade, however, cash was a benefit. They could sell the products of their own labour and retain some kind of independent income in that way. In some cases economic individualization countered the trend towards increasing dependence of the women (Poewe 1981).

We are now in a position to understand why the association of virilocal marriage and migrant labour with extramarital affairs was made in so many *ngoma* songs. The migrant labourer must not have made a dependable husband: the missionaries noted that "he is inclined to get another woman (in the town or plantation/pp) who may please him more than his real wife. The wife at home when she does not get the things she needs will naturally look out for another man".[30] Especially when the couple had settled virilocally, the woman had few independent sources of income, since she could not draw on the labour of her own lineage for agricultural production. The message of the second female initiation song is clearly economical: if your husband is in Morogoro, better find another household asset. As has been pointed out in other cases (Bledsoe and Mandeville, cited in Strobel 1982: 117, 120), the cash economy

---

[30] MP, Casus Matrimonii: "Enquiry into African Marriage", not dated (probably around 1940; English original).

made boyfriends, and the active sexual power to attract them, more of an economic necessity for women whose marital and kinship network broke down under its influence.

Thus, the business conducted at the "coming out" ceremony must have changed under the influence of the cash economy. The alliance between lineages was no longer paramount, and increasingly replaced by the exchange of commodities: the kind of "paying for the woman's vagina" recorded by Caplan for the Swahili of Mafia Island (which also goes together with teaching the girl that sex is a powerful social lever; 1976: 28). In terms of "techniques of the body", this implies a shift from the breast (*tombo* [kil.], a homonym for "lineage") to the vagina, and Luguru female *ngoma* routines were sufficiently flexible to stress alternative means of reproducing the household when the lineage as source of land and labour became less important as a means of domestic production. While a girl used to become a wife on her way to becoming a mother of and power in the lineage, now she became a wife or mistress to complement the diminishing power of the lineage. This partly explains why seclusion – the domestication of the girl for the lineage – more or less disappeared under the pressure of mission and government, while *mkoleni* lessons and *mlao* transactions are still very much alive.

THE *MWALI* AND THE MISSION

Each time that the subject of female initiation cropped up in my conversations with Mama Mkoba and Mzee Mloka, I felt that they disagreed on its necessity. Mzee Mloka couldn't understand the need for the rite: as a true Christian, he denounced its superstitions and thought the girl was only spoiled by its sexual lessons. While he argued, Mama kept quiet and exchanged knowing, and slightly amused, glances with her daughter or granddaughter, although she agreed that seclusion was often unhealthy and did not seem to regret its disappearance. Likewise on a larger scale: the attempts of the missionaries to prohibit the rite in the 1930s were supported by Christian men and opposed by their women (cf. Swantz 1986: 247). The latter argued that they were *not* heathens and that the rite was "tradition" (*mila*), independent of "religion" (*dini*), and could not be skipped.

The Alsatian missionaries seem to have acted against it most severely: they cut down the *mkole* trees (which was also a way of obstructing the boys' *ngoma*), and fulminated against the rite itself, especially against the girls' seclusion.[31] Their Dutch successors were a little bit less severe. In October 1940, Father De Vries, the first Dutch Superior of Matombo mission, issued the following proclamation:

1: Each Christian mwali has to be sent to Church to hear Mass on Sunday as befits all Christians.
2: If she is really ill on Sunday she will pass the news on to the Mother Superior (of the German Sisters/pp) on that day.
3: The religion commands that bad customs and bad teachings are left out.
4: The mwali will be taken care of by her mother or by Christian relatives, not by non-Christian relatives.
5: The mwali will be sent to the Mother Superior on each day she goes to Church.
6: The mwali will be trained to work and to walk about so she will not be unable to come to Church on Sundays.
7: If the mwali fails to live up to this law she will be penalized by the mission.[32]

Father De Vries' proclamation was supported by a similar announcement by Sultan Kingo, which the Father hoped would be spread among the Christians by the Catholic (lay) Action committee, which consisted, as noted in chapter two, only of men. Indeed, De Vries' proclamation, and the actions of his colleagues, were in line with Catholic ideas about accomodation: removing those traits of a custom that are offensive to the Faith in order to "Christianize" it.[33] Bishop Hilhorst emphasized that the missionaries ought to go slow in their attempts to abolish the rite. In Mgeta,

---

[31] MD 19.6.27, 6.12.27, 30.12.27, SD 21.7.40, KD 12.10.46; FN: Mzee Stefani Sabini, Kiswira, 10.10.89, Mzee Petri Mloka, Kiswira, 19.11.89.

[32] MD Oct. 40.

[33] Compare this Catholic tolerance to the fate of Kingo's decree, which, though inspired by DC Hutchins, was not endorsed by the Provincial Commissioner, who saw it as a covert accomodation to a rite which civilized people could not approve (TNA 61/87/B: PC Eastern Province to Hutchins, 24.9.38, 4.10.38, Hutchins to PC Eastern Province, 30.9.38, 20.10.38).

special masses for *wali* were held so they would not have to sit in church together will all those for whom they were ritually dead. A special congregation of marriageable girls was formed which was to develop into a girls' boarding house. Confession allowed a woman to admit her presence at the *mkole* tree and be readmitted to communion after her penalty.[34] The thing that could *not* be accomodated to in a "Christian" way was female power over women's bodies.

Nowadays, most missionaries stress the fact that they opposed the rite because of its ill effects on the girl's health, and because it prevented them to come to church. However, they were also suspicious of the *ngoma* because of its obscenity and what it did to the sexual consciousness of the girl. Although it is not clear to what extent the missionaries shared knowledge about the sexual teachings in the rites, Father De Vries' proclamation mentioned and prohibited "bad teachings". The Bishop's council advised to have pre-puberty sex instruction replace the teachings of the *ngoma*, especially when the girls were in the mission boarding house (*utawa*). Boarding pupils could not be initiated. In the 1960s, some of them asked a Father to give them sexual instruction in order to remove this disadvantage *vis-á-vis* the *wali*.[35]

The *utawa* was run by the Sisters of the mission and provided at least a number of Christian girls with an alternative to the *ngoma*. One of the most often recounted conversion stories of the missionaries was that of Magdalena of Mgeta, who refused to live with her future husband before her marriage, was refused by him, his family, and her own parents in return, and fled to the mission to become the first Luguru Sister.[36] Other girls, too, resisted the wrath of parents and future in-laws and fled to the mission because they wanted to continue their education to become either a teacher or a Sister.

---

[34] MD Oct. 40, see also SD 4.8.40, 8.8.40; IPAC 1b: 285; KMM 77.710: 6; MP, Reports Diaconal Meetings Matombo, 27.1.43; MP, Decreta et Documenta, Theological Conference Morogoro 9.9.48, Program Big School Safari by Fr. Scheerder, n.d.

[35] IPAC 1b: 000; IPAC 14b: 131; KMM 710/1a:166; KMM 447/2a: 342; MP, Reports Diaconal Meetings Matombo, 13.6.45.

[36] KMM 77.710: 6; BHG 28 (1932): 172–3, 38–42 (1946): 142–3.

The Singiza diary recounts several stories of girls fleeing from becoming a *mwali* and, when a Father brought them to the Mhonda or Ilonga secondary schools, being pursued by their relatives all the way. There is even one story of a girl who, after a struggle, was allowed to remain in the *utawa* by her parents. However, when she visited them for a few days, believing they had given up their opposition, she was drugged and immediately secluded. (She went mad and died young.) Some missionaries say she was not the only victim of such excessive parental care.[37] Thus, the harsh way in which the authority of the elder women could be objectified in the *ngoma* alienated some of the girls and led them to seek a different life through the channels of the mission.

MARRIAGE, CHRISTIANITY AND CHURCH LAW

One of the most important strategies of the missionaries towards conversion can be summarized by the concept of the "Catholic family". Good Catholic unions would produce children raised in a good Catholic milieu, and because Catholic rule, both within and outside of the mission's field of operation, depended on an indigenous Catholic elite which had gone through all the church's disciplinary institutions (school and seminary in particular), it was only through the Catholic family that the required recruits could be produced. Catholic marriage was the precondition of Catholic family life, and therefore marriage troubles were the missionaries' prime concern. *Safaris* and council meetings were mostly devoted to marriage problems. Because many Waluguru preferred a trial marriage, many young Christians were, at one time or other, excluded from the sacraments because the boy and the girl were already living together without having married in church. The boy and girl had to separate, confess, do penance, and preferably marry before they could be allowed to receive the sacraments again. The missionaries were on their guard to prevent "immoral" contact between the betrothed, whether they were working together in the field or

---

[37] SD 31.1.44, 13.1.45, 12.11.51, 22.12.51, 7.1.52, 1.9.52, 18–20.10.52, 12.2.54.

living together at the girl's parents' house. It was only shortly before and during Vatican Two that the missionaries started to discuss the fairness of the law that was so strict about "concubinage" (*hokken*, NL).[38]

Once a couple was married, it should be kept together, even in those cases where that was not really fruitful or just. It was the example that counted, because only through the example of married men and women could their children be persuaded to follow the same path. When a "good" Catholic girl had remarried after divorcing her impotent first husband, all her "goodness" could not prevent the missionary from refusing her the sacraments, however much he sympathized with her. A dying man who wanted to be converted had to send away the woman who cared for him because she was his second wife, despite the fact that the priest felt it was "inhuman" and "weird" to have to do so. When fiancés started to live together before the marriage had been concluded in church, their parents, mother's brothers and other relatives who were thought to be in a position to force the children to rectify the situation, could not receive the sacraments either. It was a *sheria kali*, a harsh law.[39]

It was the *legal* aspect of marriage which differed most profoundly from Luguru practice. Marriage in church retained something of its initiatory dimension: it brought the initiands into a new world and invested them with new tasks and possibilities. But the functioning of the institution into which the newlyweds were incorporated was predicated on the use of clearly defined limits – defined by church law – that were supposed to keep the married individuals in place. It was less the *content* of church laws than the *legal form* itself that changed the life of those who fell under its jurisdiction. The content of church law had, in practice, to be interpreted, and was regularly evaded by both missionary and Mluguru (as I argued in chapter two). While Bishop Wilson trusted the Fathers' discretion in solving marriage problems, Hilhorst (who

---

[38] KMM 710/1a: 260; MP, Reports Diaconal Meetings Matombo, 1942–7: passim; IPAC 15a: 512, 15b: 000, 270, 16b: 088.
[39] KMM 43/1a: 245, 708/2a: 187; FN: Mzee Petri Mloka, Kiswira, 5.2.90.

graduated *cum laude* in Canon Law) never gave them as much free-dom. The incest prohibition on cross-cousin marriage was cheerfully ignored by some Fathers, and those who dared could always keep silent about a marriage that, though "legally" dubious, did not harm the general strategy of creating and maintaining Christian families. Hilhorst, on his part, tried to avoid complications by declaring all "pagan marriages" to be "doubtful" (which left considerable leeway for admitting pagans into the church), but his opinion was not a legal act and did not carry weight with his missionaries.[40] But these conflicting interpretations and attempts to evade the contents of church law were probably a major means of making the legal form itself practically relevant to marriage in Uluguru.

Church law spelled out that Catholic marriage should be based on a *matrimonium legalis naturalis* – in this case, a "legal" Luguru marriage. To make sure his Fathers did the right thing, Bishop Hilhorst asked one of the veteran Alsatians, Father Lemblé, to out-line this Luguru "law". This is Lemblé's report on Matombo area:

> *Matombo*: stabilité de l'union admise comme idéal et préferable en divorce – monogamie semble prévaloir parmi la jeune géner-ation païenne (...) La dot consolide l'union (...) La 1ère union est la seule légitime – la femme de la 1ère union est appellée mkubwa ou mke wa haki (...).[41]

This version of Luguru norms was instituted as "legal natural marriage" (or *ndoa ya sheria*) and consecrated in church. But its legality was imported: the Bishop raised a set of Luguru practical norms to the status of "laws" existing independently of practice and intended to regulate it. Although Father Lemblé still formulated some of his answers "normatively", in terms of an idealized regular-ity rather than an absolute standard for conduct (*admise comme idéal, semble prévaloir*), when legalized, the ideal formulated and employed *in* practice was now used to "rule" *over* practice.[42]

---

[40] MP, Casus Matrimonii: Dubia Matombo, October '40, De Vries to Hilhorst, 22.1.41, Hagenaars to De Vries, 4.2.41.

[41] MP, Casus Matrimonii: Lemblé to Hilhorst, 12.7.36.

[42] "Norms", unlike "rules", cannot be "broken" and are used like weapons in a duel (Greenhouse 1982: 61, 64). Legal anthropologists often confused rules,

Just as the commodity form "serves to 'extinguish' the 'memory' of use-value and concrete labour, so too the legal form functions to extinguish the memory of different interests and social origins" (Balbus 1977: 576). If money measures and creates fetishized goods – commodities – then law measures and creates fetishized bodies: in-dividuals (1977: 575, 579). In church law, married individuals were created by a careful management, a trimming-down, of their personal histories and the network of relationships it had produced. Take the case of Luanda Ngogole, who could not be baptized together with his second, faithful and pious wife because his legal wife Teresia (baptized when they were still married) had left him. Despite the fact that Luanda was not able to understand why he had to suffer for his wife's misdemeanours, he was not admitted to the sacraments. The limits imposed on his biography by the legal form of marriage effectively excluded the fact that he was not responsible for the divorce, as it excluded his subsequent pious life. The opposite happened to Bernardi Mkude, who wanted to marry in church despite having been a Muslim for some time. On the pretext that he hadn't received a Muslim baptism (another form that could be, but wasn't, legally inscribed in his biography) his Muslim history was declared null and void so Bernardi could marry. The legal form asked for an either/or decision on whether an act was going to be registered in someone's official individual biography – if so, the rest of his or her history, including the accumulated multiplicity of roles on which so much of the women's power depended, could be deleted.

The choice of such legal limits in relation to Luguru practice (which was meant to counter the proliferation of desertions and divorces) was difficult. Because the brideprice was never paid at once, Father Lemblé's statement that it was the consolidation of

---

norms and practices by arguing that behaviour is "governed" by "implicit" rules or norms (see, for example, Bohannan 1967: 45). Such "fallacies of the rule" (Bourdieu 1977: 22) have been criticized (Comaroff and Roberts, 1977, 1981; Nader and Yngvesson 1973). The distinction of rules, norms and the regularities of practice is especially crucial to the study of colonial legal history (Chanock 1982).

marriage had insufficient legal status because it did not fix a point in time from where someone could be said to be married. Father Scheerder insisted on the full payment of the brideprice, but this was far too burdensome and often unjust. Therefore, other Fathers chose a point somewhere in between, when, for instance, only half had been paid. Again, it was not so much the actual content as the legal form of the limit that transformed a historical process of exchange between lineages into the fetish of the married individual.

Legal treatment, and especially *baraza* and confession, also modified the allocation of blame. If something went wrong in a Luguru marriage, this was discussed by the lineages: it was their relationship which had been disturbed and their representatives should rectify it. The fact that the whole network of relatives was denied the sacraments because of the sins of one Catholic married, or not-yet-married, couple shows how conscious the missionaries were of this process of rectification. But in Catholic marriage, these lineage relations were no longer sufficient: whereas at the *baraza*, the presence of Catholic elders guaranteed that considerations of Luguru "law" were duly taken care of, the Father had the final word. He defined both sin and penance individually, in private consultation with one of the spouses during confession. Thus, the mission shifted the emphasis in Luguru marriage practice from lineage relationships to the married individual.

Moreover, in the event of transgression of church law, one's relatives became a liability instead of an asset, a disciplinary, rather than an enabling institution. If fiancés refused to obey church laws by living apart until they were married, the missionaries pressurized them through their relatives who, even when innocent of the decision, could not receive the sacraments while the couple lived in sin. Thus, legal intervention created an antagonism between individuals and their family groups that, while meant to strengthen discipline along family lines, also worked to achieve the opposite: an escape from family control. If a girl was unhappy with a partner which her parents' lineages forced on her, the church ceremony provided the only way to publicize this effectively: when the officiating Father asked the girl whether she wanted this man as her lawful wedded husband, she could deny it in front of the whole

Christian community.[43] This was impossible before the church ceremony, for if the girl told the missionary of her preferences, he
would inform the parents, who could then informally coerce the
girl to obey anyway. In contrast, the girl's public and quasi-legal
refusal while the marriage ceremony was in full swing promised a
freedom from the demands of the lineages similar to that of the
girls fleeing to the mission's *utawa*.

Lastly, Catholic marriage law cancelled the positive contribution of "instable" and multiple liaisons to someone's social position.
As we have seen, Father Lemblé tried to "fix" the "real" wife of the
polygynist. Polygyny in Uluguru was mostly restricted to big men,
who enhanced their power base by the multiplication of relationships through marriage. Although most Waluguru were monoga-
mous, the fact that a new marriage did not necessarily cancel out
the relationships of a previous one made this multiplication of relationships important to many more than just the small élite of big
men. I profited from it because my second guide, Camillus, had an
astounding number of in-laws (*shemeji*) held over from previous
relationships (none of them ever consecrated in church). Although
Camillus was required to help his (former) in-laws in some
respects, it was more important that these relationships smoothed
his, and therefore my, entry into places in Uluguru where my work
was little known or understood. Similarly, they were an asset in
Camillus' usual work as a travelling tailor. This marriage flexibility
also benefited women, because the uxorilocal settlement of children
generally guaranteed some support from their father even after the
mother had returned to her own lineage or remarried in another
location (Brain 1969: 176). Thus, Catholic marriage law, by setting
limits to the multiplication of relationships and inscribing these
limits in someone's biography, helped produce a shift from the
"dividual" personalities of initiation to the fetishized individuals of
Christian discipline.

Women suffered more from this form of individualization
than men. Men had easier access to individual power – selling labour
for cash is, after all, an individualistic economic practice. Men were

---

[43] Examples in SD 27.7.51, 29.12.52, 26.11.53.

away more often, and therefore less subject to supervision by the mission. Individual men working in Morogoro were hard to press into faithfulness to their wives, while the women who stayed behind were close to their relatives through whom missionaries enforced their sanctions. If the mission's legal practice reinforced the process of male individualization which the cash economy and the British demand for tax (from male householders) had set in motion, the collective defense of women against the uncertainties of marriage to a migrant labourer through the teachings of female initiation was outlawed by the mission. The commercialization of sex was of course out of the question; neither did the mission improve life for the women by condemning *onanismus conjugalis* (which satisfied the husband during the two-year period in which Luguru custom proscribed genital sex between the birth and weaning of a child). Moreover, many missionaries' attempts to hold a married couple together were biased against women, for most accounts of "beating up a marriage" (see p. 97) or of peaceful attempts to reconcile a couple refer to the culprit in the feminine.[44]

CONCLUSION: INITIATION AND DISCIPLINE

As argued in chapter three, Catholic marriage indicated Christian life and cash cropping: at times of large-scale migration or threat of migration (as during the Second World War), girls were less interested in marriage since it hampered their ability to respond to that situation. In areas such as Kasanga and Singiza, where cash cropping was not as important as wage labour, the resistance of girls against marriage was notorious: "You will die with this same man" (*utakufa na bwana huyuhuyu*), the girls told the Father, implying that it was better to be flexible and not tie yourself permanently to a single husband.[45] In Matombo, where cash cropping – based on lineage land holdings – was more intense, and where the women

---

[44] IPAC 6b: 139; 9b: 326, 355. MP, Reports Diaconal Meetings Matombo, 27.1.43; MP, Decreta et Documenta, Theological Conference Matombo, 19.8.49.
[45] MP, Reports Diaconal Meetings Matombo, 4.1.45.

themselves needed no help to bring their produce to the Mtamba market (only 45 minutes away), unions seem to have been more stable. As we have seen in the previous chapter, the attractions of Christian life appear to have been more intimately related to cash cropping, while labour migration, on the contrary, tended to diminish its relevance.

We have seen how the female *ngoma* incorporated the possibilities of this situation. Both the boys' and the girls' *ngoma* addressed the shift from a position in lineage relationship to a more individualized participation in the politics and economy of the colonial world. For the men, the diminishing relevance of local power balances between the generations led to the gradual disappearance of their *ngoma*. For women, the decreasing importance of their ties to the lineage produced by the colonial administration's stress on male command of land distribution, by virilocal marriage, or by male labour migration, decreased the number of resources on which they could fall back while increasing their domestic uncertainties. The female *ngoma* adjusted to this by reducing (if under pressure) the length of the period of seclusion – which "domesticized" the girl – and by introducing a commercial note into its teaching of female sexuality. The continuing tensions between the sexes in the domestic balance of power – if anything, exacerbated by the fact that male migration has now become ubiquitous (Van Donge 1993) – explains why this *ngoma* is still a viable element of Luguru education and has not disappeared like its male counterpart.

The resistance which elder women put up against the missionaries' attempts to abolish their *ngoma* shows how strongly they felt the mission was working against their interests. The struggle over Catholic marriage shows that mission Christianity could not always be simply imposed. Maybe even more important is, however, that it points to a distinction between different microphysics of power. Luguru initiation exemplifies the production of power as embodiment of societal possibilities. Initiation is a surrender to the transformations that others, more powerful, exert on the body, but it is transient and the body comes out "dividual", armed against the vicissitudes, multiple roles and shifting patterns of social life. In contrast, the mission's marriage strategies legalistically created and

CHAPTER FIVE

From *Mkubwa* to *Mwalimu*.
Mission Schools and the
Commodification of Knowledge

If one talks to former teachers about the history of mission education in Eastern Uluguru, one may notice an interesting correspondence between their account and a lineage head's account of clan history. Just as a lineage head starts the history of the clan with a recitation of all those who took the name of the clan founder, and of the *mama* or *bibi* of the clan, just so teachers may open up the history of education with a recitation of the Matombo Middle School's list of headteachers. The list of teachers is recited with similar solemnity, and authorizes the historical account by establishing the reciter's credentials, just as it authorizes the lineage head's account of his own predecessors. Indeed, a teacher (*mwalimu*) was a big man (*mkubwa*) among local Christians, even when he remained the inferior (*mdogo*) of the priest.[1] Many Waluguru perceived a continuity between *mkubwa* and *mwalimu*.

But there is also a significant difference between the two terms. Former teachers often retain the title *Mwalimu*, even if their age and career qualify them to be addressed as "elder" (*mzee*). *Mwalimu* is preferred: it conveys a modern form of authority also bestowed on the first head of state of Tanzania, Mwalimu Julius Nyerere, who taught at Catholic schools before devoting himself fully to the cause of Tanganyikan independence. This modern form of authority was not compartmentalized in a "religious" sphere: through the teacher and the school, the missionaries not only produced Catholics, but the colonial state's new citizens as well. The Holy Ghost Fathers' teachers followed the government syllabus in

---

[1] Alexander 1990: 1; FN: Mwalimu Leo Marki, Kiswira, 9.1.90; Adriani Nyawale, Morogoro, 31.1.90.

their primary schools, which from Standard III onwards included "citizenship" (*uraia*). The teachers themselves were taught citizenship as follows: "The school as microcosm of the state. The teacher as a village leader and his house as a model to the village. How we are governed and the work of the various government departments".[2] The *mwalimu* was (together with the Native Authorities) the embodiment of modern African power.

On the one hand, mission education in Uluguru produced (as elsewhere in Tanzania) a shift away from the political authority of a *mkubwa* to that of a *mwalimu*. On the other, this shift was not possible if missionaries and teachers did not somehow accomodate to the powers that were. Before educational discipline could try to transform Luguru bodies into "docile" and "useful" citizens (Foucault 1979: 13, 137), they had to be brought within its sphere of operation by strategies of exchange with, and accomodation to, Luguru practices of power. This sphere of exchange and accomodation can be highlighted by concentrating on the material mediations of the educational project (something that is rarely done in studies of colonial education).[3] For a school to produce Catholics, there had to be a plot on which a school was built, a teacher to direct it, and pupils to attend it every day. The missionaries could get none of these without active engagement and partial identification with the old *wakubwa* and the new Native Authorities.

If the missionaries could only set up their education system by accomodating to local authorities, they could not maintain this monopoly without increasingly incorporating the colonial state's curriculum (including *uraia*) and using its financial assets as well. Government supported the schools mainly by paying teachers' salaries, and its

---

[2] MP, Schools-Syllabus: "Syllabus of instruction for the Vernacular Teacher's Certificate – 3 years' course", n.d.

[3] Studies of colonial education deal predominantly with policy, motives and initiatives of government and mission (Beidelman 1982: 95–6, 120–1, 196–70; Buchert 1994; Gould 1976; Oliver 1952; Santandrea 1980), of Africans (Gray 1990a: 144, 182–9; Ranger 1965), or their struggle over the curriculum (Anderson 1970; Ball 1983; Sifuna 1977–8). Berman (1975) gives a competent overview.

demands tended to secularize the mission school by thus increasing its control of teachers' qualifications. Because grants were given to missions, not to the church, the missionaries had to reconstitute themselves as employers of African white collar workers (Oliver 1952: 282). A distinction between religious and profane teaching was introduced at secondary school level around 1926, and institutionalized by the separation, in the late 1950s, of primary school from catechetical centre (the latter being dedicated to religious teaching only).[4]

Thus, the shift from the power of *mkubwa* to that of the *mwalimu* implied the increasing hold of commodified forms of authority – power objectified in diplomas, curricula and money – on the process of education in Uluguru.[5] As I hope to show in the following chapter, such commodified power could only be introduced on the basis of a prior development of forms of discipline. Such microphysical manipulation corresponded, at the bush school level, with Luguru forms of initiation; at the other extreme of the system, at the Teacher Training School (TTS) it corresponded with the most severe of European disciplinary regimes, that of the public school and the seminary. These two extremes of the system were in existence from the 1920s, the beginning of the period under review. The middle sectors, primary and middle school, through which the individualizing, commodifying and secularizing influence of the state's subsidies, diplomas and curricula were brought into the Uluguru mountains during the 1940s and 1950s, were added later. I will first sketch the construction of the schooling system in Uluguru that independent Tanganyika inherited in 1961. Then we will have a closer look at the material mediations of the school (plot and building, catechist, and pupils) and their social implications. Lastly, I shall briefly discuss the disciplinary regime of the higher echelons, the TTS in particular.

---

[4] Interestingly, a similar separation characterized the simultaneous decline of the minor seminary in the Netherlands in the 1950s and 1960s (ch. 2, p. 77).

[5] I take "commodification" to refer to the acquisition of "exchange value" by "objects, persons or elements of persons" (Thomas 1991a: 39; see also Balbus 1977).

FORGING A GOLDEN CHAIN: MISSION SCHOOL AND GOVERNMENT

The Vicar Apostolic of Bagamoyo, Bartholomew Wilson, noted the (for him) appalling lack of unity displayed by representatives of the Protestant churches during an important education policy meeting with Governor Cameron in September 1925. One of the High Church members even defected to the Catholic camp during the discussion. In contrast, the Italians, Dutch, French, Irish, Germans and Swiss of the Catholic church presented a "unanimous and neat" front which promised to do the work of schooling in return for the government's subsidies. A few months later, Wilson had already presented an elaborate plan for a Teacher Training School which, the government had proposed, should be built in Morogoro to serve the Southern and Eastern Provinces' demand for qualified teachers. Indeed, Catholic unity put a much larger source of funds at the disposal of its Tanganyikan missions than what was available for Protestants. After only a year, on December 8, 1926, the TTS in Morogoro was opened. For the next five years, it was the top teacher training school of Tanganyika Territory, receiving praise from the Director of Education in report after report. It continued to have a good reputation until Tanganyikan independence and after.[6]

Despite Protestant lack of consensus, government–mission relationships in the field of colonial education flowered through Protestant initiatives. The Christian Missionary Society had already suggested in 1921 that a system of grants-in-aid to mission schools should be introduced. Because of his switch-board position in the wiring of missionary, Colonial Office and Colonial Service interests, J. H. Oldham, secretary of the International Missionary Council, was able to direct simultaneously the governmental and missionary response to the call for "community oriented education" of the Phelps/Stokes Commission to East Africa in 1922 (Oliver 1952: 250, 263–71). Through his membership in the Advisory

---

[6] *Annales des Pères du St. Esprit* 46 (1930): 6–8, 48 (1932): 173; BG 1925–6: 122, 1927–8: 597, 1956: 382; BHG 29 (1933): 20–1.

Committee for Education in Tropical Africa (from 1923 onwards) and by writing – together with Frederick Lugard – the important statement on Education Policy in British Tropical Africa (1925), Oldham forged the link between the Colonial Office and missionary agencies, giving the former the cheapest education system they could get, and the latter much-needed government subsidies (Anderson 1970: 20; Bennett 1960: 357; Oliver 1952: 263–71). As a body, Catholics were slow to react. A Jesuit member of Oldham and Lugard's International African Institute first drew Vatican attention to the Catholic lack of organization in this respect (Oliver 1952: 273–4). Cardinal Van Rossum, the Dutch prefect of Propaganda, promptly sent out Cardinal Hinsley as Visitor Apostolic to East Africa, who, after six months of touring, told his missionaries in Dar es Salaam in August 1928 that "where it is impossible for you to carry on both the immediate task of evangelization and your educational work, neglect your churches in order to perfect your schools" (quoted in Oliver 1952: 275).

The Holy Ghost missionaries in East Africa did not need Cardinal Hinsley's exhortation. To the north, in the Vicariate of Zanzibar, Mgr. Neville had already been convinced by the arguments of the indomitable Father Witte, one of the first products of the Dutch branch of the Congregation, to start catechist training, and Kabaa school was founded under Witte's leadership in 1925.[7] Already in 1924, the Tanganyikan Bishops planned a system of education which provided for an *Ecole Supérieure* in Morogoro, and as we have seen, Mgr. Wilson was quick to act upon it. The Holy Ghost Fathers' quick response to educational developments is often attributed to the presence of the Irish Fathers, the most education-minded of all nationalities represented in the Congregation. The choice of Morogoro as location of the Teacher Training School was the result of the fact that only there, (Irish) Fathers with the degrees required for secondary education were present. Irish Fathers acted as Education Secretaries of the Vicariate until the

---

[7] De Jong 1974: 66; not 1927, as Anderson (1970: 22) assumes. For Kabaa, see p. 231–2.

Second World War, although with increasing assistance from their qualified Dutch *confrères*.[8]

However, developments towards government-sponsored education were regarded with suspicion by other missionaries. In Kenya, members of Mgr. Neville's council doubted – to the despair of Father Witte – whether the interests of religion would be served by the profane activities of the schoolteacher (De Jong 1974: 54–5). Father Scheerder recalled that his first Superior, Father Hürth of Mgeta, doubted the wisdom of having teachers salaried by government; he told his younger colleague that they were going to be "tied with a golden chain": when teachers were going to be paid by government, they would no longer think of themselves as mission teachers and neglect their religious duties. Indeed, the Tanganyikan Bishops decided in 1924 not to accept government subsidies for this reason. As we shall see, suspicion was justified, but the Fathers had no choice. The bush schools had proven themselves to be an extremely effective method of proselytization, partly because they taught reading, writing and arithmetic next to the catechism. The government was in a position to prohibit the bush schools (except for religious teachings), and the fact that Wilson held an eloquent plea for the fundamental importance of the bush-schools at the Dar es Salaam Education Conference in 1925 testifies to the fact that the missionaries were actually afraid that this might happen.[9] Thus, while some missionaries enthusiastically embraced government subsidies, those who were reluctant also had to go along with the forging of this golden chain.

At first, progress was slow in Uluguru. It seems the schools of the big mission stations were brought "up standard" (made to conform to government regulations for primary schools) in the years after the 1925 conference. Often, a Sister of the Precious Blood, a congregation with a distinctive emphasis on education in

---

[8] BG 1925–6: 48–9, 1956: 383; BHG 29 (1933): 20; TP, School and Education Matters: Education Dept. Circular 33, 1931, distributed by EdSec Butler; MP, Registration Schools/Teachers: EdSec Slevin to Fathers, 7.4.37, EdSec Wallis to Fathers, 8.2.38.

[9] BG 1925–6: 48–9; KMM 710/1a: 260; BHG 29 (1933): 150.

its spirituality, was put in charge of the mission school. The missionaries do not seem to have shared the government's emphasis on vocational and agricultural training (advocated by the Phelps/ Stokes commission), although they had to include it in their assisted schools (cf. Anderson 1970: 21; Ball 1983). Faced with a lack of cooperation on the part of administrators, some missionaries thought that Indirect Rule did not agree with native education, although other missionaries shared the Indirect Rulers' suspicion towards educated Africans. Relationships with the British were ambivalent in other respects: some of the Fathers found inspections too critical and directed at minimizing the efficiency of the Catholic schools. They thought this was caused by envy: even though the missionaries spent much less money on a school, theirs were better than those set up by the government.[10]

The move to create assisted schools in the Vicariate was brought to a halt by the Depression. The Education Secretaries of the missions were told that the financial position of the Territory made an increase in grants-in-aid for 1931 impossible. At the same time, the Vicariate sought to alleviate its financial troubles by insisting that every responsible Father should exert himself to turn his mission schools into assisted ones. The Matombo Fathers responded to this by trying to turn Kisemu (Gozo), Tawa, Mtombozi and Mtukila into assisted schools in 1932, but they failed (these schools were only registered in 1937). Registered schools were introduced ten years after the first contract between government and mission in 1925. An assisted school fulfilled government standards when it was built of bricks and sheet-iron, equipped with "writing accomodation" (slates and pencils, mats or benches), four Standards and

---

[10] The Matombo mission school was subsidized in 1928 at the latest (MD 18.12.28). In 1926, the Education Department tried but failed to subsidize the Matombo carpentry workshop as a vocational school (MD 17.11.26). On suspicion towards educated Africans: Ball 1983: 247; Chief Patrick Kunambi, FN i. On relations with government, BG 1927–8: 92; BHG 29 (1933): 168; KMM 710/2a: 030, 099; TD 17.3.39; in 1946, Government spending for the same education was still about double of mission expenditure (TP, School and Education Matters: Central Ed. Comm., 11.9.46).

two teachers with a certificate from a Teacher Training School (while the other teachers should be licensed). If these conditions were met, the government paid 75 per cent of the teachers' salaries (the mission took care of the rest) and gave grants for equipment and buildings. The registered school was somewhere in-between the assisted and the bush-school, without subsidy but liable to get a grant soon. Registration was possible when the school possessed a licensed teacher: someone who had not obtained a TTS certificate but possessed some teaching experience or other qualifications. A registered school should have a good building, two standards teaching the government syllabus and writing accomodation for standard II.[11]

In retrospect, the creation of the registered school appears like a symbolic move by the government to increase its hold on mission education. A registered school did not receive subsidy, it was not inspected; in fact, the government did not do anything about it except registering it and licensing its teachers. Nevertheless, the missionaries complied. In 1937, the Holy Ghost Fathers' Education Secretary urged the Fathers to apply for licenses, as the conditions to obtain them were very easy. In the same year, the Matombo Fathers wanted to register eight schools. Other, more remote missions responded slower. In 1943, the Education Secretary (now a Dutch Father) urged the speedy application for licenses, as conditions were becoming increasingly strict.[12]

By that time, the general slump in which Depression and World War had plunged education policy in Tanganyika was coming to an end. In 1944, there were plans "to upgrade the school movement". A Central Education Committee of the Vicariate was erected in order to

---

[11] Teachers could get a license when they sat for the TTS exam but failed, spent at least two years at the Training School, had a year experience in an assisted school or were otherwise qualified (e.g. failed seminarists). BHG 29 (1933): 151; TP, Schools and Education Matters: Education Dept. Circular 33 (1931), Central Ed. Comm., 31.7.44; MP, Meetings: Vicariate Council, 20.11.32; MP, Registration Schools & Teachers: Lemblé to EdSec (draft), 1937, EdSec Slevin to Fathers, 7.4.37; MD 20.11.32, 30.11.32, Jan. 33.

[12] MP, Registration Schools/Teachers: EDSec Slevin to Fathers, 7.4.37; Lemblé to EdSec (draft), 1937; EdSec Hagenaars to Father Willem, 30.4.43; SD 19.5.39, 23.7.39, 11.6.40.

coordinate the work with an eye on continuous improvement in line with government demands. The aspirations of the Committee clearly show a shift from religious interests towards more profane concerns:

> Every school should grow to the best type [...] Better half a school than none at all. Better a school without catechism than none at all. Those who refuse religious instruction (e.g. Muslims/pp) should remain in the classroom and be given other work to do.[13]

New schools should be opened where there was a possibility of visiting them several times a year. No school should be closed without permission of the Bishop. Teachers should be sent to Holland or England to learn school methods and obtain proficiency in English. The Committee urged the Vicariate to take its share in the forming of a Catholic African elite by sending "real good and promising boys" to Tabora and even Makerere to get university level training, and carrying the cost of their education.[14]

It was a timely move. In 1945, Hilhorst received reports that several government officials were opposed to mission education and wanted to take over the schools. The fear turned out to be unfounded, but the government did accelerate the development of education, partly in response to complaints by a UNESCO committee in the early 1950s about the poverty of Tanganyikan education. In 1945, the Vicariate had only seventeen primary schools divided over twenty-three parishes; since 1926, none of the outlying bush or registered schools had become an assisted one. The Education Secretary expressed the hope that those schools which could be brought up to standard in four years would get grants; in the case of Matombo, the number of assisted schools would then rise from one to seven. Missionaries were urged again not to minimize the importance of the government's demands and to have more and better schools.[15]

---

[13] TP, School and Education Matters: Central Ed. Comm., 31.7.44.

[14] TP, School and Education Matters: Central Ed. Comm., 31.7.44; also MD 8.8.44; MP, Meetings: Hilhorst to Sup. Matombo, 31.8.44.

[15] KD 12.6.45; MP, Registration Schools/Teachers: EdSec Hagenaars to Retera, 6.11.45; MP, Reports Diaconal Meetings Matombo, 13.6.45; TP, Schools and Education Matters: Central Ed. Comm., 8.1.45, 11.9.46.

At the same time, the first complaint about insufficient religious knowledge among certificated teachers appeared. The replacement of all Europeans by natives in the lower Standards decreased personal surveillance of teachers by the missionaries. When English was introduced in Standard V, the missionaries feared that, on the one hand, it would make their teachers desert to other, better-paying jobs, and on the other, lead to increased moral dangers through making a wider field of reading available to them. The Central Committee maintained that paying at least a percentage of the teachers' salaries was necessary to prevent them from becoming government teachers completely. Some Native Authorities, in Muslim regions in particular, applied for a government school, which did not provide sufficient religious instruction for Catholic pupils. Every year, rows between government and mission occurred when state and mission schools which had been built close to eachother seemed to cater for the same population. The missionaries often defended themselves with the argument that they had been there first (which was true in most cases).[16]

Despite opposition and mistrust, however, government-assisted schools remained a *conditio sine qua non* for the missionaries' work, while the government also had no choice but to cooperate with Christian voluntary agencies. Government measures increasingly enveloped the missionaries' schools. In 1946, the Education Department ordered that all teachers' salaries should be brought up to government standards, depriving the Education Secretary of his right to fix them and forcing him to raise them all. The legal status of registered schools began to take practical effect when the government announced that children on the roll of a registered school could be forced by the Native Authorities to attend it. (The missionaries had to be assured that, despite the fact that a bush school was not provided for by law, it was not illegal. However, it *was* illegal to force bush school pupils to attend it.) In 1949, the prohibition to have licensed teachers work in assisted

---

[16] TP, School and Education Matters: Central Ed. Comm., 8.1.45, 30.7.45, 28.1. 46, 11.9.46, 8.9.48; Annual Returns Bush Schools 1951; MP, Government and Schools: District Ed. Comm. Matombo, 6.12.51; SD 12.3.49.

schools forced the missionaries to have certificated teachers work double sessions. The conditions for grants-in-aid were sharpened: from 180 to 200 schooldays a year, a minimum roll of ninety-five with thirty pupils in Standard I and a minimum average daily attendance of seventy-five per cent. That daily attendance was difficult to maintain in several outschools, which again increased the dependence of the missionaries on the Native Authorities and their capacity to enroll students and force them to attend the school.[17]

The mission school system could no longer function without grants. While the first applications for grants of the Tawa, Kibungo and Kitungwa schools in Matombo parish were refused because of government shortage of funds in 1946, in 1947 they were all, including Mtombozi school, assisted for fifty per cent while the grant for the mission school itself had gone up to eighty-five per cent of the teachers' salaries. While the remoter missions (Kasanga, Tegetero) also got their school assisted, the percentage paid by the government went up to ninety per cent in 1948 and ninety-five per cent in 1950 for the large mission schools and seventy-five per cent for the smaller outschools. (In the latter case, twenty per cent was paid by the Vicariate, while the local mission had to provide the remaining five per cent.) In 1953, the number of assisted schools (seventy) had quadrupled since 1945; assisted school pupils made up thirty-six per cent of the total number of mission school pupils, as compared to ten per cent in 1945. In addition, the mission administered two Teacher Training Schools (one for boys, one for girls), two Middle Schools (nil in 1945), Bigwa industrial school, two girls' boarding schools (in Mgeta and Matombo), 27 registered schools (62 in 1945) and – still – 289 bush schools (303 in 1945).[18]

At the same time, government wanted the missionaries to involve Waluguru in the support of the schools by introducing

---

[17] MP, Education Meetings & Varia: Central Ed. Comm., 28.1.46; TP, School and Education Matters: Central Ed. Comm., 11.9.46, 22.9.49; MP, Government and Schools: Mishahara ya Waalimu, by B. Leechman, 15.12.48; R.B. Armstrong, Inspection of Schools: General Remarks (1949?).

[18] MP, Registration Schools/Teachers: EdSec Hagenaars to Retera, 18.2.46, EdSec Schelen to Retera, 17.2.47; TP, School and Education Matters: Central Ed. Comm., 11.9.46, 8.9.48, 29.8.50; KD March '48, TD 3.1.49; BG 1956: 303, 343.

school fees. Parents and pupils should be instructed about the fees: "People should learn and know that it won't do to expect everything to be got for nothing. Let them get some selfrespect". During the early post-war years, small fees were introduced, at first for richer parents only: 10/- for the TTS in 1946, 1/- for primary schools in 1948. By 1949–50, the fees for the TTS, industrial school and girls' secondary education were at 100/- or more, while primary school fees had risen to 4/- and continued to rise. Although poor pupils could always be helped, and study material would be distributed free of charge, the new problem of how to devise sanctions for those people who did not pay school fees emerged from 1949 as one of the missionaries' prime concerns.[19]

By that time, the explosive growth of assisted mission schools had been checked. The exams for the Matombo and Morogoro Middle Schools in the Fall of 1955 were the worst of the whole Eastern Province, and the Provincial Education Officer, echoed by the Mission's Education Secretary, admonished the Fathers not to apply for new grants, but improve existing schools first.[20] More important was that these years saw the demise of the bush school. While the Singiza Father in 1952 already complained that the "bush-school movement" was a "languishing lot", in 1955 the law (dating from 1937) that all schools which taught secular education beyond reading need to be registered was finally enforced. That meant that catechetical centres could remain, but all bush schools would have to be registered. The missionaries were advised to register if their bush schools influenced pagans and Muslims (who might not be inclined to follow the predominantly religious lessons in catechetical centres). In that way, the gap between religious and secular education, which had already grown to the point

---

[19] Generally, fees for bush schools were not thought advisable. TP, School and Education Matters: Central Ed. Comm., 11.9.46, 8.9.48, 22.9.49, 29.8.50, Standing Ed. Comm., 5.5.52, EdSec to Fathers, 26.8.55, Acting EdSec to Fathers, 10.9.57; KD 6.1.56, 3.2.56, 6.2.56; MP, Education Meetings and Varia: District Ed. Comm. Matombo, 19.8.49; MP, Decreta et Documenta: Van Elswijk to Superiors, 20.11.53.

[20] The bad results, however, may also have been part of the revolt against the Uluguru Land Usage Scheme in July 1955 (Brain 1979).

where the Matombo Fathers complained about the "neo-paganism" of the primary school teachers, was finally institutionalized.

The missionaries feared a loss of control of the schools when in 1954, school-councils (*halmashauri ya shule*) were established with the *mndewa*, a government employee, as chairman, but these councils rarely obstructed the missionary's work, and then only through angry young TANU leaders.[21] The teachers remaining at the bush schools (now "catechetical centres") were admired by younger Fathers because of their "sacrifice": they could have earned a lot more elsewhere. Despite these enthusiasts, the mission relied for its religious instruction more and more on the discipline of the mission boarding school (*utawa* – up to St. IV); the boys or girls educated there would be able to go straight to the Sisters' school or into the minor seminary.[22] The mission tried to retain its hold and even extend it in the territory's political life by organizing its teachers in a Catholic Union and allowing them to participate in other unions, but the divergence between missionary and teachers' interest continued to grow. In 1959, the Bishop's Secretary wrote to the Fathers that there seemed to exist no harmony between clergy and teachers in many places in Uluguru. When the first African Education Secretary, Father Canute Mzuanda, told the Fathers that the government forced him to nominate African inspectors to the schools, he added that he was not afraid of *Uhuru* (Tanganyikan independence), but feared communism: "If we do not treat our teachers well, they will become our worst enemies."[23]

BUSH SCHOOL: LUGURU LAND AND MISSION POLITICS

The process described in the previous section could not occur except on the basis of the previous establishment of bush

---

[21] KD 1.11.54; IPAC 16a: 514.

[22] KD 3.4.53, 7.1.55, 20.8.54, 1.11.54, SD 10.3.52, 27.8.54, 29.9.54, MD 27.11.55; MP, Government and Schools: District Ed. Comm. Matombo, 13.4.55; TP, School and Education Matters: Standing Ed. Comm., 5.5.52; EdSec to Fathers, 26.8.55, 3.10.55, 30.11.55; IPAC 1b: 226, 16a: 514.

[23] TP, School and Education Matters: EdSec Hagenaard to Fathers, 25.2.59, Bishop's Secretary to Fathers, 27.2.59, EdSec Mzuanda to Fathers, 28.3.61.

schools by the missionaries, and despite the introduction of grants-in-aid and registration, "covering the land" (as Father Scheerder put it) by the foundation of unregistered bush schools remained the primary interest of the missionaries until about 1940. Afterwards, the war limited the Vicariate's financial ability to expand the number of catechists. After the war, the movement to create more and more assisted schools became more important and consequently, the number of schools went down because an assisted school had four classrooms and could therefore accomodate a much larger number of pupils.

In 1925, Matombo mission already had a large number of schools, but expansion continued despite the fact that many schools were transferred to new parishes like Singiza and Kasanga. The development of a parish such as Singiza shows that the placement of schools was largely determined by the wishes of the native Christians themselves: not only were flourishing schools like Lukange and Mgata already in existence before the foundation of the mission, the opening of new schools was very often determined by migration of groups of Christians to the plains areas in the south towards Kisaki.[24]

In this section I shall concentrate on one of the material preconditions of mission education in Uluguru: the plot for a school building. In Matombo, Singiza, Kasanga, and environs, the mission rarely ran into trouble acquiring it. Luguru Christians were generally eager to have a school (also because it meant a regular visit by a Father), usually granted a plot voluntarily, and built the school-chapel "á la native" (six poles and a thatched roof) for free. The main obstacle in the way of expansion was financial: Father Scheerder

---

[24] See ch. 3 and KMM 710/1a: 415; in 1927, Matombo had 51 schools (MD 30.12.27), in 1928 54 (MD Oct. 28), in 1933 (after Singiza split off) 49 (BHG 29 (1933): 168), in 1935 again 54 (MD Jan. 35), and 44 during the war (Kasanga split off in 1936; MD 11.5.40, 8.8.44); Singiza had 8 schools in 1931 (SD 4.8.31), 17 in 1933 (SD 31.7.33), 18 in 1934˙(SD 7.7.34), 22 in 1935 (SD 30.6.35), 24 in 1936 (SD 7.6.36), 28 in 1937 (SD 6.2.37, 16.5.37, Aug. 37) and 29 in 1938 (SD July 38), after which the movement petered out (in 1951, Singiza had 21 schools – SD Jan. 51). Especially in 1937 and '38, schools were founded on the request of Christians migrating south.

could no longer afford to pay his catechists when his funds ran out and had to close his schools twice, in 1939 and 1945. Although the other missions do not report such a drastic measure, the fact that Hilhorst ordered the schools to be closed in September 1939 because of the outbreak of the World War shows that the financial balance of school work was precarious as long as the mission still relied on funding from Europe instead of government grants.[25]

The ease with which expansion went on, however, conceals to what extent these peaceful negotiations relied on local power relationships. The establishment of a school was always accompanied by the introduction in the village of a new powerful role, that of the catechist or teacher (who will be dealt with in the next section). Most missionaries were not intimately involved in these power relationships, because they usually followed the wishes of a group of Christians and quickly withdrew when the situation was perceived as precarious (as in the case of the Kisaki *mndewa*, whose request for a school was not supported by his predominantly Muslim subjects). The schools of Tegetero mission, however, always faced stubborn opposition from the local Muslim community. A year after the mission was founded, Father Van de Kimmenade had six schools; his successor, Father Bukkems, had only three in 1944, while Father Guffens had only two schools open during 1950 (two others reopened in December; eight schools remained closed). In 1952, the number of open schools was back to five. The example of the Tegetero schools is the exception that proves the rule that most school establishments in Uluguru were based on tacit agreements between missionary and Waluguru about local power relationships, and I will examine them in detail to bring out these tacit agreements.[26]

---

[25] SD 16.1.39, 28.5.39, 3.7.39, 7.9.39, March '45, KD 6.9.39; after grants for building primary schools became available for outschools, the readiness to build for free declined (see MP, Diaconal Meetings Matombo, 19.8.49, MD 24.11.47, TD 2.6.50, 6.11.50, 5.12.50).

[26] SD 4.9.34; MP, Schools: Mtukila School, 20.9.55 is an example of peaceful negotiation about a plot. TD 11.10.35, Jan. '44, Jan. '52; TP, School and Education Matters: Annual Returns Unregistered Schools, 1950.

Father Van de Kimmenade was the first to experience Muslim resistance in Tegetero, when the school under construction in Nyachiro was pulled down by a brother of the new (Muslim) *mndewa* and the successor to the lineage head of the area. They argued before the DC's court that the former *mndewa* had had no right to give the plot to the Christians, and the school had to be built again on the teacher's land, which diminished the latter's status in the community considerably. Shortly afterwards, the Father recorded that, first, the new *mndewa* of Ng'enge, and later, the *mndewa* of Zinga and the lineage head of Tegetero itself, were building mosques to combat the building of the church (which in Uluguru combined, like a mosque, the functions of worship and education). When Van de Kimmenade was replaced by Piet Bukkems, relations with the Tegetero lineage head, Magoma, improved (up to the point that Magoma granted Bukkems the *milunga* – see the introduction). But Bukkems also noted Islamic opposition and his teachers found it more and more difficult to keep the schools open in the face of Muslim resistance and Muslim parents' preference for government schools. After the war, many Muslims consented to follow the mission schools but often refused to learn the catechism. The British school inspector noted in 1951 that mission school attendance was always below standards because of the large number of Muslim residents.[27]

In 1945 a new school was opened in Kisambwa, near the Kiroka plains, where Christians from the higher Matombo slopes (between Kibogwa, Tawa, Kibungo and Konde) had settled. It continued to grow while more and more migrants arrived. In 1950, the school fell in during the rains (a regular occurrence) and the owner

---

[27] TP, Lettres de la Boma: v. d.Kimmenade to Hutchins, 4.10.36, 10.11.36; Hutchins to v. d.Kimmenade, 23.10.36, 6.11.36, 18.11.36, 15.12.36; TD 2.10.36, 22.1.37, 7.5.37, 26.6.37, 6.7.38, 3.12.41, 14.12.41, 11.1.42, 16.1.42, 6.2.47, 9.2.47; TP, School and Education Matters: Tegetero School Inspection, 7.3.51. This rise in interest for the schools among the Tegetero population coincided with Bukkems "initiation" (see chapter one), which may therefore (given the resulting dispute with the mission teachers) be interpreted as part of a move to restore respect for traditional authority which was on the wane because of the school's increasing popularity.

of the plot refused to have it rebuilt. He did not turn up when Father Guffens wanted to discuss the subject with him and the *mndewa* of Kisambwa, Mwinyimvua. Those were the opening moves in a political game which sorely tried Father Guffens' patience.[28] Throughout the negotiations, Father Guffens displayed faith, bordering on naivety, in a solution on the basis of local power relationships, without taking recourse to government power (as most other Fathers would have done). Because of this faith, and the opposition of the Muslims to his school, the Kisambwa case brings into the open the tacit agreements on which most other negotiations about plots and schools were based, and I need a fully detailed description of its development to spell out these agreements.

At a first baraza in Kisambwa (June 1950), Guffens invited former Sultan Kingalu Mwanarubela, in order to convince the owner of the plot that Kingalu was his overlord and could decide on it. It didn't work (understandably, since the area belonged to a Wakumbulu lineage, not to Kingalu's Wabena). Kingalu was solemnly asked for another plot and, earning Guffens' admiration, granted one after consultation with a second landowner, Kihangire. In August, a Muslim, Salim, claimed the plot and denied that Kingalu and Kihangire had any say in the matter. Moreover, the (Muslim) *mndewa*, Mwinyimvua, was angry about the fact that Kingalu (who had held no official government position since his deposition in 1936; see Pels 1996) was involved. Guffens tried to appease him, but Mwinyimvua refused to grant the plot. The dispute came before the (Muslim) *mtawala*, who misinterpreted it: he thought that Guffens wanted to buy the plot (which, since the 1930s Uluguru Land Survey, had been prohibited to Europeans) and refused. Guffens argued that the right to the land would remain with the native owners. Despairing, he complained to the Bishop, who wrote that he had to go on, have patience and pray a lot.[29]

In November, Guffens reminded Mwinyimvua of his duties – in vain. Then, he threatened him with government action and an episcopal decree which precluded Muslims from attending the

---

[28] TD 11.6.45, 7.3.47, 11.9.47, 16.6.48, 15.8.49, 11.2.50, 10.5.50.
[29] TD 17.6.50, 12.8.50.

school, whereupon the *mndewa* consulted a few elders and asked for time to discuss the plot with its owners. In December, Guffens heard that Kihangire had gone to talk to Salim (Mwinyimvua having agreed, it seemed, to have the school), but Salim refused to part with it. In January 1951, Sultan Sabu castigated Mwinyimvua, and a few days later, the Kisambwa Muslims told Guffens that they were willing to grant a plot – but they didn't want the teacher, Augustini, to teach their children. A meeting was planned, but Mwinyimvua did not turn up. Guffens demanded an explanation, but none was given. The Father issued an ultimatum: if no complaints were received at the mission, work on the plot would start on February 12. On the 11th, Mwinyimvua called the Father to a *baraza*, to be held on the 16th. (Guffens had to be persuaded by the Christian elders to go.) At the *baraza*, Mwinyimvua and some elders offered Guffens another plot; Salim's was not available as it had been planted. However, the teacher said that it was a sham and that all of Salim's palm-tree shoots and beans had already shrivelled and died. The Father wanted to go and have a look, but Mwinyimvua refused because Salim would not believe them (which, Guffens noted, was rather unlikely when he would be confronted with six witnesses). After consultation with his Christians, Guffens decided to accept the new plot, but then it turned out that the people living on it still had to move, which would take time. Mwinyimvua made an offer of a plot across the Mbezi river, which was, according to the teacher, too far away. The Father opted, again, for calling in Salim.[30]

A *baraza* was to be held on the 23rd; neither Salim nor Mwinyimvua appeared. Mwinyimvua said he would be in Kisambwa on the 25th, but postponed it again to the 28th. Guffens let him know that both he and Salim would get a present (*zawadi*) if he would get the plot. The *baraza* was held, but Salim did not show up. Mwinyimvua promised he would call Salim the next day to the *mtawala*'s *baraza*, but Salim did not turn up. Another try was made on March 9: nothing happened. Mwinyimvua wrote that he would be in Kisambwa on the 16th where he didn't show up either. By that time, the shrivelled shoots on Salim's plot had disappeared in the

---

[30] TD 24.11.50, 4.12.50, 11.1.51, 14.1.51, 11.2.51, 16.2.51.

long grass. Guffens told Mwinyimvua to come to the mission on the 20th, with or without Salim. Otherwise, the Father would call in government support, but he still hoped they would be able to settle the question "in peace" (*kwa wema*); in that case the promise of the *zawadi* was retained. The *mndewa* did not turn up; later, the message came that he was ill. On the 25th, Mwinyimvua wrote Guffens that as soon as he recovered, "You will get the plot and you will build the school."[31]

Salim finally appeared at a *baraza* in Kinole at Kingalu's house on April 6, and, again, refused to part with the plot. Mwinyimvua reprimanded Salim for his repeated absences. Salim said that Kihangire was his inferior (*mdogo*) and had no right to decide on the plot. Another relative, Dihalile, tried to shut up Salim and a long discussion ensued over Kumbulu lineage authority in which the actual *mkubwa* of the lineage, Kumbulu, kept silent because he did not dare to antagonize any of his relatives. Dihalile, some argued, gave plots to the Kisambwa immigrants, so he would also be the one to grant this plot to the Father. Salim stoutly maintained his opposition, but under the combined pressure of Kingalu and the *mndewa* he finally said that he would reconsider his decision after he had returned from a trip to Dar es Salaam.[32]

Another month passed before Guffens finally decided to call in the authorities. He asked the Sultan to order his subordinate to grant the plot, enclosing Mwinyinmvua's letter of March 25 in which he made his promise. In the meantime, Salim had already given in, but was too late to prevent the Sultan from ordering Mwinyimvua to grant the plot (May 21st). On June 8th, Guffens gave Mwinyimvua a firm dressing-down, which, after a year of *upole* (calm) and *uvumilivu* (patience) was necessary "*propter prestigium Missionis*". *Mtawala* Ali Selemani said he would settle the issue the next week, but nothing happened. On the 22nd, it turned out that Mwinyimvua had accused Guffens before the court, among other things with the lie that he had been told by the Father to "abandon his religion" (*acha dini yako*). The court case had to be settled first.

---

[31] TD 23.2.51, 25.2.51, 25.2.51, 9.3.51, 16.3.51, 20.3.51, 25.3.51.

[32] TD 6.4.51.

On July 1st, Sultan Sabu ordered Ali Selemani to give Guffens the plot, but several abortive attempts were necessary before, on the 25th, a large *baraza* was held in Kisambwa with Kingalu, the *mtawala*, Guffens and a number of *wandewa*. Salim tried to change the plot again, but the *mtawala* measured it then and there and reconciled Guffens and Mwinyimvua. Guffens counselled his Christians not to laugh at the Muslims and left for his new mission (Tununguo) when Father Bukkems returned to Tegetero on the 27th. On October 24, Bukkems consecrated the new school under great rejoicing of Kisambwa Christians.[33]

I have presented the case in such detail to show the number of tacit agreements on which other grants of plots to the mission were based. First, there had to be a stable balance of power within the lineage controlling the land. In this case, the lineage was divided between Kihangire and Dihalile on the one hand, and Salim on the other, with a scared Kumbulu in between. Second, the mission needed the cooperation of Native Authorities. Here, it was not forthcoming because *mndewa* Mwinyimvua was on the Muslim side, as is suggested by his covert support of Salim, his persistent stalling, and occasional lie. Neither did *mtawala* Ali Selemani cooperate, probably because he was already committed to a Government School in Kinole (see note 33) and did not want to antagonize his predominantly Muslim subjects. Third, there had to be a stable balance of power between lineage leaders and Native authorities. In this case, Kingalu, the deposed Sultan, reasserted his authority as ex-sultan, lineage head and powerful rainmaker against the power of

---

[33] TD 13.5.51, 1, 8, 10, 22 June '51, 1, 3, 6, 11, 25, 27 July '51, 24.10.51; TP, School and Education Matters: Sultan to EdSec, 21.5.51; despite this victory, Bukkems warned already in 1951 about further trouble with Kisambwa Muslims when the latter applied for a Government School. This fear materialized in 1956 when Kisambwa could not be registered because it was only a 20 minutes' walk to the Government School at Kinole (TP, School and Education Matters: Ann. Ret. Bushschools, 1951; EdSec to Sup. Tegetero, 15.5.56, Sup. Tegetero to EdSec (draft), 21.5.56). There was further trouble about a plot in 1961 between a certain Bugano Mussa and his mother's brother Kumbulu (TP, Baraza: Baraza la Mkuyuni, Shauri 64 ya 1961, 11.10.61). In 1990, the parish priest of Tegetero told me that Kisambwa was still a trouble spot.

government positions (as is witnessed by Mwinyimvua's anger about calling him in).[34] Throughout, Guffens preferred to rely on a local combination of lineage leaders and Native Authorities, which he thought gave the power to grant a plot. Faced with opposition, however, he used threats and coaxed with *zawadi*, thus having recourse to means of negotiation common between unrelated strangers, in Uluguru and elsewhere (see Pels 1996; we shall see that such presents to *wandewa* were common mission policy). Only his lack of success forced him to fall back upon the highest Native Authority. Thus, we see that the missionary depended on Luguru power relationships, whether of the lineage, of the give-and-take of threat and *zawadi*, or of Native Authorities appointed by government. This was even more true of the catechist.

MKUBWA, CATECHIST AND TEACHER

The Holy Ghost Fathers often remember their catechists fondly. Without the *mwalimu*, the mission would not have been built up; they were the *trait d'union* between mission and people. Fond memories, however, go back mostly to the village catechist, the *mkubwa* of the local Christians. His successor, the certificated teacher, is less fondly remembered, while an earlier, short-lived personage, the catechist who was *mkubwa* in the more general sense of "big man" (drawing upon other than just the missionaries' spiritual power) is forgotten.[35]

The first catechists (often ex-slaves) profited from the close relationship between mission and colonial authorities. A Tununguo man, Martini Kauseni, was the first teacher of the Matombo mission school, but soon became tax-collector for the Germans and later headman (*akida*) of the Matombo area, a position which he held until the introduction of Indirect Rule. Other catechists were

---

[34] This came to a head when Kingalu Mwanarubela's sons and successor led the 1955 revolt against British soil conservation measures (Brain 1979: 185–8). I will deal with these events in a separate book.

[35] KD 1.4.55, 23.3.57; BHG 30 (1934): 119–22; OO 33 (1955): 29; IPAC 16b: 000–035; KMM 710/1a: 102.

appointed as *jumbes* (local headmen subordinate to the *akida*) by the Germans, even when they held no specific claim to local authority (such as *jumbe* Marie Pauli of Tawa). This association with colonial authority, however, was not a happy one for the Fathers: many times, a teacher who became *jumbe* took more than one wife. The Fathers would fire him, but he could only be removed from the jumbeship by the Germans, and often was not. Polygyny is significant because it seems to have been an uncommon occurrence in Uluguru *except* for big men (lineage heads in particular): it enabled them to increase their network of relationships and economic potential. Becoming a teacher or *jumbe*, or taking a second wife are all attempts to concentrate a diversity of power resources in one person.[36] In one exceptional case, the fired catechist could even raise sufficient support to get people to demolish the school by stealing wood and grass; he managed to have the schoolchildren harass his successor to such an extent that the latter resigned. Generally, however, such a concentration of power was rare. The Matombo Fathers soon saw that the mix of power resources produced bad examples for their Christians. They stopped recommending Christians for government service in 1910.[37]

The taking of a second wife happened usually in the early years of a mission (in Matombo, before the First World War; in Singiza and Kasanga, before the Second). We can assume that the practice did not continue because it guaranteed the loss of one's job. Although the catechist occupied a powerful position, his was a derived power. His resistance to the missionary's demands was limited to subterfuge (like spending his time in his fields instead of in school), desertion to better-paying jobs in Morogoro, or, occasionally,

---

[36] These cases should be distinguished from the dismissal of catechists with a *mchumba* (see ch. 4; KD 10.10.42, KD 5.7.37, SD 10.7.57, 11.8.57, 19.12.57, TuD 16.7.42) or that of "adulterers" whose own wife was barren (KD 11.7.40).
[37] MD April. 07, Aug. 08, 21.8.10, 23.6.12, 18.11.17, 11.2.24, KD 10.5.40, 9.7.40, 2.1.44, TD 22.3.42; FN: Mzee Daudi Maduga, Kiswira, 17.8.89; Chief Patrick Kunambi, Dar es Salaam, 12.4.89; Akida Martin, however, remained true to the Faith and amassed sufficient wealth – by depositing his savings at the mission – to start several shops when he had to retire from the *akidat* in 1925 (FN: Mzee Morisi Martini, Kiswira, 14.12.89).

strikes (when they thought their salary was insufficient).[38] Like the missionary, the catechist had to rely on the independent powers of lineage head and government *mndewa* for support, which explains why there are so few cases of open conflict between catechist and traditional or neo-traditional authorities on record (the Tegetero cases are instructive exceptions; the early Christian *jumbes* may also have been engaged in more struggles than the later catechists).

Thus, catechists had not much opportunity to act independently and were, in fact, scared of stirring up conflict within the village. A recurring qualification of a good catechist was that he was "not afraid" (even when his teaching left a lot to be desired). The catechist was often a young man, still very conscious of the respect due to the elders of a village, especially when he did not teach in his own village. As we have seen in the previous chapter, Father Schaegelen of Matombo appointed *wasimamizi* or overseers as helpers of the catechists to increase the latter's influence, especially among the elder candidates for baptism. Catechists were often afraid to act against people's wishes; they refused to open a school among Muslims; they feared trouble when accusing parents of truants before the court; they were afraid to teach soil conservation when Waluguru had just revolted against it. When a succesful offensive of the catechist Paulo Juma against Muslim truants was followed by Paulo's sudden death (by poison?), these fears seemed justified. Because of the rumours about the succesful bewitching of Paulo, Father Bukkems despaired of getting another man for the post.[39]

Thus, when a catechist was engaged in struggle, it was most often a struggle with one of his predecessors who had been replaced for some reason or other. The former catechist of Ukwama took a second wife and, after his demotion, even dared to resist the

---

[38] MD 19.2.29, 8.4.29, KD 15.3.57.

[39] KD 19.6.46, 2.8.47, 18.8.47, 15.9.47, TD 12.3.44, 20.10.46; TP, School and Education Matters: Central Ed. Comm., 29.8.50; MP, School Inspections: Inspection Kitungwa, 12.9.55, Inspection Konde, 6.9.55; the case of Mwandogwe, a catechist who moved from Ilonga to Vidunda after his ten-year-old son had died, also suggests that witchcraft fears existed between catechist and local population (BHG 30 (1934): 120).

Father himself. Some people of Singiza led by former catechist Petri (a leader of Catholics in other functions, such as the Legio Mariae) wanted to oppose the mission school teacher Fortunati in his work of chairing the *baraza* and inspecting minor schools. In Taragwe in Ukaguru, a headteacher feared poison because he had accused another teacher of laziness; in at least one other case the problems with a school were the result of the opposition of a former catechist (who, by the way, retained the title *mwalimu* even when deposed). Thus, even if a catechist derived most of his power from the missionary, he built up and retained influence after his deposition, to the extent of feeling strong enough to oppose his successor.[40]

The fact that the catechist wielded a derived power suggests a comparison with *jando* leaders, circumcizers in particular, who also derived their authority from the teachings of a superior and whose transmission of authority was, like the catechist's, relatively autonomous from lineage relationships. The continuity between *ngoma* camp and bush school practice that this suggests seems to have been there in other respects as well. In his recollections, a former teacher, Mzee Pius Wendelini, wrote that he entered a bush school for the first time in 1926, only to leave it the same day because the teacher gave all his pupils a beating when only one of them made a mistake. He remembers that these schools had no classes, and that one simply studied there until one reached the age of getting betrothed. He himself reentered school in 1930 (under another teacher) to leave it four years later on being baptized and ascending to the post of junior teacher, the first step in a long career in mission and government service (Wendelini 1990: 54–5). This shows that, as in the *ngoma* camp, all pupils sat in a single class, only left the school by a rite of passage (betrothal and/or baptism), and future school leaders were initially educated locally and put to work locally.

The example of Mzee Pius also shows that, in the 1930s, the gap between bush school and the disciplinary apparatus of higher,

---

[40] KMM 708/1b: 000; SD 1.3.41, 20.3.53, KD 10.5.40, 9.7.40, 2.1.44, 19.1.55; one teacher wielded additional power because he could bargain with parents to obtain children for other schools, and was in that way able to serve other teachers (FN: Mwalimu Edward, Lusangalala, 21.9.90).

government-regulated education was still large. The level of learning of the bush school was variable, determined locally rather than standardized by the syllabi of primary and middle school. Mzee Pius went straight to Standard IV after his exam, but a pupil of Konde school who thought he could not learn more at the bush school (after three years) had to join Standard II of the Matombo primary school. He maintained, however, that someone who left the Konde school after baptism knew well how to read, write and reckon, mainly because it took four years (of religious instruction, but also the three r's) before one could be baptized.[41]

Bush school teaching was in many ways close to the mimesis through songs and riddles (*mizungu*) of the initiation camp. Pupils were often taught by song, and those who were new simply joined the chorus. They sang the alphabet in sequence, copied the letters onto a slate and sang them again. Counting was taught by showing a number of sticks, at which the class had to chant the number; the procedure was then adapted to advance into calculation (which, however, hardly reached figures beyond 100; some of the teachers, my informant claimed, could not even write 1000). From the perspective of European ideals of education, this was not a didactic without dangers. The missionaries regularly lamented the "parrot-work" to which it could lead. They complained that both children and catechists recited the catechism like a gramophone, repeating it "senselessly" without being able to give the necessary explanation.[42] Some missionaries attempted to improve the catechist's methods, but without avail, because in 1949 the Education Department's general inspector complained that many teachers, and especially the uncertificated bush school teachers, made their pupils learn a whole page or blackboard by heart, so that a certain prompt word or symbol would set them off chanting it and they would be memorizing songs rather than recognizing symbols for reading. The absolute

---

[41] FN, Mzee Petri Mloka, Kiswira, 28.1.90.

[42] Given the perspective advanced in the introduction, "senseless" is not the right way to formulate it. Father de Rooij made an interesting statement in this respect: he wanted to teach the schoolchildren, who, he said, "read with their *ears*" to "*see*" (KMM 47/1b: 157; emphases mine).

sign of backwardness of a school was that pupils could not answer the first question of the catechism (*Mungu wangapi?* How many Gods are there?), showing that they had merely chanted the words without reflecting on their meaning. Similarly, in initiation ritual, both boys and girls learnt *mizungu* by heart, to come to understand them only much later. The criticism voiced by the school inspector suggests that this "parroting" was fairly widespread in the bush schools.[43]

Luguru enthusiasm for the bush school decreased shortly before and during the Second World War, coinciding with the slump in enthusiasm for Catholic marriage and baptism (see chapter three and the next section). In Kasanga it was noted that the older catechists lacked their former zeal. Their replacement by younger men, "better educated, more energetic, more impressive", often improved teaching.[44] While certificated teachers took over the didactical training of the older catechists from the missionary, the power of the bush teacher diminished. But the power of the *mwalimu* also underwent a qualitative change. The catechists' power in the community was based on the fact that they were (one of the) leaders of the local Christians, which involved many relationships beyond those of teacher and pupil. Younger teachers were, by dint of their formal qualifications, more divorced from the local community: they could be, and were, transferred more often and their transfer was more determined by their diploma than by the influence they could wield in a specific community. The catechists sometimes refused to teach outside of their own area and the missionaries tried to counteract this by giving a catechist a lower salary when he lived in his native village. Appointment and dismissal of qualified teachers were much more determined by the government; catechists who held a responsible position as inspectors of the local schools were

---

[43] MP, Government and Schools: Inspection of Schools, General Remarks, no date (1949?), by R. B. Armstrong; KD 3.10.42, 14.10.46, 2.7.54, SD 17.6.50, 18.11.51; BHG 31 (1935): 172; KMM 77.710: 11; FN, Mzee Petri Mloka, Kiswira, 14.12.89; Richards (1956: 128) makes similar remarks about the girls going through a *chisungu*.

[44] KD 6.7.38, 6.5.40, 17.11.46.

replaced by qualified school inspectors, and certificated teachers were moved from post to post according to the desires of the education authorities. Thus, it comes as no surprise that younger teachers were less involved in religious matters. Missionaries complained that they became more and more interested in money and had "no higher idea about their duties" and "little faith".[45]

The new teachers had some reason to be less motivated: before the levelling of mission and government teachers' salaries, those who held a grade from the Teacher Training School were conscious of the fact that their colleagues in government schools earned more. The problem of defection to other jobs was sufficiently serious for the missionaries to contemplate (in 1944–5) some kind of contract which tied the teachers into the service of the mission after they had received their – largely mission-paid – certificate. Although the contract was legally possible, the Education Department advised against it because it doubted its efficacy (Africans were not thought to be very susceptible to the legal weight of contracts). The practice (at at least one mission) to have the teachers pay for their education by cutting their wages for some time was illegal and had to be abolished. The levelling of wages of mission and government teachers probably checked this tendency to desert the mission for a better-paid job.[46]

The mission tried to keep the teachers within the orbit of the mission by others means: near the end of the war, a Catholic Association of Teachers (CAT) was started to keep them from enrolling in other, government sponsored organizations, and to keep them convinced of the greatness of their vocation which was perceived to be in competition with the "material outlook" of the

---

[45] MD 4.2.49, TD 1.1.39, SD 1.3.41; IPAC 16a: 600–720; KMM 710/1a: 102; MP, Diaconal Meetings Matombo: School Safari Report by Fr. Scheerder, no date (1944?); Generalia: Govt. notice no. 192, 29.6.56; FN, Mwalimu Bartolomeo Lukoa, Kiswira, 21.8.89.

[46] TP, School and Education Matters: Central Ed. Comm., 31.7.44, 8.1.45, 30.7.45; MP, Diaconal Meetings Matombo: Scheerder report, no date (1944?); before 1946, no pupil was required to pay schoolfees at the Teacher Training School.

latter. The CAT had its own journal, *Mwalimu*, which among other things reported on refresher courses, meetings of the CAT Central Board and printed obituaries. Most of its pages were, however, devoted to warnings to the teachers not to read things which were "poison" to the (religious) mind and exhortations about the teacher's "vocation". The teacher should not be a *mwalimu-kibarua* (referring to working *kibaruani*, on wage-labour) and his calling should protect him from the dangers of indifference to and ignorance about his task.[47]

The teachers, even when their salaries were paid by government for more than ninety per cent, were still said to be mission employees; they were told that every teacher should be a good catechist just as every catechist should be a good teacher. But the tide was against religious instruction. In the lower echelons of bush schools and catechetical centres, salary raises were proposed in 1944 to keep the catechists from running off to better jobs. In 1951, missionaries complained about the fact that catechists were "giving their money's worth", that is, did not do anything for their meagre salary. It became more difficult to get catechists for the bush schools, partly because the pupils themselves were no longer satisfied with the minimal education they provided and were looking for government or Native Authority Schools for their education instead.[48]

In the schools that provided better education the relationship between teachers and missionaries was also deteriorating. In 1955, the Education Secretary wrote to all teachers that many of them, especially youngsters, no longer deserved to work on a mission school as helpers of the Fathers. A true helper of the Fathers, an "apostle" (*mtume*) only second in status to him, had to teach through his example and his deeds, not just through words, because

---

[47] *Mwalimu* 3, Sept. 1952; on CAT: TP, School and Eeducation Matters: Central Ed. Com., 30.7.45, 31.3.46, 8.9.48; MP, Reports Diaconal Meetings Matombo, 19.8.49.

[48] SD 18.11.51, 31.8.57; MP, Diaconal Meetings Matombo, 19.8.49; TP, School and Education Matters: Central Ed. Com., 31.7.44, 8.9.48; some supposed catechists too lazy to look for better paying jobs elsewhere (SD 18.11.51), but others that their remaining at the catechetical centres proved they were ready to make sacrifices for their faith (IPAC 1b: 226).

that is the way in which one learns the road that leads to Heaven. (The teachers seemed to have resented the letter very much.) The Fathers wanted to fine teachers who misbehaved, but were warned by the Education Secretary that "we need them more than they need us ...". Some years later, "more democracy" between teachers and missionary was urged. Beyond that, the missionaries could only influence teachers through the refusal to grant increments. The CAT was reported to be "dead" in most missions.[49]

Exhorting teachers to remain true to their "vocation" and to hold on to their role as "prophet" to the people was evidently insufficient to counter the changes resulting from the shift from a local (if derived) position of power to one largely determined by syllabus, certificate and salary of the government – the commodities that determined a career in education. The education policy of the mission slowly shifted from local power relationships to a more bureaucratic domain that had its centre of gravity outside the mountains, in Morogoro and Dar es Salaam. A similar shift is apparent when we turn to the way in which the schools secured for themselves the necessary number of pupils to train.

BUSH AND PRIMARY SCHOOL ATTENDANCE

Mzee Pius' memoirs show that, despite corporal punishment, attendance at bush schools could not always be enforced, and was often a problem. In the late 1920s in Matombo, average attendance was sixty per cent, while in Tegetero in the 1940s and 1950s attendance at bush schools and registered schools wavered between 65% and 75%.[50] Low average attendance is explained by the fact that the

---

[49]KD 1.3.57; TP, School and Education Matters: EdSec to All Teachers, 12.2.55, EdSec to Fathers, 26.8.55, EdSec to Fathers, Nov. '56; MP, Generalia: EdSec to Fathers, 16.7.55.

[50]Primary schools were required to have a minimum average attendance of seventy-five per cent – see p. 207 above. The percentage for Matombo was obtained by comparing the numbers of pupils of 1928 (roll) to the number of pupils of 1929 (average attendance): MD July '28, July '29. For Tegetero, see TP, School and Education Matters: Annual Returns Assisted Schools, Annual Returns Registered Schools, Annual Returns Bush Schools: passim.

school had many local competitors. One of them, Islam, was, as we have seen, spurred into more intensive action by the Christian initiative to build school-chapels, so that Tegetero saw a significant increase in mosques. Muslims did not follow the school because they feared they would be forced to accept baptism, despite denials of such pressure by the missionaries. As an example, Father Guffens publicly denied that Muslims could be forced to receive baptism, but privately hoped Muslims would be converted, once told Muslim children to come to church on Sunday, and at another occasion forced them to pray at school.[51] Thus, even if Guffens' attitude was more combative than that of his colleagues, the substance for rumor was there. Many Muslims told their children to stay away from the missionaries' schools, or to neglect the study of the catechism. Fathers regarded the Muslim request for a government school and the defection to it once it was established as being "against morality".[52]

Another competitor to the mission school was seasonal work (*kibaruani*) on the plantations near Morogoro or Kisaki to earn cash for clothes (or food in times of scarcity). This period usually fell within the school holidays; as the holidays usually coincided with the long rains (March–April), younger children could assist their parents at chasing the birds from the ripening harvest (*kuhamia ndege*, "moving the birds"). The missionaries often had to follow the desires of Waluguru in that respect: during *kuhamia ndege*, an empty school was better closed, to save the money of the teacher's salary. In times of scarcity, the problem would be aggravated: in Kasanga, post-war famine (due to a prolonged drought all over Tanganyika) led to the absence of most children; the missionaries complained that after four months of closed schools, the desire to learn the Faith was diminishing among the people. In 1938, hunger in Tegetero had the same effect.[53] Although the

---

[51] TD 11.1.51, 13.6.51, KD 16.10.46.

[52] TD 5.1.42, 6.2.47; TP, School and Education Matters: Inspection Tegetero Mission School, 7.3.51; MP, Generalia: Circular Educ. Office, 12.6.54.

[53] KD 9.2.42, 17.1.46, Feb. '46, 9.3.53, SD 1.12.52, TD 7.11.38, MD 22.5.48; MP, Diaconal Meetings Matombo, 9.1.46; MP, Government and Schools: General Remarks of Inspection of Schools, by R. B. Armstrong (1949?).

mission diaries do not mention this, another reason for boys to stay away from school must have been the necessity to stay in the *ng'ula* or *jando* camp when these ceremonies were still held.

As we have seen, for girls, *ngoma* was also a reason for truancy: the *mwali* only came to church on Sundays. Waluguru seem to have been more reluctant to send girls to school: in Matombo, boys generally made up sixty per cent of the number of pupils (figs. 9 and 10 p. 154–5), while in Tegetero, Islamic influence brought this figure up to seventy per cent. The missionaries regularly complained that they could not get girls to attend their schools and it was a mark of succes when they could. Moreover, parents often hesitated to send their girls to missionary institutions outside the mountains (see chapter four). The fact that the missionaries regularly reported that especially female pupils were "stupid", that is, did not know their lessons, may be tied to this reluctance to see them leave the mountains: in one case at least, it is reported that parents told their children to flunk their exam for the Middle School so they would not leave for Matombo or Morogoro.[54]

Thus, the problem arose how to fill the school. To some extent, teachers and missionaries relied on *viboko* to punish truants (although not as arbitrarily as Mzee Pius' first teacher). Occasionally, the missionaries held a "raid" to "arrest" truants. At other times the catechists were exhorted to impress upon their pupils their duties towards the faith and the necessity of baptism. To what extent exhortation was taken as command (as was often the case in government-Luguru relationships) is not clear, but the emphasis on religious duties was, in this case, succesful: the empty schools filled up again and pupils reappeared in church on Sunday.[55] Nevertheless, the most effective and widely adopted measure was to rely on the Native Authorities. This was not always legal: the missionaries had

---

[54] TD 16.1.39, 4.6.46, 30.8.46, 22.6.50, KD 19.10.46, 18.8.47, SD 4.8.56; TP, School and Education Matters: Annual Returns Schools, passim; when a Matombo girl died in a Morogoro school, witchcraft fears reduced Matombo girls' attendance to almost nil (MD 1.2.34).

[55] KD 8.9.42, Feb. '46, 1.3.46, TD 10.6.51, TuD 9.12.43; FN: Mzee Petri Mloka, Kiswira, 18.11.89.

no right to compel children to come to school except when pupils had enrolled for a registered or assisted school. In a situation where the large majority of schools were still of the bush school type, many of the missionaries' measures of compulsion were of doubtful legal status.

Mtawala Hega held his first school *baraza* in Singiza in 1940, when it got its first registered school: attendance immediately jumped from 42% to 77%; in Kasanga, too, he filled the schools by force (*nguvu*). As we have seen, Father Guffens also relied on the Native Authorities, although less than his precursors and successors in Tegetero. In Matombo, too, the visits of the Sultan himself usually led to an increase in school attendance. Reliance on Native Authorities also meant that the local *mndewa* had to be well-disposed towards the mission, and this was achieved by presenting him with a "salary" or with (regular) presents. Thus, to some extent the missions relied on exchanges and gifts (the dealings of Guffens with *mndewa* Mwinyimvua noted above are another example). For many bush schools, however, N.A. help was only a temporary stop-gap: in some cases the school had to close again shortly afterwards (as happened to Kisolo and Hewe schools in Tegetero).[56]

The majority of examples given above are from the war years: attendance was at that time so low that the mission needed regular support. Before that time, many missionaries seemed to have resigned themselves to a sixty to seventy per cent average attendance. Like marriages and baptisms *extra periculo mortis* (which, I argued, were indicative of Christianity as *ngoma* – figs. 2 and 4), the number of pupils dropped around 1940, only to rise again sharply around 1946 (fig. 9, p. 154 and fig. 11). The sharp increase after the war is not simply a return of Christianity's earlier popularity, but also the increasing impact of compulsory school attendance. In Tegetero mission school, for instance, average attendance jumps to 80% and higher from 1950 onwards, when a grant

---

[56] SD 11.6.40, KD 19.6.44, 4.12.44, TD 15.6.37, 20.6.37, 12.4.38, 8.1.38, 8.2.39, 9.7.43, 22.7.43, 13.10.43, 9.3.44, 17.9.45, 4.6.46, 30.8.46, 22.1.51, MD 17.8.44, 18.8.44, 29.8.44, 5.9.44, 14.9.44, 8.10.45, 22.7.46, 9.9.46, 22.5.48; MP, Diaconal Meetings Matombo: Scheerder Report, not dated (1944?).

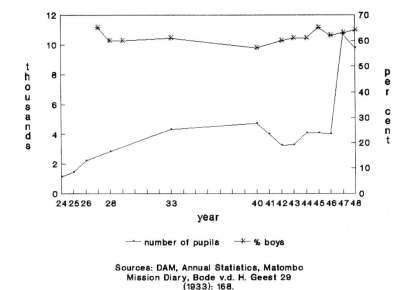

FIGURE 11   *Matombo, schools, 1924–48*

for the school was contemplated (and given; fig. 12). Attendance at the bush schools remained around 70% (fig. 13). Discipline increased, and transformed the local, initiation-like bush school into a learning factory on the European model.

Discipline worked by individualization: pupils were joined on the basis of their individual level of achievement ("Standard" I, II, etc.), and only secondarily because they lived in the same community. The bush school collectivity, a homogeneous unit which one left after baptism or betrothal, disappeared. The increase in the number of schooldays prevented the boy or girl from going *kibaruani* or *kuhamia ndege*. Parents could be fined by the court when their children skipped school or when they did not pay their school fees. Teachers, not Fathers, were to accuse truants before the court, and those who opposed the teacher's authority should be dealt with by the same legal apparatus.[57] In other words, Christian and local

---

[57] KD 15.12.52, 9.3.53, 11.4.56, 8.7.56, 10.1.57; TP, School and Education Matters: Central Ed. Com., 29.8.50.

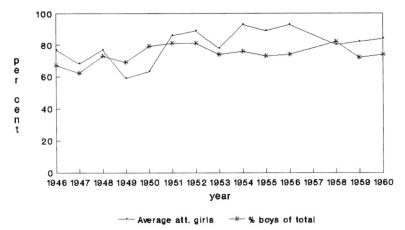

Source: TP, School and Education
Matters: Annual Returns Ass. Schools,
passim.

FIGURE 12   *Tegetero mission school, 1946–60*

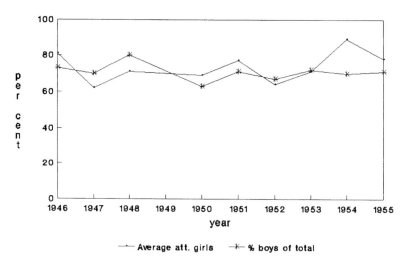

Source: TP, School and Education
Matters: Annual Returns Bush Schools,
passim.

FIGURE 13   *Tegetero bush schools, 1946–55*

authority increasingly retreated, while the authority of certificates and diplomas, backed by the disciplinary power of the state, took over.

DISCIPLINE AND TEACHER TRAINING

Before the war, a future teacher was immediately put into Standard IV, or, if he had had the chance to attend an assisted school, into Standard V. The Teacher Training School still consisted only of Standard IV to VIII. Later, a separate Middle School was created and the TTS became a "college" (Standards IX to XII). At both Middle School and TTS, boys from different tribes and denominations were put together, regardless of their origin. Entrance standards for both major and minor seminary and TTS were the same (except for the religious aspect), and the one often received pupils from the other (although the direction of transfer was, as far as I can tell, mainly from seminary to TTS).[58]

As we have seen above, the TTS was set up by Irish Holy Ghost Fathers. This may account for the fact that the disciplinary methods used reflected the patterns of supervision of the English public school. The prefect-system worked to single out talented boys, and, as in the public school, train them as responsible leaders.[59] Shortly before the war, it passed into the hands of the Holy Ghost Fathers' most renowned and controversial education expert: Michael Witte, founder of the Kabaa school in Kenya. We should have a glimpse at the foundation and running of Kabaa before we turn to the way in which the disciplinary methods of the TTS in Morogoro were perceived by its pupils.

Witte wanted education to form "character" through discipline and regularity, to such an extent that good results of study became secondary to drill, handicraft and agriculture. His Bishop had to caution him not to sacrifice literary studies to the school's

---

[58] Wendelini 1990: 55; IPAC 17b: 000, 083, 241; FN: Mwalimu Bartolomeo Lukoa, Kiswira, 21.8.89, Mwalimu Leo Marki, Kiswira, 9.1.90; SD Nov/ Dec. '35; MP, Schools: Entrance examinations, St. Peter's seminary, 1956; TP, School and Education Matters: Central Ed. Com., 8.1.45.

[59] KMM 708/1a: 215; IPAC 11a: 087.

physical education (De Jong 1974: 81, 94, 99). A visitor to Kabaa said that "no one is ever allowed to remain idle. The pace is terrible…" (1974: 73). In the beginning, this antagonized many pupils. In the first few years, three out of four deserted in the first two weeks and regular journeys to find new recruits were necessary. Grumbling and strikes recurred, especially after long periods of manual labour (which many pupils regarded as women's work). Abundant food, and meat in particular, usually restored order again (1974: 69, 84). In the course of several years, Witte managed to gather a core of pupils around him, and held them in tight control (they were kept at school during holidays, because Witte thought their home was not an "ennobling environment" – 1974: 71). The motto of the school was *jishinde ushinde* ("control yourself and you will win") and to reach that goal manual labour and drill (the latter for "quick thinking, quick obedience and heeding others") were thought to be most appropriate (1974: 78, 94).

The TTS under Witte also emphasized pace, physical conditioning and closure. The students got up at five a.m. and were kept busy until nine p.m, just as the seminarists in the Netherlands (see chapter two). Students were not kept at school during holidays, but letters written home were scanned by the missionaries; those who tried to circumvent the censor were punished. No exceptions to the rule were allowed: Muslim students followed Christian service just like the others (which may have led to the conversion of some Tegetero boys in 1948). Some students remember Witte with gratitude: they say he taught them to work (that is, manual labour) and accept discipline and obedience. Witte did not have to do much to keep order: when the dormitory was not quiet, he simply passed underneath its window smoking his pipe and the smell would produce immediate silence. Also, many students remember Witte's brass band with fondness. Another Father recalled that the students were a hundred per cent motivated and never baulked at their studies; the only trouble he remembered were tensions between students from different ethnic backgrounds (they came, apart from Uluguru itself, from as far as Tabora, Ukerewe, Kondoa-Irangi and Shinyanga).[60]

---

[60] De Jong 1974: 174; TP, School and Education Matters: Central Ed. Com., 30.7.45; IPAC 11a: 095; KMM 708/1a: 215; TD 20.7.48; FN, Chief P. Kunambi, Dar es Salaam, 12.4.89; Mwalimu Bartolomeo Lukoa, Kiswira, 21.8.89.

The desire for education and resentment of discipline and manual labour is evident from Mzee Pius Wendelini's memoirs. After a year of training in the Matombo primary school, he passed the exam for the Morogoro TTS, which at that time (1937) was led by Father Michael Witte. Witte was not universally popular: many disliked his many and harsh rules, his corporal punishments, the requirement to be silent, to avoid being in company of less than three, to do much and hard agricultural work and handicrafts. Many boys deserted after having been punished regularly. Mzee Pius himself resented that others were brought to watch his prowess in agricultural work, since he felt that they were made to act like overseers that hurried him in his work (showing that the position of first among equals of the prefect system was not always a joy). He recalled, however, that the school taught him to work hard and to obey hard commands in a strange environment (Wendelini 1990: 55). Mzee Pius was not the only one to interpret the tough learning environment as an advantage in later years.[61]

PLATE 14   *Drill at the Teacher Training School in Morogoro (from BHG 28 [1932]: 283)*

---

[61] FN, Chief P. Kunambi, Dar es Salaam, 12.4.89; Mwalimu Bartolomeo Lukoa, Kiswira, 21.8.89.

Michael Witte was transferred back to Kenya during the war, and physical discipline seems to have been somewhat lighter under his successor Loogman. In the 1950s, the contribution of manual labour to TTS discipline had been decreased to one hour a day (drill remained – see plate 14), which had its effect on the willingness of pupils to stay. At the time, the need for qualified teachers in primary schools was highest and the TTS could hardly manage to keep up with the demand.[62]

CONCLUSION

In this chapter, I have tried to concentrate on the material mediations (plot, teacher, pupils) of colonial education, in an attempt to bring out the microphysics of colonial contact needed for a development of forms of authority and power that had their centre of gravity outside of the Uluguru mountains and the social routines of its inhabitants. Studies of colonial curricula and education policies have, by the nature of the subject matter, tended to concentrate on European initiative in education policy, and African resistance to it. But such struggles over policy depended on the prior establishment of a contact zone to which they could be applied, a zone that was constructed in the cooperation between missionaries and Africans. Ignoring this contact zone implies missing much of what can be called "resistance without protest" (Scott 1987), the grassroots negotiations that allowed Africans and missionaries access to each other's routines of power – the possession of knowledge for both religious and secular positions of power in colonial society on the one hand, the access to land, to children, and to lineage and Native Authority hierarchies on the other. However, this negotiation was decisively influenced by the colonial administration's remote control of education by subsidy, which increasingly stressed that power resided in money, curricula and diplomas, commodities divorced from local power relationships, that could be

---

[62] FN, Mwalimu Bartolomeo Lukoa, Kiswira, 21.8.89.

replaced at will by one of equal (exchange) value, and that one could possess like property (Ball 1983: 259). The source of authority, where such commodities were invested with the power they henceforth wielded in Uluguru, had thereby shifted to centres outside of the mountains, at the TTS in Morogoro or the Education Department in Dar es Salaam.

One might wonder why Waluguru, with the exception of Muslims, rarely protested against this attempt to wrest control over their children from them. I think the answer lies in the way the career of *mwalimu* was the most accessible form of social advancement under colonial rule that did not depend on lineage authority, precisely because its authority was derived from an external source. Through the position of catechist, someone could become a leader of local Christians, but because his position was based on a derived power (and remained derived because missionaries prohibited its extension by other power resources) it did not interfere with or usurp other local sources of power. When government regulations decreased this dependence on Christianity, education as such replaced it, creating a political economy based on commodity forms (money, knowledge, diplomas) and largely divorced from local relationships.

Apart from the changes involved, a specific kind of continuity should be pointed out. In many respects, Waluguru gained a new career in education not because of the content of the knowledge they passed on, but because of the authority they derived from the *act* of passing on knowledge. Despite the fact that the missionaries tried to obliterate "parroting" in primary school practice, the emphasis was (as in most education systems) on the mimesis of information as such. Because social mobility was largely monopolized by the education system, (secular) professional and commercial advancement were underdeveloped (Ball 1983: 248). The classes into which Africans *wanted* to move were not the near-absent professional and commercial ones: their examples of people in power were priests and administrators, both products of systems of education and discipline (in which commerce was suspected). Someone who failed to reach a next Standard several times could be asked: "So now you won't become a white man (*mzungu*)?"[63] This, I feel, explains why most Africans insisted on literary instead of industrial and agricultural education (Anderson 1970; Ball 1983): the latter did not promise a career. We might say that "parroting" (with its promise of becoming the head parrot) was, for Waluguru, the obvious way to advance under colonialism. Not the content, but the power of education (*elimu*) was important, and *elimu* is, to this day, discussed as something one possesses like a commodity. This perspective was shared by the Europeans to the extent that they stressed discipline, and, consequently, mimesis and obedience, above learning.

This lends a peculiar flavour the words of Father Mawinza (as he compares Luguru initiation to modern education):

> To-day there seems a superstition of education among our inhabitants. The people ascribe elementary book-learning power in school to form character, make good citizens, keep family more pure, elevate morals, establish individual character, civilize barbarians and cure diseases. The parents apply schooling as a remedy *for every social factor which they do not like* (Mawinza 1963: 23, my emphasis).

Many Waluguru are now convinced that someone with only Standard III "has nothing" as far as education is concerned (*hana elimu*). Educated Waluguru phrase their diagnoses of social wrongs (including their characterization of oppressive colonizers) in terms of "lack of education".[64] In other words, there is a real kind of "superstition" about education: education is a mimesis that is thought to help one get along in life without the process of this "getting along" being taken into account. It reminds one of the mimetic magic that characterized certain stages in the initiation ceremonies. To the extent that it only taught pupils to reproduce, not to use, knowledge, the school provided a similar kind of mimesis of power. The next chapter explores the extent to which missionaries were otherwise entangled in magic.

---

[63] FN: Adriani Nyawale, Morogoro, 24.1.90.
[64] FN, Mzee Emili Daudi, Kiswira, 21.1.90; Chief Patrick Kunambi, Dar es Salaam, 12.4.89.

CHAPTER SIX

White Magic: The Missionary in the Field of *Uganga* and *Uchawi*

Matombo oranges are large, sweet and famous as far north as Lake Victoria. Thus it is not surprising that the missionaries' orchard attracted illegitimate consumers. On the advice of the boys of his football club, Brother Rudolf hung a tuft of grass in one of the orange trees as *zindiko* (kil. *kago*; see plate 15), a magical guard against thieves. The device worked to the Brother's satisfaction, but gave rise to a vehement dispute in the mission's refectory. Most Fathers said that Rudolf was spreading superstition. His reply was on the same practical level as the measure itself: "who is eating these nice oranges here?"[1]

The event illustrates three important aspects of the missionary engagement with magic. First, it shows that there was no consensus among the missionaries about the ways of cordoning off "religion" from "superstition", and that disbelief in Luguru magical routines did not prevent missionaries from practical participation in them. Second, it makes clear that such debates about the necessity and efficacy of magic were not just the privilege of the missionaries, but were at least partly shared by some Waluguru (in this case, the boys of the football club). Third, it indicates that the missionaries' struggle against "superstition" took place within a larger field of social practice where it could, paradoxically, be rejected and promoted by them at the same time, and where the missionaries' interest in the proper approach of the spiritual interfered with its more worldly mediations (such as the protection of property). Following Luguru usage, I designate this field with the Swahili words *uganga* and *uchawi*, words which one can freely translate as (both social and individual) "healing" and its destructive opposite, "witchcraft".

---

[1] IPAC 3a: 402.

PLATE 15   *A* kago *charm guarding a field of cassava (photograph taken by author at Mlono 1989)*

Such a translation is highly problematic, however. Given that *uganga* is not only concerned with the integrity of individual, but also of social bodies, it is always a practice of gaining and explaining political and economic power as well. Moreover, since one person's *uganga* (Rudolf's protection of his crop) may be another's *uchawi* (the illness it would produce in the orange thief), the positive and negative, causal and moral, connotations carried by the English terms healing and witchcraft cannot be easily distinguished. Lastly, given that at least some missionaries willingly identified themselves as healers or medicine men (*waganga*) and most were identified by Waluguru as such, we may wonder to what extent they practised "witchcraft" as well. To untangle some of these problems, it will first be necessary to locate them in anthropological discourse on magic and witchcraft. This clarification of the difficulties of translation will make it easier to outline the field of Luguru *uganga* and *uchawi*, position the missionaries in relation to it, show how their activities helped to promote a secularization of magic in Uluguru, and lastly, show their relation to new conceptions of evil that arose in late colonial Uluguru.

MAGIC, WITCHCRAFT AND THE COLONIAL ENCOUNTER

During the past decade, studies of magic and witchcraft have stressed the resilience of ideas about the occult in the face of processes of modernization that, according to previous paradigms, should have diminished their relevance (De Blécourt 1990; Comaroff and Comaroff 1993; Fields 1982b; Fisiy and Geschiere 1991; Geschiere 1995; Meyer 1995; Rowlands and Warnier 1988; Wiener 1995). As a result, the hegemony of the term "witchcraft", established by Evans-Pritchard's work (1937), has given way to a proliferation of terms. The problem of description appears in the tentative use of alternatives like "occult forces" or "ritual", or in the observation that terms like witchcraft and sorcery were or have become part of the vocabularies studied, whether those of colonial discourse or those in which Africans today talk about magic and witchcraft. Thus, the field which was given a certain consistency by the label "witchcraft" has become more difficult to describe, and this may account for the fact that studies of missions in Africa rarely address the issue of magic and witchcraft head-on. Some continue equating witchcraft with African tradition (Beidelman 1982); others rest content with pointing out that witchcraft and magic form an important background for understanding the construction of colonial society (Comaroff 1985; Fields 1985).

Of course, students of missionary discourse have stressed the role of notions of magic and witchcraft, or "superstition", in the world view of missionaries. In much mission propaganda, the "witch-doctor" is presented as the missionary's most perfidious antagonist, and magic and witchcraft are described as a scourge of fear that the divine love of the Christian religion will remove (Corbey 1989b: 53, 90–1; Corbey and Melssen 1990; Erivwo 1975). However, such merely discursive analysis is insufficiently critical (cf. Bal 1990). Although we shall see that derogatory images of African healing in terms of "magic" and "witchcraft" played a role in the work of missionaries in Uluguru, there was, one the one hand, too close a symbolic correspondence between Christian worship and the figure of the African healer (cf. Schoffeleers 1982, 1988), while on the other, missionaries were already always practically involved in Luguru routines of healing. As with colonial administrators, the denial of witchcraft by missionaries went along with a much more murky practice (Fields 1982b).[2] Unfortunately, the anthropological notion of witchcraft – which, I argue below, derives at least in part from the Witchcraft Ordinances of the British colonial administrations – seems to have obstructed the analysis of this field for quite some time.

The demise of the largely structural-functionalist witchcraft paradigm (Marwick 1972) was signalled by arguments that the application of the English term "witchcraft" to other cultures may have been a big mistake (Crick 1973). To my knowledge, however, nobody has asked *why* the term became employed in such a way and

---

[2] This is, of course, an implicit critique of Fields' rigid opposition of "revolutionary" missionaries and "accomodating" administrators (Fields 1982a).

why it nearly completely displaced the alternative term "magic" in the 1930s. Whereas anthropologists like Frazer and Malinowski used "magic" (usually in comparison with science and religion; Frazer 1911; Malinowski 1925, 1935a), and even Evans-Pritchard initially presented his Azande studies in these terms (Evans-Pritchard 1929), in the first edition of *Witchcraft, Oracles and Magic among the Azande* (1937) the order of priority firmly privileges "witchcraft" while "magic" only figures as a derivative activity – a response to witchcraft beliefs. Later, the vanishing act of "magic" was completed by translating the activities it referred to by "sorcery" (Evans-Pritchard 1970).

However, if we look into the theoretical meaning that the terms carried at the time the shift from magic to witchcraft was made, the displacement of the former by the latter is by no means self-evident. In terms of Malinowski's 1935 essay, which was eclipsed by Evans-Pritchard's book of two years later, "magic" stood for a universal human attempt to call up a desired future, reducing anxiety about an uncertain prospect by "institutionalizing human optimism". In contrast, "witchcraft" pointed to a system of belief held by particular other peoples about a mystical substance which some people carried and which enabled them to harm others by jealousy and envy. Although both paradigms had the same aim – explaining the apparently irrational by calling on universal human traits – Malinowski and Evans-Pritchard worked by diametrically opposed textual strategies. Malinowski first presented a universal theory of the magical word, reducing the apparent irrationality of magic by arguing that all people learn the magical and pragmatic uses of words from infancy, and pointing out the modern European magic of advertising and political rhetoric before presenting his data on Trobriand garden magic. Evans-Pritchard's strategy of "disenstrangement" (Geertz 1988: 69) started out from a particular belief in nonexistent entities held by "others" and then embarked on a series of comparisons that showed why it was rational, consistent and pragmatically feasible to hold such beliefs. In 1930s anthropology, therefore, "magic" indicated a universal human act; "witchcraft", a faulty belief held by "others", and we may wonder what was the use, for anthropologists, of replacing the former by the latter.

As an initial step towards understanding the sudden hegemony of "witchcraft", we need to understand two things.[3] First, Malinowski's pragmatic notion of "magic" may not have appealed to an academic audience whose lack of a theory of practice made them define their object in terms of a system of beliefs (cf. Bourdieu 1977). Just as Malinowski's pragmatic legal anthropology was ignored until recently (Comaroff and Roberts 1981), so his pragmatic theory of magic may not have seemed as attractive as it does now. But that does not yet explain why "witchcraft" came to academic attention, and I feel – and this is my second point – that its emergence in anthropology cannot be explained without taking its prior emergence as an object of colonial rule into account. British governments in Africa had been engaged in the proclamation of Witchcraft Ordinances – that declared witchcraft to be a mistaken set of beliefs, and accusations of witchcraft as punishable – in the years before the Sudan Government invited Evans-Pritchard to its territory. British administrators had written books on African "witchcraft" that anticipated Evans-Pritchard's arguments (Melland 1923; Fields 1982b: 582). Evans-Pritchard first argued that witchcraft was mistaken belief in an introduction to a special issue of *Africa* in which these administrators also wrote (1935), and he saw his writings about witchcraft as serving colonial administration (1935: 421; 1937: 3). As in so many other cases, colonial ethnography prepared the way for its academic successor (Pels and Salemink 1994).

If the notion of witchcraft as mistaken belief indicates that witchcraft was initially a colonial object, it should be clear that the concept changed content in the course of its academic career. For a colonial administrator like Frank Melland, witchcraft was important for its support of political power (Melland 1935; see Fields 1982b). To Evans-Pritchard, political power was a side issue, since he interested himself in the collusion of moral and causal explanations of

---

[3] For a full explanation of the shift, we probably have to delve deep in the history of British anthropology, and its uses of related terms like fetishism and animism, to find out why "magic" lost its former popularity in the 1930s. I hope to do this in another essay.

misfortune, and *Witchcraft, Oracles and Magic among the Azande* owes much of its punch to the fact that it is also about the sociology of perception and knowledge. After the second world war, the epistemological dimension of reflecting on processes of explanation was sidestepped as anthropologists became preoccupied with witchcraft as (inexplicable) evil, in other words, as a reinforcement of collective morality by the inverse definition of it. The epistemological discussion was only revived by the time the witchcraft paradigm was already on the wane (Douglas 1970: xv 1980; Wilson 1970). But if "witchcraft" could cover different approaches to the topic, there were certain elements of the functionalist paradigm that remained fairly constant and should be spelled out since they might stand in the way of the study of magic and witchcraft in the Uluguru missions.

Firstly, "witchcraft" remained a sign of the otherness of Africans, to the extent that "recurring reminders" that the anthropologist did not share their beliefs were deemed necessary (Marwick 1952: 122). Thus, the possibility that something akin to witchcraft could occur in the anthropologist's own society (as envisaged by Malinowski's notion of "magic") was preempted from the start. It was therefore made unlikely that, for instance, modern European missionaries could be involved in it. Related to this is the persistent definition of witchcraft as "supernatural" or "mystical". This was perhaps obvious among Azande, whose notion of a witchcraft substance within the body raised Western naturalist doubts, but in at least some parts of East Africa (Uluguru included), witches (*wachawi*) are distinguished by motive (unprovoked malevolence) rather than supernatural or mystical methods (Lienhardt 1968: 51, 53, 58). In such cases, witchcraft is not more nor less than a notion of evil, disconnected from mystical or naturalist explanation and from the Western definition of what is and is not possible in the field of the latter. *Uchawi*, therefore, may be translated by "witchcraft", but it is not a mistaken belief, except if we are prepared to agree that present-day European stereotypes of ritual child abuse, heroin junkies, or coloured immigrants can also be classified as such (see, for example, La Fontaine 1992).

Finally, understanding witchcraft as a collectively held system of beliefs defined it atemporally, and produced the problem of how to account for change in these beliefs. From the 1930s onwards, two opposed notions of witchcraft functioned in British anthropology and colonial discourse: witchcraft as a contribution towards social health, and witchcraft as a symptom of a sick society (Douglas 1970: xxi). In the 1935 issue of *Africa* mentioned above, Evans-Pritchard argued that witchcraft would disappear together with the institutions supporting it (Evans-Pritchard 1935: 421), while Audrey Richards argued that witchcraft and magic increased when colonial rule "shattered tribal institutions and moral codes" (Richards 1935: 458). Thus, the functionalist view disallowed change of witchcraft beliefs from within African society, by means of debates about (the efficacy of) witchcraft taking place along indigenous cultural fissures. By emphasizing the conservation of a system of beliefs or of the institutions on which it was based, it theorized a collective clinging to "tradition".

Malinowski's notion of magic, in contrast, emphasized a magical act and individual agency directed at the future, as an "institutionalized expression of human optimism" (1935a: 139; Tambiah 1990: 42). This formula allows for a creative *bricolage* of existing beliefs about natural and moral causation and leaves open the possibility of new imaginings of the future. The problem of accounting for the modernization of African conceptions of magic, healing and witchcraft is thereby displaced: it is no longer a question of detribalization and social breakdown, but of how different generations of Africans belonging to different sections of society reimagined their contact with colonial society and reinvented the institutionalization of the hopes to influence that contact (see below). Since that contact involves both sides of the encounter, we can also work much better with a theory that starts out with defining a magical act, the behavior that needs explaining, than with a system of beliefs that supposedly explains the behavior, since cross-cultural correspondences occur at the level of the magical act that may be absent at the level of belief – as Brother Rudolf showed in the defense of his oranges. Moreover, we shall see (in the section below on *Uganga* and the Missionary) that magical acts created a correspondence between missionary work and Luguru magic and witchcraft that the comparison of beliefs would only deny.

Lastly, I feel that Malinowski's idea of magic as an "institutionalization of human optimism" is sufficiently vague as to the specific mystical or natural causation involved to allow for a better understanding of what occurs in the history of the Luguru missions. For if a certain compartmentalization occurred under the influence of European agency, it did not follow the lines of "supernatural" versus "natural" beliefs, or "mystical" versus "commonsense". In the fourth section on witchcraft eradication (which I prefer to call "medicine hunting"), I hope to show that the magical acts which both missionaries and administrators interpreted as religious (that is, acts involving something which European common sense defined as mystical), were regarded by Waluguru as down-to-earth political issues that were the responsibility of the state rather than of the missionaries. Witchcraft (*uchawi*, human malevolence) was, for Waluguru, something to be countered by secular means and they failed to see why missionaries had to interfere, and government was loath to cooperate, in a secular measure for the common good. This, of course, raised suspicions about Europeans, since their non-cooperation seemed to defend witches, and the last section shows that such suspicions were also voiced in different social circumstances, leading eventually to the conclusion that we may be better off translating *uganga* and *uchawi*, not as magic, healing or witchcraft, but as "good" and "bad contact", respectively.[4]

UGANGA: HEALING AND POWER

Uganga was the practice of preventing or countering misfortune. It healed and protected individual and social bodies. It was practised by means of both ritual and medicines, to cure and protect individuals as well as to protect the crops on lineage land and keep the lineage healthy, to guarantee the efficacy of the changes wrought

---

[4] Which might mean that, in situations of colonial contact, the contagious or metonymic dimension of magic becomes more important than the homoeopathic or metaphoric one – an inversion of the hierarchy proposed by Frazer (1911: 54).

by initiation on the younger generation, to make rain, to make war magic, to protect the community against witches and to exorcize bad spirits. During the colonial period, however, the emphasis on collective (lineage) rituals and medicines (*tambiko* and *zimbo*, see below) slowly decreased, while more individualized treatment of both social and physical disorders remained (cf. Swantz 1986: 180). This change also implies a commodification of healing, in the sense that treatment by consumable objects that could be purchased from a healer became more and more important (see Swantz 1986: 72, and the section on Nguvumali below).

In Luguru etiologies of evil, the change meant a shift from explanations in terms of spirits (*mizimu*), those of the ancestors in particular) to explanations in terms of medicines (*dawa*; Lienhardt 1968: 166–7, 180–1). Before the introduction of European overrule, Luguru politics seems to have consisted of two complementary practices: that of power within the lineage (kil. *lukolo*), expressed in a discourse of kinship, and that of power between lineages, expressed in terms of precarious balances of both physical and magical threats on the one hand, and obligations incurred through gift-giving and receiving on the other (Pels 1996: 744–9). *Lukolo* discourse was, and to some extent still is, dominated by the notion of ancestral spirits, while inter-lineage balances of magical power were usually explained in terms of the magic of medicines. The shift from lineage ritual and medicine to individualized treatment by a healer or medicine-man (*mganga*), and from spirits to medicines, is therefore also a symptom of the decreasing power of the lineage in day-to-day affairs.

Healing the lineage rested on two modes of treatment, usually combined: communion or reconciliation with the ancestors (*tambiko*) and treatment with lineage medicine (*zimbo*). Each year, the lineage head performed a sacrifice of food and beer accompanied by prayer (see Bombwe 1983), in order to keep the ancestors from disturbing the fields and to procure sufficient rain. Such reconciliation (*kutambika*) was done at an ancestral shrine (*changa*) located in a place where their spirits were supposed to dwell, usually a clump of trees containing their graves. In the same place, a pot was kept with lineage medicine, an often rotting and foul-smelling concoction of magical stones and cooked medicines (*miti*, "trees"), the recipe of which was supposedly inherited from the first lineage head to settle in the area. Lineage medicine belonged to one lineage branch (sw. *ziwa*; kil. *tombo*) or to a cluster of them, all descended from the same ancestor. The possession of lineage medicine often depended on the history of a specific lineage: all Wabena of Nyingwa, for instance, drank the same *zimbo* except for a Mbena group that arrived much later from another direction. According to some, the lineage had to maintain itself through regular, yearly or two-yearly, application of lineage medicine; others say it was used when a lineage member fell ill; in that case, all lineage members had to use the medicine to cleanse themselves of ancestral wrath. Among the Matombo Wanyani (and probably elsewhere), a similar medicine (*mepo*) was prepared by the leading Mama for the women of the lineage.[5]

The lineage head himself could be a healer, but if not, he depended on a local *mganga* to prepare lineage medicine if any mishap occurred to the pot in which the substance was kept. The healer in question had to be a member of the lineage, however, in order to be able to commune with the relevant ancestral spirits. Not all spirits, however, were ancestral. Waluguru distinguished a category of nature-spirits, like Lunyagi who resided in the cave that gave the Matombo area its name. His origin is unknown and he is now said to have fled from the presence of the Catholic Fathers. If Waluguru talk of mysterious or dangerous areas such as swamps or volcanic springs, they call it a place of spirits (*pana mzimumzimu*).[6]

More interesting are those spirits that occupy a place in between: the spirit Muhangalugome, the spirit of Kingalu's shrine

---

[5] MSS Vermunt 5.4: "MZIMU. Spirit shrines" and "MZIMU. Matambiko"; 6.0 "Zimbo"; FN, Mzee Stefani Sabini, Gubi, 10.10.89, Mzee Mahumbo, Kiswira, 15.10.89, Mzee Petri Mloka, Kiswira, 8.10.89, Mzee Mnyingwa Mwanabwakira, Zava, 23.11.89, Mzee Daudi Maduga, Kiswira, 14.12.89, Mama Mkoba, Kiswira, 30.1.90.

[6] Other nature spirits were Nyaluwere, Salambwe, and Mundo; MSS Vermunt 5.4: "Mzimu. Oaths and Curses", 6.0: "Matambiko"; FN, Mama Mkoba, Kiswira, 1.10.90, 30.9.90, Mzee Ngomani, Zava, 21.11.89.

in Unguru, and the spirit of Kolero (Bokero or Boka). Muhangalugome used to be the spirit of the Watonga of Eastern Uluguru and was in some mysterious way split up between Msumi, the Watonga lineage head, and his (Mbena) son Mleke (who later became Kingalu the first) when the latter went to Kinole (Mzuanda 1958: 74). In Kinole, Muhangalugome seems to have merged with the ancestral spirit of Kingalu. For an unknown reason, its shrine was moved from Kinole to the Unguru mountains in the North where it catered to a large audience including other Luguru lineages, Wazaramo, Wakutu (Swantz 1986: 173), Wakwere, and Wanguru (Brain 1971: 832). Muhangalugome fulfilled a role similar to that of Bokero (or Bokera, or Boka), the snake-spirit of Kolero which was related to the Maji Maji rising (Gwassa 1972; Iliffe 1979: 169; Swantz 1986: 173). The shrine of Kolero was guarded by a Wamlali lineage and the officiant at the shrine had to be a Mlali virgin. These spirits, mid-way between ancestral and natural, were invoked in particularly difficult witchcraft or possession cases, rows between healers, and when droughts threatened the crops of a number of lineages. Richard Burton wrote in 1857 that the Kolero spirit cured barrenness, produced good harvests and war magic and drew pilgrims from as far as Uzaramo. Some people claim that all healing power, although derived from God, is mediated by the Kolero spirit.[7] It seems the transformation from lineage to nature-spirits accompanied the rise of a particular lineage-head (such as Kingalu, or in the case of Kolero, Hega) to a "big man" position of power beyond that of the particular lineage concerned.

Big men magic could be supported by the fusion of ancestral and nature-spirits, but there were other ways. Most important of these was the possession of secret medicine that got its name from the small gourd (sw. tunguli; kil. nunguli). Uganga wa nunguli could be used to cure illness, to divine the right place to build or to

---

[7] MSS Vermunt 5.3: "Kolero", 6.0: "Kolero and the snake cult"; MS Faridi Dossi, "The History of Kolelo Spirit", 1989; TNA MF 19, MDB: "The Waluguru", by F. v. d. Kimmenade, "Extract from Burton, The Lake Regions of Central Africa", by R. H. Gower; FN, Mzee Mikaeli Mlosa, Zava, 23.11.89; Swantz 1986: 173.

influence the words used by a party in a dispute. Its major function, however, was martial: the war leader or lineage head (who were not always the same person) sprinkled the medicine on the shoulders of warriors going out for a raid, or used it to hide his dwelling-place from an approaching enemy. The interesting thing about this *dawa* for inter-lineage purposes was that it is usually said to have non-Luguru origins: acquired from Wanyamwezi, or, in the case of a Matombo warleader from the last half of the previous century, from the Wambunga, the descendants of the Wangoni who settled near Kisaki and harassed Uluguru shortly before the Germans established military dominance (see Von Prince 1914: 92–8; Mzuanda 1958: 17 ff.).[8]

If lineage healing can still be reconstructed through people's reminiscences of the inhabitants of the spirit world and of inter-lineage relationships before colonial rule, the history of the treatment of personal problems is less easy to uncover. For example, I never met or even heard of a healer who engaged in exorcizing the Kinyamkera demon, despite Father Vermunt's repeated references to it. This form of possession may have disappeared.[9] More important, however, is that the professional practice of healers seems to have changed. While in former times, communion with ancestors still occupied a prominent place in healing, from the late 1960s onwards witchcraft diagnoses and treatment by means of medicines became more prominent. The change is related to several historical processes with which we are not directly concerned here: the political shift away from lineage authority characteristic of the post-independence and post-Native Authority period, and the *Ujamaa* villagization programme that brought much more people into frequent daily contact than before, thereby heightening witchcraft

---

[8] Wanyamwezi probably had contact with Waluguru through the caravan trade, as is proved by their joking-relationship (*utani*; see Christensen 1963). MSS Vermunt 6.0: "Foreword. Religion and Uganga", "Nunguli"; FN, Mama Mkoba, Kiswira, 1.10.90.

[9] MSS Vermunt, 5.4: "Spirit Shrines", 6.0: "The Bible and Uganga", "Uganga and Uganga". Another explanation might be that spirit possession was more common in more individualized societies like the Zaramo (Swantz 1986: 215–7).

suspicions (Brain 1981: 11). I will try to show, however, that the process itself is important for understanding the extent to which the mission influenced changes in healing practice.

Most healers engaged in three separate but connected activities: divining (*kuagua*; kil. *kulagula*), healing (*kutibia* with ancestor ritual and medicines) and protecting (*kuzindika* by charms, amulets and the like).[10] Although, according to Father Vermunt, the functions of diviner (*mlaguzi*) and medicine-master (*mganga*) need not be combined, I never heard of a healer who was only a diviner. Divination and treatment, however, are always separated by specific verbal conventions, that is, by an explicit request from the patient for a treatment of the causes divined.[11] Thus, on the one hand, room is made for a choice of a different healer than the one who diagnosed the problem. On the other, the diviner has the possibility to influence that choice by his explanation of the causes of the illness, and consequently, to influence his income – treatment is, as far as I know, much more expensive than divination.

There are many ways to divine in Uluguru. The most common is "hitting the board" (*kupiga bao*): the diviner traces lines in ashes sprinkled on a wooden board, and if the line continues to the end of the board, the answer is negative, if it stops mid-way it is positive. Another method is by means of a small gourd through which a double string runs: one end of the string is tied to a beam in the roof, the other is held by the diviner, who throws the gourd up to the roof-beam where it miraculously stops.[12] The gourd slides along the string and if it stops by itself, it agrees, if the diviner has

---

[10] Cf. Schoffeleers' distinction of "diagnostic", "therapeutic" and "prophylactic" activities (1988: 160).

[11] MSS Vermunt, 6.0: "Uganga and Uganga", "Divination", "Appendix Uganga", "Divination. Kulagula zimbitzi. Ndagu", "Uganga. Kago", "Uganga. Zindiko"; TNA MF 19, MDB: "Notes on the Waluguru and Wakami", by E. Hutchins and G. Debenham; Mzuanda 1958: 114.

[12] This was *kupiga ramli*, the only divination I witnessed myself. By showing me the gourd, the diviner allowed me to discover its mechanics: the string was hooked behind a little cross-bar concealed in the gourd, stopping it through friction when the diviner pulled the string tight. His skill in doing this effectively concealed this conjuring (*kiinimacho*).

to stop its downward slide manually, it denies. Yet another form is through *mbizi* (kil. *zimbitsi*) or *ng'ondo* (kil.), rattles or bells which induce a spirit trance in the diviner. In all cases, the outcome is said to be directed by the spirit by which the diviner is possessed.[13]

Father Mzuanda has given an example of the negotiation of etiologies that characterize divination (1958: 114):

> *Mganga*: Did he (the patient/pp) step on *huto* (a place where twins or misfigured children were buried)?
> Answer: (silence).
> M: Did he quarrel with someone?
> A: (silence).
> M: Did he step on God?
> A: *Tawile*.
> M: Did he eat *kago*?
> A: *Tawile*.
> M: Did he quarrel with deceased fathers?
> A: (silence).
> M: Did he steal people's property?
> A: oooooo.
> M: Did he break a *mwiko* (taboo/pp)?
> A: oooooo.
> M: Did he unnecessarily swear on the name of an ancestor?
> A: *Tawile*.[14]

In this case, Father Mzuanda says, the patient is probably suffering from a stomach-ache, because that is something most easily explained by the fact that the patient has stolen something (to eat) from a field which had been magically protected. It is possible to reconcile four of the suggestions with which the representatives of the patient agreed by affirmative humming or formal

---

[13] Mzuanda 1958: 114; MSS Vermunt 6.0. "Appendix Uganga", "Divination. Kulagula zimbitzi. Ndagu"; Wendelini 1990: 13–4; Michael Martiniani, Kiswira, 6.10.89, 8.10.89.

[14] Both my sources and my fieldwork failed to produce a translation of *tawile*, despite repeated attempts by both the missionaries and myself to elicit an explanation of the word (but see Johnson 1939: 389 on *tawileni*).

agreement (saying *tawile*): *kago* (sw. *zindiko*) is a taboo (*mwiko*) put in physical form by someone who has employed a healer to defend his field.[15] Because all taboos come from God in the end, he "stepped on God", too. Only the idle swearing on the name of an ancestor is less easy to fit in this otherwise clear etiology.

We can say that divination is in the first place a communication between healer and (representatives of) the patient in which the diviner tries to determine the causes of a specific misfortune:[16] death, illness, barrenness, difficult birth, theft; to find lost or stolen objects, defend a field against harm, detect firebrands or predict the course of a journey. Father Vermunt lists four types of explaining misfortunes: afflictions brought by God (*vibi vya Mlungu kagwa*, kil.), by the wrath of the ancestors (*vibi vya mitsimu*, kil.), possession by Kinyamkera or another demon, and harm done by one's fellow-humans through witchcraft (the case cited belongs to this category).[17] As I wrote above, Kinyamkera or other demons no longer seem to play an important role in Uluguru; *Mlungu* is only accepted as exclusive explanation in the case of a death of old age. Healers therefore usually employ the explanations by means of ancestral spirits or witchcraft.

However, younger healers, who started their career in the early 1970s (and whose popularity was definitely on the wane when I was there in 1989–90), never mentioned the category of ancestral spirits when I asked them to tell me about causes of misfortune (see plate 16). They did employ the word *mzimu*, but only to refer to the spirit whom they controlled or by whom they were possessed. The activities of these "modern" spirits not only governed divination but also the efficacy of medicines. They explicitly compared their medicines to the European type: whereas the latter is

---

[15] MSS Vermunt 6.0: "Uganga. *Luhungo*".

[16] Catholic Luguru sceptics say that diviners have no spirit: *wanabuni tu*, "they merely construct" an answer through their questioning and through their knowledge of the circumstances of the patient (FN, Mama Mkoba, Kiswira, 30.9.90; Camillus Kunambi, Kiswira, 30.9.90; Wendelini 1990: 13).

[17] MSS Vermunt 6.0: "Uganga and Uganga", "Divination", "Mwiko. Vibi. Uganga".

PLATE 16 *Mzee Mtimkavu, a* mganga *living near Kitungwa (photograph taken by author, 1989). Note the cap of colobus-monkey hair on the left, and the wildebeest tail fly whisk he is holding. Mtimkavu trades in roots, but also in more exotic medicines such as the coral standing on his right. He has spent some years in Dar es Salaam and sometimes strengthens his reputation by showing a popular booklet, widely sold on the streets of Dar in 1989, about a* mganga *of Kolero spirit, which is also the spirit of Mtimkavu*

"cool" (*baridi*), the former, through spiritual influence, is very hot (*motomoto*) or strong (*kalikali*). The spirit through which they healed was not the spirit of an ancestor, but one of the bigger, almost-nature spirits such as the spirit of Kolero or the spirit of the West Uluguru big man, Mbago. These men and women were mostly former Catholics, and Catholics disagreed about whether they were frauds or not. One of them was said to have fled Dar es Salaam after his medicine killed a patient by accident; another to have lost the support of his spirit when he committed adultery; yet another was discredited when people found out that the sounds his spirit made were produced by an accordion buried under the floor of his hut. It is significant that these younger healers (and most others of the generation born around 1950) never referred to the ancestors as a cause of illness of misfortune.[18]

In contrast, one of the few surviving older healers told me that misfortune was caused either by demons (*shetani*) unleashed by a witch, sometimes through the help of an evil healer, or by the deceased ancestors (*marehemu*). In the former case, treatment could only proceed through washing away evil, and by working counter-magic through medicines; in the latter, one had to combine reconciliation with ancestors and the consumption of medicine (*miti*, "trees").[19] If reconciliation with ancestors was necessary, the healing involved the presence of lineage members since *tambiko* implies that most lineage members are reconciled at the same time. As Lloyd Swantz has brought out in his study of urban healers among Wazaramo, the modern healer is oriented to a social situation where individual antagonisms, more than relations within the extended family, determine the process of healing: "there is a change from kinship support to individual responsibility, a change from the extended family and cult member support to individual and nuclear family support in the treatment of illness and misfortune" (Swantz 1990: 139; see also Swantz 1986). In Uluguru, too, lineage relationships became less important after independence destroyed the political power of Native Authorities, based as it was on reinvented lineage traditions (see Pels 1996). This situation was aggravated by the fact that Waluguru were ordered to live together in villages instead of scattered hamlets during the *Ujamaa* villagization scheme in the early 1970s (the period during which these younger healers rose to prominence). But one cannot fully understand this change in healing practice without tracing the influence the missionaries exerted in the spiritual realm.

---

[18] Mzee Mtimkavu, Kitungwa, 20.10.89; Luvumbe Mbena Mbago, Zava, 24.10.90; Faridi Dossi, Morogoro, 20.12.89; Thomas Martiniani, Kiswira, 21.9.89, 9.10.89; Father Winkelmolen, Morogoro, 10.12.89, 30.10.90; Mzee Petri Mloka, Kiswira, 11.9.89, 12.12.89, 5.2.90; Adriani Nyawale, Gervas Nyawale, Morogoro, 18.12.89, 27.8.90; Mama Mkoba, Kiswira, 30.1.90, 24.9.90, 29.9.90, 30.9.90; Camillus Kunambi, 30.9.90.

[19] Mzee Mumba, Tambuu, 18.10.90.

UGANGA AND THE MISSIONARY

In missionary propaganda, the *mganga* was a "witch-doctor", and in many ways the personification of evil. Father Witte wrote that where a church in Africa remained empty, it was the result of the fact that the village headman was at the same time its witch-doctor. A witch-doctor was someone essentially and uncompromisingly opposed to the Christian mission, for "peace, love [and] God's light" could not merge with "pagan fear, ignorance and hate". A missionary could, according to mission propaganda, "open hostilities" towards witch-doctors without provocation. After the war, propagandists in the Netherlands tried to uphold the opposition by denying that the era of the fetish and the sorcerer was over and maintaining that missionaries were confronted daily with the problems they created. During the 1950s, the image of the evil sorcerer slowly gave way to that of the evil communist, although the two could be combined (as in descriptions of Mau Mau and the 1962 Katanga rising in Zaïre).[20]

Although it was propaganda in the first place, and, as we shall see, the practice was different, to some missionaries the negative image of the *mganga* was valid. If a more respectable missiological publication made a careful distinction between healer and witch that was usually lacking in mission propaganda, the writer could still argue that the healer was a quack, a charlatan and an exploiter out for personal gain (De Rooij 1946: 95–6; the terminology used may reflect the fact that this writer often used medical skills to promote Christianity). Another missionary opposed the healer's work because it was similar to the belief in "swastika's and mascots" which he thought were having an evil influence on European politics at the time (in 1934). A third thought the fight against healers was his foremost duty, probably inspired by the common thought that pagan fears and superstition would survive if the power of the "medicine-man" was not broken (De Rooij 1946: 97; Melchior 1950: 245). Missionaries thought in the 1930s that the rumours

---

[20] Witte, in BHG 44 (1948): 74; other references in BHG 28 (1932): 22, 31 (1935): 110–1, 38–42 (1946): 64, 46 (1950): 70–1/95; AC 48 (1952): 2/inside back cover, 49 (1953): 5, 51 (1955): 14, 58 (1962): 10.

about the *mumiani* or white vampire (see below) were spread by witchdoctors to slander missionaries.[21]

Magic and religion were an important part of missionary ethnographies (see Pels 1994). Compared to the accounts of administrators, the missionaries rarely used the concept of "witchcraft" (NL: *hekserij*).[22] Their interest in magic was not legal and secular, and contrary to some administrators, they saw little use in acknowledging positive aspects of it. Magic was put in the context of "religion", but as a negative, satanic kind of religion. The articles in the *Holy Ghost Messenger* generally labelled Luguru discourse on the spiritual world "superstition" (NL: *bijgeloof*). Unpublished accounts often took more interest in "African religion", but the negative approach never disappears. Some accounts move from descriptions of the spirits and "ancestor worship" to the Luguru conception of a Supreme Being.[23] Father Vermunt seems to have had the intention to write a separate book about Luguru traditional religion, which contextualized the spirit-world by the Luguru conception of a Supreme Being, but which excluded *uganga*.[24] Scheerder and Tastevin separate God from the spirits by including the latter in the section on "magicians" (1950: 271–9). All accounts exemplify the tendency towards a selective, non-holist representation: the spirits, "ancestor worship", or *uganga*, are presented separately and often described as evil, while the conception of the Supreme Being is treated as original revelation. In the conclusion, we shall see that this influenced Luguru capacities for producing instances of revelation.

Both propaganda and ethnographies showed that the healer was perceived as a direct competitor of the missionary in the spiritual

---

[21] KMM 447/1a: 302, 447/1b: 338; BHG 30 (1934): 70/134–5; TNA MF 19, MDB: "Mumiani or Chinjachinja", by E. Hutchins.

[22] Father de Rooij used *tooverij* ("sorcery"; 1946).

[23] TNA MF 19 MDB: "The Waluguru", by Father v.d. Kimmenade; De Rooij, KMM 75.447; see also De Rooij, in BHG 43 (1947): 68.

[24] MSS Vermunt, 5.1: "Religion. Introduction"; this table of contents, however, was probably produced after Vermunt's retirement and was influenced by the ideas of accomodation to indigenous religion of the years after Vatican Two (see also Vermunt 1967).

field: his practice violated the First Commandment.[25] The missionaries, especially in the early years, opposed anything connected to the power of spirits or demons, whether they were ancestral, or called up by vegetable medicine (*pepo*), or brought by Koran sorcery (*jinni*). They forbade amulets (*mahirizi*), charms to protect the fields (*zindiko*), divination, rain-making, and appeals to ancestors in general. They were particularly disturbed by the popular appeal of travelling medicine hunters (about which more below). But if some held on to their Alsatian Superiors' conviction that all idolatry was a "sacrifice to the devil", others started to suspect that the indigenous distinction between healer and witch implied that not all were idolaters in the same way, and that at least a number of healers fought evil influences as much as the missionary did. From the outset, some missionaries recognized that a number of healers possessed real medical skills (against early stages of leprosy, for instance), and even made use of it. They never forbade "cooking medicine" (*dawa ya kupika*). Moreover, the missionaries came into conflict with healers only sporadically, partly because the Christians hid their involvement with them from missionaries, and partly because the missionaries sensed that it was not very fruitful to launch an out-and-out attack on these practices, as they would continue anyway. After Vatican Two, some Fathers even disdained defining *uganga* in terms opposed to the faith (calling it "psychotherapy" instead), or were prepared to affirm that for African Christians, some witches and demons were real and that Christianity should help in opposing them (cf. Erivwo 1975).[26]

Missionary opposition to healing was further qualified by the fact that – even if some Fathers refused to honour their Christians' requests for oaths on the cross, witchcleansing by holy water, or

---

[25] "Thou shalt have no other gods before me", Exodus 20: 3.

[26] MP, Decreta et Documenta: Safari report Scheerder, n.d. (1944?); KMM 111/1b: 400, 111/2b: 071, 514/1b: 197, 710/1a: 200; SD 1.12.41, 2.12.57, TD 23.11.50, MD 30.12.27, 3.6.53; Mzee Stefani Sabini, Gubi, 10.10.89; BHG 28 (1932): 163, 30 (1934): 39–41, 32 (1936): 59; MSS Vermunt 6.0: sections on *uganga*, the Bible, and fetishism; IPAC 1b: 430, 2a: 548, 5b: 156/447/555, 7a: 250, 8a: 224, 12a: 404/511, 13b: 394–580, 14a: 396, 15b: 020–126.

holding a novena to pass an exam – the Catholic church possessed its own "institutionalizations of human optimism" (see p. 54). Waluguru maintained relations with the ancestors in ways sufficiently similar to Christian worship for them to be partly adapted to the latter (Bombwe 1983). Missionaries could replace the rainmaker and other social healers by reading Mass in order to make rain (*oratio imperata propter pluviam*), to appease unruly ancestors, to procure good harvests, and in exceptional cases even to disarm witches. Reconciliation with the spirits of the ancestors was Christianized by the ceremony of the "beer of the cross" (*pombe ya msalaba*) on All Saints' or All Souls' day. The role of charms could be taken over by blessings, rosaries and medals.[27] The Bishop advised that "parochial devotions nourish the life of faith and are an excellent antidote against superstitious practices" (Hilhorst 1937: 14).

Blessings were used to combat superstition, but like many forms of combat, they took over some of the traits of the opponent: the branches blessed on Palm Sunday, for instance, were put over the door of a house just like a protective charm (*zindiko*). The Bishop also favoured the free distribution – sometimes leading to scrambles among the faithful – of medals at baptism, rosaries at first communion and scapulars at confirmation (Hilhorst 1937: 15) and these to some extent replaced the protective charms worn on the body (*mahirizi*). Moreover, whereas Brother Rudolf's defense against orange thieves may not have been explained in Christian terms, other forms of magic were. Father Bukkems, for instance, was convinced that it was the praying of a chaplet which gave the Tegetero people a good harvest (while Muslims and a group of recalcitrant Christians obtained a bad crop). One missionary held a novene to obtain a Brother for the understaffed mission of Tununguo (and succeeded). Holy water, coveted by the African Christians, was also used by the German Sisters to bless the seeds,

---

[27] FN 173; IPAC 2b: 071, 3b: 470, 14a: 000; BHG 32 (1936): 71/138; MP, Decreta et Documenta: Hilhorst to Superiors, n.d. (1953); SD 3.6.43, 28.2.55, MD Jan. '41, 12.1.43, 17.1.43, 6.12.43, 4.2.46, 24.9.53, 6.2.55.

while they employed the statue of St. Joseph to have the chickens lay more eggs.[28]

Whether they liked it or not, the missionaries were in many ways white *waganga*, and healing was part of the appeal that Christianity had for Africans (Schoffeleers 1988: 165). Of course, the practical efficacy of European medicines had a lot to do with that. Once a Father cured a man from a festering wound after the latter had been from healer to healer without getting relief, his reputation as *mganga* was made. Many simple European medicines had an immediate effect which Luguru healers often found hard to equal (such as the purgatives that Father de Rooij used when treating people for worms).[29] Their role as medical doctors provided them with unusual power: some managed to assure access to otherwise secret initiation ceremonies in this way, and it gave others the opportunity to threaten that only those whose children went to school would be treated. Father de Rooij even once advised – just like a Luguru healer – a woman to observe a taboo (*mwiko*; in this case, not to sleep with other men than her husband) after he had cured her. He explicitly compared himself with the *mganga* as opposed to the *mchawi*.[30]

Once medicine was used to apply pressure on people, "white magic" – here, in the sense of healing for benevolent purposes – began to shade into black magic or *uchawi*. The Father of Kidodi, in nearby Uvidunda, threatened the Muslims of the area that he would turn the river into holy water (which Muslims regarded as poison) after hearing a rumor that some of them wanted to set fire to the mission. Even if one regards the action as justified, it was hardly

---

[28] IPAC 3b: 470, 4a: 000/030/416, 5b: 156–236, 7a: 372; MSS Vermunt 6.0: "Uganga. Vumbala or Mapvumba"; BHG 29 (1933): 15, 32 (1936): 10/102, 47 (1951): 155; SD 13.8.35, 15.8.35, TD 5.12.36, 30.3.47, 15.11.49, TuD Apr. '49.

[29] As one Father put it: "[In Europe] doctors are already quite magical figures, but there [in Africa] it is much worse" (KMM 708/1a: 408). The magic of European medicine is evident in the case of a Father who acted *as if* he could cure people (BHG 32 [1936]: 140).

[30] KMM 708/1a: 316/408, 447/1a: 034/302, 447/1b: 338; IPAC 11a: 478; some European medicines and appliances, such as antibiotics and injections (*sindano*), have acquired decidedly magical properties for some Waluguru.

benevolent. Neither, at times, was the Christian God: when a woman who wanted to divorce lost two children, a Father told her that "God isn't laughed at" (*Mungu haichekwi*); in another case, a Singiza headman who had lied to the Father "paid for" that lie when God took the life of his daughter. If these were mere warnings about general conduct, in yet another case God intervened in a struggle between a missionary and one of his enemies: after the former told the latter that he would be punished for making trouble against him, the man promptly lost both hands in an explosion (and was brought to hospital by his "enemy"). That missionary magic could, in Luguru thinking, shade into witchcraft is also apparent from the fact that a man was accused of *uchawi* because he hid old medals and rosaries under his bed. The charity (in this case, free distribution of food) of the Mgeta Sisters was misinterpreted, by the lepers who were supposed to receive it, as a way to bewitch people so they would all become Christians.[31]

When asked, however, most Catholic Waluguru deny that missionaries could be witches.[32] Reminiscences of attitudes among Matombo Waluguru towards missionary healing in the 1930s do not stress the possible evil intent of missionaries, but the ambivalence about, and danger of, sacred substances such as the host, holy water, medals and rosaries. If holy water could free a field of black magic, it is obvious that non-Christians should be careful not to touch it (a Muslim would jump back when, during a blessing, drops of holy water flew about). Pagan children would warn their fellow-schoolmates of a boy who had already been baptized: don't touch him (*msiguse*)! People recall that if one touched a goat or chicken with a rosary or medal, pagan elders would refuse to eat it and give the animal to a Christian (after beating up the person who did the touching). The animal was classified in the same way as a baptized Christian: *amekula matema*.[33]

---

[31] BHG 28 (1932): 211, 31 (1935): 110–1, 47 (1951): 170; KMM 447/1b: 237; IPAC 3a: 644, 4a: 030/320/416; KD 9.10.38.
[32] Catholic Waluguru say the *shehe* (Koran teacher and healer) is a witch who had to kill to obtain his powers. I guess one would hear the same about a priest from a Muslim.
[33] IPAC 4a: 030; P. Winkelmolen, Morogoro, 23.11.89; Mzee Petri Mloka, Benedicta Bunga, Kiswira, 14.12.89.

Kula matema was an early translation of "to baptize" (whereas now, the swahili *kubatiza*, loaned from the English, is commonly used, Johnson 1939: 31). The word *matema* is interesting: I suspect it was initially a bantuized form of the French *baptême*, introduced by the Alsatian Fathers, but this was not confirmed by the Waluguru whom I asked about it. They referred to the verb *ukutema*, to cut (kil.). *Kula matema* (itself a hybrid, because *kula*, to eat, is Swahili) could in that case be translated as "to eat cutting stuff". This translation is contextualized by one of my informants' memory of the profound ambivalence with which candidates for baptism approached the church: on the way, they would hesitate, and debate whether it was good to *kula matema* or not.[34] This suggests that conjecture about the magical power of Christian subtances provoked a debate about contact and the cutting of contact; after all, a Christian was supposed to observe a number of taboos which cut him or her off from ordinary Luguru practices of healing, and therefore, of sociability and power as well.

By itself, the concept of *kula matema* is flimsy evidence for these debates about magical contact, were it not that according to Father Vermunt, one of the basic concepts of Waluguru for explaining and discussing healing was *luhungo*, which he translates as "contact", or, alternatively, as "an act by which a friendly relation is established" between persons or between a person and an object. "Friendly relation" is evidently similar to Frazer's "sympathy", because Vermunt also wrote that contagious magic is an example of *luhungo*. *Tambiko* was *luhungo*; calling the name of an ancestor is to contact him or her. Children who were scared of, for instance, a European car or house are comforted by letting them touch it: *luhungo* again. Showing trust in someone by eating his or her food and using his or her house or possessions was also *luhungo*. The idea of contact also figures in explaining charms: they are defences against bad *luhungo*. Where misfortune occurs, good *luhungo* has to be restored.[35] Knowing this, the

---

[34] Adriani Nyawale, Morogoro, 16.12.89.

[35] MSS Vermunt 5.4: "Luhungo. Mwiko. Dawa", 6.0: "Uganga: Mapembe. Gamahembe", "Uganga: Luhungo". Johannes Fabian (personal communication) suggested that *kula* – to eat – is semantically similar to *luhungo* in other Bantu languages (accede to power, strike a friendship, marriage, having sex). Indeed, Catholic baptism was followed by communion – shared food.

ambivalence about baptism is explained by the fact that it not only brought someone into contact with a new, powerfully present way of life but it also tended to cut many relations with the old one.

Judging from the dearth of witchcraft accusations against missionaries (but see below) and from present-day discussions about them, Waluguru were led to think that missionaries brought good contact, but were not very efficacious against *bad* contact. The Catholic priest is now called a "corrector of sin" (*mrekebishaji dhambi*). He cannot give effective protection against witchcraft (*si kazi yake*, "that's not his job"). Blessings and other forms of Catholic healing are necessary but do not give certainty (*uhakiku*) in warding off evil influences. The only certainty the missionaries could give was the oath on the bible or the cross, which people took clothed in black, just as a Mass for the deceased was attended in black. Black cloth (*kaniki*) is worn by healers claiming to possess a spirit, by children in the spirit-world of an initiation camp, and by lineage elders going to commune with ancestors. Someone who lied while taking the oath on the Bible in that dress would die on the spot. Thus, it seems Christianity severed contact with local spirits to replace them by the worship of God and the Saints. The missionaries were, however, not able to immunize people to against witchcraft.[36] The ambiguity of the field of *uganga* and *uchawi* guaranteed that, had they been effective against witches, they would have to have power to harm, too, and lose their status as white *waganga*. Instead, they reinforced the split between spiritual and secular power which both missionary institutions (see chapter two) and governmental control of education (see chapter five) introduced in Uluguru.

The younger healers mentioned in the previous section may have adapted to the presence of the missionaries by dropping the claim to restore contact with wrathful ancestors, or to cure ordinary

---

[36] Adriani Nyawale, Morogoro, 18.9.89; Thomas Martiniani, Kiswira, 6.12.89; Camillus Kunambi, Kiswira, 30.9.90; Mama Mkoba, Kiswira, 30.9.90. See Schoffeleers (1988: 163, 167); the split may also explain the absence, in Uluguru, of the millenarian image of Christ as a slain healer known elsewhere in Africa (1988: 169–71).

disease (which European missionaries and medicine claimed to do better). Instead, they concentrated on the non-spiritual residue of evil and misfortune against which missionaries were not thought to be effective. These healers dealt in wordly magic, a politics of threat and counter-threat which did not *heal* so much as reinforce existing inequalities. They shared this realm of magical action with travelling witchfinders (whose example they followed). Such secular magic was dominated more by the concept of medicines (*dawa*) than that of spirit (*mzimu*). It seems Luguru healing split into two: one form drawing the practice of contact through spirits into European practices of worship, the other retaining the link of medicines – the possession and exchange of (magical) objects – to worldly power. Nothing symbolizes this latter field better than the name adopted by the healers who cleansed Uluguru of evil medicines in the late 1950s: Nguvumali, "Force of property".[37]

NGUVUMALI THE MEDICINE HUNTER

One of the few places where one could find modernity coupled to witchcraft in colonial anthropology is in the phrase "modern witchfinding" (Brain 1964; Richards 1935). Witchfinding was "modern" to the extent that the breakdown of society under colonialism – especially the prohibition of older systems of witchcraft control – was thought to lead to African anxieties about an increase in witchcraft (Douglas 1963; Marwick 1950). Thus, even an analysis of "witchcraft eradication" movements that provided for the possibility of social innovation (by picturing them as "proto-institutions") remained caught in the presupposition of the structural-functionalist paradigm that envisaged African societies as being caught in the "prison" of traditional beliefs (Willis 1968, 1970: 133). In contrast, historians of witchcleansing movements have stressed their novelty, especially in transcending older forms of organisation

---

[37] The translation is problematic. "Force of" and "force to obtain" property are both possible (Johannes Fabian, personal communication); in the second translation, power is not (yet) completely commodified.

(Gwassa 1972; Iliffe 1967; Larson 1974, 1976; Ranger 1966, 1972). I feel this tallies with the argument (p. 141–2) that "witchcraft eradication" can better be seen as the search for and neutralization of medicines in the possession of people whose previous position of power had been overturned by a sudden upheaval in political relationships (cf. Parkin 1968). Medicine in the possession of people who were not in a position to heal socially increased the possibility for uncontrolled magical malevolence. Modern witchfinding's exclusive emphasis on medicine (*dawa*) as both source and cure of evil shows that it implied a modernization – a further commodification – of Luguru healing. The mobility of medicines like Kinjekitile's *maji* and the *usembe* of Ngoja and Nguvumali allowed for an application that was as translocal as the (colonial) source of the political upheaval it tried to counter.

When, therefore, the preparation for the general elections in 1957 had shown that African nationalism put a new generation in power in Uluguru, a *mganga* was needed from the outside to neutralize the loose medicines of the previous powerholders. The man who originally adopted and popularized the name Nguvumali was a Mmatumbi from south-eastern Tanganyika, an adept of the *uliro* magic of the shrine of Bokero, near Kilwa Kivinje, who died in a car accident in 1957 (Lienhardt 1968: 71–2, 195). The name passed on (maybe to former retainers or servants of the original), probably much as the name and spirit of an ancestor could be transferred to a descendant, and to such an extent that some of my informants thought "Nguvumali" was the generic name for such healers.[38] On the 26th of July 1958, the Singiza Fathers suddenly heard that Nguvumali had arrived with twelve aides and government permission to cleanse Uluguru of witchcraft. The Fathers recorded that everyone had to take his medicine (*usembe*) or be faced with death through witchcraft. They wrote that tales went round about large numbers of people surrendering baskets full of evil gourds (*nunguli*) and horns (*mapembe*). The medicine which Nguvumali confiscated – rumored to include human skulls and bones to which

---

[38] MP, Government and Schools: Duff to Procura, 2.12.58; IPAC 16b: 166; Mzee Mikaeli Mlosa, Zava, 23.11.89.

the flesh still clung – would have to be collected and shown by Nguvumali at the district headquarters. People could be immunized against witchcraft for seventeen years by the application of powdered *usembe* on their tongues and foreheads. Men paid one shilling, women 1/20 because they were thought to be more prone to practice witchcraft.[39]

Next day, "Christ wept over Singiza", as the Fathers wrote: it was the feast of the Bishop's silver jubilee as a priest, but the collection only amounted to sh. 13/25 while the day before at least sh. 100/- had been brought to Nguvumali. The Fathers refused the sacraments to those who had been to the medicine hunter and closed the mission dispensary. "The Father wants us to die", some people said. Others argued that they had no choice but to go to Nguvumali because they were ordered to by government. The Fathers got the headman and schoolteachers to inquire about the "government permission" that Nguvumali claimed to have. Subchief Hega told the Father Superior that, to the contrary, he had ordered the people *not* to receive the *mganga*. People would not believe the headmen who read the subchief's order and suspected it had been issued by the mission. In Kolero, some who refused to take *usembe* were beaten up. On August 1, the Fathers barred people from confession. The following Sunday, the faithful were told they had been cheated by Nguvumali and that they had sinned against the First Commandment, for which they had to pay a fine equivalent to what they had given Nguvumali. Few paid the fine, however, and people even dared to argue with the Fathers that Nguvumali would have to return to Singiza: his work guaranteed collective obedience to the Fifth Commandment ("Thou shalt not kill" each other by witchcraft).[40]

In the meantime, the Native Authorities had arrested Nguvumali and brought him to Morogoro, but the District

---

[39] SD 26.7.58; I suggest the suspicion of women was based on the colonial modification of male–female relationships (ch. 5): love magic may have increased to alleviate uncertainty about the migrant husband's economic contribution to the household.

[40] SD 27.7.58, 29.7.58, 1.8.58, 3.8.58, 10.8.58.

Commissioner, Patrick Duff, was not legally empowered to detain Nguvumali. Early in November Nguvumali was at work on Matombo mission territory, whence the Matombo Fathers had him removed by the Mtamba police. Nevertheless, Nguvumali continued his work, extending it along the Mfizigo river up towards Kibungo. There, he inflated his credibility with the claim that the Bishop in Morogoro had given his permission, but was stopped by "the Giant" Father Winkelmolen and sent scuttling back to the lower slopes. The Christians of higher-up Nyingwa now had to do without Nguvumali's presence (although he sent his deputies) and were so angry with Winkelmolen that, according to one informant, they were at the point of "doing something to him". Father Winkelmolen himself told me that he preached against Nguvumali because he destroyed both the devotion and the common-sense that the missionaries had tried to build up, but that his preaching was ill received by the people of Kibungo.[41]

Meanwhile, Nguvumali's deputies had returned to the Singiza area, where the Fathers tried in vain to get the people of Vihamvi to testify against them in the subchief's court. Like the Kibungo people, Vihamvi Christians denied the Fathers' right to interfere with Nguvumali and *usembe*-dealing, and they only reconciled with the mission four years later (after the Bishop himself had intervened). The DC wrote to the Fathers that he was unable to do something about it as long as Nguvumali was invited by the people themselves to hold "a simple cleansing ceremony". He could only be prosecuted when he would start to impute witchcraft to people, but Sultan Sabu and his deputy, Patrick Kunambi, had advised Duff that Nguvumali was not interested in smelling out witches. The Singiza Father interpreted this as meaning that Nguvumali received permission from the DC, and indeed, Duff's letter prohibiting Nguvumali to trespass on mission land can be read as providing this permission (and no doubt Nguvumali was shrewd enough to use it as such). Nguvumali continued to harass the Kasanga and Singiza

[41] SD 3.8.58, MD 7.11.58; Mzee Mikaeli Mlosa, Nyingwa, 23.11.89; Mzee Alfonsi Kigundula, Nyingwa, 26.9.90; F. Winkelmolen, Morogoro, 30.11.89, 19.12.89, 14.8.90.

Fathers until July 1959, when he fell fatally ill. Nguvumali spent his last days in Morogoro hospital, where a Holy Ghost Father visited him for a friendly chat and found Nguvumali quite charming and not at all as boastful of his witchfinding powers as he had expected.[42]

I went into this story in detail, because it is through detail that we can untangle some of the confusion which Nguvumali used to his advantage. In the first place, the reaction of the missionaries shows that they classified medicine hunting as a religious practice antagonistic to their own. The reaction of the population, however, shows they thought it had nothing to do with religion and that the missionaries had no right to interfere. Government attitudes conformed to the missionaries' view, but with inverted results: government should not interfere in matters of religion ("a cleansing ceremony"). This had not always been the government's attitude, however. The visit, in November 1926, of Nguvumali's predecessor in Uluguru, Ngoja bin Kimeta (see p. 141), was cut short by the Provincial Commissioner who ordered Ngoja to confine his movements to Dar es Salaam. Most administrators thought Ngoja's work was "detrimental to good order" and feared a recurrence of Maji Maji (apart from the connection through *uliro* medicine, apparently called *usembe* in Uluguru, Ngoja's father was reported as having been an important man in the Maji Maji rebellion). After Ngoja died in 1932, numerous other travelling witchfinders were reported to have toured parts of Eastern Province, but none of them created the stir among administrators that Ngoja did (Fields 1982b: 585; Larson 1974). Administrative fears abated and during the war, witchfinding was classified as "religion".[43] This classification was, I feel, wrong.

---

[42] SD 19.11.58, 5.12.58, 22.1.59, 22–25.4.59, 3–5.7.59, 22.7.59, 6–8.8.59, 22.2.60, 23.7.62, KD 23.1.59; MP, Government and Schools: Duff to Procura, 2.12.58; IPAC 12b: 498; the letter from Sultan Sabu to the subchief of Matombo on Abdallah Mpangile "Nguvumali" explicitly says he has permission to practice in Matombo before detailing that he should not do so on mission land (MP, Correspondence: Sultan to Mtwala Matombo, 3.12.58).
[43] See TNA 12333, "Ngoja bin Kimeta", *passim*. After a complaint about a popular witchfinder by a Catholic Bishop, the Mahenge DC told his PC that "we are dealing here with a conflict between two rival bodies wishing to abolish

The coming of Ngoja after the introduction of Indirect Rule, and Nguvumali after the rise of African nationalism in the wake of the Uluguru Land Usage Scheme riots, indicate that it was political crisis that provoked the demand for a medicine hunter. Moreover, they were called in by the villagers themselves, and the fact that other large-scale witchcraft accusations and requests for government help in moving in a *mganga* were reported at the same time, testify to the fact that it was a political conjuncture feeding this local demand, rather than the self-advertising of Ngoja and Nguvumali, that created the movement.[44] Moreover, the credibility, to Waluguru, of the medicine hunter's claim to carry permission of the government itself indicates his "secular" intentions. The indignation of Waluguru when confronted with missionary resistance to medicine hunting shows that they thought Nguvumali's work did not conflict with "religion" (see Hasani 1968: 178, 180; Lienhardt 1968: 74).

Apart from perceiving a threat to their religion, the missionaries thought Nguvumali brought discord among Waluguru because he pointed out witches. It may be significant that Chief Sabu and his deputy Patrick Kunambi denied that such accusations occurred, when they advised Duff not to prosecute Nguvumali, and reported he was merely holding "cleansing ceremonies". Although, indeed, Nguvumali sought out medicines rather than witches, both Sabu and Kunambi knew this was only part of the story, and their reticence suggests they were trying to conform to the wishes of the people whom they represented. On arrival, Nguvumali never directly pointed out a witch, but would start to look for the horns (*mapembe*) and gourds (*nunguli*) that contained the worldly magic of combat and defense used in the inter-lineage politics of threat,

---

black magic by supernatural means, and as a Government servant I do not feel it right for me to favour the methods of one at the expense of the other ... what is religion and faith to one is magic and superstition to the other" (a point of view which the PC was loath to present to the Bishop in such terms): TNA 61/128: Witchcraft, 1932–39: *passim*.

[44] TNA 11676/I: Ann. Rep. Eastern Province, 1927; TNA 26/223/3: Anonymous letter from Kibwe village, July 1957, Anonymous letter, August 1957; Mzee Alfonsi Kigundula, Nyingwa, 26.9.90.

attack and gift-exchange. Thus, to say that Nguvumali did not point out witches is a half-truth: he identified them through digging up their medicines, because those who possessed *mapembe* or *nunguli* clearly meant to harm others. (The word *usembe*, which Waluguru used for Nguvumali's benevolent counter-magic, had been in use for magic that countered *dukula*, an evil medicine used to deprive someone of his crops at another's advantage).[45]

Thus, it seems that Nguvumali's work was intended to counter the medicines of people engaged in regaining their lost secular power. Political upheaval upset the balance of power and medicine: whereas those who were in power were usually thought to be in a better position to obtain medicine for protection and attack, changes in the allocation of power implied that people who lost power still possessed dangerous medicines. The political imbalance was thought to lead to an increasing use of these medicines, and this posed a threat to the community as a whole: *mapembe* are said to roam about at night, liable to hurt an innocent passer-by; they can even harm the person that possesses them.[46] It was on this field of worldly magic – but including intra-lineage issues of family politics and economic jealousies – that the younger healers of the 1970s concentrated by offering a tremendous scala of medicines (see plate 16), but although they imitated the travelling medicine hunters in their alomst exclusive reliance on cure by commodity, they were never as successful as Ngoja or Nguvumali.

MUMIANI: IMAGINATIONS OF CONTACT

It is significant that missionaries were never mentioned as employing such worldly magic and counter-magic except in the case of Brother Rudolf, who was not a priest and did not possess the latter's spiritual defenses against evil. As a young man leading the Matombo carpentry workshop, he had to do the work of a

---

[45] Mzee Petri Mloka, Kiswira, 14.12.89; MSS Vermunt 6.0: "Mapembe. Gamahembe", "Uganga. Dukula".

[46] MSS Vermunt 6.0: "Mapembe. Gamahembe"; this 'lust' for harm can be compared to the sexual connotation of *pembe* (see p. 131).

"big man" or elder (*mkubwa* or *mzee*) while not initially possessing the respect which came with experience and old age. Lacking spiritual power – embodied by his inability to say Mass, the prerogative of the priests – he was thought to rely on certain extremely powerful medicines, and this rumor made the first year of his stay in Matombo into a severe trial. Rudolf was accused of being the *mumiani*, the white vampire who makes strong medicine out of Africans' blood. Before we bring this chapter to a conclusion, it will be necessary to consider what this tells us about the contact between Waluguru and missionaries.

Soon after Brother Rudolf was transferred from Mhonda to Matombo in 1959, a corpse was found in the river nearby the carpentry workshop. It was rumored that the *mumiani* was responsible, and suspicion fastened on Rudolf: didn't it happen shortly after he came? Hadn't things always been peaceful while his predecessors, Brothers Patrick and Nico were there? Tension mounted up to the point where a teacher felt he had to warn Rudolf not to venture outside the mission house. At one time, a mob gathered threateningly at the Mhangazi bridge which the Brother had to pass when returning from the workshop; although he passed unscathed, he was openly accused some days later. Suspicion was deflected when a geologist suddenly appeared prospecting in the Mhangazi river; he barely escaped a lynching mob by hiding in the church. Later, the murderers were identified and the Matombo people shamefully excused themselves to the Brother, but the experience had been so harrowing that for some time, Rudolf refused to return to Matombo after his leave in Holland.[47]

The Swahili word *mumiani* seems to have been an adaptation of *momiyai*, a word introduced into coastal culture by Indian soldiers serving in East Africa which designated an enormously powerful medicine made from a fluid which was extracted from human bodies. In India, *momiyai* was rumoured to be gathered by the British, especially in hospitals or mortuaries, and *mumiani* rumours in East Africa often focussed on the same institutions (Arnold 1988: 406–7;

---

[47] MD 19.12.59 to 24.11.60, MtD 25.3.60, 17.4.60; IPAC 3a: 424–603, 4a: 320; Mzee Petri Mloka, Kiswira, 8–15.10.89; this section summarizes Pels 1992a.

Baker 1930, 1946; Gordon 1929, 1933, 1934; Huntingford 1934). *Momiyai* may have been linked to African suspicions of Europeans using their bodies for magical purposes. Whereas *mumiani* rumours are said to have started in Mombasa around 1904 (where the Indian troops had their first headquarters – Hollingsworth 1960: 39–40), suspicions about the use of African bodies for cannibalistic or blood-sucking purposes were probably present as far inland as Kilosa around 1895. DC Hutchins reported that the rumours became common in Uluguru from about 1930 onwards, because according to him, a research team took blood samples for yellow-fever research at the time. Some of the missionaries heard that *mumiani* was the substance which gave European fuel the power that propelled cars and areoplanes.[48]

While *mumiani* first only referred to the magical substance itself (Johnson 1939: 314; Sacleux 1939: 625), in Hutchins' account it had already acquired the additional, present-day meaning of "white vampire" (also, "butcher" [*chinjachinja* or simply *mchinja*]; see Kamusi 1981: 198). In the Uluguru mountains, the rumour usually grafted itself on the presence of strange white men in the vicinity. Those most likely to be accused were lonely prospectors, engineers or surveyors who camped wherever they had to do their work, and especially the cattle and game officer (*bwana nyama*). They all shared the characteristics of having hardly any contact with the local community and spending a lot of their time in the bush. (The upsurge in *mumiani* rumours reported by Hutchins took place shortly after Matombo experienced a small gold-rush by white prospectors.)[49]

Holy Ghost missionaries were very seldom accused of being *mumiani*, which contrasts sharply with the findings of Luise White

---

[48] TNA 21855: "Mumiani", passim; TNA MF 19, MDB: "Mumiani or Chinjachinja", by E. Hutchins 1938; BHG 30 (1934): 119–22, 44 (1948): 44–5; IPAC 4a: 320; MD 8.12.18.

[49] Who, as a result of the accusation, could not obtain indigenous labour; TNA MF 19, MDB: "Mumiani or Chinjachinja", by. E. Hutchins 1938; BHG 32 (1936): 67–9. For the Matombo gold rush, see MD 27.12.33, 31.12.33, 28.1.34, 1.2.34, 4.9.35, 13.10.35, and p. 70.

about the "vampire priests" of Northern Rhodesia. She reports that White Fathers were accused (as a body) of the trade in blood. One interpretation of the rumour advanced by White focuses on the fact that mission labour contrasted unfavourably with the wage labour relationships to which Bemba men were accustomed in the mines (1993: 765).[50] This association of wage labour with vampire rumours is interesting even if it does not really apply to Uluguru. I only know of two Holy Ghost missionaries who were accused: Brother Rudolf, mentioned above, and Father Winkelmolen, who has not been able to shed *mumiani* accusations ever since they clung to him when he was the pastor of Kibungo in the late 1950s. Both Rudolf and Father Winkelmolen were engaged in wage labour relationships, the former through employing workers at the mission carpentry workshop, the latter through his perpetual engagement with building projects in the missions where he worked. But the fact that many other missionaries also employed Africans (see pp. 100–2) and were not accused shows that the association of *mumiani* rumours with wage labour was not a necessary one (see White 1993: 767).

Even if the association of wage labour with *mumiani* rumours was not necessarily direct, White's argument that *mumiani* rumours were linked to a "distorted" form of colonial contact is still important. Such "distortion", I would argue, took place when Europeans who employed Africans did not extend this contact to a "normal" relationship with them – according to Luguru norms. Most *mumiani* rumours fastened on people who did not (yet) engage in daily interaction with the local population. Brother Rudolf had only just arrived. Surveyors, engineers, and cattle and game wardens, all of whom employed Africans, were doing their work in the bush, which, as we have seen, was a place of danger for Waluguru (see p. 165). Father Winkelmolen, moreover, preferred to travel at night, when Waluguru think *mapembe*, *wawanga* witches (see below), and *mumiani* are about. As we have seen, his preaching against Nguvumali was interpreted as less than social. Associations with the bush and the night are qualitative, symbolic aspects of the

---

[50] For a fuller discussion of a manuscript version of her paper see Pels 1992a.

lack of contact with local human society that are easily reinter-
preted as the evil, *inverted* sociality of witchcraft, and the *mumiani*
in particular. I suggest that, when wage labour relationships were
not seen as embedded in mutual trust, embodied in acts of communication and (minimal) sharing of power and skills, Waluguru interpreted them as anti-social.

In this respect, the comparison of the *mumiani* with another
terrifying inhabitant of Uluguru, the *mwanga* witch, is illuminating:
in Uluguru, *wawanga* are old men or women who are out at night
for their evil work. They feed on corpses dug up for the purpose,
feed unsuspecting people with human meat so they will die, or carry
them away to till the *wawanga*'s mysterious fields until dawn, when
the victim wakes up tired but oblivious of any nocturnal exertion.
Wawanga are always naked, although only very strong counter-
medicine can make them show their nakedness during the day.
Some people suspect the *mwanga* is more powerful than any of his
"good" opponents, the *mganga* in particular.[51]

The *mumiani* is in many ways similar to the *mwanga*: he is
also out in the bush at night; his power is secular, as it is derived
from the ability and willingness to sacrifice fellow-humans (and not
from the spiritual support claimed by lineage healers, headmen and
Catholic priests). Both the *mwanga* and the *mumiani* occupy an
imaginary realm of anti-social consumption of human bodies which
contrasts with the destruction of the body of political rivals which
is the result of *mapembe* sorcery; whereas *mapembe* can be combated by the healer, he is (nearly) powerless in relation to *mwanga*
and *mumiani*. There is a significant difference, however, in that the
mwanga uses human bodies for food, or for labour (in which case
the victim escapes tired but unharmed). The *mumiani*, in contrast,
uses the blood of his victim as a commodity: as medicine or as fuel.

The significance of the difference between *mwanga* and
mumiani becomes clearer when we acknowledge that both seem to

---

[51] Camillus Kunambi, Mama Mkoba, Kiswira, 30.9.90; MSS Vermunt 6.0:
"Uganga. Mwanga". It seems the *mwanga* occupies a less prominent place on
the Swahili coast: according to Lienhardt (1968: 61), they are "minor sorcerers"
who cannot compete with medicine men or witches.

be reflections on the exploitation of labour. However, if the *mwanga* sucks people's energy for nocturnal agriculture, the white vampire transforms labour power by killing victims and turning them into medicine. Not only did *mumiani* rumours fasten on people who employed Africans (gold prospectors, surveyors, engineers, Brother Rudolf, Father Winkelmolen), they usually cropped up when Waluguru were forced to engage in wage labour: seasonally, in February and March, when food was scarce, and historically, when cash cropping was suffering from the Depression (1931–8), when the government conscripted Africans for the army (1941–3), and during the 1947 famine.[52] When we realize that, for Waluguru, wage labour was a kind of surrender of the body to a labour discipline far removed from the exchange of labour in lineage relations of production, it becomes easier to understand why the rumors coincided with increases in wage labour relationships.

To a predominantly cash cropping economy, wage labour must have been a mixed blessing. It took away labour power and those who went away returned with an independent income which, as we have seen in chapters three and four, threatened existing relationships within the (extended) family, and consequently, the existing relations of agricultural production. In a society where wage labour was exchanged through kinship and reciprocal obligation, and marked by reconciliation through *tambiko*, the mere exchange of labour power for money must have appeared as a *lack* of contact between employer and employee. Moreover, both plantation labour and the public works for which Europeans needed labour were characterized by a disciplinary organization and goals of work far removed from Luguru experience. Road works and sisal plantations for which Waluguru had no use, and work discipline wholly determined by Europeans and their overseers, must have given the impression that wage labour was a kind of surrender of one's body

---

[52] TNA MF 19, MDB: "Mumiani or Chinjachinja", by E. Hutchins 1938; SD 17.10.40, KD 3.11.43; IPAC 7b: 161. Compare this to the evidence on wage labour collected in chapter three. Increase in wage labour among Waluguru does not explain the cases from the late 1950s, although tension between Africans and British was of course strong before independence.

to Europeans which was not matched by an equal participation in these relations of production.

The *mumiani* can be taken as a metaphor of these relationships: the surrender of one's body for money equalled its commodification as medicine or fuel. Moreover, the African's *blood* was significant, because it indicated, within the relations of production characteristic of Luguru society, bonds which were at the core of these relationships: descent (seen as the sharing of blood) and marriage (which was concluded by the sharing of blood between husband and wife; see p. 180). In this sense, blood was *luhungo*, contact. The *mumiani* took the African's blood, but the *mwanga* either ate the African's body or used his labour power (without killing him) for agricultural production. In other words, while this black witch cannibalized Africans in relations of production and reproduction familiar to Waluguru, the white witch produced blood in relations of medical or industrial discipline from which they were alienated.[53]

This also explains why the missionaries in Uluguru were not often accused of being the *mumiani*. They deplored wage labour when it induced boys to go to work on the plantations and play truant from the mission school. Catechists were wage labourers, but I have tried to show in chapter five that they were also "big men" because they worked as overseers of the local Christians: they actually organized the new relations of religious production, rather than being subordinated to a strange and uncontrollable labour discipline. The arguments of the missionaries against the *mwalimu-kibarua* (see chapter five) show that they tried to counteract wage labour relationships in this field, too. In chapter two, I have shown that the Brothers' relationship with their workers was either based on local routines which did not draw the labourer away from home, or, in the case cited in that chapter, on Vidunda family relations of production. The carpentry workshops, moreover, trained Waluguru,

---

[53] Cf. Arnold (1988), who shows that during the plague epidemic of 1896–1900, Indian *momiyai* rumours were triggered by the impact of a European medical discipline on Indian bodies. Cf. also Fisiy and Geschiere's account of a Cameroonian magic for the exploitation of labour (1991).

and therefore taught a trade even if they imposed labour discipline. In other words, the mission's wage labour relationships were contextualized by a proliferation of contacts and therefore less alienating than the mere exchange of physical energy for money.

The missionaries who were accused of being the *mumiani* engaged in wage labour relationships which were more one-dimensional. Brother Rudolf's case can be explained by the fact that he was still relatively unknown to Matombo Waluguru when the murders occurred. Moreover, as I indicated above, the discrepancy between his youth and his superior position may invited speculations about his superior powers. Father Winkelmolen did not engage in the exchange of Christian magic which did so much to produce contact with Waluguru, and his quick temper may have tempted him to cut off relationships in a way that did not agree with Luguru etiquette.[54] Thus, we might argue that *mumiani* rumours were ways to debate a form of colonial contact which Waluguru experienced as a lack or distortion of contact.

CONCLUSION

In summary, I have tried to argue that to understand the engagement of missionaries with Luguru magical practice one starts with an advantage when departing from a Malinowskian theory of the magical act rather than from a theory of witchcraft as a system of belief. Missionaries took up a specific place in the field of action and discourse that Waluguru call *uganga* and *uchawi*, and where their acts created a kind of continuity between Luguru practices and Catholic worship (through blessings, rosaries, and other materials of communication), both the debates of missionaries and those of Waluguru about *uganga* and *uchawi* displayed various types of explanations ranging from disbelief to speculations on how *uganga* and *uchawi* worked. On the discursive level, however, there were

---

[54] His temper was regarded as *moto*, in contrast with Luguru norms of proper "cool" (*baridi*) behavior; it is interesting that the *mwanga*, when discovered, spits fire.

few points where missionaries could agree with Waluguru. While Waluguru generally tried to combine foreign expertise in the spiritual with existing practice, the missionaries were as jealous as their God in guarding His exclusive right to worship and supplication. As in so many other colonial situations, the Europeans' dichotomous view of the colonial world was contextualized by a practice of translating, merging, accomodating, inverting and reinventing "traditional" and "modern" routines.

If the missionaries' intervention in Luguru healing nevertheless produced a dichotomy, a split in the Luguru world between spiritual and secular activities, then this had less to do with the missionaries' understanding of worship and healing than with the way in which their acts spoke to Waluguru about the separate spheres of competence of healers in the spiritual and healers in the secular realm. By consistently undercutting the spiritual basis of lineage *uganga*, demonstrating their power in the biomedical curing of illness, and more or less consistently acting in the realm of benevolent magic only, the missionaries excluded a large part of the Luguru treatment of misfortune from their activities. This part was taken up by a novel kind of *mganga*, who almost exclusively concentrated on the treatment of affliction by medicines. The model of such healing seems to derive from the travelling medicine hunter. Thus, the largest part of Luguru healing was divided between three new roles, all three based on expertise or commodities from outside Uluguru: the (bio)medical doctor or dresser, with whom I have not dealt here, the missionary (the priest in particular), and the travelling medicine hunter. What this means for the development of religion, power and social discipline in Uluguru we shall discuss in the conclusion.

CHAPTER SEVEN

Conclusion:
The Underdevelopment
of Luguru Revelation

Pope Pius XI may not have had a missionary like
Father Bukkems in mind when he said that Catholic mission implied
a "politics of presence" (cited in Oliver 1952: 274), but the phrase
adequately captures the mission strategy of the Roman church in
Uluguru, of which Bukkems was only one, and a rather eccentric,
representative. The task they took upon themselves brought
Catholic missionaries closer to Africans than most other Europeans
were prepared to come (Oliver 1952: 242; Forster 1986: 101). Such
an ideological and practical emphasis on colonial presence contrasts
with the mediation through ethnographic representation by which the
British administrators of Uluguru constituted their contact with its
inhabitants (Pels 1994; 1996). To the Holy Ghost missionaries, their
personal presence, and the expansion of that presence, were more
important to the spread of Christianity than knowledge and expertise of converts and conversion. As their spiritual father, Francis
Libermann, said: "... This African race will not be converted through
the exertions of capable and clever missionaries, but through holiness and sacrifice". In the end, the missionaries' task would not be
accomplished by adequate representations of those they were to
convert, and strategies of conversion based on them, but by the way
the mission embodied a Divine gift. Catholic missions were founded
on the sacrifice of the self, not on the study of the other.[1]

Any analysis of missionary work in terms of the adequacy of
its ethnographic representations – often, modernized versions
of the argument that the "Missionary point of view" on Europe's

---

[1] Libermann cited in BHG 44 (1948): inside cover. Cf. C. G. Seligmann (cited
in Lewis 1976: 76): "Field research in Anthropology is what the blood of the
martyrs is to the Church".

others consists of paraphrases of "customs none, manners beastly" (Malinowski 1922: 10) – is therefore bound to be somewhat one-sided. Of course, Catholic missionaries at home sometimes adopted a politics of ethnographic representation, as is witnessed by, for instance, Father Schmidt's journal *Anthropos* (1906), the participation of Catholics in the International African Institute (1926), or the more or less relativistic notions of Father Charles' "plantation" missiology (see p. 74-5). Moreover, a few Holy Ghost Fathers in Uluguru, as other Catholic missionaries elsewhere, enjoyed doing research and applied their ethnographic expertise in the mission area itself. But while Bishop Hilhorst urged "every missionary" to "try to make a study of the native customs in his own district, in order to be able to abolish those which are contrary to faith and good morals" (Hilhorst 1937: 18), the majority was content to abstain from ethnography (understood as a practice of writing and reflection) and stick to a kind of practical knowledge, taught by their Alsatian Superiors at the dinner-table, and not enlarged by systematic research (Pels 1994: 337).

However, if the core feature of mission is the movement towards to a place in order to rectify a perceived deficiency or lack in that place (cf. pp. 11, 45), we find that the "politics of presence" of the missionaries turns out to be again dependent on a representation of difference – in our case, of Africans as being ignorant of true revelation. In this conclusion, I shall try to interpret the significance of the findings in the preceding chapters for our understanding of colonial contact, by returning to some of the issues addressed in the introduction, and especially to the relation between representations of colonial contact, and the physical contact itself. Throughout the chapters, I have tried to contrast missionary images of otherness with their practical engagement with others in the mission field. We have seen how notions of sacrifice and exoticism were complicated by the practice of moving to the missions, and how the missionaries' distinctions of self and other and spiritual and secular were transformed by the necessity to maintain the mission. In chapter three, I have tried to show how Christianity was indigenized through initiation practices to which the missionaries felt they could not accommodate, and in chapter four, how their images of female emancipation and legal control had to cope with resistance through such routines. In chapter five, the missionary strategy of educational control turned out to have unintended secularizing consequences even for the missionaries themselves, and in chapter six, an indigenous practice of healing turned out to influence Luguru perceptions of colonial contact through the mission in ways the missionaries also could not fathom. Throughout, the missionaries' strategies were submerged in a *bricolage* of improvised tactics and unintended consequences.

In this conclusion, I hope to tie together some of these half-conscious tactics and unintended consequences by an interpretation of their combined effect on Luguru society. I will start by returning to the topic of colonial representation, in a kind of reversal of the Luguru point of view on colonial contact described in the previous chapter. I will analyze the missionaries' notions of appropriate colonial contact by concentrating on the ethnographies they produced, and try to show that they exemplify a kind of magic of representation and registration meant to turn Waluguru into "individual" subjects amenable to conversion. These representations of individuality were a self-evident complement to the missionaries' unquestioning acceptance of European disciplinary practices. However, that discipline of registration and (self-) representation could not be simply imposed on Waluguru: it had to interfere with their lives along the lines of Luguru routines. This complicated practice eventually led to the subordination of Luguru routines to those of an encompassing colonial society, but by processes of commodification which neither missionaries nor Waluguru intended or controlled. In the final section, I try to argue that these processes of commodification led to an underdevelopment of the capacity of Waluguru to provide their own revelations of the constitution of the world. Ironically, this produced a nostalgia for a better past that even the missionaries who initiated this underdevelopment were, at times, inclined to share.

INDIVIDUALITY AND THE MAGIC OF REPRESENTATION

As I have argued at length elsewhere, the mode of production and contents of the missionaries' ethnographies differed considerably from those of professional anthropologists or British administrators of Uluguru.[2] In chapter two I argued that the missionaries learned most of the cultural competences necessary for dealing with the inhabitants of Uluguru not by the book but in practice, by trial-and-error and the coaching of their superiors. Of course, there were exceptions: some missionaries fought boredom and the sin of *acedia* (sloth, lethargy) by engaging in ethnographic work as a hobby. At headquarters, Bishop Hilhorst followed up on his own exhortation to his missionaries to produce ethnography by asking Father Lemblé for a canonically legal notion of "Luguru" marriage. As we saw in chapter four, this set up a version of Luguru marriage that, like administrative ethnography in the field of politics, functioned like a "pidgin" discourse, fusing elements from the substrate Luguru discourse on marriage and the superstrate discourse of Church law, that continued to exist next to and in permanent conflict with the discourses from which it was derived (cf. Pels 1996).

Even those exceptional essays in missionary ethnography, however, differed considerably from their administrative counterparts. Bishop Hilhorst's request for ethnographic research stressed a *selective* activity ("…in order to be able to abolish those [native customs] which are contrary to faith and good morals"; Hilhorst 1937: 18), which resembled late nineteenth-century conceptions of anthropology, rather than the more functionalist and holist notions common among early twentieth-century anthropologists and colonial administrators.[3] Unlike the administrators of Uluguru, the missionaries rarely displayed an interest in defining a "Luguru" ethnicity, using the term "Luguru" in a more purely geographical sense, and preferring to talk of "Africans" when they discussed issues of

---

[2] The following section relies largely on previous publications (Pels 1994, 1996). For references to research material, the reader should consult these.

[3] For Edward Tylor, for instance, "the office of ethnography" was "to expose the remains of crude old culture which have passed into harmful superstition, and to mark these out for destruction" (Tylor 1873, II: 453). Hilhorst's different practical interests show in his replacing "crude old" by middle-aged and even young culture.

cultural difference. This racialist marking of the individual "African" rather than a tribalist "Luguru" collective reflects the missionaries' interest in the conversion and ministry – the personal transformation – of individuals, and it contrasts with the administrators' preoccupation with engineering an evolution from "tribal" patterns of "Luguru" authority to something like British local government. When discussing political authority, missionaries mostly restricted themselves to the realm of family and lineage relationships, and rarely touched upon the issues of chiefship and tribal dominion that were the administrators' prime concern.

In fact, even Bishop Hilhorst's concern with ethnic demarcation – in defining a specifically *Luguru* marriage – was scarce among the Holy Ghost Congregation's grassroots ethnographers. While at headquarters there was a legal necessity to identify a boundary in "tribal" terms that could work to keep converts from entering in un-Christian marriage practices, at the grassroots level, missionary ethnographers were mostly concerned with the generalizations of individual biographies (see chapter four). In their unpublished papers and their occasional publications in Dutch mission propaganda journals, missionary ethnographers concentrated on the lifecycle of individuals, their names, and the obstacles these presented to successful conversion. Many of the articles in the *Holy Ghost Messenger* and *Africa Christo* feature ethnographic accounts interspersed with stories of the success or failure of the writer's attempts to bring his ethnographic subjects into the Christian fold. Thus, these accounts do not distance Waluguru from the culture and society of the author in the same way as ethnographies by twentieth-century anthropologists and administrators do: rather than stressing an "other" life that is both spatially and temporally distant from that of the author, they emphasize the coevalness of missionary and (potential) convert, their participation in a common project of civilization and Christianization (cf. Fabian 1983a). If, as we have seen in chapter three, Christianity changed the rhythm of Luguru life, missionary ethnographers often wrote in a way that was closer to Luguru rhythms of life as well.

At first sight, the missionaries' representations of Luguru society give the impression of a somewhat indiscriminate collection of "customs" and discrete instances of behavior that seem to have little connection with each other (one of the Holy Ghost Fathers' most experienced ethnographers of Uluguru, Father Vermunt, tried but never succeeded to collate his observations in a systematic account). Yet there was a method in this collectors' mania, and one that we can discern precisely because the missionaries often presented the practical context of their observations in the same texts. A striking generic trait of the missionaries' ethnographies is the recurrence of long lists of clan names and their derivations.[4] Father de Rooij's translation and adaptation of a paper by one of his Irish predecessors explains why this is so: he argues that the missionary serves, in Africa, as a pioneer "registrar's office" (*Burgerlijke Stand*). The novice would encounter unforeseen difficulties in finding, for instance, the names of a betrothed couple in the church register. But to the experienced missionary, that is not an obstacle:

> [H]is knowledge of family names provides him with the key to pagan society and many social laws. ... As soon as the missionary hears the family name, he sees at once to which family group or clan his bride or groom belong. Of course he does not know whether there are impediments to marriage, but solely the knowledge of their family names assures him that there is no *pagan* impediment to marriage. (BHG 29 [1933]: 69).

The "pagan impediment" referred to is the prohibition on clan endogamy, but the passage as a whole shows a practical puzzle which all Fathers had to learn to solve: the identification of Luguru individuals. Women were fairly easy to identify, because they usually had a *lukolo* or lineage name: Maria Mlamchuma was simply "Maria, daughter of a Mchuma lineage". But if Maria married a son of a Mwenda lineage, her son received a name from his father's lineage (*mtala*), which could vary from Johani Kung'alo to Johani Mkude, Johani Nguo, Johani Miduli, Johani Mgonza, or Johani Mizambwa, and so forth, all surnames being metaphors or metonymies of the

---

[4] TNA MF 19 MDB: "Waluguru Sibs", by Father Wallis; "The Waluguru" by Father v. d. Kimmenade; MSS Vermunt 2.2: "A Short History of the Uluguru Clans", and 2.4: "History of the Clans"; Father de Rooij in BHG 29 (1933): 69, Scheerder and Tastevin 1950: 249–53, 256.

original *Mwenda* (kil.), "cloth". If this gave rise to problems among Waluguru (when, for instance, Johani moved house to a place where another Johani Kung'alo lived), they simply chose another surname from the available alternatives.

Chapter four documented the missionaries' interest in managing the histories of individual Waluguru, and to do this they had to be able to identify them in their registers. It is no coincidence that most missionaries who engaged in ethnography as a hobby (like Fathers Van den Kimmenade, De Rooij and Scheerder) were exceptionally keen on good church registration. The quote from Father de Rooij's article clearly brings out the bureaucratic and legal context of this interest in clan names, and explains why the majority of missionary ethnographies contain sections on the topic and long lists of *mtala* names. This interest in individuals is also apparent in another important generic trait of the missionaries' Luguru ethnography: the "life-cycle" account, listing rituals surrounding birth, initiation, marriage, the initiation into *mlunga* rank, and death. The life-cycle account thus represented stages directly connected to the administration and refusal of sacraments: birth implied baptism, all initiations could involve refusal of absolution and communion, while marriage and burial required the missionaries' ministrations. The predominance of the life-cycle account seems to be partly fostered by the work of saving individual souls, just as the focus on clan names shows its administrative side.

I want to submit that this concern with the registration of individuals, just as the colonial administrators' concern with establishing "tribal authority" (cf. Pels 1994), is a form of what one can call "the magic of representation". Representation works by the assumption of a difference between representation and referent, or picture and reality, an assumption that sets up the latter as the original or factual (cf. Mitchell 1991: 60–1). The former can only become congruent with the latter by the work of observing the latter: in our case, by ethnographic research. But every such research activity needs to account for the distinction between representation and referent, and assumes certain elements of its terminology to be more neutral and to belong to the realm of referent and reality rather than that of representation. Thus, British administrators thought "chiefs" and "tribes" were the reality behind the different political languages of Tanganyikan societies, and the repetition of this formula in the practice of administration subsequently created many of these "tribes" (cf. Iliffe 1979: 318 ff.). Missionaries assumed that the individual "soul" going through a "life-cycle", and identifiable by a "name", was the neutral term on the side of the real, and this formula conjured up the individuals that it desired as well, although not always and everywhere.[5] Both administrators and missionaries, therefore, practised ethnography as a kind of contagious magic, an "expression of human optimism" (Malinowski 1935a: 239) institutionalized in ethnographic formula. A magic, moreover, that often worked.

In assuming an objective correspondence between terms like "tribe" and "individual" and social reality, this conception of ethnographic formula did not differ very much from Trobriand magical spells that assume an original coevalness between magical words and the reality they are supposed to influence (1935a: 229). It may be important to realize that this "representative" form of contagion – in both ethnographic and Trobriand form – is clearly dependent on the assumption of a simultaneous distinction of, and relation between, the representation or word and the reality it stands for and calls up: for Trobrianders, this relation lay in a mythical past, for missionaries, in a personal past: the assumption that the duration of their stay in Africa gave them privileged access to its secrets.[6] It is therefore different from another form of contagious magic which one may call "tactile" – the "politics of presence" of the missionaries; or the form of contact covered by the Luguru

---

[5] Individuality was also implicit in the missionaries notion of "conversion" (as opposed to *plantatio* theory, see p. 75–6), and in the reduction of the family to the husband. The kind of male–female complementarity that characterized, for instance, the sharing of *milunga* power by husband and wife in Uluguru (see pp. 2, 109), was recognized by missionaries like Placide Tempels, but rejected by church orthodoxy (cf. Fabian 1971).

[6] The knowledge of missionaries was supposed to improve the longer their "experience" in Africa, and this argument was often employed against the claims of academic ethnographers: IPAC 2b: 071, 12a: 464, 17b: 463; KMM 43/1b: 076; 708/2a: 091; BHG 29 (1933): 69; see also Van der Geest (1990).

term *luhungo* (see p. 261) – a contagion by touch, by physical co-presence.

Evans-Pritchard has argued that these different forms of magic – which he condensed to the spell, and the bit of medicine, respectively – reflected different societies, as, indeed, they do to some extent (Evans-Pritchard 1929). But the missionaries seemed to rely on both. Their ritual presence was supposed to work towards salvation of Waluguru in its own respect, although the missionaries could only use mystical notions ("holiness", "sacrifice") to account for this working. This overarching consciousness of an Infinite beyond observer and observed, or missionary and missionized, made conversion into an event that always escaped the consciousness and engineering of participants, and enchanted their work by leaving a considerable amount of it to mysterious powers. And indeed, notwithstanding all differences in interpretation, Waluguru saw the process in a comparable way. Both missionaries and Waluguru saw missionizing as a gift: for the missionaries, the gift of themselves ("sacrifice"); for Waluguru, the gift of religion (*dini*) or "the light" (*nuru*; f.e. Wendelini 1990: 34). Both thought this gift could not be fathomed by the merely human participants in the process, since it worked partly through spiritual influences. Both thought the giving of the gift (in the form of a departure for Africa [chapter two]; or of baptism or *kula matema* [chapter six]) would irreversibly rupture their relations with their previous home.[7]

But as we have seen above, the missionaries' magical repertoire also included bringing persons under "a new and more subtle enchantment" (Mitchell 1991: 62): the modern state's routines of representation. By fixing people's names in the church register, charting their life-cycles, and reducing their biographies to a set of official legal events, the missionaries tried to create the individuals to which their Western notions of conversion and discipline could apply. As with other forms of verbal magic, this statement of individuality was "untrue" and "in direct opposition to the context of

---

[7] In contrast, while colonial administrators thought of their work as the bringing of law and order, Waluguru commonly perceived it as extraction of tax and labour.

reality" (Malinowski 1935a: 239), in so far as Luguru persons were, as I argued in chapters three and four, rather "dividualities" made up of a range of potential embodied dispositions, than the single bodies containing the single souls that the missionaries aimed to convert and discipline.

DISCIPLINE, INITIATION AND COMMODIFICATION

Michel Foucault wrote that discipline dissociates power from the body, making the latter into an object that could be counted, policed and made industrious (Foucault 1979: 138; see also Mitchell 1991: 127). This commodification of the human body – both for installing obedience and purposes of self-control – was, as we have seen, central to the conduct of the mission itself. The doctrine of sacrifice urged the young recruits of the mission to subject themselves to its central strategy of moving personnel to a place where ignorance of original revelation had to be eliminated. A similar kind of discipline was, in varying degrees of intensity, applied to Waluguru in the schools and the church. In chapter four, I argued that this application of discipline was never completely successful. The example of Luguru women's resistance to the abolition of their initiation practices indicated the impossibility of a complete take-over of Luguru routines of initiation by the mission's regime of legal and bureaucratic representation and its corresponding form of discipline. The disembodiment of power which discipline entails was resisted by Luguru women, and this may serve as a reminder that the microphysics of colonial contact are always more complex, and never a mere reproduction, of the microphysics of colonial discipline.[8] The general Luguru suspicion towards such forms of individual discipline appears in their stories about *mumiani*, the white vampire (pp. 269 ff.).

Yet, we have also seen that the women's resistance of missionary discipline was partly motivated by their adaptation to the men's

---

[8] See also Hirschkind's (1991) critique of Mitchell (1991), and Pels (1996).

engagement in plantation labour discipline: while (migrant) labour discipline worked on men at the plantations, their absence led towards a partial commodification of the female body in terms of sexual services. I believe that this can be generalized to a level at which the irony of this process becomes more apparent. On the one hand, the presence of the missionaries, despite their efforts, did *not* produce the regime of Christian discipline which they earnestly hoped would emerge. On the other, the efforts of Waluguru to selectively adopt and resist what the missionaries and other Europeans had to offer were not very successful. Instead, colonial society was characterized by a increasing penetration of the commodity form in many sectors of life, in a way that most participants in the process neither intended nor controlled. The value of the "tactile" perspective used in this book is precisely that it brings out the extent to which the process of Christian missionization was characterized by a shift from embodied to commodified power and knowledge. Luguru authority increasingly ceased to depend on initiation, which invested the body with power by condensing the training in natural and social dispositions in a single enactment of physical transformation. Instead, economic power came to rely increasingly on cash crops and money, political power on impersonal skills of writing and ascriptions of political office, legal power on proper recording and registration, intellectual power on knowledge commodified as diplomas, syllabi and certificates, and healing power on the trade in medicines.

This penetration of society by commodity forms was, of course, not absolute. On the one hand, commodification – the turning of objects, persons or knowledge into exchange values – is not restricted to capitalist societies (Appadurai 1986). On the other, even if under capitalism the commodity form increasingly spreads from the market sector of society (because an "economy" of "things" is a central cultural feature of modern governmentality: Foucault 1991: 92–3), it can never completely extinguish use- and other values, only (attempt to) subordinate them to a regime of exchange. Lastly, one must be aware of the fact that different forms of commodification can stand in a relation of contradiction.

The latter is, for instance, the case with the missionaries, whose seminary training did two different things: on the one hand, it depersonalized the young recruit, divesting him as much as possible of family history, personal will and identity in order to produce a pliable and humble instrument that would willingly accept any labour regime the Lord would impose. On the other, he was invested with professional powers of ministry equivalent to all his *confrères*, especially when Swahili examinations and the resulting legal qualifications confirmed his rights and duties as a priest in East Africa. In chapter two, I have tried to show how this commodification of the body through monastic discipline came into conflict with the commodification of skills necessary for professional ministry. It shows, on the one hand, the objectification of the body of the recruit, divested of personal will in order to become one of the many exchangeable instruments of Divine will. On the other, it shows the objectification of the skills of the priest, making him independent from, as well as exchangeable for, any other *confrère* in the work of ministry.[9]

In chapter three, I tried to show how the initiation of Luguru boys disappeared, and in chapter five, how a more commodified form of socialization – the school – was established. Taken together, the process implied that the most important expressions of successful socialization in Uluguru became more and more dependent on disembodied skills, objectified in the syllabi and diplomas of the school, while the work on the body characteristic of initiation lost most of its relevance. In chapter three, I have argued that this was to a large extent because the bodies of young men were increasingly valued separately from the lineage relationships they were supposed to embody, by the commodification of their bodies as labour power in the plantations where they earned the money that made them more independent from the lineage. In chapter five, another aspect of this process of commodification was visible in the attempts by school inspectors to shift teaching methods from the embodied mnemonics of the chant to the more disembodied reproduction of the signs of literacy. As we have seen, while

---

[9] Of course, the fact that a priest was first ordained – that is, initiated – in the Netherlands complicates the matter, but this needs to be spelled out in a more detailed study of Dutch 20th-century Catholicism than I can offer here.

Luguru women resisted the missionary attacks on female initiation, they commodified the sexual services of the female body. Their personal power was further alienated by the practice of missionaries commodifying marriage by legal registration, divesting it of the history that women and men embodied both personally and in terms of lineage ties. Chapter six showed that the process of disembodiment and objectification also took place in the sphere of healing, where cures based on embodied characteristics – that is, descent from a certain set of ancestors – gave way to cures based on powers objectified as medicines that one could buy and sell.

Of course, the process was impossible without intermediate forms in which the shift from embodied to objectified power could be negotiated. In the sphere of politics, this appeared as the respect British administrators gave to hereditary authority – a seemingly embodied form of power. Yet, they reinvented heredity to such an extent that it became legalized, exchanged among administrators in the form of ethnography, and imposed on Waluguru in the form of (re)invented headmenships and chiefships (Pels 1996). In chapter four, we have seen that the missionaries' conception of "Luguru marriage" functioned in much the same way: as a commodified form which reinvented and redirected the content of a certain relationship. Such intermediate forms functioned on the Luguru side, too: I argued in chapter three that Christianity – in whatever commodified form it arrived – had to be appropriated by Waluguru by making it analogous to the forms of embodied power that characterized Luguru *ngoma*. Likewise, the monetization of young men's labour power was "domesticated" and embodied in female initiation by the cultivation of the girls' sexuality. Thus, the process of commodification of power, which, one may suggest, occurred globally, took specific routes according to the interests, routines and imagined futures of the actors concerned.

The process of transformation which this analysis of the microphysics of colonial contact uncovers seems to operate, therefore, through an appearance of commodified objects rather than an "appearance of order" (Mitchell 1991: 60). I feel that the general and world-wide diffusion of a discourse of representation exists – as Timothy Mitchell shows brilliantly and in remarkable detail – mostly

in the abstract, homogenized order of exhibitions, carceral buildings, shopping malls, or the social engineer's maps of cultures and
societies. In contrast, the processes of colonization pioneered by
the mission display rather less systematic developments. The missionary movement was heterodox from the start, a specifically
Dutch *bricolage* of discourses of exploration and adventure, magical
exchanges with the supernatural, true Catholic devotion and vocation, and material benefits. It could only work in East Africa by
exploiting such diversity further, in order to create new *ad hoc* com-
binations of devotion, magic, adventure and reward. In our case, the
process of commodification of persons and things – which eventually can lead to a situation in which each thing and person is primarily treated as an object representing an order of exchange values –
depended on the prior establishment of a certain correspondence
between Luguru modes of investing bodies with social power, and
Catholic forms of initiation and education.

This process started earlier, but it was given an important
boost when Waluguru took the initiative to have themselves initiated
into Christianity in the late 1920s and early 1930s. In retrospect,
we might say that this step was an attempt by Waluguru to incorporate or embody novel elements of a social situation with which
they were objectively confronted. In this situation, the original
"gift" of the missionaries – the gift that came, in many ways, in
commodity form – turned out to have more value for Waluguru
when the British fused the policy of encouraging cash cropping
with the political apparatus of indirect rule. Thus, the process in
which Waluguru increasingly lost the capacity to identify power
personally, in embodied relationships, reached a critical point at
which its acceleration could no longer be controlled by any participant in the process. Waluguru thus lost embodied power in a
way that was rarely compensated for by a corresponding gain in
the possession of the goods in which social power was newly
materialized. They experienced this as a loss of integrity of personal
and social bodies, and in conclusion, I hope to address that sense
of crisis.

THE UNDERDEVELOPMENT OF
LUGURU REVELATION

There is a remarkable correspondence between the religious processes taking place in the Catholic Netherlands and in Uluguru in the 1950s and 1960s. Both societies experienced a process of secularization, understood as a shift from religious institutions to the state in the management of welfare and education (Van der Veer 1995: 8), and in both societies, the process went together with the appearance of a "generation gap": the loss of control over socialization processes by the previous generation, and open critique and resistance of their power by the new. Obviously, the two are connected, for secularization in the Netherlands implied the break-up of the total institution of the (Protestant, Catholic or Socialist) "pillars", working through family and domestic relationships, by state-directed welfare and educational services, while in Uluguru, the family and domestic arrangements of lineage ties and ancestral religion were similarly ruptured by the appearance of education and the independence which migrant labour provided to young adults.

However, the latter example already shows that such correspondences should not lead us to assume a global process of homogenization. Luguru young men gained their independence partly because the plantations, not the state, provided alternative opportunities outside the family network. More important, however, may be that, while secularization in the Netherlands often implied a move from established religion into the diverse forms of individual growth promised by the new occultism, the corresponding increase in occult activity in Uluguru was not based on the promise of individual growth and independence, but on the threat of witchcraft gone rampant. In the Netherlands, the generation gap opened over an abyss of affluence; in Uluguru, it was a response to affliction.

To understand the novelty and specificity of such affliction, and the sense of crisis it produced in Waluguru, it is necessary to realize that processes of commodification, by objectifying power, also made the repositories of power more *mobile*. Commodities can – are – alienated; their transfer across social boundaries does not meet the same obstacles as the transfer of values by words or by personal appearance. Such mobility of the repositories of power was long familiar to Waluguru: big persons profited from their trade with the Swahili coast to support their position of power at home, while Waluguru generally believed that strong medicine, the commodified form of *uganga*, came from outside Uluguru. However, the increasing dependence on power in commodified form, all manufactured outside Uluguru – medicines, syllabi, diplomas, political positions, money, goods – was matched by a corresponding decrease in the capacity of Waluguru to know, and consequently to protect, the integrity of the social and individual body. As Waluguru increasingly relied on commodified and imported social and individual health care, they experienced an underdevelopment of their own capacity to reveal the sources of affliction.

As we have seen in chapter six, missionary ethnography usually separated indigenous concepts of the Supreme God, exemplifying (for them) "true" revelation, from the worship of ancestor spirits or *uganga*, which were the work of "witchdoctors" or the devil (p. 254; Scheerder and Tastevin 1950: 271–9). The gift of Christian revelation, of *dini*, was therefore often accompanied by active opposition to the revelatory practices which were constitutive of Luguru *uganga* (cf. Schoffeleers 1988). Among anthropologists, Victor Turner has pioneered the study of revelation in African society. He argued that Ndembu conceptions of "making visible" (*kusolola*) can be classified as either divination, "the disclosure of what has previously been concealed", or revelation, "the manifestation of what resists conceptualization" (1975: 15). This contrast is drawn too sharply to be applicable to Uluguru. In fact, Turner's way of thinking about revelation and divination very much resembles post-Vatican Two reinventions of "traditional" African religion. In the 1960s, many Roman Catholics – and Turner was one himself – started to appreciate collective ritual as a kind of "social" revelation.[10] In contrast, Turner's idea of divination, which he supposed

---

[10] Understood as mystique, "communitas" or "proto-philosophy" (Turner 1975: 21–3). One of the younger Holy Ghost Fathers called *tambiko* a "sacramental structure" (IPAC 13b: 496).

was based on a "scheme of delusory persecution" (1975: 24), is a conception which brings to mind the missionary's dislike of the "fears" supposedly inculcated by "witch-doctors".

Nevertheless, Turner's attempt to outline African notions of revelation is crucial. He links revelation to four Ndembu practices: making the invisible (such as hidden game, angry spirits, or witches) visible in real or symbolic form; making the forgotten, the ancestors in particular, remembered; making the unspoken spoken (confession); and making the hidden known to all (bringing about successful birth, displaying initiation medicine [1975: 143–4]). If we compare this to Luguru *uganga*, Turner's stark contrast between divination and revelation becomes difficult to maintain: a Luguru diviner identified a forgotten ancestor to recommend a healing ceremony in which the patient had to adopt the ancestral name (*kutawala jina*); he pointed out the influence of witches or demons; he asked the family members for confessions of the deeds that led to someone falling ill. In other words, the Luguru *mganga* was both diviner and revealer and Turner's opposition between revealing ritual and paranoid divination does not apply to him (but see below).

Waluguru are, unlike Ndembu, not "distrustful of *all* that is withdrawn from public view or company" (Turner 1975: 16, emphasis mine). The statement applies to their thoughts about evil and misfortune, but there are also things hidden to which their attitude is respectful. As far as I know, Waluguru do not oppose revelation and divination but revelation and the secret (*siri*; kil. *swiri*), a concept crucial to Luguru authority in all stages of life. The revelation, or "open showing" (*kuonyesha wazi*) of secrets happens at every initiation and is therefore basic to all political authority and integrity within Luguru lineages; moreover, it is crucial in uncovering the causes of both social and individual affliction. In the boys' initiation, the *mizungu* and other lessons reveal the secrets of adult life to the boy; in the female *mwali* rite, the same is done for the girl; the climax of the *milunga* rite is the initiated elders' sharing of the secret leaves of power with their initiand. In the field of sickness and misfortune, as we have seen, the secrets which a healer had to reveal consisted of the covert influence of ancestors or demons and the hidden medicines of witchcraft (*mapembe, uganga wa nunguli*). In the realm of evil, secrecy was ascribed to the initiation into the society of *wawanga*, and the vampirism of the *mumiani*.

Thus, secrecy and its revelation were intimately connected to power: the former as the support of authority, and the latter as a way of sharing it out. Such simultaneous affirmation and sharing of authority was emphasized by all initiation rituals through secrecy, just as the secret knowledge and possession of strong medicine was thought to give lineage leaders, healers and witches their power. Acts of revelation such as *tambiko* and the unfolding of secrets in initiation reduced this inequality by either reconciling the lineage members through the ancestors, or by incorporating someone among the powerful, be it the society of adult men, of mature women, or of *wenye mlunga*. Within the context of lineage relationships, therefore, all Waluguru experienced forms of revelation, during initiation or during collective curative ritual. The presence of witches, demons, and *wawanga*, however, guaranteed that not all could be or would be revealed.

The previous chapters show the different levels at which missionization worked to reduce the capacity of Waluguru to affirm and share out authority by the revelation of the hidden constitution of the world. On the one hand, the mission started a process in which initiation practices were partly superseded by a socialization of young Waluguru into the "secrets" of society as they were determined by the colonial government's syllabi and diplomas, thus creating the "superstition" of education that I noted at the end of chapter five. On the other, the missionaries themselves tried to monopolize access to the spiritual, by incorporating Luguru ancestors into Catholic ritual, and selectively opposing those Luguru practices in which the secrets of ancestral powers and dispositions were used to heal or transform Luguru bodies. They tried to turn both initiation and confession into a communion with a higher, absent source of authority, represented by the missionaries themselves and the commodities they introduced, thus divesting revelation of the immediate use-value it had in local relationships. If the missionaries were unsuccessful in solving the problems created from day to day by secret evil agencies, their increasing monopoly of the spiritual realm forced Waluguru to rely more and more on the secular healing by the medicines that traveling healers like Nguvumali had to offer. In a sense, the presence of the mission increasingly turned divination into the paranoid practice which the missionaries (and Victor Turner) believed it was.

To some extent, then, Nguvumali and the missionary were both agents of the commodification of revelation, the former by selling medicines which would counter witches regardless of the local relationships which produced them, the latter by giving out sacraments no longer tied to the use-values conveyed by revelation of local ancestral ties. Both Nguvumali and the missionary embodied the "underdevelopment" of revelatory practice in Uluguru: evil became less manageable by local experts and professionals and commodities from outside Uluguru had to play a larger and larger role. Schools further reinforced the underdevelopment of revelation as a social rite by the educational stress on commodified knowledge as something to be possessed and exchanged by individuals. Whereas the earlier catechists still embodied a respectable position in the relations of production of Christian revelation, later teachers earned their secular authority and power from the possession of knowledge and diplomas certified outside the mountains.

Ironically, a similar development characterizes the position of the missionaries themselves: while they came to Uluguru invested with a capacity for revelation that, in Holland as well as in Uluguru, extended over the complete field of primary and secondary education, this authority was already on the wane before they handed over the local church to African priests. While the missionaries alienated Waluguru from the capacity for revelation by embodying, as priests, an outside authority, their own capacity for revelation was subsequently alienated in the educational field when they lost control over the content of the knowledge dispensed within the schools to the Education Department in Dar es Salaam. Thus, the success of the mission is qualified by the fact that the way in which the church was planted in Uluguru resulted in a decrease of its power to guide social life. As in Holland, Christianity was compartimentalized, set aside as a kind of private and domestic "religious" socialization distinct from public welfare and education.

Such an underdevelopment of the capacity for producing revelation was nostalgically perceived by many Waluguru, as the loss of the powers which their grandparents could still employ against those who threatened the health of persons and society, and a rueful reflection on the incapacity of missionaries and, even more, of their African successors, to equal such defenses. Elder Waluguru often also contemplated their own loss of power over the younger generation, exemplified by the disappearance of the boys' *ngoma*, and the loss it entailed of the capacity of locally reproduce and incorporate wider social forces. Present-day elder Waluguru may therefore talk of the "gift" of religion by the missionaries, but they understand that this gift presented ambiguous benefits. In German and Dutch a *Gift* may also be a poison, and the commodity form in which the gift came did, indeed, tap the strength of the uses Waluguru had for it, and subordinated them to alien systems of exchange.

Many members of the younger generation embraced this shift of political and economic initiative to centres outside the mountains, exemplified by their *waganga* turning to acquired medicines rather than embodied spirits for their cures, or their implicit trust in the secular magic of colonial and especially postcolonial education and welfare. But even among those younger people who wholeheartedly joined in the independent Tanzanian government's plans for "village" development, one can discern a yearning towards the restoration of a lost integrity and of a self-sufficiency projected back on to the period before the Germans had intervened. Many people interpreted Julius Nyerere's notion of "familyhood" or *Ujamaa* as such a restoration of self-sufficiency, and it could serve as an antidote against the sense of crisis and loss, a sense also implicitly maintained by notions of evil and witchcraft like *mumiani*. But the "villages" to be "restored" were a social form quite different from the hamlets and valleys in which Waluguru had been organized: colonial and postcolonial policies actually tried to bring these villages into existence. Perhaps it has become easier, now that the market values of neo-liberalism have also destroyed Luguru faith in self-sufficient *Ujamaa* villages, and increasingly demoralize life in the Luguru countryside (cf. Van Donge 1993), to see that *Ujamaa* villagization was a new way to cope with the crisis that shifted power to outside the mountains. Waluguru may have perceived this crisis in terms of a nostalgia towards a self-sufficient (but historically novel) "village". I hope to have shown that this sense of crisis itself reflects a real loss of embodied power, of the capacity to manage one's own affairs without the mediation of things that one cannot manage oneself; and that this crisis was initiated by the microphysics of the mission of the Holy Ghost.

Abbreviations; Notes on Archival Sources

AC	*Africa Christo*, the propaganda journal of the Dutch Holy Ghost Fathers; successor to the *Holy Ghost Messenger* (see BHG) since 1952.
AC/WvA	*Africa Christo, Werkers voor Afrika*, special 1957 issue of AC promoting the work of religious Brothers ("workers for Africa").
BG	*Bulletin General*, the internal journal of the Congregation of the Holy Ghost produced by the mother-house in Paris.
BHG	*Bode van de Heilige Geest* (*Holy Ghost Messenger*), the propaganda journal of the Dutch Holy Ghost Fathers since 1904. Renamed *Africa Christo* in 1952.
CAT	Catholic Association of Teachers (in Tanganyika).
CS	Chief Secretary (to the Tanganyikan Governor).
Cssp	(Member of) the Congregation of the Holy Ghost.
DAM	Diocesan Archives Morogoro; contains (copies of) some of the diaries of the Uluguru missions and the annual statistics. Most diaries of Uluguru missions founded after 1949 are missing, nor are the statistics complete. Because I only had access to the archives through an intermediary, I cannot say what else the archives contain.
DC	District Commissioner; head of the administrative officers of a Tanganyikan district. Subordinate to PC.
FN	Field notes; were kept in Dutch by the present author during twelve months of fieldwork in Uluguru (see introduction, note 34) and include some interviews done in Morogoro and Dar es Salaam. References normally specify the informant except when the latter's name needed to be protected.
IPAC	Interviews for the project "Africa Christo"; eighteen long interviews collected by the author to complement the KMM material (see there). References

	give the number, the (a or b) side of the cassette tape and the clock number.
KD	Kasanga mission diary; see under DAM.
KMM	KomMissieMemoires; a large-scale project of some 800 interviews with Dutch Catholic missionaries (Fathers, Brothers and Sisters) gathered in order to have their experiences on record and made accessible (on tape) at the Katholiek Documentatie Centrum of the University of Nijmegen, the Netherlands. The material quoted concerns interviews with Holy Ghost missionaries only; references give the interview's accession number, the number and side of the tape and the clock number. See also under IPAC.
MDB	Morogoro District Book; in the district book, information collected in the interests of the district administration was deposited when it was thought to be relevant for future administrators. The Morogoro District Book contains much ethnographic information.
MD	Matombo mission diary, see under DAM.
MF	microfilm.
MP	Matombo parish files; the present author has, with the help of Father Gumbo, unearthed a number of parish files from the mission's library and office. These files have been sent to the diocesan archives (DAM) in 1996.
MS v/d Poel	Short typewritten manuscript with reminiscences of mission life by Father Frans van der Poel; a copy was given to the author by the Father.
MSS Vermunt	Ethnographic papers about Uluguru by Father Cornelis Vermunt CSSp. The original papers have been sent to the Congregation's mother house in Paris; copies are kept in Morogoro, in the Dutch Spiritans' headquarters in Gemert, and by the present author. The author hopes to edit and introduce the papers for publication in the near future.
MtD	Mtombozi mission diary, covering only 1959–67; one of the few surviving diaries of Uluguru missions founded after 1949; see under DAM.
OO	Ons Orgaan, internal newspaper of the Dutch province of the Congregation of the Holy Ghost.

PC	Provincial Commissioner, superior of several DCs, directly subordinate to the CS and the Governor.
SD	Singiza mission diary, see DAM.
SVD	(Member of) Society of the Divine Word.
TANU	Tanganyika African National Union, the party that, under the leadership of Julius Nyerere, took over Tanganyikan government after Independence in 1961.
TD	Tegetero mission diary, see under DAM.
TNA	Tanzania National Archives.
TP	Tegetero parish files; a small number of files collected with the help of Father Kubahari; it is hoped they will be sent to the diocesan archives (DAM).
TTS	Teacher Training School, founded in Morogoro in 1926; after the additions of Standards IX to XII, it became the Teacher Training College.
TuD	Tununguo mission diary, see under DAM.
UDSM	University of Dar es Salaam library; contains the papers of Hans Cory, Government Sociologist of the Tanganyikan administration.
ULUS	Uluguru Land Usage Scheme; a British soil conservation project instituted in 1950, turned into community development after riots in July 1955 prevented its further implementation (see Brain 1979; Young and Fosbrooke 1960).
VPRO	Tape-recording of a radio-programme about Dutch mission folklore of the Vrijzinnig Protestantse Radio Omroep in the series 't Spoor Terug, 20.11.90; permission to quote from the programme is gratefully acknowledged.

Chronology

1864 Foundation of Bagamoyo Mission by Holy Ghost Fathers (HGF) from Zanzibar.

1870 Kisebengo conquers Morogoro and subjects Luguru clan heads. Wambunga raids on Eastern Uluguru.

1882 Foundation of Morogoro by HGF from Bagamoyo.

1884 Foundation of Tununguo Mission by HGF from Bagamoyo.

1884 Imposition of German rule: *Deutsch Ost-Afrika*.

1897 Foundation of Matombo, central mission of Eastern Uluguru, from Tununguo Mission. Bishop Allgeyer shifts mission strategy from Christian villages to catechists.

1904 French HGF found minor seminary in Weert, the Netherlands.

1905 Foundation of Mgeta, central mission of West Uluguru. Maji Maji revolt passes by Eastern Uluguru but involves major clan heads (Mbago and son) of Western Uluguru.

1906 Vicariate of Bagamoyo splits off from Vicariate of Zanzibar. Appointment François Xavier Vogt as Vicar Apostolic (August). Mbago and son arrested for partaking in Maji Maji.

1917 British troops chase German soldiers under Von Lettow Vorbeck from Uluguru mountains.

1918 Many German and Alsatian HGF interned by British. Mgr. Vogt moves his residence from Bagamoyo to Morogoro.

1920 Mgr. Munsch and others Fathers not allowed to return to their missions. German Sisters of the Precious Blood have to leave Tanganyika. Irish HGF appointed for East African missions.

1922 First Dutch HGF appointed for East Africa, Vicariate of Zanzibar (Michael Witte, Alfons Loogman). Mgr. Vogt resigns as Vicar Apostolic of Bagamoyo and is appointed for Cameroun.

1923 First Dutch HGF appointed for Vicariate of Bagamoyo (Jan de Rooij, Gerard Brouwer, Martinus v.d. Kimmenade). Sisters of the Precious Blood return to East Africa.

1924 Bartholomew Wilson, Principal Superior of HGF of the Vicariate of Bagamoyo, appointed as Vicar Apostolic.

1925   Donald Cameron appointed as Governor of Tanganyika. He arrives in July and starts to introduce Indirect Rule at once. Kingalu Mwanamnguo appointed as Sultan of South Uluguru; Kingo appointed as Sultan of North Uluguru. Education Conference of Mission and Government in Dar es Salaam in September. Some mission schools get government grants. First minor seminarians of Vicariate of Bagamoyo sent to Tabora.

1926   Ngoja bin Kimeta practices in Uluguru in November. On December 8th, the Teacher Training School of Morogoro is opened.

1927   Spectacular growth of number of catechumens in Eastern Uluguru.

1931   Recognition of separate Dutch province of the Congregation of the Holy Ghost; appointment of Bernard Hilhorst as first Provincial Superior.

1932   Vicariate Bagamoyo allotted to Dutch province.

1933   Mgr. Wilson resigns.

1934   Bernard Hilhorst appointed as first Dutch Vicar Apostolic of the Vicariate of Bagamoyo.

1936   Kingalu Mwanarubela deposed as Sultan of South Uluguru. Kingo becomes first Sultan of the whole of Uluguru. Foundation of Native Sisters' Congregation in Mgolole.

1937   Many mission schools registered.

1938   Minor seminary moved to Morogoro. Foundation of Native Brothers' Congregation.

1942   Ordination of the first African priest of the Vicariate of Bagamoyo, Pascal Juma.

1943   Sabu bin Sabu becomes Sultan of Uluguru after the death of Kingo.

1948   Many registered schools turned into assisted schools. Enormous growth of government-sponsored education.

1950   Start Uluguru Land Usage Scheme.

1952   Native Brothers' Congregation disbanded.

1953   The Vicariate of Bagamoyo becomes Morogoro Diocese and Mgr. Hilhorst its first resident bishop.

1954   Herman van Elswijk appointed as Bishop of Morogoro Diocese. Mgr. Hilhorst dies in Mgolole.

1955   Uluguru Land Usage Scheme riots (13 July and after). TANU mushrooms in Uluguru mountains.

1958   Nguvumali practices in Uluguru mountains. Deputy Sultan of Uluguru, Patrick Kunambi (independent candidate), defeated by Julius Nyerere (TANU) in Eastern Province elections.

1959 Sultan Sabu dies, is replaced by Patrick Kunambi.

1961 Uhuru/Independence for Tanganyika.

1964 Tanganyika and Zanzibar unite in Tanzania.

1967 Mgr. Van Elswijk resigns. Adriani Mkoba becomes first African bishop of Morogoro Diocese.

Glossary

T his glossary lists Kiluguru and Swahili words appearing more than once in the text. Their Swahili or Kiluguru origin is tentatively indicated, but there was and is much interchange between the languages, which are, like neighbouring Kizaramo and Kikwere, much alike; while Swahili words may get a specific meaning in Kiluguru speech. The meanings given are often not the only ones possible, but the ones in general use in Uluguru.

akida	(Sw.) senior native official under German rule; a position abolished under Indirect Rule.
bangili	(Sw.) bracelet; in Uluguru, it indicates that a person has taken an ancestral name.
baraza	(Sw.) council meeting; also verandah in front of a building.
baridi	(Sw.) cold, cool.
bibi	(Sw.) married woman, grandmother; in Uluguru it is rarely used in the first sense.
bululu	(Kil.) hamlet.
dawa	(Sw.) medicine, but can refer to any substance used in chemical preparations.
dini	(Sw.) religion.
galigali	(Kil.) the lessons given to the initiand in the last phase of female initiation.
jando	(Sw.) circumcision ritual.
jina	(Sw.) name (pl. *majina*); in Uluguru, often a synecdoche for having taken an ancestor's name (*kutawala jina*).
jumbe	(Sw.) headman; in Uluguru it usually refers to a headman appointed as local ruler under German rule and subordinate to an *akida*; today, *mjumbe* refers to the "head of ten houses", the lowest official in the organization of the party.
kago	(Kil., but see Johnson 1939: 166, under *kaga*) magical guard against evil; cf. *zindiko*.
kali	(Sw.) hard, sharp.

kanga	(Sw.) the common female dress; a double coloured cloth, one piece worn tucked in above the breasts and the other draped over the head or shoulders.
kibaruani	(Sw.) "on the chit": wage labour measured by a labour card which lists the days of the month.
kifungo	Opening gift by parents of boy for bride-price negotiations.
kizungu	(Sw.) "of the white man"; adverb of *mzungu*.
kuchumbiwa	(Sw.) being courted; refers to the marriage negotiations, the passive suffix *wa* referring to the girl (for a boy, the same process would be *kuchumbia*).
kufungwa	(Sw.) being secluded; refers to the period of seclusion of an initiand in Luguru female initiation.
kuhamia ndege	(Sw.) "to move the birds": chasing birds from the ripening harvest.
kula matema	(probably kil.) an older Luguru translation for baptism, probably constructed from the Swahili for "to eat" and a derivation of the French *baptême*; for a further explanation, see p. 261.
kumbi	(Kil.) the place where initiands are secluded during initiation. May have become homologous with the Swahili *kambi* (from "camp").
kupiga bao	(Sw.) method of divination by which lines are traced of a board (*bao*); often used as gloss for divination in general.
kutambika	(Sw.) reconciling with, sacrificing to, the ancestors; see *tambiko*.
kutawala jina	(Sw.) "to rule a name"; the ceremony in which someone adopts the name of an ancestor, either in a healing ritual or in the rite of passage to the position of *mwenye mlunga*. Derived according to Brain (1971: 820) from the Kiluguru *kuhala tawa*, "to take the name", but he is not supported by any informant or writer in the field.
kuzimu	(Sw.) the place of the spirits (*mizimu*); can refer to any place where ancestors or nature-spirits are thought to dwell, but often carries the temporal connotation of the liminal period in rites of passage (see *kumbi*).
limba	(Kil.) obstacle at the entrance of an initiation camp; can only be passed if one knows its secrets.

luhungo	(Kil.) "contact", or "an act by which a relation is established" between persons or a person and an object (MSS. Vermunt 5.4 "Luhungo; Mwiko, Dawa"; 6.0 "Uganga. Luhungo"). See p. 261–2.
lukolo	(Kil.) mother's clan; the most encompassing concept of descent, from which a Mluguru gets his or her name and which guides practices of exogamy (see *tombo* and *mtala*).
lungu	(Kil.) powerful medicine used in boys' initiation ritual; resonates with *Mulungu* ("God").
lusona	(Kil.) boys' initiation ritual; predates *jando* and may be synonymous with *lwindi*, *ng'ula*, and other names for Luguru boys' initiation (see ch. 4).
lwindi	(Kil.) boys' initiation ritual; see *lusona* and *ng'ula*.
mahirizi	(Sw.) plural of *hirizi*, protective charms worn on the body.
mali	(Sw.) property, goods, wealth; in Uluguru, it often means "bride-price".
marehemu	(Sw.) deceased.
mapembe	(Sw.) plural of *pembe*; see there.
mchawi	(Sw.) witch, sorcerer, someone who harbours evil intentions towards his fellow human beings.
mchumba	(Sw.) lit. "roommate"; refers to a partner to whom one is not (yet) married.
mdogo	(Sw.) "smaller one"; in general, someone inferior; in particular, someone lower down in the line of descent.
mganda	(Sw.) a big drum; also, a rhythm played on festive occasions which mimics the rhythmic surface of European march rhythms.
mganga	(Sw.) healer, medicine person.
mhunga (mkulu)	(Kil.) generic name for guardian of initiand and leader of initiation ritual, but usually refers to a leader in female initiation; if several *wahunga* are present, one of them is the leader, the 'big' one (*mhunga mkulu*).
mila	(Sw.) "tradition".
miti	(Sw.) plural of *mti*, 'tree', but the plural often refers to vegetable medicine in general.
milunga	(Kil.) plural of *mlunga*.
mizungu	(Sw.) riddles whose secrets are revealed to initiands in *ngoma* before they can come out (but see Johnson 1939: 281–2).

mkole	(Kil., but see Johnson 1939: 286) tree which often serves as fertility symbol and which is necessary for female initiation.
mkoleni	(Kil.) "at the mkole tree", the place where many of the lessons of female initiation are given to the *mwali* on the night before coming out.
mkubwa	(Sw.) 'big person'; generic name for someone in a position of power or authority.
mlao	(Kil.) the 'coming out' ceremony which closes a *ngoma*.
mlunga	(Kil.) ceremonial object, the possession of which indicating that one has adopted an ancestral name and has been initiated as an elder of a specific area.
moto	(Sw.) fire, but also "heat", "anger" or "aggression".
mpingu	(Kil.? Sw. *mpingo*) the ebony tree.
mtala	(Kil.) father's clan.
mtama	(Sw.) millet.
mumiani	(Sw.) bloodsucker, vampire; usually a white man.
mwali	(Sw.) initiand.
mwalimu	(Sw.) teacher.
mwanga	(Sw.) a kind of nocturnal witch who, in the company of his fellows, feeds on corpses and lets people work on his fields in their sleep.
mwenye mlunga	(Kil.) someone initiated as member of the society of elders of a specific area.
mwiko	(Sw.) taboo.
mzee	(Sw.) 'elder'; term of address of senior person.
mzimu	(Sw.) spirit.
ng'ariba	(Sw.) circumcizer.
ng'ariba mkuu	(Sw.) head circumcizer; in Uluguru, the one who taught all other *mang'ariba* of the area.
ng'ula	(Kil.) boys' initiation ritual; see *lusona* and *lwindi*.
ngoto	(Kil.) land rent paid yearly to lineage heads by non-lineage squatters on their land.
nguvu	(Sw.) force, strength, power.
ngoma	(Sw.) dance, rhythm, drum; Kil. *ingoma* also means ritual or rite of passage.
nunguli	(Kil.) gourd containing medicine, usually obtained from foreign sources.
pepo	(Sw.) spirit, usually evil or demonic.
pembe	(Sw.) "horn", but in boys' initiation, an occult word for "penis"; the plural *mapembe*, however,

	usually refers to evil medicine, kept in a horn, which is used to harm others and can move of its own accord.
pombe	(Sw.) native beer, usually made of maize or millet; also, beer-feast, as in *pombe ya msalaba*, "beer of the cross", held on the closing day of the mourning period on which a cross is planted on the grave; in Matombo, it is also held on All Souls' day to commemorate the ancestors.
sadaka	(Sw.) religious offering, sacrifice, act of charity.
sae	(Kil.) boys' initiation ritual held on the higher slopes of the mountains, possibly incorporated into *lusona*, *lwindi* or *ng'ula* in the areas closer to the plains.
safari	(Sw.) journey.
shauri	(Sw.) (issue of) discussion or debate.
tambiko	(Sw.) any occasion on which the ancestors are propitiated; sacrifice to the ancestors.
tombo	(Kil.) breast; also, a local lineage of a specific clan.
uchawi	(Sw.) witchcraft, sorcery; harm done to others out of malevolence.
uganga	(Sw.) healing, medicine.
uhuru	(Sw.) freedom; written with a capital, it means independence from colonial rule.
ujamaa	(Sw.) kinship, brotherhood; with a capital letter, the doctrine of kinship which ought to characterize Tanzanian society under one-party rule.
urembo	(Sw.) adornment, ornamentation, cosmetic beauty.
usembe	(Kil.) cleansing medicine against *uchawi*.
utawa	(Sw.) seclusion, a religious way of life; in the Uluguru missions, it meant the boarding house of the mission for pious boys or girls.
viboko	(Sw.) plural of *kiboko*, hippopotamus; but usually, strokes with the hippopotamus-hide whip, and later, a generic term for corporal punishment in general, synonymous to *fimbo* (cane).
wachawi	(Sw.) plural of *mchawi*.
waganga	(Sw.) plural of *mganga*.
wakubwa	(Sw.) plural of *mkubwa*.
wali	(Sw.) plural of *mwali*.
wasimamizi	(Sw.) plural of *msimamizi*, overseer.

wenye mlunga   (Kil.) plural of *mwenye mlunga*.

zawadi   (Sw.) gift, present.

zindiko   (Sw.) magical protection against evil and misfortune; covers both amulets and medicine hidden above the lintel of the door or put up to guard the harvest in the fields.

zimbo   (Kil.) medicine to protect and restore the health of the lineage or its members.

JANDO SONGS

This appendix lists some *jando* songs recorded by Cory (1947, 1948) to show to what extent *jando* was connected to Swahili culture and the coast. I have added some of my own interpretations in line with the argument advanced in chapter three. The translations and clarifications between brackets in the right hand column are Cory's, and not always sufficiently accurate or convincing. One must bear in mind that Cory gathered his songs from a number of tribes (Waluguru among them) and that inter-pretations in terms of Luguru culture are tenuous. None of Cory's main informants, however, was from a coastal group (1947: 159).

※

(Song sung right after circumcision:)

Kwa Mnazi Wake Sitamburu	On his coconut tree the red hat
Kuremba Sanduku Kwa	Is to decorate the box for
Miaka Mbali	many years to come
Wavaa Nguo Moja Kwa	They dress in one cloth to
Kulala Pwani	sleep on the coast

This is half of Cory's third song. Cory states that the first two sentences refer to the reddish glans which will decorate the penis after circumcision (Cory 1947: 162; I could find no dictionary confirmation of his translation of *sitamburu*). The coconut tree was not common in Uluguru, and probably elsewhere in the hinterland, until the 1960s, and is a thing of the coast. "Kwa Kulala Pwani" might carry the connotation, not noted by Cory, of "having sex on the coast", that is, with women of the coast.

※

315

(Song sung when male visitors are around:)

Wali, Niende Zangu	Novices, might I go
Bandari Dar es Salaam	to the port of Dar es Salaam
Kaenda Kumwaga Mama	(To join a *Jando*) He went to say
	goodbye to mother

First half of Cory's song no. 11 (1947: 164). The latter two sentences show that to say goodbye to mother when going on a trip to Dar es Salaam is likened to going into *jando*. It also suggests the rift between the female and male realm created by *jando*.

٭

(Song of an ordinary visitor to the camp:)

Ohoo, Ohoo, Mambo Leo	Ohoo, a novelty
Pwani Tulipondwa	On the coast (*Jando*) we
	have been crushed

The first two sentences of Cory's song no. 12a (1947: 165). Here, the coast *is* the jando. *Mambo Leo* is, I feel, better translated as "the things of today", and gives, in line with the argument of chapter four about the influence of colonial society, a peculiar connotation to the second sentence.

٭

(Song sung when the boys, recovered, visit the village from the camp:)

Sungura Mjanja	The hare (penis) is a
	smart boy
Wallahi Si Mjanja	(but) by God, he is
	(sometimes) not a
	smart boy
Kafa na Uerevu Wake	He died of his smartness
Kenda Kulawa	He went to come out
Kenda Kurudi na Feza	He went to come back with
	money

Wanawake Njooni	You women come here
Mlole Wengine na Mali	Have a look at a changed one
	(penis), a man of fortune

Cory's song nr. 20 (1948: 81–2). "To die" is, for many Waluguru, a metaphor for going away from the mountains. The association between someone going away to earn money (on the coast, but also on the European's plantations) and someone going away to get circumcized is apparent; his attractiveness to women, too.

✽

(A different version of the same song:)

Kafunga Safari Yake	He embarked on a journey
Kaenda Unguja	He went to Zanzibar (he entered the *Jando*)
Kaenda Kulima Shamba	He went there to cultivate a field (he went there to undergo circumcision)

The three middle sentences of Cory's song nr. 21, which follow on the first two sentences of the previous one (1948: 82). Again, *jando* is associated with the coast, this time with Zanzibar. *Kulima Shamba* has, among Waluguru, the connotations of "going into business" and "having sex".

✽

(Song of entertainment:)

Mwana Marinde, Kiazi Chema	Marinde's son, he has a proper potato (genital)
Amempeleka Mke, *Mke Hukulema*	He offered it to a woman, she did not agree (because he was not circumcised)
Kafunga Safari Mrima	He went on a journey to the coast (he entered a *kumbi*)

Mkadamu Mbele, Mwari Nyuma	The instructor in front, the novice following behind
Anakulembela Wendako Kuna Mamba	He follows to the place where the crocodiles assemble (the novices live in the *kumbi*)
Mamba Kaja, Jahazi Kwa Mbauza Chuma	Now the crocodile came back, a ship with iron planks (Now the novice came back as a strong man)
Akianza, Kamtaka Mwanamke Mwema	If he starts, a nice woman becomes fond of him (After circumcision he has no difficulties in making the acquaintance of nice girls)

Cory's song nr. 70 (1948: 91). Again the *jando* is likened to the coast; in another sentence, the crocodiles suggest the river where the novices are supposed to bath after circumcision. The most interesting sentence is the one that mentions 'a ship with iron planks'. Ranger has shown to what extent the Beni *ngoma* in Mombasa was influenced by the marine brass band and how the organisations that developed around the *ngoma* used the image of European warships in their competitive parades (1975: 20–32). In Tanganyika, British warships bombarded Bagamoyo during the First World War, which made a lasting impression on the coastal peoples, an impression which must have been passed on into the hinterland.

✢

(Song of entertainment:)

Pweza	The cuttle fish (penis)
Mwenye Matereza	The slippery one
Akaapo Hutereza	Where he stays, he slides

Hukaa Chini Ya Jiwe	He likes the place underneath the stone
Panapo Kombe na Chaza	Where is found the shell-fish (female sex organ) and the oyster (its secretion)
Maji Marangaranga na Mchanga Mwangaza	There is heavy water and shining sand (sperm)
Mchokozi Si Mchinga	The daring man is no fool (the boy who undergoes circumcision is clever)
Mwerevu Tumwerevushe	The clever man, let us make him more clever

Cory's song nr. 71 (1948: 91). Again, the metaphors used connect the *jando* to the coast. Among Waluguru, *mchokozi* has a negative connotation: someone who quarrels, and who through his strong will makes life difficult, in particular for his elders to whom he ought to pay more respect. The ambiguous attitude of Waluguru to wage labour life outside the mountain villages makes the epithet particularly appropriate here.

*

(Song of entertainment:)

Pwani Kuna Mashindano	At the coast there exists a competition
Ya Kurukia Ngamia	Of jumping over a camel (in the *kumbi* there is a difficult competition of learning)
Mwezaji Kurukia	The clever jumper (the novice who knows his lesson)
Atapata Reale Mia	Will receive hundred reale (will receive a handsome gift)

Last four sentences of Cory's song nr. 72 (1948: 91). The reference to the camel is intriguing: camels were not used except by nomads far north of Tanganyika, in the Kenyan and Somali deserts. *Mwezaji kurukia* is better translated as "he who can jump". *Reale* comes from the Portuguese real; the reference to a reward *in money* is, I feel, significant.

*

References

Abbink, Jan (1985) Anthropology and the Missions: A Critical Epistemological Perspective, *Methodology and Science* 18: 253–269.
—— (1990) Anthropologists, Missionaries and Rationality, in: R. Bonsen, H. Marks, and J. Miedema (eds.), *The Ambiguity of Rapprochement. Reflections of Anthropologists on their Controversial Relationship with Missionaries*. Nijmegen: Focaal.
Ackerman, Robert (1987) *J. G. Frazer: His Life and Works*. Cambridge: Cambridge University Press.
Akkerman, Tjitske, and Siep Stuurman (eds.) (1985) *De Zondige Rivièra van het Katholicisme. Een lokale studie over feminisme en ontzuiling*. Amsterdam: USA.
Alexander, Mzee Pius (1990) *Historia Fupi ya Kanisa ya Kibungo*. Ms.
Anderson, John (1970) *The Struggle for the School. The Interaction of Missionary, Colonial Government and Nationalist Enterprise in the Development of Formal Education in Kenya*. London/Nairobi: Longman.
Ankersmit, Frank (1993) *De historische ervaring*. Groningen: Historische Uitgeverij.
Appadurai, Arjun (1986) Introduction: Commodities and the politics of value, in: A. Appadurai (ed.), *The Social Life of Things. Commodities in Cultural Perspective*. Cambridge: Cambridge University Press.
Arbuckle, Gerald A. (1978) The Impact of Vatican II on the Marists in Oceania, in: J. Boutilier, D. Hughes, S. Tiffany (eds.), *Mission, Church and Sect in Oceania*. Ann Arbor: University of Michigan Press.
Arnold, David (1988) Touching the Body: Perspectives on the Indian Plague, 1896–1900, in: R. Guha and G. Ch. Spivak (eds.), *Selected Subaltern Studies*. New York: Oxford University Press.
Asad, Talal (1993) *Genealogies of Religion. Discipline and Reasons of Power in Christianity and Islam*. Baltimore: Johns Hopkins University Press.
Baker, E. C. (1930) Mumiani, *Man* no. 57.
—— (1946) Mumiani, *Tanganyika Notes and Records* 21: 108–9.
Bal, Mieke (1990) Showcase, in: R. Corbey and P. v.d. Grijp (eds.), *Natuur en Cultuur. Beschouwingen op het raakvlak van antropologie en filosofie*. Baarn: Ambo.

Balbus, Isaac D. (1977) Commodity Form and Legal Form: An Essay on the "Relative Autonomy" of the Law, *Law and Society Review* 11: 571–88.

Ball, Stephen J. (1983) Imperialism, Social Control and the Colonial Curriculum in Africa, *Journal of Curriculum Studies* 15: 237–63.

Bateson, Gregory (1979) *Mind and Nature. A Necessary Unity.* New York: Bantam Books.

Bax, Mart (1983) 'Us' Catholics and 'Them' Catholics in Dutch Brabant: The Dialectics of a Religious Factional Process, *Anthropological Quarterly* 56: 167–79.

———— (1984) 'Officieel geloof' en 'Volksgeloof' in Noord-Brabant; veranderingen in opvattingen en gedragingen als uitdrukking van rivaliserende clericale regimes, *Sociologisch Tijdschrift* 10: 621–647.

———— (1985) Popular Devotions, Power, and Religious Regimes in Catholic Dutch Brabant, *Ethnology* 24: 215–228.

———— (1986) Terug naar donkere tijden? Over het falen van een voorgeschreven kerkelijke orde in hedendaags ruraal Brabant, in: G. Rooijakkers and T. v.d. Zee (eds.), *Religieuze Volkscultuur.* Nijmegen: Sun.

———— (1989) Fighting with Sacraments. The Evolution of a Roman Catholic Regime in Dutch Brabant, in: J. Boissevain and J. Verrips (eds.), *Dutch Dilemmas. Anthropologists look at the Netherlands.* Assen/Maastricht: Van Gorcum.

Bax, Mart en A. Nieuwenhuis (1982) Peasant Emancipation in the Roman Catholic South of the Netherlands: The Shattering of a Tableau-Vivant, *The Netherlands' Journal of Sociology* 18: 25–45.

Beidelman, Thomas O. (1974) Social Theory and the Study of Christians Missions in Africa, *Africa* 44: 235–249.

———— (1981) Contradictions between the Sacred and the Secular Life, *Comparative Studies in Society and History* 23: 73–95.

———— (1982) *Colonial Evangelism. A Socio-Historical Study of Missions at the Grassroots.* Bloomington, Indiana: Indiana University Press.

Benjamin, Walter (1977) Über den Begriff der Geschichte, in: *Illuminationen.* Frankfurt: Suhrkamp Verlag.

Bennet, George (1960) Paramountcy to Partnership: J. H. Oldham and Africa, *Africa* 30: 356–60.

Berman, Edward H. (1975) Christian Missions in Africa, in: E. H. Berman (ed.), *African Reactions to Missionary Education.* New York and London: Teachers College Press.

Bettelheim, Bruno (1954) *Symbolic Wounds*. Glencoe, Ill.: The Free Press.

Bloch, Maurice (1987) The Political Implications of Religious Experience, in: G. Aymer (ed.), *Symbolic Textures. Studies in Cultural Meaning*. Göteborg: Acta Universitatis Gotoburgensis.

Blok, Anton (1991) Zinloos en zinvol geweld, *Amsterdams Sociologisch Tijdschrift* 18: 189–207.

Bombwe, Rev. Fr. Gaspar (1983) *Luguru Ancestor Cult and Christian Morals*. Rome: Pontificia Universitas Urbaniana.

Bohannan, Paul (1967) The Differing Realms of the Law, in: P. Bohannan (ed.) *Law and Warfare. Studies in the Anthropology of Conflict*. New York: Natural History Press.

Bonsen, Roland, Hans Marks, and Jelle Miedema (eds.) (1990) *The Ambiguity of Rapprochement. Reflections of Anthropologists on their Controversial Relationship with Missionaries*. Nijmegen: Focaal.

Bourdieu, Pierre (1977) *Outline of a Theory of Practice*. Cambridge: Cambridge University Press.

Brandewie, Ernest (1983a) Ethnology and Missionaries: The Case of the Anthropos Institute and Wilhelm Schmidt, in: Salamone, Frank, and D. Whiteman (eds.) *Missionaries, Anthropologists and Cultural Change*, 2 vols. Williamsburg, Virginia: College of William and Mary, Studies in Third World Societies nrs. 25/26.

——— (1983b) *Wilhelm Schmidt and the Origin of the Idea of God*. Baltimore: University Press of America.

——— (1990) *When Giants Walked the Earth. The Life and Times of Wilhelm Schmidt SVD*. Freiburg: University Press Fribourg (Studia Institui Anthropos no. 44).

Brain, James L. (1964) More Modern Witchfinding, *Tanganyika Notes and Records* 62: 44–48.

——— (1969) Matrilineal Descent and Marital Stability: a Tanzanian Case, *Journal of Asian and African Studies* 4: 122–31.

——— (1971) Kingalu: a Myth of Origin from Eastern Tanzania, *Anthropos* 66: 817–38.

——— (1978) Symbolic Rebirth: the *Mwali* Rite Among the Luguru of Eastern Tanzania, *Africa* 48: 176–188.

——— (1979) The Uluguru Land Usage Scheme: Success and Failure, *Journal Dev. Areas* 14: 175–90.

——— (1980a) Boys' Initiation Rites among the Luguru of Eastern Tanzania, *Anthropos* 75: 369–382.

———— (1980b) Luguru Bird Names, *Tanzania Notes and Records* 84/85: 123–6.

———— (1981) *Witchcraft and Development*. Dar es Salaam: Dar es Salaam University Press, Inaugural Lecture Series no. 31.

Brown, G. Gordon (1944) Missions and Cultural Diffusion, *American Journal of Sociology* 50: 214–219.

Brown, Judith K. (1963) A Cross-Cultural Study of Female Initiation Rites, *American Anthropologist* 65: 837–55.

Bücher, Karl (1902) *Arbeit und Rhythmus*. 3rd enlarged edition, Leipzig: B. G. Teubner.

Buchert, Lene (1994) *Education in the Development of Tanzania, 1919–1990*. London/Dar es Salaam/Athens: Currey/Mkuki na Nyota/Ohio University Press.

Callaway, Helen (1987) *Gender, Culture and Empire. European Women in Colonial Nigeria*. Basingstoke and London: MacMillan.

Caplan, Patricia (1976) Boys' Circumcision and Girls' Puberty Rites among the Swahili of Mafia Island, Tanzania, *Africa* 46: 21–33.

Chanock, Martin (1982) Making Customary Law: Men, Women, and Courts in Colonial Northern Rhodesia, in: M. J. Hay and M. Wright (eds.) *African Women and the Law: Historical Perspectives*. Boston: Boston University Papers on Africa, VII.

Chernoff, John Miller (1979) *African Rhythm and African Sensibility. Aesthetics and Social Action in African Musical Idioms*. Chicago and London: University of Chicago Press.

———— (1991) The Rhythmic Medium in African Music, *New Literary History* 22: 1095–1102.

Clifford, James (1982) *Person and Myth: Maurice Leenhardt in the Melanesian World*. Berkeley: University of California Press.

———— (1983) On Ethnographic Authority, *Representations* 1/2: 118–46.

———— (1992) Traveling Cultures, in: L. Grossberg, L. Nelson, P. Teichler (eds.), *Cultural Studies*. New York/London: Routledge.

Cohn, Bernard S. (1987) *An Anthropologist among the Historians and Other Essays*. Delhi: Oxford University Press.

Coleman, John A. (1978) *The Evolution of Dutch Catholicism, 1958–1974*. Berkeley: University of California Press.

Colie, Rosalie Little (1966) *Paradoxia Epidemica: the Renaissance Tradition of Paradox*. Princeton: Princeton University Press.

Collingwood, R. G. (1961) *The Idea of History*. London: Oxford University Press (orig. published 1946).

Colson, Elizabeth (1970) Converts and Tradition: the Impact of Christianity on Valley Tonga Religion, *Southwestern Journal of Anthropology* 26: 144–55.

Comaroff, Jean (1985) *Body of Power, Spirit of Resistance. The Culture and History of a South African People*. Chicago: Chicago University Press.

Comaroff, Jean, and John L. Comaroff (1991) *On Revelation and Revolution. Christianity, Colonialism and Consciousness in South Africa*, vol.1. Chicago: University of Chicago Press.

——— (1992) *Ethnography and the Historical Imagination*. Boulder: Westview Press.

——— (1993) *Modernity and Its Malcontents. Ritual and Power in Postcolonial Africa*. Chicago: Chicago University Press.

Comaroff, John, and Simon Roberts (1977) The Invocation of Norms in Dispute Settlement: The Tswana Case, in: I. Hamnett (ed.) *Social Anthropology and Law*. London: Academic Press.

——— (1981) *Rules and Processes. The Cultural Logic of Dispute in an African Context*. Chicago: University of Chicago Press.

Coombes, Annie E. (1994) *Reinventing Africa. Museums, Material Culture and Popular Imagination in Late Victorian and Edwardian England*. New Haven and London: Yale University Press.

Cooper, Frederick (1992) Colonizing Time: Work Rhythms and Labour Conflict in Colonial Mombasa, in: N. Dirks (ed.), *Colonialism and Culture*. Ann Arbor: The University of Michigan Press.

Cooper, Frederick, and Ann Laura Stoler (1989) Introduction: Tensions of Empire, *American Ethnologist* 16: 609–21.

Corbey, Raymond (1988) Alterity: the Colonial Nude. Photographic Essay, *Critique of Anthropology* 8: 75–92.

——— (1989a) Pictorial Narratives: The Christian Frontier in Colonial Africa. Amsterdam: Paper for conference on Social History and Photography.

——— (1989b) *Wildheid en beschaving. De Europese verbeelding van Afrika*. Baarn: Ambo.

Corbey, Raymond, and Fred Melssen (1990) Paters over Papoea's. Narratio, Macht en Ideologie in Kaiser-Wilhelmsland, 1896–1914, *Antropologische Verkenningen* 9: 11–27.

Cory, Hans (1937) Some East African Native Songs, *Tanzania Notes and Records* 4: 51–64.

———— (1947) Jando, part I, *JRAI* 77: 159–166.

———— (1948) Jando, part II, *JRAI* 78: 81–94.

Crick, Malcolm (1973) Two styles in the study of witchcraft, *Journal of the Anthropological Society of Oxford* 4: 17–31.

Daniel, E. Valentine (1991) *Is There A Counterpoint to Culture?* The Wertheim Lecture 1991. Amsterdam: Centre for Asian Studies Amsterdam.

De Blécourt, Willem (1990) *Termen van Toverij. De veranderende betekenis van toverij in Noordoost-Nederland tussen de 16de en 20ste eeuw.* Nijmegen: SUN.

De Boeck, Filip (1995) Bodies of Remembrance: Knowledge, Experience and the Growing of Memory in Luunda Ritual Performance, in: G. Thinès and L. de Heusch (eds.), *Rites et Ritualisation.* Paris: Librairie Philosophique J. Vrin, 114–38.

De Certeau, Michel (1984) *The Practice of Everyday Life.* Berkeley: University of California Press.

De Heusch, Luc (1985) *Sacrifice in Africa.* Bloomington: Indiana University Press.

De Jong CSSp., Rev. Fr. Albert (1974) *Michael Witte CSSp. Pionier van het schoolwezen in Oost-Afrika.* Nijmegen: M. A. Thesis Catholic University Nijmegen.

Delfendahl, B. (1981) On anthropologists vs. missionaries, *Current Anthropology* 22: 89.

De Reeper MHF, Rev Fr. J. (1955) De missionaris en de Priestermissiebond, *Het Missiewerk* 34: 12–16.

De Rooij CSSp, Rev. Fr. J. (1946) Tooverij en toovenaars?, *Het Missiewerk* 25: 86–97.

Diamond, Stanley (1974) *In Search of the Primitive. A Critique of Civilization.* New Brunswick, NJ: Transaction Books, E. P. Dutton.

Dirks, Nicholas B. (1992) Introduction: Colonialism and Culture, in: N. B. Dirks (ed.), *Colonialism and Culture.* Ann Arbor: The University of Michigan Press.

———— (1995) The Conversion of Caste: Location, Translation, and Appropriation, in: P. v. d. Veer (ed.), *Conversion to Modernities: The Globalization of Christianity.* New York/London: Routledge.

———— n. d. Is Vice Versa? Historical Anthropologies and Anthropological Histories. Unpublished manuscript.

Dirkse, P. (1983) Tentoonstellingen van zending en missie, in: *De heiden moest eraan geloven. Geschiedenis van zending, missie en ontwikkelingssamenwerking.* Utrecht: Het Catharijneconvent.

Donatus OFM Cap, P. (1949) Over aanpassing aan de religieuze mentaliteit der Dajaks, *Het Missiewerk* 28: 32–41, 84–101, 209–224.

Douglas, Mary (1963) Techniques of Sorcery Control in Central Africa, J. Middleton, and E. Winter (eds.), *Witchcraft and Sorcery in East Africa*. London: Routledge and Kegan Paul.

—— (1970) Introduction: Thirty Years after *Witchcraft, Oracles and Magic*, in: M. Douglas (ed.), *Witchcraft. Confessions and Accusations*. London: Tavistock.

—— (1980) *Evans-Pritchard*. Glasgow: Fontana Paperbacks.

Eagleton, Terry (1990) *The Ideology of the Aesthetic*. Oxford: Basil Blackwell.

Eco, Umberto, and Thomas E. Sebeok (1983) (eds.) *The Sign of Three. Dupin, Holmes, Peirce*. Bloomington and Indianapolis: Indiana University Press.

Erivwo, Samuel U. (1975) Christian Attitude to Witchcraft, *Afer* 17: 23–31.

Etherington, Norman (1977) Social Theory and the Study of Christian Mission in Africa: A South African Case Study, *Africa* 47: 31–40.

—— (1983) Missionaries and the Intellectual History of Africa: A Historical Survey, *Itinerario* 7 (2): 116–143.

Evans-Pritchard, Edward E. (1928) The Dance, *Africa* 1: 446–462.

—— (1929) The Morphology and Function of Magic, *American Anthropologist* 31: 619–41.

—— (1935) Witchcraft, *Africa* 8: 417–22.

—— (1937) *Witchcraft, Oracles and Magic among the Azande*. Oxford: Clarendon Press.

—— (1970) Sorcery and native opinion, in: M. Marwick (ed.), *Witchcraft and Sorcery: Selected Readings*. Harmondsworth: Penguin.

Eves, Richard (1991) Ideology, Gender and Resistance: A Critical Analysis of Godelier's Theory of Ideology, *Dialectical Anthropology* 16: 109–24.

Fabian, Johannes (1971) *Jamaa: A Charismatic Movement in Katanga*. Evanston: Northwestern University Press.

—— (1978) Popular Culture in Africa: Findings and Conjectures, *Africa* 48: 315–34.

—— (1979) The Anthropology of Religious Movements: From Explanation to Interpretation, *Social Research* 46: 4–35.

—— (1981) Six Theses Regarding the Anthropology of African Religious Movements, *Religion* 11: 109–126.

—— (1983a) *Time and the Other. How Anthropology Makes its Object*. New York Columbia University Press.

—— (1983b) Missions and the Colonization of African Languages: Developments in the Former Belgian Congo, *Canadian Journal of African Studies* 17: 165–187.

—— (1985) *Language On The Road: Notes on Swahili in Two Nineteenth Century Travelogues*. Hamburg: H. Buske.

—— (1990a) *Power and Performance. Ethnographic Explorations through Proverbial Wisdom and Theater in Shaba, Zaire*. Madison: University of Wisconsin Press.

—— (1990b) Presence and Representation: The Other and Anthropological Writing, *Critical Inquiry* 16: 753–772.

—— (1991) Ethnographic Objectivity Revisited: From Rigor to Vigor, *Annals of Scholarship* 8: 381–408.

Fernandez, James (1964) The Sound of Bells in a Christian Country – in Quest of the Historical Schweitzer, *The Massachusetts Review*, Spring 1964: 537–562.

—— (1978) African Religious Movements, *Annual Review of Anthropology* 7: 195–234.

—— (1982) *Bwiti: An Ethnography of the Religious Imagination in Africa*. Princeton: Princeton University Press.

Fields, Karen (1982a) Christian Missionaries as Anti-Colonial Militants, *Theory and Society* 11: 92–108.

—— (1982b) Political Contingencies of Witchcraft in Colonial Central Africa: Culture and State in Marxist Theory, *Canadian Journal of African Studies* 16: 567–593.

—— (1985) *Revival and Rebellion in Central Africa*. New Jersey: Princeton University Press.

Firth, Raymond (1936) *We, the Tikopia*. Reprint. Boston: Beacon Press.

—— (1968) Social Anthropology, *International Encyclopedia of the Social Sciences*. New York: Macmillan/The Free Press.

Fisiy, Cyprian, and Peter Geschiere (1991) Sorcery, Witchcraft and Accumulation – Regional Variations in South and West Cameroon, *Critique of Anthropology* 11: 251–78.

Forster, Peter G. (1986) Missionaries and Anthropology: The Case of the Scots of Northern Malawi, *Journal of Religion in Africa* 16: 101–20.

—— (1989) *T. Cullen Young: Missionary and Anthropologist*. Hull: Hull University Press.

Foucault, Michel (1979) *Discipline and Punish. The Birth of the Prison*. New York: Vintage Books.

—— (1980) *The History of Sexuality. Volume 1: an Introduction*. French orig. 1976. New York: Vintage Books.

────── (1991) Governmentality, in: G. Burchell, C. Gordon, P. Miller (eds.), *The Foucault Effect. Studies in Governmentality*. Chicago: University of Chicago Press, 87–118.

Fox, Robin (1967) *Kinship and Marriage. An Anthropological Perspective*. Harmondsworth: Penguin Books.

Frazer, James G. (1911) *The Golden Bough. Part I: The Magic Art and the Evolution of Kings*. Vol. I. London: MacMillan.

Freitag SVD, Rev. Fr. Anton (1953) *Die neue Missionsära. Das Zeitalter der einheimischen Kirche*. 2. Auflage. Kaldenkirchen: Steyler Verlagsbuchhandlung.

Geertz, Clifford (1973) *The Interpretation of Cultures*. New York: Basic Books.

────── (1988) *Works and Lives. The Anthropologist as Author*. Stanford: Stanford University Press.

Geschiere, Peter (1995) *Sorcellerie et politique en Afrique. Le viande des autres*. Paris: Karthala.

Gluckman, Max (1963) Rituals of Rebellion in South-East Africa, in: *Order and Rebellion in Tribal Africa*. London: Cohen and West.

Goddijn, Walter (1973) *De beheerste kerk. Uitgestelde revolutie in R. K. Nederland*. Amsterdam/Brussel: Elsevier.

Godelier, Maurice (1986) *The Making of Great Men*. Cambridge: Cambridge University Press.

Goldberg, David Th. (1990) Introduction, in: D. Th. Goldberg (ed.), *Anatomy of Racism*. Minneapolis: University of Minnesota Press.

Goody, Jack (1961) Religion and Ritual: The Definitional Problem, *British Journal of Sociology* 12: 142–64.

Gordon, D. H. (1929) Momiyai, *Man* no. 160.

────── (1933) Some Further Notes on Momiyai, *Man* no. 163.

────── (1934) Momiyai and Silajit, *Man* no.83.

Gould, W. T. S. (1976) Patterns of School Provision in Colonial East Africa, *Etudes d'Histoire Africaine* 8: 131–148.

Gray, Richard (1990) *Black Christians and White Missionaries*. New Haven: Yale University Press.

Greenhouse, Carol (1982) Looking at Culture, Looking for Rules, *Man* (n.s.) 17: 58–73.

Gregorius OFM Cap, P.Dr. (1955) Enige beschouwingen over het aanpassingsvraagstuk, *Het Missiewerk* 34: 47–50.

Gwassa, G. C. K. (1972) Kinjikitile and the Ideology of Maji Maji, in: T. Ranger and I. Kimambo (eds.), *The Historical Study of African Religion*. London: Heinemann.

Haddon, Alfred Cort (1921) *The Practical Value of Ethnology*. The Conway Memorial Lecture. London: Watts & Co.

Hafkin, Nancy J., and Edna G. Bay (eds.) (1976a) *Women in Africa. Studies in Social and Economic Change*. Stanford: Stanford University Press.

Hafkin, Nancy J., and Edna G. Bay (1976b) Introduction, in: N. Hafkin and E. Bay (eds.), *Women in Africa. Studies in Social and Economic Change*. Stanford: Stanford University Press.

Hammersley, Martyn, and Paul Atkinson (1983) *Ethnography; Principles in Practice*. London and New York: Tavistock.

Hannerz, Ulf (1987) The World in Creolisation, *Africa* 57: 546–59.

Harlow, Vincent, and E.M. Chilver (eds.) (1965) *History of East Africa, vol. 2*. Nairobi: Oxford University Press.

Hartwig, Gerald W. (1969) The Historical and Social Role of Kerebe Music, *Tanzania Notes and Records* 70: 41–56.

Hasani bin Ismaeli (1968) *Swifa ya Nguvumali*. Oxford: Clarendon Press.

Hay, Margaret J., and Marcia Wright (eds.) (1982) *African Women and the Law: Historical Perspectives*. Boston: Boston University Papers on Africa, no. VII.

Heise, David R. (1967) Prefatory Findings in the Sociology of Missions, *Journal for the Scientific Study of Religion* 6: 49–63.

Hertlein, Siegfried (1976) *Wege Christlicher Verkündigung*, vol. 1. Münsterschwarzach.

───── (1983) *Wege Christlicher Verkündigung*, vol. 2 and 3. Münsterschwarzach.

Hezel, Francis X. (1978) Indigenization as a Missionary Goal in the Caroline and Marshall Islands, in: J. Boutilier, D. Hughes, S. Tiffany (eds.), *Mission, Church and Sect in Oceania*. Ann Arbor: University of Michigan Press.

Hiebert, Paul (1978a) Introduction: Missions and Anthropology, in: W. Smalley (ed.), *Readings in Missionary Anthropology* vol. II. South Pasadena: William Carey Library.

───── (1978b) Missions and Anthropology: A Love/Hate Relationship, *Missiology* 6: 165–180.

Hilhorst CSSp, Mgr. Bernard (1937) *Directory for the Use of Fathers and Brothers Working in the Vicariate Apostolic of Bagamoyo*. Morogoro: Vicariate Apostolic of Bagamoyo.

Hirschkind, Charles (1991) 'Egypt at the Exhibition': Reflections on the Optics of Colonialism, *Critique of Anthropology* 11: 279–298.

Hocart, A. M. (1914) Mana, *Man* 14, no. 46.

Hollingsworth, L. W. (1960) *The Asians of East Africa*. London: MacMillan & Co.

Horton, Robin (1970) African Traditional Thought and Western Science, in: B. Wilson (ed.), *Rationality*. Oxford: Blackwell.

—— (1971) African Conversion, *Africa* 41: 85–108.

—— (1973) Paradox and Explanation, parts I and II, *Philosophy of the Social Sciences* 3: 231–56 and 289–312.

—— (1975) On the Rationality of Conversion, parts I and II, *Africa* 45: 219–235 and 373–98.

Huber, Mary T. (1988) *The Bishops' Progress. A Historical Ethnography of Catholic Missionary Experience on the Sepik frontier*. Washington and London: Smithsonian Institution Press.

Hubert, Henri, and Marcel Mauss (1964) *Sacrifice: Its Nature and Function*. 1st French edition 1898. London: Cohen and West.

Hughes, Daniel T. (1978) Mutual Biases of Anthropologists and Missionaries, in: J. Boutilier, D. Hughes, S. Tiffany (eds.), *Mission, Church and Sect in Oceania*. Ann Arbor: University of Michigan Press.

Huntingford, G. W. B. (1934) Momiyai, *Man* no. 22.

Hvalkof, S., and P. Aaby (eds.) (1981) *Is God an American? An Anthropological Perspective on the Missionary Work of the Summer Institute of Linguistics*. London: IWGIA and Survival International.

Ifeka-Möller, Caroline (1974) White Power: Social–Structural Factors in Conversion to Christianity, Eastern Nigeria, 1921–1966, *Canadian Journal of African Studies* 8: 55–72.

Iliffe, John (1967) The Organisation of the Maji-Maji rebellion, *Journal of African History* 8: 495–512.

—— (1973) (ed.) *Modern Tanzanians. A Volume of Biographies*. Nairobi: East African Publishing House.

—— (1979) *A Modern History of Tanganyika*. Cambridge: Cambridge University Press.

Isichei, Elizabeth (1970) Seven Varieties of Ambiguity: Some Patterns of Igbo Response to Christian Missions, *Journal of Religion in Africa* 3: 209–227.

Jackson, Michael (1983) Knowledge through the Body, *Man* (n.s.) 18: 327–345.

Janzen, John (1991) 'Doing *Ngoma*': A dominant trope in African religion and healing, *Journal of Religion in Africa* 21: 290–308.

—— (1992) *Ngoma. Discourses of Healing in Central and Southern Africa*. Berkeley: University of California Press.

Jewsiewicki, Bogumil, and David Newbury (eds.) (1986) *African Historiographies. What History for Which Africa?* Beverly Hills: Sage Publications.

Johnson, Frederick (1939) *A Standard Swahili-English Dictionary* (founded on Madan's Swahili-English Dictionary). Reprint 1986. Oxford: Oxford University Press.

Jones, A. M. (1945) African Music: The Mganda Dance, *African Studies* 4: 180–188.

Jubileumblad SPM (1950) *Jubileumblad 25-jarig bestaan Sint Paulus Missieclub*. Weert: Missiehuis van de H. Geest.

Jubileumuitgave (1929) *Jubileumuitgave 1904–1929. Missiehuis van den H. Geest te Weert, Limburg*. Weert: Missiehuis van de H. Geest.

Julien, Dr. Paul (1940) *Kampvuren langs de evenaar. Herinneringen aan tien jaar bloedonderzoek in West- en Centraal Afrika*. Amsterdam: Scheltens & Giltay.

—— (1949) *De eeuwige wildernis. Herinneringen aan tien jaar bloedonderzoek in Equatoriaal Afrika*. Eindhoven: Uitgeversmaatschappij "De Pelgrim".

Junod, H. P. (1935) Anthropology and Missionary Education, *International Review of Missions* 24: 213–228.

Kamusi (1981) *Kamusi ya Kiswahili Sanifu*. Dar es Salaam/Nairobi: Oxford University Press.

Keil, Charles (1979) *Tiv Song*. Chicago and London: University of Chicago Press.

—— (1987) Participatory Discrepancies and the Power of Music, *Cultural Anthropology* 2: 257–283.

Kieran, J. A. (1969) Some Roman Catholic Missionary Attitudes in 19th Century East Africa, *Race* 10: 341–359.

—— (1971) Christian Villages in North-Eastern Tanzania, *Transafrican Journal of History* 1: 24–38.

Kimambo, Isaria N. (1991) *Penetration and Protest in Tanzania*. London: James Currey, Tanzania Publishing House, Heinemann Kenya, and Ohio University Press.

Kimambo, Isaria N., and A. J. Temu (eds.)

—— (1969) *A History of Tanzania*. Nairobi: East African Publishing House.

Koren CSSp, Henry J. (1983) *To the Ends of the Earth*. Pittsburgh: Duquesne Studies.

Kramer, Fritz (1987) *Der rote Fes. Über Besessenheit und Kunst in Afrika*. Frankfurt: Athenäum.

Kunst met een Missie (1988) *Kunst met een Missie*. Maarheeze: Werkgroep Musea-Missie-Medemens.

Kuklick, Henrika (1991) *The Savage Within. The Social History of British Anthropology*. Cambridge: Cambridge University Press.

La Fontaine, Jean S. (1982) Introduction, in: A. Richards, *Chisungu. A Girl's Initiation Ceremony among the Bemba of Zambia.* Reprint, 1988. London: Routledge and Kegan Paul.

—— (1985) *Initiation.* Harmondsworth: Penguin Books.

—— (1992) Concepts of Evil, Witchcraft and the Sexual Abuse of Children in Modern England, *Etnofoor* 5: 6–20.

Larson, Lorne (1974) Witchcraft Eradication Sequences among the Peoples of the Mahenge Ulanga District, Tanzania. Unpublished ms.

—— (1976) Problems in the Study of Witchcraft Eradication Movements in Southern Tanzania, *Ufahamu* 6/3: 88–100.

Lee, Anthony A. (1976) Ngoja and Six Theories of Witchcraft Eradication, *Ufahamu* 6/3: 101–117.

Lévi-Strauss, Claude (1975) *The Raw and the Cooked. Introduction to a Science of Mythology, Vol.1.* New York: Harper and Row.

Lewis, Ioan M. (1976) *Social Anthropology in Perspective. The Relevance of Social Anthropology.* Harmondsworth: Penguin.

Lienhardt, Peter (1968) Introduction and Appendix, in: Hasani b. Ismaeli, *Swifa ya Nguvumali.* Oxford: Clarendon Press.

Linden, Ian, and Jane Linden (1974) *Catholics, Peasants and Chewa Resistance.* London: Heinemann.

Luzbetak, L. J. (1961) Toward an Applied Missionary Anthropology, *Anthropological Quarterly* 34: 165–176.

Magubane, B. (1971) A Critical Look at Indices used in the Study of Social Change in Africa, *Current Anthropology* 12: 419–45.

Malinowski, Bronislaw (1911) Review of G. C. Wheeler, "The Tribal and Intertribal Relations in Australia", *Man* 11, no. 15.

—— (1912) The Economic Aspects of the *Intichiuma* Ceremonies, in *Festsckrift tillegnad Edvard Westermarck.* Helsingfors: Simelli, pp. 81–108.

—— (1922) *Argonauts of the Western Pacific.* Reprint. London: Routledge and Kegan Paul.

—— (1925) Magic, Science and Religion, reprinted in B. Malinowski, *Magic, Science and Religion and other essays.* New York: Doubleday Anchor Books, 1954.

—— (1935a) *Coral Gardens and Their Magic, vol.2: The Language of Magic and Gardening.* Reprint. Bloomington: Indiana University Press.

—— (1935b) Native Education and Culture Contact, *International Review of Missions* 24: 480–515.

—— (1967) *A Diary in the Strict Sence of the Term.* Reprint. Stanford: Stanford University Press.

Marwick, Max (1950) Another Modern Anti-witchcraft Movement in East Central Africa, *Africa* 20/2.

—— (1952) The Social Context of Cewa Witch Beliefs, *Africa* 22: 120–135, 215–233.

—— (1972) Anthropologists' Declining Productivity in the Sociology of Witchcraft, *American Anthropologist* 74: 378–385.

Masson SJ, Joseph (1978) The Legacy of Pierre Charles SJ, *Occasional Bulletin of Missionary Research* 2: 118–20.

Mauss, Marcel (1973) Techniques of the Body, *Economy and Society* 2: 70–88 (French original 1934).

Mawinza, Rev. Fr. Joseph (1963) *The Human Soul. Life and Soul-Concept in an East African Mentality Based on Luguru*. Rome: Pontificia Universitas Urbaniana.

McCracken, John (1977) Underdevelopment in Malawi: The Missionary Contribution, *African Affairs* 76: 195–209.

Melchior, Adolf (1950) *Schoonheid en Bijgeloof in Oost-Afrika*. Haarlem: De Spaarnestad.

—— (1957) *Gekluisterd Congo?* Haarlem: De Spaarnestad N. V.

Melland, Frank (1923) *In Witchbound Africa. An Account of the Primitive Kaonde Tribe and their Beliefs*. Reprint, 1967, London: Frank Cass & Co.

—— (1935) Ethical and Political Aspects of African Witchcraft, *Africa* 8: 495–503.

Merriam, Alan P. (1959) African Music, reprinted in: A. P. Merriam, *African Music in Perspective*. New York and London: Garland Publishing, Inc, 1982.

Meurkens, Peter (1985) *Bevolking, economie en cultuur van het Oude Kempenland*. Bergeijk: Stichting Eicha.

—— (1989) Catholic Ethics and Private Behaviour in Old Kempenland, in: J. Boissevain and J. Verrips (eds.), *Dutch Dilemmas. Anthropologists look at the Netherlands*. Assen/Maastricht: Van Gorcum.

Meyer, Birgit (1992) 'If You are a Devil, You are a Witch and if You are a Witch, you are a Devil.' The Integration of 'Pagan' Ideas in the Conceptual Universe of African Christians, *Journal of Religion in Africa* 22: 98–132.

—— (1995) *Translating the Devil. An African Appropriation of Pietist Protestantism*. Ph.D. Thesis, Anthropology, University of Amsterdam.

Miller, Daniel (1987) *Material Culture and Mass Consumption*. Oxford: Basil Blackwell.

Minamiki, George (1985) *The Chinese Rites Controversy from its Beginnings to Modern Times*. Chicago: University of Chicago Press.

Mintz, Sidney (1985) *Sweetness and Power: The Place of Sugar in Modern History*. New York: Penguin.

Missievereeniging Hoeven (1924) *De Katholieke Missie in wezen en ontwikkeling*. Hoeven: Missievereeniging Grootseminarie St. Franciscus Xaverius.

Missievereniging Roermond (1939) *Priester en Missie*. Roermond: Missievereniging van het Grootseminarie te Roermond.

Mitchell, J. Clyde (1956) *The Kalela Dance. Aspects of Social Relationships among Urban Africans in Northern Rhodesia*. Rhodes-Livingstone Paper no. 27. Manchester: Manchester University Press.

Mitchell, (Sir) Philip E. n.d. *Governments and Missions in Africa: The Case for Cooperation*. London: Church Missionary Society.

Mitchell, Timothy (1991) *Colonizing Egypt*. 2nd ed. Berkeley: University of California Press.

Mlahagwa, Josiah R. (1974) *Agricultural Change in the Uluguru Mountains during the Colonial Period, with particular emphasis from 1945–1960*. M. A. Thesis, University of Dar es Salaam.

Mluanda, Martin (1971) Traditional Practices Among the Luguru in Eastern Tanzania, *Bulletin of the International Committee for Urgent Anthropological and Ethnological Research* 13: 57–65.

Moore, Henrietta (1988) *Feminism and Anthropology*. London: Polity Press.

Mudimbe, Valentin (1988) *The Invention of Africa. Gnosis, Philosophy and the Order of Knowledge*. Bloomington/ London: Indiana University Press/James Currey.

Mulders, Dr. Alphons (1950) *Inleiding tot de missiewetenschap*. 2nd rev. ed. Bussum: Brand.

—— (1953) Nederland en de missie sinds het herstel der bis-schoppelijke hiërarchie, *Het Missiewerk* 32: 193–210.

—— (1955) Na vijf en twintig jaar, *Het Missiewerk* 34: 193–201.

Müller, F. Max (1873) On Missions, in: F. Max Müller, *Chips from a German Workshop*, vol.2. London: Longmans.

Müller SVD, Karl (1980) The Legacy of Joseph Schmidlin, *Occasional Bulletin of Missionary Research* 4: 109–13.

Mzuanda, Rev. Fr. Canute (1958) *Historia ya Uluguru*. Morogoro: Diocese of Morogoro.

Nader, Laura, and B. Yngvesson (1973) On Studying the Ethnography of Law and Its Consequences, in: J. Honigmann (ed.), *Handbook of Social and Cultural Anthropology*. Chicago: Rand McNally.

Needham, Rodney (1967) Percussion and Transition, *Man* *(n.s.)* 2: 606–14.

Ngokwey, Ndolamb (1978) Le désenchantement enchanteur ou d'un mouvement religieux á l'autre, *Les Cahiers du CEDAF* 8.

Nida, Eugene A. (1959) The Role of Cultural Anthropology in Christian Missions, in: *Readings in Missionary Anthropology* II, ed. W. Smalley. South Pasadena, Cal.: W. Carey Library, 1978.

—— (1966) Missionaries and Anthropologists, *Practical Anthropology* 13: 273–7, 287.

Nolan WF, Francis P. (1972) History of the Catechist in Eastern Africa, in: A. Shorter and E. Kataza (eds.), *Missionaries to Yourselves. African Catechists Today.* London: Geoffrey Chapman.

Obbo, Christine (1981) *African Women: Their Struggle for Economic Independence.* London: Zed Press.

Ochieng, William R. (1972) Colonial African Chiefs, *Hadith* 4: 46–70.

Ogot, Bethwell A. (1967) *History of the Southern Luo, Volume 1: Migration and Settlement, 1500–1900.* Nairobi: East African Publishing House.

Okonjo, Kamene (1976) The Dual-Sex Political System in Operation: Igbo Women and Community Politics in Midwestern Nigeria, in: N. Hafkin and E. Bay (eds.), *Women in Africa.* Stanford: Stanford University Press.

Oliver, Roland (1952) *The Missionary Factor in East Africa.* London: Longmans (1965 edition).

Olivier de Sardan, Jean-Pierre (1992) Occultism and the Ethnographic 'I'. The Exoticizing of Magic from Durkheim to 'Postmodern' Anthropology, *Critique of Anthropology* 12: 5–25.

Oppong, Christine (ed.) (1983) *Female and Male in West Africa.* London: George Allen & Unwin.

Park, Robert E. (1944) Missions and the Modern World, *American Journal of Sociology* 50: 177–183.

Parkin, David (1968) Medicine and Men of Influence, *Man* (n.s.) 3: 424–39.

—— (1985) (ed.), *The Anthropology of Evil.* Oxford: Blackwell.

Peel, J. D. Y. (1977) Conversion and Tradition in Two African Societies, *Past and Present* 77: 108–41.

—— (1990) The Pastor and the *Babalawo*: the Interaction of Religions in 19th Century Yorubaland, *Africa* 60: 338–69.

Pels, Peter (1989) Africa Christo! The use of Photographs in Dutch Catholic Mission Propaganda, 1946–1960, *Critique of Anthropology* 9: 33–47.

————— (1990a) Anthropology and Mission: Towards a Historical Analysis of Professional Identity, in R. Bonsen, H. Marks and J. Miedema (eds.), *The Ambiguity of Rapprochement. Reflections of Anthropologists on their Controversial Relationship with Missionaries*. Nijmegen: Focaal.

————— (1990b) How Did Bishop Arkfeld Get His Feathered Mitre? Review of Huber 1988, *Critique of Anthropology* 10: 103–12.

————— (1992a) *Mumiani*: the White Vampire. A Neo-Diffusionist Analysis of Rumour, *Etnofoor* 5: 165–87.

————— (1992b) Review of Kimambo 1991, *Africa* (in press).

————— (1994) The Construction of Ethnographic Occasions in Late Colonial Uluguru, *History and Anthropology* 8: 321–56.

————— (1995) The Politics of Aboriginality. Brian Houghton Hodgson and the Making of an Ethnology of India, *Yearbook 1994, International Institute for Asian Studies*: 141–62.

————— (1996) The Pidginization of Luguru Politics. Administrative Ethnography and the Paradoxes of Indirect Rule, *American Ethnologist* 23/4: 738–61.

Pels, Peter, and Lorraine Nencel (1991) Introduction: Critique and the Deconstruction of Anthropological Authority, in L. Nencel, and P. Pels (eds.), *Constructing Knowledge. Authority and Critique in Social Science*. London: Sage.

Pels, Peter, and Oscar Salemink (1994) Introduction: Five Theses on Ethnography as Colonial Practice, *History and Anthropology* 8: 1–34.

Poewe, Karla O. (1981) *Matrilineal Ideology. Male-Female Dynamics in Luapula, Zambia*. London: Academic Press.

Powdermaker, Hortense (1966) *Stranger and Friend*. London: Secker and Warburg,

Pratt, Marie Louise (1985) Scratches on the Face of the Country, or: What Mr. Barrow Saw in the Land of the Bushmen, *Critical Inquiry* 12: 119–143.

Prins, Gwyn (1980) *The Hidden Hippopotamus. Reappraisal in African History: The Early Colonial Experience in Western Zambia*. Cambridge: Cambridge University Press.

Quiggin, A. Hingston (1942) *Haddon the Head Hunter*. Cambridge: Cambridge University Press.

Rafael, Vicente L. (1988) *Contracting Colonialism. Translation and Conversion in Tagalog Society under Early Spanish Rule*. Ithaca: Cornell University Press.

————— (1992) Confession, Conversion and Reciprocity in Early Tagalog Colonial Society, in: N. Dirks (ed.) *Colonialism and Culture*. Ann Arbor: The University of Michigan Press.

Ranger, Terence O. (1965) African Attempts to Control Education in East and Central Africa, 1900–39, *Past and Present* 32: 57–85.

—— (1966) Witchcraft Eradication Movements in Central and Southern Tanzania and their Connection with the Maji Maji Rising. Unpublished ms.

—— (1972) Mchape: A Study in Diffusion and Interpretation. Unpublished Ms.

—— (1975) *Dance and Society in Eastern Africa*. London: Heinemann.

—— (1987) An Africanist Comment, *American Ethnologist* 14: 182–5.

Ranger, Terence O., and Isaria N. Kimambo (1972) Introduction, in: T. O. Ranger and I. N. Kimambo (eds.), *The Historical Study of African Religion*. London: Heinemann.

Richards, Audrey (1935) A Modern Movement of Witch-finders, *Africa* 8: 448–61.

—— (1956) *Chisungu. A Girl's Initiation Ceremony among the Bemba of Zambia*. Reprint with an introduction by J. S. La Fontaine, 1982. London: Routledge and Kegan Paul.

Rigby, Peter (1981) Pastors, and Pastoralists: The Differential Penetration of Christianity among East African Cattle Herders, *Comparative Studies in Society and History* 23: 96–129.

Rivers, W. H. (1920) Anthropology and the Missionary, *Church Missionary Review* 71: 208–215.

Roberts, Andrew (ed.) (1968) *Tanzania Before 1900. Seven Area Histories*. Nairobi: East African Publishing House.

Robertson, Claire, and Iris Berger (eds.)

—— (1986) *Women and Class in Africa*. New York: Africana Publishing Company.

Roes, Jan (1974) *Het Groote Missieuur, 1915–1940. Op zoek naar de missiemotivatie van de Nederlandse katholieken*. Bilthoven: Ambo.

Romijn, Patricia (1989) *Een revolutie in de kloosterwereld. De wordingsgeschiedenis van een 19e-eeuwse zustercongregatie vanuit een antropologisch perspectief*. Amsterdam: Ph.D. Thesis, Free University of Amsterdam.

Rowlands, Michael, and Jean-Pierre Warnier (1988) Sorcery, Power and the Modern State in Cameroon, *Man (n.s.)* 23: 118–32.

Sacks, Karen (1982) *Sisters and Wives. The Past and Future of Sexual Equality*. Urbana: University of Illinois Press.

Sacleux CSSp., Rev. Fr. Charles (1939) *Dictionnaire swahili-français*. Paris: Institut d'Ethnologie.

Sahlberg, Carl-Erik (1986) *From Krapf to Rugambwa. A Church History of Tanzania*. Nairobi: Evangel Publishing House.

Said, Edward W. (1978) *Orientalism*. Harmondsworth: Penguin Books.

—— (1989) Representing the Colonized: Anthropology's Interlocutors, *Critical Inquiry* 15: 205–25.

Salamone, Frank, and D. Whiteman (eds.) (1983) *Missionaries, Anthropologists and Cultural Change*, 2 vols. Williamsburg, Virginia: College of William and Mary, Studies in Third World Societies nrs. 25/26.

Sanjek, Roger (1992) The Ethnographic Present, *Man* (n.s.) 26: 609–628.

Santandrea, Rev. Fr. Stefano (1980) Catholic Education, Language and Religion in the Western Bahr el Ghazal, South Sudan, 1905–1955, *Transafrican Journal of History* 9: 91–102.

Scheerder CSSp., Rev. Fr. G., and Rev. Fr. Tastevin CSSp. (1950) Les Wa lu gu ru, *Anthropos* 45: 241–86.

Schieffelin, Edward (1981) Evangelical Rhetoric and the Transformation of Traditional Culture in Papua New Guinea, *Comparative Studies in Society and History* 23: 150–6.

Schlieben, Hans Joachim (1941) *Deutsch Ost-Afrika, einmal ganz anders. Eine fünfjährige Forschungsreise*. Neudamm/Berlin: Verlag J. Neumann.

Schneider, David M. (1961) The Distinctive Features of Matrilineal Descent Groups, in: D. M Schneider and K. Gough (eds.), *Matrilineal Kinship*. Berkeley: University of California Press.

Schoffeleers, Matthew (1975) The Interaction of the M'Bona Cult and Christianity, in: T. O. Ranger and J. Weller (eds.), *Themes in the Christian History of Central Africa*. London: Heinemann.

—— (1982) Christ as the Medicine-Man and the Medicine-Man as Christ: a tentative history of African Christological Thought, *Man and Life* 8: 11–28.

—— (1988) Folk Christology in Africa: The Dialectics of the Nganga Paradigm, *Journal of Religion in Africa* 19: 157–83.

Schoffeleers, Matthew, and Ian Linden (1972) The Resistance of the Nyau Societies to the Roman Catholic Missions in Colonial Malawi, in: T.O. Ranger and I.N. Kimambo (eds.), *The Historical Study of African Religion*. London: Heinemann.

Scholte, Bob (1986) The Charmed Circle of Geertz' Hermeneutics: a Neo-Marxist Critique, *Critique of Anthropology* 6: 5–15.

Schwartz, Stuart B. (1994) *Implicit Understandings. Observing, Reporting, and Reflecting on the Encounters Between*

Europeans and Other Peoples in the Early Modern Era. Cambridge: Cambridge University Press.

Scott, James C. (1987) Resistance without Protest and without Organisation: Peasant Opposition to the Islamic *Zakat* and the Christian Tithe, *Comparative Studies in Society and History* 29: 417–52.

Shapiro, Judith (1981) Ideologies of Catholic Missionary Practice in a Postcolonial Era, *Comparative Studies in Society and History* 23: 130–149.

Sheriff, Abdul (1987) *Slaves, Spices and Ivory in Zanzibar*. London: James Currey, Tanzania Publishing House, Heinemann Kenya, and Ohio University Press.

Sifuna, Daniel N. (1977) The Mill Hill Fathers and the Establishment of Western Education in Western Kenya 1900–1924: Some Reflections, *Transafrican Journal of History* 6&7: 112–128.

Skorupski, John (1975) Comments on Professor Horton's "Paradox and Explanation", *Philosophy of the Social Sciences* 5: 63–70.

Smith, Edwin W. (1924) Social Anthropology and Missionary Work, *International Review of Missions* 13: 518–531.

—— (1934) The Story of the Institute: the First Seven Years, *Africa* 7: 1–27.

Stipe, Claude E. (1980) Anthropologists versus Missionaries: The Influence of Presuppositions, *Current Anthropology* 21: 165–79.

Stocking, George (1985) Philanthropoids and Vanishing Cultures: Rockefeller Funding and the End of the Museum Era in Anglo-American Anthropology, in: G. W. Stocking (ed.), *Objects and Others. Essays on Museums and Material Culture*. History of Anthropology vol. 3. Madison: University of Wisconsin Press.

—— (1991) Maclay, Kubari, Malinowski: Archetypes from the Dreamtime of Anthropology, in: G. W. Stocking (ed.), *Colonial Situations. Essays on the Contextualization of Ethnographic Knowledge*. History of Anthropology vol. 7. Madison: University of Wisconsin Press.

Stoler, Ann Laura, and Frederick Coooper (1997) Between Metropole and Colony: Rethinking a Research Agenda, in: F. Cooper and A. L. Stoler (eds.), *Tensions of Empire. Colonial Cultures in a Bourgeois World*. Berkeley: University of California Press.

Strayer, R. W. (1973) Missions and African Protest: A Case Study from Kenya, 1875–1935, in: R. W. Strayer *et al.*, *Protest Movements in Colonial East Africa: Aspects of Early African*

Response to European Rule. Syracuse: Syracuse University Press.

Strathern, Marilyn (1988) *The Gender of the Gift. Problems with Women and Problems with Society in Melanesia*. Berkeley: University of California Press.

Strobel, Margaret (1982) African Women, *Signs* 8: 109–131.

Swantz, Marja-Liisa (1986) *Ritual and Symbol in Transitional Zaramo Society, with Special Reference to Women*. Uppsala: Scandinavian Institute of African Studies (orig. published 1970).

Swantz, Lloyd (1990) *The Medicine Man among the Zaramo of Dar es Salaam*. Uppsala: Scandinavian Institute of African Studies/Dar es Salaam University Press.

Tambiah, Stanley Jeyaraja (1990) *Magic, Science, Religion and the Scope of Rationality*. Cambridge: Cambridge University Press.

Taussig, Michael (1987) *Shamanism, Colonialism and the Wild Man. A Study in Terror and Healing*. Chicago: University of Chicago Press.

—— (1991) Tactility and Distraction, *Cultural Anthropology* 6: 147–153.

—— (1993) *Mimesis and Alterity. A Particular History of the Senses*. New York/London: Routledge.

Temple, Paul (1972) Soil and Water Conservation Policies in the Uluguru Mountains, Tanzania, *Geografiska Annaler* 54: 110–123.

Temple, Sir Richard Carnac (1914) *Anthropology as a Practical Science*. London: G. Bell and Sons Ltd.

Temu, A. J. (1972) *British Protestant Missions*. London: Longman.

Thoden van Velzen, H. U. E. (1973) Robinson Crusoe and Friday: Strength and Weakness of the Big Man Paradigm, *Man* (n.s.) 8: 592–612.

Thomas, Keith (1971) *Religion and the Decline of Magic*. Harmondsworth: Penguin Books, 1978.

Thomas, Nicholas (1989) *Out of Time. History and Evolution in Anthropological Discourse*. Cambridge: Cambridge University Press.

—— (1991a) *Entangled Objects. Exchange, Material Culture, and Colonialism in the Pacific*. Cambridge, Mass.: Harvard University Press.

—— (1991b) Against Ethnography, *Cultural Anthropology* 6: 306–322.

—— (1992) Colonial Conversions: Difference, Hierarchy, and History in Early Twentieth-Century Evangelical Propaganda, *Comparative Studies in Society and History* 34: 366–389.

——— (1994) *Colonialism's Culture. Anthropology, Travel and Government*. London: Polity Press.

Thornton, Robert J. (1988) The Rhetoric of Ethnographic Holism, *Cultural Anthropology* 3: 285–303.

Tomas, David (1991) Tools of the Trade: The Production of Ethnographic Observations on the Andaman Islands, 1858–1922, in: G. W. Stocking (ed.), *Colonial Situations. Essays on the Contextualization of Ethnographic Knowledge*. History of Anthropology vol. 7. Madison: University of Wisconsin Press.

Turner, Victor (1967) *The Forest of Symbols. Aspects of Ndembu Ritual*. Ithaca and London: Cornell University Press.

——— (1975) *Revelation and Divination in Ndembu Ritual*. Ithaca and London: Cornell University Press.

Tylor, Edward B. (1873) *Primitive Culture*. 2nd edition. New York: Brentano's (1924).

Vail, Leroy (1989) Introduction: Ethnicity in Southern African History, in: L. Vail (ed.), *The Creation of Tribalism in Southern Africa*. London/Berkeley: James Currey/The University of California Press.

Van Baal, Jan (1981) *Man's Quest for Partnership*. Assen: Van Gorcum.

Van den Bercken SJ, M. (1952) Enkele gedachten over aanpassing, *Het Missiewerk* 31: 55–68.

Van den Brink, Gabriel (1991) 'De arbeid is alles, de mensch niets...' Aard en ontwikkeling van het boerenbedrijf in de Kempen, *Tijdschrift voor sociale geschiedenis* 17: 50–72.

Van den Eerenbeemt, André (1953) *Missieactie en Missieproblemen*. Tilburg: Drukkerij van het R. K. Jongensweeshuis.

Van der Geest, Sjaak (1988) Baarden, *Etnofoor* 1/2: 73–81.

——— (1990) Anthropologists and Missionaries: Brothers under the Skin, *Man* (N.S.) 25: 190–207.

Van der Geest, Sjaak, and John Kirby (1992) The Absence of the Missionary Factor in African Ethnography, 1930–1965, *African Studies Review* 35 (3): 59–103.

Van der Kooy SMA, J. n.d. *Trommels van Kroekroe*. Utrecht: N. V. Uitgeverij de Lanteern.

Van der Veer, Peter (1995) Introduction, in: P. v. d. Veer (ed.), *Conversion to Modernities: The Globalization of Christianity*. New York/London: Routledge.

Van Dijk, Rijk, and Peter Pels (1996) Contested Authorities and the Politics of Perception: Deconstructing the Study of Religion in Africa, in: R. Werbner and T. O. Ranger (eds.),

Postcolonial Identities in Africa. London: Zed Books, pp. 245–270.

Van Donge, Jan Kees (1993) *Trapped in Decline: A sociological analysis of economic life in Mgeta, Uluguru Mountains, Tanzania*. Wageningen: Agricultural University, Ph. D. Thesis Agricultural and Environmental Sciences.

Van Doorn, J. A. A. (1958) De emancipatie van de Nederlandse Rooms Katholieken in de sociologische literatuur, *Sociologische Gids* 5: 194–204.

Van Gennep, Arnold (1960) *The Rites of Passage*. (Orig. French, 1908.) London: Routledge and Kegan Paul.

Vansina, Jan (1984) Review of Fernandez 1982, *Journal of African History* 25: 228–230.

Vencken, Harry n.d. *Rover-Bisschop*. Heemstede: Hofboekerij.

Vermunt CSSp, Rev. Fr. Cornelis (1967) The Idea of God among the West Waluguru, *Dini na Mila* 2/2-3: 1–6.

Viswanathan, Gauri (1989) *Masks of Conquest. Literary Study and British Rule in India*. New York: Columbia University Press.

Vogt CSSp, Mgr. François X. (1909) *Directoire de la mission*. Bagamoyo: Vicariat Apostolique de Bagamoyo.

Von Prince, Tom (1914) *Gegen Araber und Wahehe. Erinnerungen aus meiner ostafrikanischen Leutnantszeit*. Berlin: Mittler u. Sohn.

Welbourn, F. B. (1971) Missionary Stimulus and African Responses, in L. Gann and P. Duignan (eds.), *Colonialism in Africa* vol. 3, Cambridge: Cambridge University Press.

Wendelini, Mzee Pius (1990) *Milango ya History ya Uluguru. Zamani Mpaka Siku Hizi*. Ms.

Westermann, Diedrich (1931) The Missionary as an Anthropological Fieldworker, *Africa* 4: 164–77.

White, C. M. N. (1953) Conservatism and Modern Adaptation in Luvale Female Puberty Ritual, *Africa* 23: 15–24.

White, Luise (1993) Vampire Priests of Central Africa, or: African Debates about Labour and Religion in Colonial Northern Zambia, *Comparative Studies in Society and History* 35: 746–772.

Wiener, Margaret (1995) *Visible and Invisible Realms. Power, Magic, and Colonial Conquest in Bali*. Chicago: University of Chicago Press.

Wilensky, H. L. (1964) The Professionalization of Everyone?, *American Journal of Sociology* 70: 137–157.

Willis, Roy (1968) Kamcape, an Anti-Sorcery Movement in South-west Tanzania, *Africa* 38: 1–15.

———— (1970) Instant Millenium. The Sociology of African Witch-cleansing cults, in: M. Douglas (ed.), *Witchcraft Confessions and Accusations*. London: Tavistock.

Wilson, Bryan R. (ed.) (1970) *Rationality*. Oxford: Basil Blackwell.

Wipper, Audrey (1972) (ed.), Special Issue on Women in Africa, *Canadian Journal of African Studies* 6/2.

Wolf, Eric (1982) *Europe and the People Without History*. Berkeley: University of California Press.

Wolf, Eric, and Joseph Jorgensen (1970) Anthropology on the Warpath in Thailand, *New York Review of Books* 15, November 19: 26–35.

Wyllie, R. W. (1976) Some Contradictions in Missionizing, *Africa* 46: 196–204.

Young, Roland, and Henry Fosbrooke (1960) *Land and Politics among the Luguru of Tanganyika*. London: Routledge and Kegan Paul.

Zuure WF, Bernard n.d. *Naar de Vreemde Landen*. Hillegom: Van Dijk.

Subject Index

Name Index